Animal Victims in Modern Fiction
From Sanctity to Sacrifice

The Darwinian revolution profoundly altered society's conception of animals. Marian Scholtmeijer explores the ways in which modern literature has reflected this change in its attempts to deal with the reality of the autonomous animal and the animal victim.

Scholtmeijer considers works of fiction dealing with animal victims in the wild and in urban settings, how they are used to represent human sexual dilemmas, and how the hopes and disillusionments invested in myth generate animal victims. A broad range of authors is represented: Jack London, Thomas Mann, Ernest Hemingway, Frederick Philip Grove, Mary Webb, Gustave Flaubert, Timothy Findley, John Steinbeck, D.H. Lawrence, Jerzy Kosinski, Stephen King, and many others.

Her analysis suggests that the issue of the victimization of animals is much more tangled than we might like to believe. Scholtmeijer finds that animals resist assimilation into cultural products, and that, regarded with due attention, they possess a certain power over the themes and narratives that contain them.

MARIAN SCHOLTMEIJER has taught English at Simon Fraser University and Mount Allison University.

Animal Victims in Modern Fiction

From Sanctity to Sacrifice

Marian Scholtmeijer

UNIVERSITY OF TORONTO PRESS
Toronto Buffalo London

© University of Toronto Press Incorporated 1993
Toronto Buffalo London
Printed in Canada

ISBN 0-8020 2832-2 (cloth)
ISBN 0-8020-7708-0 (paper)

Printed on acid-free paper

Canadian Cataloguing in Publication Data

Scholtmeijer, Marian Louise
Animal victims in modern fiction

Includes bibliographical references and index.
ISBN 0-8020-2832-2 (bound) – ISBN 0-8020-7708-0 (pbk.)

1. Animals in literature.   I. Title

PN3352.A55S29 1993   809'.9336   C93-093220-X

75382

Cover illustration: detail from *Peaceable Kingdom*;
Edward Hicks; National Gallery of Art, Washington;
Gift of Edgar William and Bernice Chrysler Garbisch

Contents

CHAPTER FOUR
The Urban Context: Dispossessed People and Victimized Animals

CHAPTER FIVE
Animal Victims and Human Sexuality: Body Trouble

CHAPTER SIX
*Myth, Disillusionment, and Animal Victims: Modern Variations
upon Animal Sacrifice*

CHAPTER SEVEN
The Doubly Victimized Animal

Acknowledgments

As an eclectic work, this book reflects the kind interest and constructive criticisms of many people. Through every stage of the writing, I drew inspiration from discussion with friends, colleagues, and students in my classes on culture and animals. For their suggestions of animal stories and for their comments on ideas and theories, I am grateful to Michael Steig, Vince Godfrey, Kathy Mezei, Pamela Black, Jim Rugg, Bev Molson, Chin Banerjee, Joan Chadwick, Michael Bresalier, Alan Rudrum, and Herbert Korte. Deep appreciation goes to Jerry Zaslove, the range of whose knowledge of cultural criticism helped me to realize the depths to which the victimization of animals is ingrained in culture.

Thanks are due, as well, to the administration at Simon Fraser University, for financial support during the early stages of the work.

For their tireless attention to all the administrative intricacies associated with the publication of this book, and for their unfailing supportiveness, I thank Suzanne Rancourt, Beverly Johnston, and Prudence Tracy at the University of Toronto Press. The final work rests also on commentary of anonymous readers of the manuscript who understood the aims of the study and who suggested changes. Astute and patient editing by Judy Williams has improved the text in both large and fine details. Any remaining shortcomings and errors are, of course, mine.

Allan W. Eckert gave his gracious permission to quote from his extraordinary book *The Great Auk*. Quotations from Carol J. Adams' impressive study, *The Sexual Politics of Meat: A Feminist-*

Vegetarian Critical Theory, copyright © 1990 by Carol J. Adams, are reprinted by permission of The Continuum Publishing Company. The Stanford University Press has allowed me to use theories on sacrifice delineated by René Girard in *Things Hidden since the Foundation of the World* (English translation © 1987, The Athlone Press), and The Johns Hopkins University Press gave permission to quote from Margot Norris' *Beasts of the Modern Imagination*. Permission to use Philip P. Hallie's discussion of the dimensions of victimization in his book *Cruelty* has been granted by The University of New England Press, and Bantam Books has allowed me to quote from Morris Berman's *Coming to Our Senses*. These critical materials have been of signal importance to the analysis.

Heartfelt gratitude goes to my parents, who laid the groundwork for my respect for animals with their own. My loving thanks are also extended to my life's companion, Ted Altar; his support and his acumen in analysis of the issues involved in human and animal relations have been an inestimable influence upon the work.

I offer, finally, appreciation deeper than gratitude to the individual animals who came across my field of attention as the work progressed and reminded me of the true aims of the book. They stood, and stand – as do all animals – as a touchstone for truth and dignity.

ANIMAL VICTIMS IN MODERN FICTION

Introduction

Oxen that rattle the yoke and the chain or halt in the leafy shade, what
   is that you express in your eyes?
It seems to me more than all the print I have read in my life.
                          Walt Whitman, *Song of Myself,* lines 235–6

A fish is only a fish if it is socially classified as one ... [A]nimals are ... a
blank paper which can be inscribed with any message, any symbolic
meaning, that the social wishes.
                          Keith Tester, *Animals and Society,* ch 2, p 46

Even a perfunctory look at cultural history reveals that conceptions of nonhuman animals have wandered erratically from one
extreme to another. Animals have been regarded as gods and as
fiends, as the trustees of Edenic innocence and the prototypes of
ignorance and evil. Sometimes they resonate with totemic significance; more often, they are merely stock, resources to be managed
and 'harvested.' Sometimes, as in fables, or children's stories, or
the gentler sentiments, they are none other than ourselves with
fur, whiskers, and a tail; sometimes, as in Cartesian philosophy,
they are soulless automata. They have aided human thought in
multifarious ways, as symbols, metaphors, ritual objects, elements
of the decor (in the home, or in art), public attractions, regulators
in ecosystems, tools of scientific research, and repositories of genetic material. Each conception, as it emerges, represents itself
as the comprehensive truth of the animal. And now, as culture
purports to examine its own constructions, we have the 'real' truth

of nonhuman animals: they are the 'blank paper' on which human beings write messages to themselves. Cultural solipsism has shifted to a higher level: it is not just that we have treated other animals as blank paper, we are entitled to do so because that is what they are. If, as Whitman suggests, the animals that we see around us disclose a fatal insufficiency in cultural representation, then the 'blank paper' argument stands as the apotheosis of that insufficiency.

During all the centuries that culture has been doing this ideational dance around them, animals have remained constant. They have gone about their business unaware of the ideas humankind has of them. The indifference to cultural constructions which they preserve in the abstract might well abide as a living reality for them, were it not that the selfsame arbitrariness of conceptual uses reflects the arrogance with which we have physically used them and wreaked havoc upon their environments. Certainly, humankind has imposed ideas upon animals which validate its own materialistic interests. Casting animals as enemies of civilized ideals, or as nonsentient bodies, manifestly supports habitual raids upon their reserve. Yet even blatant discord within conceptions of animals has passed unexamined: the metaphysical contortions necessary to reconcile, for example, the symbolic significance of the lamb as the son of God with the steaming leg of lamb that sets people's mouths watering at the dinner table defy the powers of reason and the limits of practical reality. In the past, such contradictions did not matter greatly because human authority persisted unopposed. Contradictions and capriciousness simply attested to the totality of human power over natural animals.

A plausible case can be made that cultural sovereignty over animals still obtains. As long as animals live on the planet by human sufferance, as in some sense they undeniably do, then the liberties we take with them are self-authenticating. Because, as we have presumed, animals cannot inform us as to the nature of their experience or press their interests upon us, the human mind seems to be left all alone, seeking among its own devices for the value or truth of any given view of animals. The anarchy within the history of human thought on animals by itself appears to confirm our freedom to pick and choose among images of them. When ethical philosophers like Tom Regan assert that animals have intrinsic value, that they are 'subjects of a life' (see 'Honey

Dribbles Down Your Fur,' p 105), the counterargument can be made that this view of them, too, is an invention of the human imagination. As a last resort, we can always say that we simply do not know what their reality consists in, whether they suffer from pain and deprivation or not, or are sufficiently conscious to enjoy their own lives, and take our lack of knowledge as an excuse for maintaining the *status quo.*

Obviously, human beings have a prior investment in continuing to believe that we have no access to the literal animal. One might set such denial down to pure self-interest; refusal to recognize animal reality is a hedge against the guilt we would feel as we make use of their bodies were we to see them as sentient individuals rather than commodities. Furthermore, as Richard Tapper (citing Claude Lévi-Strauss) observes, animals 'are good to think with' (p 50). As living beings, whose content we have decided is inaccessible, animals are peculiarly primed to vitalize thought without – so we think – impeding its freedom. We have a liking for the effect of animals upon our thoughts, as long as they do not challenge their instrumentality as mediators of culture. In all cases, there is a certain amount of presumptuousness behind the philosophical position that the human mind constructs reality. That presumptuousness reaches a critical point, however, when we involve other living beings in our cultural projects. Relativity among perspectives on the natural world has led to the conclusion that reality is remarkably flexible, that it is infused with spiritual meaning, or is merely a source of empirical data, or displays any other particular tendency, accordingly as human attitudes and experiences change. But confidence that human thought participates in the making of reality should receive a setback when a scan of the natural world encounters another animal. Here, all of a sudden, is a being with a competing consciousness, whose own reality has an autonomy and holism that hinders the freeplay of human construction. Even if the animal is a domestic animal, Whitman's oxen perhaps, existing in circumstances human beings determine, having thoughts biased by domestication, his or her quintessential self-possession eludes our fabrication. Conceptual enculturation of nature founders in the presence of animals. Animals divest human relations with the given world of human authority and nudge the projections of culture back into the human mind.

It is this sense of the magnitude of what (I should say, 'whom') human beings assault when they victimize nonhuman animals that explains the focus of this book. The animal victim poses fundamental dilemmas existing right at the root of other representations of animals. Indeed, as the second chapter of the book seeks to demonstrate, the animal victim could well be argued to stand at the root of civilization, inasmuch as human beings have had the habit of defining civilization by its pre-eminence over other animals and their ways of living. The very use of animals within products of culture can be seen as a variant of the acts of appropriation which humankind practises in reality over the natural world. It is no easy matter to abandon the conceptual traditions which authorize the victimization of nonhuman animals. One cannot just by fiat assert that we must be kind to animals and assume that sufficient cultural work has been performed to dislodge the human sense of entitlement. To redress the imbalance caused by human dominion and the belief systems that support human dominion, culture must somehow be brought to acknowledge not only the resistance of animals to victimization but the definite challenge they represent to the seeming omnipotence of culture itself. Culture can bestow power upon animals, but the greater challenge to human dominance comes from the recognition that animals, in themselves and as they stand, possess by nature their own power to argue against the conventions in thought which license human aggression.

In an underground fashion, the intrinsic power of animals is making its way into the consciousness of culture. Animals *count* in modern Western culture,[1] and the injuries that we do to them likewise have meaning and impact. I intend this assertion to have the strongest possible connotation: that nonhuman animals literally contest the anthropocentrism on which modern Western culture is founded, and that the meaning that animals possess, whether they are victimized or not victimized, shakes what seems to be an almost congenital persuasion in humankind that nothing has value unless it has value for us. The belief that the human species is the focus of life on earth is gradually disintegrating.

Anthropocentrism received a severe blow with the advent of the theory of evolution. The full implications of the theory of evolution remain abstractions in modern sensibilities. We are not yet truly prepared to look on other animals as family, or to experience ourselves as one kind of animal among others. Even as an abstraction, however, the idea of continuity between human and nonhuman animals has significant effects upon the modern psyche. The status of animals has changed. The difference is not simply that they hold keys to human origins and identity, but that we are obliged to relate to them 'humanly.' Much of human thought and action has originated in the belief that a gulf exists between the human world and the nonhuman. Beings who once stood across that divide are now meaningfully related to us; they have an influence upon culture. Indeed, animals have a definite impact upon culture, for the location of the 'gulf' has shifted out of the realm of the real and into the realm of the hypothetical and ideational. Animals are no longer answerable for the distinctions we have assumed and operated upon. As humankind scrambles to preserve pre-Darwinian orientations towards life, it cannot cite deficiencies of meaning in the external world as the grounds for its beliefs. Impediments to meaning rest with culture, not with nature, and certainly not with animals. Evolutionary theory has not negated differences between the human species and other animals; it has not secured the import of animals once and for all. In fact, evolutionary theory has had the opposite effect: nonhuman animals have become the more dynamic in modern thought because they mean a great deal but refuse to acquiesce to specific conventions or conventionalism in general. As an idea, the theory of evolution confounds human relations with other animals; it does not normalize those relations.

The influence of the theory of evolution is the reason that the publication date of Charles Darwin's *Origin of Species,* 1859, is used here to mark the beginning of the modern period in thought about animals. Darwin's theory is less straightforward and richer than subsequent popularizations would suggest. I spend some time, therefore, on specifics of Darwin's philosophy in the discussion of theoretical approaches to animal victims. In a general way, however, Darwinian theory is treated here not as an isolated event but as a crystallization of pre-existing forces in the history of ideas. The opening chapter of the book offers description of the growing confluence of feeling and belief which brings thinkers in Western culture to the realization that animals can in fact *be* victims. Its status as science notwithstanding, Darwinian evolution can be argued to spring in part from the sensibilities which were already finding animals worthy of consideration. Darwin effects a decisive change because he gives utterance to the new world-view which was gradually unfolding in any event. The dilemmas posed by that world-view would not have been nearly as troubling as they are had Darwinian theory not emerged upon the scene. Darwin gives us the necessary push in the direction of accepting nonhuman animals as important beings.

Literature has caught the effects of the new status of animals in advance of other fields of thought. While even the most up-to-date among the sciences continue to view animals as inferior beings, and philosophers and anthropologists continue to deprecate them in order to assert human eminence, modern literature treats animals as a genuine problem. In modern literature, but more crucially in modern fiction, animals contend with the conceptual devices that seek to subsume them. Their resistance to enculturation influences the nature and profundity of the difficulties literature addresses. In fiction, animals steer the course of events into imaginative complications upon which human powers of resolution falter. In fiction, animal victims do not die passively; they fight back by creating dilemmas that surpass human control. They impress their reality upon narrative, not by the stability but by the instability of their presence. They refuse to be incorporated neatly into the cultural field.

The quarrel between culture and the animal victim is the guiding principle behind the analysis of the works of fiction in this book. Chapters are arranged accordingly as the animal victim poses an increasing threat to cultural construction. Thus, the first chapter of literary analysis (chapter 3) looks at animal victims in their own territory, the wild, where human beings are interlopers and know themselves as such. The following chapter (chapter 4) examines the problems raised by the presence of animals in our territory, the city; uprooted from the natural world, animal victims call into question the capacity of the human psyche to find a home even in the self-created, urban environment. Human sexuality is the focus of the fifth chapter; tangled as our attitudes towards sexuality already are, animal victims in modern fiction add further complications to pre-existing anxieties. They disrupt the most intimate among our efforts to bend physical desires to cultural purposes. Moving from this highly personal subject to a much wider domain, I examine in the next chapter the arguments that the animal victim gives to myth and the creation of myth. Under the critical gaze of the animal, much that is taken for truth in culture is revealed as myth, as fabrications designed to prop up anthropocentric interests. The final chapter analyses works of fiction that exercise that double tyranny over animal victims which humankind has in the past felt free to exercise. In these works, the author compels the animal victim to serve the conventions on which his art is founded. The failings of stories covered in this chapter point to the strengths in other works which do honour the animal.

Categories of animal victims and literary examples discussed in the book are diverse and free-ranging, but not exhaustive. Other approaches to analysis of culture and nonhuman animals can and, I hope, will be proposed. The aim of the book is to offer some principles for criticism of cultural conceptions of animals and to initiate further thought upon ideas about animals we have taken for truths but which now stand in urgent need of questioning. Just as once-marginalized groups of people are demanding and finding their place in culture, so too are nonhuman animals gaining the recognition they deserve. Animals abound in modern literature; they are all around us in life. Attention must be paid to them. Paying attention is the first among the ethical acts which should one day lead us to stop victimizing them.

I The Animal Victim in Its Cultural Context: *A Brief History*

INTRODUCTION

The animal victim has a secure hold upon the modern psyche. Images of dead or dying animals are so abundant that the animal victim has become a virtual institution in modern thought. Over the past three centuries these images have increased in number, in variety, and in violence. Early images prepared sensibilities for attention to the extent and degree of human trespasses against other animals. Until this century, sentiment focused upon relatively 'civilized' offences. Feeling for animals attached itself to caged birds pining for freedom, to liquid-eyed stags dying under the gaze of the hunters who shot them, to overburdened horses beaten by their drivers, to flies with their wings torn off by malicious boys, to dogs cringing beneath their masters' furious assaults, and to foxes run to exhaustion by packs of hounds. The modern mind has to cope with uglier and more widespread violations of the animal's peaceful existence. Consciousness has opened up to the pervasiveness of our victimization of animals. Now we confront images of baby seals clubbed into semi-consciousness and skinned by fishermen; of oil-soaked sea-birds and Beluga whales killed by the chemicals in the St Lawrence river; of dolphin massacres off the coast of Japan and elephants slaughtered for their tusks, their mutilated corpses rotting in the African sun; of tigers driven mad by confinement in zoos, pacing back and forth, back and forth behind the bars of their cages; of calves yanked off their feet and bound hard with ropes in rodeos; of rats skittering painfully over the electrified bars of Skinner boxes and cats with electrodes implanted in their brains; of battery hens jammed by the hundreds into rows of tiny cages, and carcasses of cows and pigs swinging from meat hooks. Almost everywhere we turn these days, there is evidence of the deliberate or unthinking harm we do to other animals. Other, grimmer images live their furtive lives on the fringes of culture and consciousness, in jokes – 'What is red and green and moves at 400 miles an hour?': 'A frog in a blender' – in news items about the torture of companion animals, and in sexual perversions as inconceivable anatomically as they are psychologically. Animal victims reach deep into modern sensibilities.

In recent years, even images of animals in the wild carry the cultural freight of victimization. Set apart from humankind, wild animals should be most free from the idea of victimization, and yet the emotions and values which realize a place for the animal victim in modern consciousness extend also into domains which at one time were properly the animal's and not ours. In the closing years of the last century and the first half of this one, 'the wild' typically meant unrelenting predation among animals, with human participation taking the form of trophy and sport hunting. The thrill of the hunt appeared to isolate aggression in the wild from the moralism of civilized life. In the past twenty years, however, the educative presentation of the lives of natural animals has come to convey the sadness of dwindling numbers, the tenuousness of the wild animal's hold upon its existence. Nature programs almost invariably raise issues of extinction and loss. We are becoming cognizant of the vastness of the damage we have done to the lives of other animals, even in their own regions.

So universal, then, is the conception of the animal as victim that it has become difficult to separate the animal from that particular role. Every animal we see is likely to appear intrinsically defeated, a victim of human dominance. Almost nothing remains to animals that has not been constrained, pruned, injured, or eradicated by humankind. The modern person is most likely to accept the animal's status as victim as definitive, forgetting that the bulk of what is 'animal' in animals has nothing whatever to do with victimization.

It is true, as the above examples illustrate, that animals are made victims when they collide with civilization. In a material sense, of course, animal domains disappear as human populations swell and human demands upon natural resources increase. But it is also true that culture creates the consciousness which perceives the animal as victim. While we might conceivably ignore the threat to our species implicit in evidence of the damage we do to other animals, modern belief impresses upon us a set of values from which the animal victim emerges as a source of distress to philosophy and feeling. A product of the advance of civilization, the animal victim is simultaneously a product of cultural history. Signs of cultural prompting do not deny the reality of animal victims; they suggest, more likely, that the human animal is obtuse and requires external aids to conscience.

THE SLOW GROWTH OF SENSIBILITY

Providing aids to sensibility has not been the method of those infrequent pre-enlightenment philosophers who preach consideration for nonhuman animals.[1] From the time of Pythagoras and the Buddha in the sixth century BC to the start of the eighteenth century, thinkers found it necessary to propose rational arguments for kindness to animals. Those arguments were directed at human concerns and had little to do with the rights of animals as animals. Granted, the transmigration of human souls into the bodies of animals (Pythagoras' position) may not seem particularly rational, but humankind had become so accustomed to using animals in whatever way it chose that extraordinary justifications were required to make any progress against entrenched habits. The greatly attenuated debate over animal souls, or lack of souls, evidently had little power to induce the populace to treat animals well. The centuries of Christian dominance occasionally produced arguments to the effect that wanton cruelty to animals was an affront to God. Appeals to systems under God, however, could be used equally well to support insensitivity to animals, as Augustine's observations on injuries to animals attest: 'We can perceive by their cries ... that animals die in pain, although we make little of this since the beast, lacking a rational soul, is not related to us by a common nature' (in Passmore, p 197). Quite plainly, people 'made little' of the suffering of animals, tales of gentle animal-loving saints notwithstanding. If, as Keith Thomas reports, the fifteenth-century mystic Margery Kempe 'had a vision of Christ being beaten' whenever she saw someone striking a horse (p 152), such visions were not the privilege of the ordinary person. Butchering, blood-sports, and the routine torture of animals on ceremonial occasions inured the public to whatever divinity each animal was supposed to possess by the visions of saints and mystics. How could the tormented animal represent Christ, when torments proceeded unrelentingly? God's world would be unthinkably cruel if animals warranted the same moral concern as humans. Of necessity, Christian doctrine blinded believers to the life of animals; that blindness was a pre-condition of its triumph over competing religions. In his article 'The Historical Roots of Our Ecologic Crisis,' Lynn White, Jr blames Christianity for promoting disregard for the interests of the nonhuman world: 'By destroying pagan animism, Christianity made it possible to exploit nature in a mood of indifference to the feelings of natural objects' (p 1205). Whether pagan animism would have led to greater appreciation of animals in Western culture is a question buried deep beneath centuries of nonpagan thought. In any event, the animal victim had to wait a long time for the emergence of the sensibility that would generate significant opposition to habitual abuse.

One philosophical variant of pagan animism which emerged from time to time was no more effective than doctrines of mercy in cultivating sensitivity to the interests of animals. This variant finds humankind at a great disadvantage on comparison with other animals. Born naked, human beings have no natural weapons and no natural knowledge. Animals live in accord with nature; they do not need the arts of reason or of medicine which human beings must achieve in order to survive. The idea of the 'happy beast'[2] occurs outside of folklore among the Cynics of the fourth century BC, and in a first-century revival of cynical philosophy. Plutarch gives extended treatment to the inferiority of humankind to animals in the dialogue *Gryllus*, and Pliny adopts the same position in his *Natural History*. The idea then apparently disappears until the sixteenth century. Its most notable proponent at this time is, of course, Montaigne. In his *Apology for Raimond Sebond*, Montaigne summarizes the position:

Why do we ascribe to I know not what slavish instinct of nature those works that excel anything we can do by nature or art? Herein we unconsciously give [animals] a very great advantage over us, in making Nature, with maternal kindness, to accompany and lead them as it were by the hand, to all the activities and conveniences of their life; whilst she abandons us to chance and fortune, and forces us to seek by art the things necessary for our preservation; at the same time denying us the means of attaining, by any education or mental effort, to the natural skills of the animals. So that their brutish stupidity surpasses in all their contrivances everything we are able to do with our divine intelligence. (p 384)

In this essay, Montaigne also addresses the perennial problem of the barrier of language standing between humans and animals: 'That defect which hinders communication between us and them, why may it not as well be in ourselves as in them?' (p 382). It is significant that Montaigne's probing of the issue takes the form of a question. His primary aim is to rattle human confidence, not to preach on behalf of animals.

While 'theriophily,' as George Boas has labelled argument based upon the idea of the happy beast, has little historical influence, it is an important theoretical marker for the spirit of the times. In his entry on 'Theriophily' in the *Dictionary of the History of Ideas,* Boas notes that 'To see society from the point of view of a foreigner ... was a favorite device for gaining distance and apparent objectivity; to see it from the point of view of an animal was even better' (4:387). Such scepticism as Montaigne demonstrates indicates the possibility for mistrust of the anthropocentric vision. If anthropocentrism can be blamed for the need to argue that nonhuman animals contain the souls of the human dead, or the need to attribute souls to animals in the first place, then doubts as to the value of definitively human qualities would undermine the authority of human-oriented arguments against the victimization of animals. The idea of the happy beast does offer the possibility of a perspective on moral issues coming from outside the anthropocentric world-view. Pity for animals may not spring directly from such scepticism as theriophily presents, but at least that scepticism shakes reliance upon those rational arguments that had been applied variously in support of and opposition to compassion. Scepticism is evidently a cultural prerequisite to empathy with animals.

Philosophical debate over the correct way to incorporate animals into moral systems continues to this day. But the sensibility which inspires modern debate becomes a stable facet of Western culture around the start of the eighteenth century. As part of their brief introduction to the collection of essays entitled *Animals and Man in Historical Perspective,* Joseph and Barrie Klaits quote in full a description of the death of a bull given in 1714 by Bernard Mandeville. They are following the lead of Wallace Shugg, who also gives the passage in full in 'The Cartesian Beast-Machine in English Literature (1663–1750).' Mandeville's description unquestionably merits attention in any history of humanity's relations with animals, however brief. It occurs in 'Remark (P.)' of his *Fable of the Bees*:

When a large and gentle Bullock, after having resisted ten times greater force of Blows than would have kill'd his Murderer, falls stunn'd at last, and his arm'd Head is fasten'd to the Ground with Cords; as soon as the wide Wound is made, and the Jugulars are cut asunder, what Mortal can without Compassion hear the pitiful Bellowings intercepted by his Blood, the bitter Sighs that speak the Sharpness of his Anguish, and the deep sounding Grones with loud Anxiety fetch'd from the bottom of his strong and palpitating Heart; Look on the trembling and violent Convulsions of his Limbs; see, while his reeking Gore streams from him, his Eyes become dim and languid, and behold his Strugglings, Gasps and last Efforts for Life, the certain Signs of his approaching Fate? When a Creature has given such convincing and undeniable Proofs of the Terrors upon him, and the Pains and Agonies he feels, is there a Follower of *Descartes* so inur'd to Blood as not to refute, by his Commiseration, the Philosophy of that vain Reasoner? (Mandeville's italics, p 181)

The attack on Descartes (who will be touched upon soon) is not the point of citing Mandeville's report on the death of the bull at this juncture. If his philosophy were at issue, one would have to place Mandeville in the camp of opponents to the animal's claim upon morality. F.B. Kaye's introduction to the edition of *The Fable* I am using states that Mandeville's 'code condemned all such acts as were caused by traits men share with the animals' (pp cxx–cxxi). There is nothing the least bit atypical about the belief that human beings are dragged down from the heights of virtue by their animal nature. Conceptually speaking, long-standing tradition cites the 'beast' as the source of evil in the world. What is new in this one passage from *Fable of the Bees* is the vivid entry into the bull's state of consciousness. All questions of argument aside, Mandeville wishes his reader to put himself or herself in the bull's place and to experience what the bull is experiencing. The bull's anguish, moreover, is animal anguish; Mandeville is not personifying the bull. Perhaps even more remarkable than this move towards identification with the animal is Mandeville's use of an everyday occurrence. This 'large and gentle Bullock' is not suffering abuse as part of a sporting event or other special occasion. It is simply being slaughtered in the customary fashion. The cruelty depicted is not of the spectacle variety which many eighteenth-century writers will decry; it is an aspect of the butchering for human use that the eighteenth century will rarely condemn. Mandeville is obviously not making a case against slaughtering livestock; nor is he particularly concerned to encourage kindness towards animals in general. He is not arguing for an ideology. Almost inadvertently, this passage instead articulates a new world-view.

Between Montaigne's time and Mandeville's, the animal had become an object of thought valuable for itself and not simply for what it had to say about humankind. The interests of animals began to arouse concern. Before Mandeville's time, the death or torment of animals would provoke hardly a twinge of conscience in the collective mind. Sentiment was unprepared to extend to animals, and cruelty was not cruelty because it was practised upon entities that did not exist in conscience as suffering beings. Various forces in the late seventeenth and early eighteenth centuries steered sensibilities towards the importance of animals in themselves. In effect, then, animals evolve into victims around the turn of the eighteenth century.

No single author augurs the change in perspective which slowly weakened established human attitudes towards other animals. Ironically, Descartes made his contribution to this change by expounding a view of animals the antithesis of that which eighteenth-century sensibilities would foster. Descartes' infamous 'beast-machine' incited vigorous counter-argument. In theory, it might be all very well to posit that animals are mere machines, without souls, without reason and without sensations, but the evidence of pain and feeling in animals, set before people who were truly observing them for the first time, would have been difficult to dismiss. No doubt the bloodbath in dissecting theatres which followed upon Descartes' assertion, graphically described by Dix

Harwood (pp 107–11), was also too much to stomach for an age that admired reason. Furthermore, the denial of souls to animals was a virtual irrelevancy, since the idea of the soul itself was losing conceptual power. Descartes' theory seems, indeed, like a last desperate effort to hold back humankind against the slide from divine status into kinship with the rest of nature. It is even possible that eighteenth-century thinkers detected a certain petti-ness in the human refusal of souls to fellow creatures. A conversa-tion reported by Joseph Spence between himself and Alexander Pope in 1743 or 1744 suggests precisely that. Spence opens by speculating that dogs have reason:

[POPE:] So they have to be sure. All our disputes about that, are only disputes about words. Man has reason enough only to know what is necessary for him to know; and dogs have just that too.
[SPENCE:] But then they must have souls too; as unperishable in their nature as ours?
[POPE:] And what harm would that be to us? (Shugg, p 289)

Likewise, Voltaire uses the occasion of his entry on animals in his *Philosophical Dictionary* (1764) to ridicule controversies over the nature of the soul in general. Despite itself, then, the Carte-sian theory of the beast-machine gave philosophical legitimacy to animals. Descartes drew attention to animals and showed the need to include them in efforts to understand the ways of the world. It was a short step from the debate over his beast-machine to the authorization of animals as having emotional and moral significance.

Philosophy moved towards asserting likenesses between hu-mankind and animals.[3] Systems of thought such as Locke's and Shaftesbury's grounded the supposedly human distinctions of knowledge and moral virtue not in divine mystery but in nature. This relocation of sources for knowledge of the human condition and of virtue curiously echoes arguments from theriophily. It shows philosophy attempting to transfer to humans the same certainty of instinct theriophily attributes to animals. Later, towards the middle of the eighteenth century, one finds Julien Offray de la Mettrie seeking to establish a primitive psychology upon biological processes: 'From animals to men,' he wrote, 'the transition is not violent' (in Thomas, p 123). Perhaps without describing their search as such, other scientists hunted for 'the missing link' between humans and nonhuman animals (Rosenfield, p 196). Donna Haraway's account of the mid-century work of the Swedish scientist Carl von Linnaeus implies that he inserted a link into his system of classification almost by main force. Haraway notes 'a dubious and interesting creature illustrated as a hairy woman' (p 8) classified by Linnaeus as *Homo troglodytes* and posited by him as belonging to the same genus as *Homo sapiens*. Linnaeus' taxonomy evidently reserves no divine or even quasi-divine status for the human species on the chain of being. Although Haraway offers the proper caution that Linnaeus' activity of naming falls into line with Christian belief, his grand system of classification participates with other scientific observations[4] in the undermining of the privileged position of humankind. These efforts assisted the collapse of the idea that the human species belongs to a different order of being from the other animals. They prepare the way for Darwin's theory of evolution and for the hold that evolutionary theory will take upon the collective mind. The extent to which this period anticipates modern thought may be judged from La Mettrie's development of methods for teaching apes to communicate using sign language (Himmelfarb, p 169).

The thought that nature might be made to speak in human terms signals the gradual closing of the conceptual gap between human and animal creation. It was only logical, therefore, that if people felt pain and deprivation, animals must feel something similar. Since the pains and deprivations of people were no longer received as a pre-heavenly given of this 'vale of tears' but were beginning to demand political attention, animal suffering was likewise converted into a correctable ill. The torment of animals was an ugliness that humankind by its better lights could eliminate, at least where that torment was needless, as in cock-fighting or bear-baiting. Although the voices of protest then and now tend to appeal to the effect on the human mind of cruelty to animals, even this argument depends upon a premise of continuity: the pain we give to animals alters our own moral and emotional state.

Recognition of similarities is oddly connected with the physical and mental distance from nature achieved in the eighteenth century. Progressive urbanization decreased the threat of the natural world. Such terrors as nature could possess for the urban sophisticate had to be reinvented in Gothic tales. That primitive intimacy which might produce genuine fear was past recall. The strange animal monsters of legend shrank dramatically to the menagerie's placid and no doubt sickly beasts confined to small cages and displayed for the amusement of the public. The kind of consumerism which drew the public to menageries produced also a diverse readership for written works of natural history (see Ritvo, pp 8–9). What Harriet Ritvo says of the contemporaneous efforts at classification may also be said of menageries: 'they embodied a sweeping human claim to intellectual mastery of the natural world' (p 12). For a large portion of European citizenry, the world really was 'man-made'; people could regard in safety a mute Nature standing ineffectual beyond city-limits.

At the same time, of course, the spread of the scientific attitude increased confidence in the human control over nature. Nature could be *known*, could be subjugated by the power of the human mind. The possibility that rationalization of the animal might itself constitute a kind of victimization would hardly have occurred to the eighteenth-century zoological enthusiast. The effect, instead, was the conceptual domestication of even the wild animal and the metamorphosis of the animal into a curiosity. Presenting thus a graspable and untroubling image to the mind, the animal could become a concern of sentiment. The sentiments necessary for seeing the animal as a victim did not, however, have to be particularly full-blooded. A mere desire for an orderly existence, completely in keeping with the scientific attitude, would have been sufficient to isolate the misery of animals as a source of disturbance. Empiricism assisted that perceptual keenness which enhanced the emotional piquancy of the plight of suffering animals.

An enlightened attitude towards animals emerges, then, out of several processes, in particular – one must grant – the scientific approach that would so irritate the Romantics towards the end of the century. While it may not be true that empiricism removes human investment from the enterprise of understanding, it is clear that humankind had to attend to the natural world before it could begin to extend moral concern to animals. Signs of recognition of the continuity between human and nonhuman animals presage the clear moral dilemma Darwinism would later place before humankind. In the Enlightenment, the attempt to apply philosophical thought to humanity's place in nature was also salutary, even where that philosophical thought came to conclusions detrimental to the nonhuman animal as Descartes' did. Regarding animals as a genuine ontological problem enhanced the sensibility that would lead to indignation at the mistreatment of animals. Urbanization also had its place in the process, despite the fact that urban people have fewer and less vital contacts with animals than their rural counterparts – an observation that is made to this day, when resentment rises against city people promoting ethical regard for animals. Perhaps urbanization led to a certain amount of hypocrisy on the score of sentimentalism over animals, with people struggling to rationalize kindness for some domestic animals and slaughter for others, scientific appreciation for curiosities of the animal world and the elimination of 'noxious' creatures. Still, the disappearance of superstition and fear of the natural world, coupled with efforts to found morality on sound rational principles, could not help but render the urban person sensitive to cruelty to animals. Worldliness in general prompted concern for animals, if only because physical suffering alone clearly stood in need of amelioration.

Nevertheless, compassion for animals was a long way from becoming a regular feature of ethics for adults. It may be sweet, and it may even constitute a cultural breakthrough, when in Laurence Sterne's novel *Tristram Shandy* (1759–67) Uncle Toby opens a window to let a fly escape instead of squashing the insect, but the act testifies more to the character's (and Sterne's) innocent eccentricity than to a practical ideal in action. Uncle Toby is not a model of expected conduct. As far as public concerns went, sentimental regard for animals was more of a decoration than a dictate. Despite empirical interests, sympathy was extended to animals only by categories. Those that were timid and harmless to humans aroused pity. Those that were useful to humans could be used without compunction. Those that defied civilization, beasts of prey like wolves and wild bears, were taken still to be legitimate targets of human hostility. Uncle Toby's fly would normally fall into the category of pests justifiably destroyed by humans. The seeds of a publicly generated political movement on behalf of the animals might be sown at this time, but the conceptual bulwark against full-scale appreciation of animals was only slightly weakened. Anthropocentrism was not yet ready to give way to the interests of nonhuman animals. People were, after all, just beginning to enjoy considerable power over nature; the sympathetic soul might bend to pity the suffering creature, but the idea that animals could truly threaten human entitlement was a long way off.

PREACHING TO CHILDREN

It was more or less safe, however, to preach to children about the need for kindness to animals. As to flies, one enlightened moment occurs in a children's story written by Dr Aiken and Mrs Barbauld. A father responds to his child's question 'What are flies good for to people?' with the logical observation that one might just as fairly ask 'What are people good for to flies?' (cited by Harwood, p 258). Conceptual reversals like this one are, of course, rare in any literature of the period. Literature for children in the later years of the eighteenth century most frequently deploys animal victims for the moral improvement of the young. At the same time as the spirit of Romanticism is beginning to emerge, pre-Romantic notions of proper conduct seem to descend into instructions to children, at least where animals are concerned. Fairy tales fell into disfavour, and in the absence of this more penetratingly imaginative mode, the animal victim becomes a somewhat rarified entity. Beings more helpless than children could induce in the child the appropriate spirit of duty towards others. Mary Wollstonecraft goes as far as to inform her readers that 'It is only to animals that children *can* do good,' since 'men are their superiors' (Wollstonecraft's italics, ch 2, p 15). Feeling for animals was represented, moreover, as a species of gentility for the poor and the middle-classes. Animals provided the disadvantaged child with access to that condescension which the wealthy could exercise in wider fields. In fact, the wealthy come in for a great deal of rebuke in children's stories of this period. Wealthy children suffer from ill-temper and poor health; not the least among their failings is cruelty to animals.

As the first lessons in Wollstonecraft's *Original Stories* relate, the healthy child can '*retrace* the image that God first implanted in him' (Wollstonecraft's italics, ch 1, p 10) in loving attention to animals. The wise Mrs Mason, who delivers these lessons, initiates instruction by stepping off the path into the high grass, to avoid crushing some snails. Her young companions are incredulous, but she counters their squeamishness with encouragement to observe the wonderful ways of such lowly creatures as spiders, worms, ants, and snails. Empirical interest will then lead to delight in nature, and to good deeds. Where other creatures 'only think of themselves,' children can set themselves on the road to godly virtue with altruistic regard for animals. The mix of attitudes and assumptions is informative: empirical objectivity leads to kindness towards animals and thence to service to God. In this chain of reasoning for children, wealth apparently stops sensibilities at the first step, for the indulged child cannot see beyond his or her own interests.

The story (1766) of the extraordinarily unselfish Miss Goody Two-Shoes suspends lectures on kindness to animals until the orphaned girl has become comfortably middle-class, a wealthy family having rewarded her for saving their lives with a position as a school-mistress. It is at this point in the narrative that the young woman's compassion for animals emerges. Her income helps: in one incident, she is able to buy animals from some boys who are tormenting them (pt 2, ch 1). This development shows considerable canniness on the part of the writer (possibly Oliver Goldsmith). Where other writers present malicious children undergoing a change of heart through talk, this one realizes the implausibility of that device. The preaching that does occur in the story is directed at children emerging from ignorance by means of books such as *Goody Two-Shoes*. The structure of the narrative imitates its ideals in predicating virtue upon learning. The following passage lays out the argument for kindness to animals:

Mrs. *Margery* [Goody Two-Shoes], you must know, was very humane and compassionate; and her Tenderness extended not only to all Mankind, but even to all Animals that were not noxious; as your's ought to do, if you would be happy here, and go to Heaven hereafter. These are GOD Almighty's Creatures as well as we. He made both them and us; and for wise Purposes, best known to himself, placed them in this World to live among us; so that they are our fellow Tenants of the Globe. How then can People dare to torture and wantonly destroy GOD Almighty's Creatures? They as well as you are capable of feeling Pain and receiving Pleasure, and how can you, who want to be made happy yourself delight in making your fellow Creatures miserable? Do you think the poor Birds, whose Nest and young ones that wicked Boy *Dick Wilson* ran away with Yester-day, do not feel as much Pain, as your Mother and Father would have felt, had any one pulled down their House and ran away with you? To be sure they do. Mrs. *Two-Shoes* used to speak of those Things, and of naughty Boys throwing at Cocks, torturing Flies, and whipping Horses and Dogs, with Tears in her Eyes, and would never suffer any one to come to her School who did so. (pp 68–9)

This passage takes the time-honoured approach: 'How would *you* like it if someone did that to you?' In its small way, the argument does reflect the new recognition of similarities between human beings and nonhuman animals, similarities at least sufficient for moral consideration. One wonders, of course, how 'naughty Boys' given to torturing animals were supposed to overcome that vice without the benefit of Mrs Margery's educational institution.

Thomas Day's *History of Sandford and Merton* (1783–9) is built upon the moral superiority of the honest labourer over the indolent person of wealth. This three-volume work records the lengthy process whereby Harry Sandford, son of a farmer, converts Tommy Merton, a gentleman's child, from mental and physical slothfulness to moral and physical rectitude. Several of Tommy's lessons come from being pitched into bogs and ponds by the frightened animals he assaults. The *History* requires that the wealthy child be humiliated. The rationale for the critique of the rich, however, is supposed to originate in nature. 'The History of the Two Dogs,' in volume I, illustrates the point. In this tale, an exchange of dogs between a rich man and a poor man produces a complete switch of character in the two dogs (pp 53–60). Two encounters with wolves prove the moral and physical inferiority of the pampered dog: while the pampered dog beats a cowardly retreat, the dog who has lived with the poor man rushes in to slay the wolf. Evidently poverty produces a natural moral courage superior to all the refinements of wealth.

Along with the heroism demonstrated in combat with wild beasts, however, *The History of Sandford and Merton* also advocates mercy. In winter, Harry sometimes goes to bed without food, having given his supper to the poor little starving birds. He never hurts the toads, frogs, and spiders that other people despise, and will walk around worms that are in his path (1: 5). Harry, it should be noted, is all of six years old at this time. Clearly, as the story insists, righteousness must have a great deal to do with diet and exercise. What other explanation could there be for such fine sensibilities in so young a child? In addition to steeling the person for

the good fight with savagery, righteousness possesses the additional benefit of instilling love in the frightened heart of the
beast. 'If you want to tame animals,' says the good Mr Barlow,
'you must be good to them, and treat them kindly, and then they
will no longer fear you, but come to you and love you' (1:122). This
advice follows an incident in which Tommy has been dragged into
the mud by a pig he has tormented for failure to respond to his
orders.

Many bribes are thus offered to young readers of the late eighteenth century. Images of a St Francis–like power to attract animals through love was one sort of bribe. Courage to defeat the
wild beast was another (for adventure-loving boys, at any rate).
Satisfaction to the soul was propped up with hints of financial
gain. If no monetary reward were forthcoming, the disappointed
child could always content himself or herself with a sense of moral
superiority over the idle rich. For all the talk of animals and their
feelings, one has the impression that the main purpose of these
stories is to promote obedience, quietness, and extraordinary tolerance for the preaching of adults. With the political and religious
bribes to the juvenile audience, the pain of the animal is largely
obscured. The animal victim is a means to foster a generalized
moral tone. The frequent references to God and humankind's dominion, however, do suggest fears that somehow the climate of
the times will conspire with the stories to elevate the animal
victim to a true object of compassion. History outside of stories for
children was gradually bestowing that independent status upon
animals which would make their suffering a genuine cause for
moral concern rather than an instrument for emotional and ethical
instruction. Romanticism is that historical development which fills
out the charitable approach to the animal.

ROMANTICISM: THE SUBLIME AND THE NARCISSISTIC

The conventional view of Romanticism as a nature-loving, pan-
theistic movement would indicate a direct connection between Romantic passions and full appreciation of the animal. In theory,
the Romantic animal should possess strength and beauty to raise
it beyond the sentimentalism inherent to Enlightenment images
of animals. The Romantic animal, in other words, should embody
that spirit of wildness which truly challenges the act of victimiza-

tion. The Romantic animal should 'fight back' conceptually and thus resist human dominance. The proper reaction to this theoretical Romantic animal should be to stand back and admire. All this might be so, were Romanticism as straightforward as the customary perspective suggests.

Many aspects of Romanticism have, however, a deleterious effect upon recognition of animal victims. Indeed, an examination of Romanticism highlights the point that there is a significant difference between appreciation of nature in general and appreciation of animals. Nature worship, for example, is possible even in the twentieth century, whereas worship of animals is an intellectual impossibility. The nature worship of the Romantics has a suspiciously self-serving quality, and that quality seems to disbar, for the most part, regard for the inherent value of animals. Raging cataracts and mountain crags worked the appropriate exaltation upon human imagination; in these landscapes, animals are incidental at best. In many of the European Romantics, one discovers that the effort to locate godhead in nature tends to undo previous ethical attention to animal victims. A counter-example to this assertion seems to occur in Goethe's *Sorrows of Young Werther* when Werther bemoans universal destructiveness: 'A harmless walk kills a thousand poor crawling things, one footstep smashes a laboriously built anthill and stamps a whole little world into an ignominious grave' (p 63). This outcry, however, is at once unusual in Goethe's works and somewhat specious. The destruction of 'poor crawling things' panders to Werther's mood of despair; the creatures themselves do not appear to matter greatly. Indeed, in Goethe's *Elective Affinities* and *Faust,* the very few places in which animals are mentioned at all occasion expressions of disgust. In *Elective Affinities,* Ottilie devotes a journal entry to her contempt for those who paint 'horrid monkeys' (p 215): 'How can anyone bring himself to expend such care on depicting horrid monkeys!' she begins (p 215). For Goethe, as for others working out Germanic idealism, contemplation of 'whole rows of inferior natural creatures' (*Elective Affinities,* p 216) apparently blocked the road to discovery of the divinity of humankind. In its religious and supernatural mode, the Romantic imagination was inclined to jump from the individual person to the panorama of nature, overleaping the animal in the process.

The panorama of nature had a curious effect upon the Romantic psyche. Instead of overawing the observer and impressing him or her with the smallness of the human person, the scene tended instead to inflate the idea of self. Grandeur could be nature's gift to the individual, and especially to the artist. In the mind of the Romantic, identification occurred between the person and the infinite in nature, between the imagination and the universal spirit moving through particular forms. Empiricism was tedious, its conception of nature lifeless and soul-destroying. The right of the artist to impose upon nature a 'new mythology,' such as Friedrich Schlegel demanded, sprung from the sublime individuality nature had granted to the human being and denied to the rest of creation.

In the euphoria of working out a new world-view, Romantic thinkers may simply have overlooked the mundane existence and plain suffering of animals. This would be a minor omission, were it not that Romanticism purports to revivify nature, purports, that is, to rescue natural phenomena from the tyranny of science and thus to restore power to the natural world. As one contemplates Romanticism's effect upon nonhuman animals, two sources of uneasiness arise. First, since the Romantic idea of nature seems in general to elide the animal in favour of the sublime, one begins to wonder if the Romantics are in fact addressing the tangled issue of concepts of nature, or have instead erected some metaphysical idea which does not enhance but substitutes for earthly existence. The second source of uneasiness comes with the possibility that the Romantic idea of nature is self-serving. The belief that the human imagination can attain extraordinary magnitude by true contact with the sublime in nature seems suspiciously like yet another attempt by humankind to become divine and to separate itself from the earthly world where animals live. Physical pain appears to have fallen out of the purview of the Romantic mind; pains are world-pains: dejection, lassitude, dysphoria. Thus, when moral concern for animal victims occurs in Romantic poetry, that concern tends to look very much like a return to Enlightenment thought.

We are, however, in the realm of culture and ideas – perhaps even more decidedly in this realm with Romanticism than with other historical movements. Since the aim here is to determine a conception of nonhuman animals that disturbs or even militates against acts of victimization, and since Romanticism is clearly still with us, one seeks in the movement crucial changes in thought which do work to the advantage of the animal victim. For one thing, the domesticated nature of science, ever obedient to human reason, was the enemy to Romanticism. The wildness in the wild animal could therefore be honoured in art, and is honoured in Blake's 'Tyger,' for instance, and Southey's 'Dancing Bear.' The wild animal is honoured also in painting, in, as examples, Antoine-Louis Barye's *Tiger* and Delacroix's *Lion Hunts*. Arnold Hauser's comments on Delacroix are informative in this context. Delacroix, Hauser says, is the 'greatest representative of romantic painting, [but] also one of the enemies and conquerors of romanticism' (*The Social History of Art*, 3:206). For Hauser, Delacroix's Romanticism resides in the fact that 'man still stands in the centre of his [the artist's] world' (p 207). Looking only at *Lion Hunts*, however, one sees 'man' thoroughly tumbled about by the wild animal; the human participants in fact seem to be at the mercy of the lions. Human control is surrendered to the animal. Even the artist himself has conceded the power of aesthetic organization to the rage of the hunted beast. Romantic idealism may bestow absolute authority upon the human psyche, but Romanticism's challenge to the authority of the scientific approach to nature yields the opposite view of the status of the human being in creation. Maintained awkwardly alongside idealism is submission of the spirit to the forces of nature. Both of these contrary strategies have serious theoretical consequences for animal victims.

Among the English Romantic poets, Coleridge was most affected by German idealism. Although the didactic element in *The Rime of the Ancient Mariner* has become something of a cliché in the course of time, its approach to the animal victim reveals the intensity of the moral struggle between Enlightenment and Romantic belief. An allegorical reading of Coleridge's *Ancient Mariner* based upon idealism could easily find symbolism in the albatross. The albatross could be a Christ-figure, for example. That kind of reading, however, risks reinforcing those qualities in the poem that have turned it into a cliché. If we forego the temptation to view the albatross as a symbol, the poem may not increase in rationality but it does gain on the score of terror and historical significance.

In some ways, of course, the poem begs for a symbolic interpretation; for most readers, I imagine, it is simply too hard to accept that the killing of a mere bird should disarrange reality as it does in *The Ancient Mariner*. The Mariner's moment of liberation, however, argues against symbolic readings of animal life in the poem: he blesses some water snakes because they are beautiful. As a Christian man, he has a thick obstruction of symbolism to overcome before he can see snakes plainly as the natural creatures that they are. Coleridge's invocation of spirits and other supernatural paraphernalia gives what seems a naïve morality of love of animals its intellectual credibility. The moral drawn from the tale improves little upon instructions given to children at this time. But the submission of the poem to the inherent value of the albatross and the snakes elevates its morality beyond previous sentimentalism. The application of Romantic principles to the ideological issue of the animal victim lends dignity and power to the animal. Whether Coleridge was aware of it or not, he has felt and imaged forth the double-sided and profound significance of the animal victim in modern life. Truly, that mindless approach to animals – if it moves, kill it – vitiates claims to superiority in civilization; wanton assaults upon animals return humanity to a primitive state wherein the occult rules. On the other side of the issue centred on the albatross, that intellectual distance which scoffs at the supernatural and neutralizes animal existence represents to the Romantic imagination the disordered universe, the universe without meaning. If we think of Coleridge's albatross as a literal albatross pure and simple, the poem as a whole addresses reality with much greater cogency than if we try to translate the albatross into some other, non-animal being or entity.

William Blake's metaphysics are too esoteric for anyone to make a confident or final interpretation of his animals. So many of his figures and beings are symbolic of abstract forces, and sometimes changing forces, that it is difficult to find trustworthy animal images among them. Like other Romantics, he places certain human capacities, poetic genius primarily, at the summit of creation. Nevertheless, out of the obscurity of his thought, he does produce some revolutionary ideas about literal animals. The small poem 'The Fly,' in *Songs of Experience*, for example, begins with the lines:

Little Fly,
Thy summer's play
My thoughtless hand
Has brush'd away.

Am not I
A fly like thee?
Or art not thou
A man like me?

'The Fly' concludes with the assertion that the poet is indeed a fly because both beings live and die in the same way. In *The Book of Thel*, Blake suggests that we should feel blessed to feed the worms after we die (line 25). The Romantic love of contrariness which Black evinces sometimes works to the benefit of animals. On the whole, however, Blake's mythology converts animals into prophetic symbols less beneficial to actual animals than to the flagging human spirit.

English Romanticism in its second phase is less inclined towards religiosity. Logic dictated to both Shelley and Byron that genuine feeling for animals demanded a vegetarian diet. While Byron practised vegetarianism only sporadically and largely out of vanity, Shelley went as far as to write philosophical treatises on the matter. In his notes to *Queen Mab,* he offers semi-scientific arguments for vegetarianism: humans, he says, are biologically 'frugivorous' not carnivorous; vegetarianism will slow the spread of disease and soften the warlike spirit. The myth which speaks to him of the change in human diet is the myth of Prometheus. Prometheus introduced humans to cooked meat, 'thus inventing an expedient for screening from his [man's] disgust the horror of the shambles.' The passage of *Queen Mab* to which these notes pertain offers a vision of humankind, no longer devouring the 'mangled flesh' of animals and becoming once again 'immortal upon earth' (VIII, lines 211–2).

In contrast to the candour of *Queen Mab,* the high Romanticism of *Prometheus Unbound* precludes talk of dietary reform. After the fall of Jupiter and the release of Prometheus, however, the 'Spirit of the Earth' does find that the previously repulsive 'toads, and snakes, and loathly worms' have become beautiful: 'And that with little change of shape or hue: / All things had put their evil nature off' (III.iv.76–7). One hears echoes of children's literature, in which empirical interest was supposed to achieve just such a change of attitude towards toads, worms, spiders, and the like, though the suggestion that a toad, or any other natural entity, was previously evil strikes a dissonant note. Shelley's allegory in

Prometheus suggests rightly that the seemingly simple change in perspective requires a virtual revolution in thought. But the disappearance of such frank political assertion as appears in *Queen Mab* has the disturbing effect of putting change beyond human intelligence and will. Myth concedes the power of reform to mystical forces in nature. The mythic dimension of *Prometheus* rests, nevertheless, upon an earthly plane where even lowly creatures assume importance. Shelley's hostility to Christianity and interest in science would have made him suspicious of any religiosity which had negative implications for animals.

Christianity's view of animals is one source of conflict in Byron's *Cain*. Byron uses the animal victim to turn Christian orthodoxy on its head. The first murderer of Christian belief becomes, for Byron, a modern figure striking out against placid acceptance of God's construction of life. The suffering of animals is the point of departure for Cain's rebellion. Something is unfair in the universe when animals, who did not sin along with Adam and Eve, must die (II.ii.153–60). Worse, it looks as though Jehovah smiles upon the sacrifice of animals. When Cain offers his bloodless sacrifice, an altar spread with fruits, as an alternative to Abel's where spring lambs have been sacrificed, the fire on Abel's altar flares upward to heaven while Cain's is destroyed in a whirlwind. According to Abel, Jehovah has shown his 'immortal pleasure' in the ritual killing of the lambs. Cain reacts:

> *His!*
> *His pleasure!* What was his high pleasure in
> The fumes of scorching flesh and smoking blood,
> To the pain of the bleating mothers which
> Still yearn for their dead offspring? or the pangs
> Of the sad ignorant victims underneath
> Thy pious knife? Give way! this bloody record
> Shall not stand in the sun, to shame creation! (III.i.297–304)

That Lucifer has encouraged Cain in his revolt is not evidence of Byron's disavowal of Cain's anger. The indictment of Jehovah is unanswered; the drama surrounding God's choice of the bloody altar itself supports Cain's revolt. The Angel of the Lord appears, not to exonerate God, but to punish Cain. And although Cain mourns in the end the death of the 'gentle race' that Abel might have begun, one senses that Byron prefers a world full of questioning, exiled Cains to one in which faith accepts blindly what reason sees clearly as injustice. That piety which does not balk at inflicting an unnecessary death on animals, when it is bad enough that animals die in the first place, presents an aspect too terrible to credit as love of God.

The request for mercy in *Cain* appears intellectually to be almost indistinguishable from pre-Romantic argument. Yet there is a way in which truly Romantic sensibility may be seen to attach to the two altars in *Cain*. Elaine Scarry's observations on sacrifice in *The Body in Pain* point to the juncture at which love of animal freedom and intellectual revolt at victimization meet. The substitution of sacrificial animals for humans is a step in the right direction. Scarry asks the reader to visualize the image of human sacrifice being supplanted by an image of animal sacrifice. She suggests, next, a second substitution:

But if one now holds steadily visible not two pictures but three – the child with the knife looming above, giving way to the lamb and the knife looming above, and now in turn the lamb moved out of that location and replaced by a block of wood under the still looming knife – so great in the transition from the second to the third picture is the revolution in consciousness that the object itself is now re-perceived as a wholly different object, a tool rather than a weapon, and the anticipated action of the object is no longer an act of 'wounding' but an act of 'creating.' (p 174)

Scarry's analysis intensifies Byron's denunciation of Jehovah. Byron's Jehovah aims to 'wound' humans by demanding the sacrifice of living beings. Jehovah rejects Cain's offer of a creative sacrifice in place of the destructive one. The spirit of Jehovah opposes Romantic creativity. Cain proposes a 'revolution in consciousness' with his bloodless sacrifice. The substitution appeals not simply to reason but to that spirit of freedom in Romanticism which honours the wild animal.

I close this short survey of Romantic animals by touching upon some of Arthur Schopenhauer's statements and images. Schopenhauer is an interesting figure in this argument because his work extends from the age of Romanticism proper to the middle of the nineteenth century, during which time agitation for the protection of animals gained momentum. Schopenhauer's early theories illustrate the negative effect upon animals of Romantic idealism, while his later thought demonstrates the foresight that could come out of the combination of Romanticism and rational ethical regard. In his best-known work, *The World as Will and Representation,* published in 1819, he establishes his hierarchy of the beautiful in art upon the typically Romantic notion of individuality combining with the universal 'Idea.' The aesthetic theory of his early work clearly places humankind at the summit of imaginative representation. Animal painting falls two grades below representation of humankind. In animal painting, 'the characteristic is wholly one with the beautiful; the most characteristic lion, wolf, horse, sheep, or ox is always the most beautiful also. The reason for this is that animals have only the character of their species, not an individual character' (p 220). In view of the Romantic glorification of artistic activity, such thought as this does not bode well for the animal victim. In Schopenhauer's aesthetic judgment, vital, imaginative one-to-one contact apparently stops short with the human species.

It is not only as an artistic subject that animals come in for disparagement in *The World as Will and Representation.* Various other denials of animal capacity prop up Schopenhauer's valorization of humankind. Animals lack reason, of course; they lack memory; and because of these two other deficiencies, they lack intentionality (2:59-61). Their lack of freedom in particular causes Schopenhauer to lump animals in with inanimate objects. 'The hungry wolf,' he observes, 'buries its teeth in the flesh of the deer with the same necessity with which the stone falls to the ground, without the possibility of the knowledge that it is the mauled as well as the mauler' (1:404). He follows up this last enigmatic assertion with the italicized conclusion that *'Necessity is the kingdom of nature; freedom is the kingdom of grace.'* The implication is that humankind belongs at least in part to the kingdom of grace. In this hierarchical arrangement, with its promise of grace for humanity, Schopenhauer backs up the central Romantic drive to elevate humankind out of animal creation and into the regions of the sublime. It is characteristic of this hierarchical arrangement that ethical concern for animals is delimited by human pleasure. In a footnote, Schopenhauer states that 'the pain the animal suffers through death or work is still not so great as that which man would suffer through merely being deprived of the animal's flesh or strength. Therefore in the affirmation of his own existence, man can go as far as to deny the existence of the animal' (1:372). Granted, later in this statement, he disallows beatings and vivisection, but the minimization of the animal's pain and the magnification of the suffering of humankind were it denied the use of animals is part and parcel of the overall idealistic aim of Schopenhauer's philosophy at this point in his life.

Among the idealists, however, Schopenhauer is atypical in several respects, one of them being that he lives long enough to record the influence of a kind of pragmatism occurring alongside the initial ardour for Romanticism. Here, I anticipate the upcoming section in this history. As will be seen in that section, various attitudes towards animal victims work themselves out simultaneously during this period. In *On the Basis of Morality,* completed in 1840, Schopenhauer takes up one of those attitudes. As in the earlier work, he maintains that human beings alone possess reason. He is willing to grant that if 'we were to discover a species of apes which deliberately made *implements* for fighting, building, or any other use, we should at once admit that it was endowed with *reason*' (his italics, p 84). I suspect that he would have been pleased with the recent observations that chimpanzees and other animals do in fact use tools. In this argument, he does not assume that the distinction of reasoning powers gives licence to humans to use animals at will. He notes the 'boundless' (p 131) egoism of the human animal as one of only three incentives to action. The basis of morality, he argues, is compassion: 'Only insofar as an action has sprung from compassion does it have moral value; and every action resulting from any other motives has none' (p 144). The extremity of the position may be characterized as Romantic. Likewise, the founding of a moral system upon emotion could be described as a Romantic gesture. The strong position, even so, could also be seen to follow from the weaker sentimentalism of the Enlightenment.

While sometimes raising the old argument that cruelty to animals leads to indifference to other people, he is also capable of viewing kindness to animals as an end in itself. Criticizing Kant's view of moral ends, he writes:

Genuine morality is outraged by the proposition ... that beings devoid of reason (hence animals) are *things* and therefore should be treated merely as *means* that are not at the same time an *end*... Thus only for practice are we to have sympathy for animals, and they are, so to speak, the pathological phantom for the purpose of practising sympathy for human beings... I regard such propositions as revolting and abominable. (His italics, pp 95–6)

He finds confirmation of his own, contrary moral position in 'the fact that *the animals* are also taken under its [his own moral system's] protection':

In other European systems of morality, they are badly provided for, which is most inexcusable. They are said to have no rights, and there is the erroneous idea that our behaviour to them is without moral significance, or, as it is said in the language of that morality, there are no duties to animals. All this is revoltingly crude, a barbarism of the West... (p 175)

The compassion he spoke of earlier in his argument is to attach itself to the ego of the animal, for animals also share in the boundless egoism of living beings. 'If any Cartesian were to find himself clawed by a tiger,' he quips, 'he would become aware in the clearest possible manner of the sharp distinction such a beast draws between its ego and the non-ego' (p 176). The difference between the wolf in the earlier work that is barely distinguishable from a stone and this image of a tiger asserting its ego with its claws marks a change in thought so radical as to project Schopenhauer's later remarks past even the presumptions of the mid-nineteenth century. His prescience can be judged from his denunciation as 'revolting' of the linguistic habit of the English of applying the pronoun 'it' to animals. This habit of speech he describes as a 'priestly trick for the purpose of reducing animals to the level of things.' He does, however, admire the English for their progressive moves to enact protective legislation on behalf of animals.

At this point in his argument, he also brings into focus the effect of scientific observation of animals upon moral conduct: 'Nothing leads more definitely to recognition of the identity of the essential nature in animal and human phenomena than a study of zoology and anatomy' (p 177), he says:

What, then, are we to say when in these days (1839) a bigoted and canting zootomist [Rudolph Wagner, according to the editor's footnote] has the audacity to emphasize an absolute and radical difference between man and animal, and goes so far as to attack and disparage honest zoologists who keep aloof from all priestly guile, toadyism and hypocrisy, and pursue their course under the guidance of nature and truth? (p 177)

Upon this pre-Darwinian assertion of identity between humans and animals Schopenhauer establishes the bond of compassion. Schopenhauer's philosophical approach to animal victims, in sum, steers an uncertain course between scientific fact and religious belief. Plain fact, sheer empirical observation, proves the interconnectedness of humans and animals; certain religions (notably Eastern religions) presuppose attentiveness to animals and bypass, therefore, the mechanisms that societies adhering to other belief systems require for the exercise of compassion. It is in compassion that he finds the human mean between the two cultural forces of science and religion. The compassion he speaks for could take either the strong form of anger at human ignorance, such as he demonstrates in his own language, or the cool form of reasoned empathy. The confluence of attitudes in his expressions of compassion indicates a fusion of Romanticism and Enlightenment approaches to the animal.

Romanticism's contribution to the whole issue of the victimization of animals is decidedly mixed. On the one hand, idealism and the search for a new mythology reinforce the conception of human power as other-worldly and hence pre-eminent over the earthly interests of nonhuman animals. Plain sentiment appears to be too puny an emotion to satisfy the Romantic desire for the sublime. On the other hand, Romanticism's appreciation of energy and freedom readies the imagination for converting the animal into a source of threat and thus into a being dangerous to tamper with. The Enlightenment prepares the ground for political reform, while Romanticism begins to work the conceptual revolution that would liberate the animal from human authority.

CLOSING IN ON THE THEORY OF EVOLUTION:
THE VAGARIES OF SOCIAL REFORM AND ARTISTIC
REPRESENTATION IN THE EARLY NINETEENTH CENTURY

For discussion of development in social attitudes towards animals manifest in the closing years of the eighteenth century and the

first half of the nineteenth, I will be drawing upon both philosophical statements[5] and examples from the visual arts. Both
sources, divergent as they are, reveal a socialized animal, one
that does not quarrel with the mores of the time. Certainly, the
philosophical arguments made for the rights of animals extend
the gradually widening circle of ethical concern beyond the limits
that would be acceptable to the general run of humanity, but the
approach to the subject of animals falls directly in line with humanitarian arguments applied to human suffering. Works from
the visual arts illustrate the tailoring of animal images to social
needs. It is in the visual rather than the written arts that growing public interest in animals is disclosed. Humanization of the
animal is apparent both in philosophical works and in artistic
creations. The eccentric people who presented arguments for
kindness to animals on the grounds of their similarities to human
beings nevertheless managed to sustain the rights view that would
base moral concern upon the animal itself. Artists, by contrast,
adapted their representations of animals to human ends. Indeed,
one of the paradoxes of the visual representations of the times is
the extent to which naturalistic images of animals could be used
to foster the aims of civilization. The desire to emancipate animals
legally and morally contends with an imperialistic urge to subsume
them under the ideals of the civilized. Although a steady stream
of political agitation on behalf of animals has its source in these
pre-Darwinian years, attitudes towards animals become increasingly polarized. Conflict exists among categories of human relations
with animals simultaneously as those categories are merging. This
is a strange and wavering period for animals.

The peak of these years, 1850, produced probably the most
famous condemnation of nature, Tennyson's characterization of
nature as 'red in tooth and claw / With ravine' (*In Memoriam*, lvi,
15–16). According to Tennyson, while humankind struggled to
maintain faith in God, nature 'shrieked against his creed' (line
16). Much of society, it appears, was determined to follow Tennyson's
advice from the same poem: 'Move upward, working out the beast /
And let the ape and tiger die' (cxviii, 27–8). If lines like these are a
sign of the spirit of the times, the perfection of the human being was
the primary project, and the achievement of this perfection was
assumed to depend upon the suppression of the qualities that animals, or at least the wild ones, were taken to represent.

At the same time, however, one finds John Oswald (1791) and David Mushet (1839) arguing that it is the 'voice of nature' (Oswald, p 38; Mushet, p 18) itself which speaks for kindness. If human beings would only heed the natural common sense and feeling with which they are endowed, they would abandon the acts of cruelty which the delusions of selfishness and superstition have permitted. Nature does not shriek at humankind but, through animals, pleads for tenderness and mercy. Oswald sees in all animals 'the tremor of desire, the tear of distress, the piercing cry of anguish, the pity-pleading look, expressions that speak the soul with a feeling which words are feeble to convey' (pp 57–8). Mushet, too, believes that animals possess natural affection, sympathy, and even benevolence (p 19); he observes eloquently that 'we might write till our hearts ached, over the exquisite qualities of animal affection left desolate and unfulfilled' (p 260). For Mushet, kindness of animals can have no other motive but 'a true tenderness of spirit.' No other voice speaks through acts of mercy to animals than that of nature which spoke to humankind before our fall from grace: with acts of mercy, 'all is silent but the voice of nature, and that guileless spirit of harmony which, when disturbing sin had not been mingled, breathes so exquisitely through the whole frame of the created world' (p 18). Taking this Christian belief in the fall of humankind even further, Mushet asserts that animals are 'the only uninjured models left of natural propriety' (p 77). Oswald, however, finds a natural will towards mercy still abiding in the human heart; he believes that 'within us there exists a rooted repugnance to the spilling of blood' (p 29). Following 'Hindoo' religion to the point of advocating vegetarianism, he states his conviction that 'of all creatures the essence is the same, and that one eternal first cause is the father of us all' (p 6). Both Oswald and Mushet clearly have a vision of world harmony in mind. As a result, both trip up in casting the spirit of wildness as the enemy. Though he has earlier noted that the word 'brutal' is an unjust designation because 'in brutes is wanton cruelty unknown' (p 6), Mushet says of vivisectionists that they 'prefer the summons of a wild and brutal will to the sweet voice of nature' (p 251). Oswald opines, conversely, that the 'advocate of mercy' would 'be traduced as a wild unsocial animal who had formed a nefarious design to curtail the comforts of human life' (pp 43–4). Even if he is enjoying an irony, he has let slip by him an insult to the wild animal. Small as they are, these mistakes indicate a muddling of categories typical of the times.

Henry David Thoreau commits a similar *faux pas* in his discussion of vegetarianism in *Walden* (1854). In speaking about his own aversion to meat-eating, he makes the generalization that the 'repugnance to animal food is not the effect of experience, but is an instinct' (p 343). Having said that such abstinence is an instinct, however, he goes on to attribute the desire for meat to a sensual appetite. From this point, he arrives at the observation that there is 'an animal' in us 'which awakens as our higher nature slumbers.' This animal is 'reptile and sensual, and perhaps cannot be wholly expelled' (p 346), but clearly it is our duty to attempt to expel it. 'Nature is hard to be overcome,' he states, 'but she must be overcome' (p 348). For all his appreciation of the wild, Thoreau's philosophical position on relations between humans and animals approximates that of Tennyson. One wonders how Thoreau could spend as much time as he did simply observing natural animals and recording their ways and still impute the worst in human nature to the animal in us.

Others circumvented the obstacle of the uncivilized animal by dividing the animals into those that should be treated kindly and those that could be used in any fashion without scruple. In his *Philosophical and Practical Treatise* of 1798, John Lawrence goes to great lengths to describe the proper care of horses. His holds horses in high esteem. They are 'the most beautiful of all four-footed creatures'; the horse's body, 'and that of every living creature, is vivified and informed by a *soul,* or portion of intellectual element super-added' (p 78). All of 'brute creation' possesses 'natural and unalienable rights' (p 84). Only blind adherence to custom explains abuses of those rights (p 118). He waxes so indignant at one point that he declares that he would be willing to see the whole body politic torn down if it could be shown to be completely 'infected' with the disease of cruelty to animals (p 155). Yet after all these fine and strong assertions, he turns around in a short second volume to note that the fox, 'which is a beast of prey, greedy of blood, a robber prowling about, seeking what creature he may devour, is not liable to a single one of the preceding objections; nor indeed to any one, in a moral view with which I am acquainted. He is a fair object of sport, who sports with the feelings of all other creatures subjected to his powers' (2:14). Obviously,

Lawrence is a victim of the fixed prejudice against foxes that is not uncommon in Britain. Horses inspire him, but foxes fall out of the purview of his compassion.

A desire to preserve such institutionalized victimization of animals as hunting and butchering creates small hypocrisies in many of these statements. In his speech to the House of Lords in 1809 on the need for legislation to protect animals, Lord Erskine denounces cruelty to all animals, but he suggests that we owe special duties to the animals that we have 'reclaimed,' that is, domesticated (in Mushet, p 295). The word 'reclaimed,' of course, is telling; it implies that we have rescued certain animals from the horrors of the wild. The belief that we are in fact saving the animals that we hunt or kill for food enters also into his rationalizations for these acts. He argues that the deaths of animals in the wild from old age, disease, or predation are much grimmer than those to which we subject them. In keeping with his general desire to advance the aims of civilization, he also speculates that if we did not kill animals they would soon overrun the earth, and that this repercussion of our laxity would be terrible. He raises the standard argument, too, that cruelty to animals produces less-than-civilized human beings – an argument which would have a natural appeal to gentlemen wishing to keep their servants in line. Despite these self-serving assertions, however, he closes his remarks with a reference to the episode in *Tristram Shandy* in which Uncle Toby releases a fly: 'it will not be left to a future Sterne to remind us, when we put aside even a harmless insect, that the world is large enough for both' (in Mushet, p 297).

The utilitarians of this age are in a better position than those who make arguments from sentiment. Arouse the compassions of the audience, and one is bound to reach a dilemma with customary uses of animals. Utilitarians bypass the issue with the weighing up of suffering and happiness. In the 1780s – evidently a period of change on many political fronts – another frequently cited line of reasoning reached the general public: Jeremy Bentham's contention that it is the capacity to suffer which includes animals in the moral community. Like many who address this issue, Bentham projects a civilized future in which animals receive the ethical regard they deserve. Noting that the French have provided legislation to protect people of colour from the 'caprice of a tormenter,' he hopes that,

It may come one day to be recognized, that the number of legs, the villosity of the skin, or the termination of the *os sacrum,* are reasons ... insufficient for abandoning a sensitive being to the same fate. What else is it that should trace the insuperable line? Is it the faculty of reason, or, perhaps, the faculty of discourse? But a full-grown horse or dog is beyond comparison a more rational, as well as a more conversable animal, than an infant of a day, or a week, or even a month old. But suppose the case were otherwise, what would it avail? the question is not, Can they *reason*? nor, Can they *talk*? but, Can they *suffer*? (His italics, p 311)

This justly famous remark is buried in a footnote to his *Introduction to the Principles of Morals and Legislation.* Unfortunately, he too suggests that the fate that nature provides for animals is less merciful than that to which humankind subjects them. Nevertheless, he proposes a rational measurement for the mitigation of cruelty to animals.

In 1840, John Stuart Mill would lift ethical regard for animals out of the footnote form and state, in his critique of Dr Whewell, that he was 'willing to stake the whole question [of utilitarianism] on this one issue' (p 187). Whewell has relied upon the distinction between humans and animals to argue that ties of 'human brotherhood' (Mill, p 186) unite humankind ethically and to ridicule any notion that we should concern ourselves with animal happiness. Mill points out that such an argument could be used to defend abuses of those human beings, such as slaves, who fall out of the 'brotherhood' of humankind. Mill's defence of utilitarianism as a whole has direct relevance to the appeals to natural sympathy made by other writers: 'The contest between the morality which appeals to the external standard, and that which grounds itself on internal conviction, is the contest of the progressive morality against stationary – of reason and argument against the deification of mere opinion and habit' (p 179). Habits of thought and practice in approaches to the animal victim clearly interfere in philosophical statements that rely upon an innate generosity in humankind. The benefits that accrue from the utilitarian position may be seen from Peter Singer's use of the utilitarian measure to argue in his landmark book *Animal Liberation* (1975) against 'speciesism' and in favour of the rights of animals.

Among the gathering forces which would eventually crystallize around Darwin's *Origin of Species,* one finds the British parliament reluctantly agreeing to minimal legal protection of specifically identified domestic animals in 1822, excluding dogs and cats.[6] In America, various states passed similar laws in the following decade. Societies for the Prevention of Cruelty to Animals began to spring up in England almost simultaneously with legislative enactments, in part, as John Turner notes, to ensure enforcement of the laws (p 40). Interest in such societies grew also in the United States, though they were not established there until the 1860s. Turner offers a theory of philanthropic work on behalf of animals which runs counter to the impression that animals were swept up in an ever-expanding circle of humanitarianism. In his reading of events of this period, 'social caution' dictated that agitation for better treatment of slaves, children, and the working poor be tempered with due consideration of economics. The 'one wholly acceptable object of benevolence,' Turner suggests, was 'the suffering beast':

Kindness to animals profaned no social taboos and upset no economic applecarts ... When other channels were blocked, the rising tide of sympathy almost inevitably flowed to animals, especially now that they had drawn concern for other reasons. Though hardly the only unthreatening outlet for humanitarian impulses, animal protection did provide an attractive one at a time when few were available. (pp 36–7)

Turner's position makes sense if one sees such appeals for kindness as did exist as a development out of the moral arguments used in children's stories. Animals victims do provide a readily available, nonthreatening object for the exercise of compassion. It must be pointed out, however, that people of this period are also conceiving of suffering animals in ways that ensure that petitions for reform will not 'profane' any 'social taboos.' Humanized animals did not challenge the ideal of a wholly civilized world which allowed human beings to feel virtuous at the same time as they were eliminating 'noxious' or vicious animals and eating domesticated ones. In fact, with a little posing and cleaning up, animals could be used to illustrate the very virtues that civilization wished to promote. Examination of images of animals in the visual arts goes a long way towards explaining why preaching kindness to animals represented no real threat to the body politic.

Among the arts, literature between Romanticism and Darwinism pays scarce attention to the animal. Fiction took up social concerns, particularly active during this period. Animals became the subject of the static art of painting. The use of the word 'static,' here, is not intended to disparage the painter's art. Certainly Delacroix's canvases show the intensity of activity that can be achieved in painting. If one is following the history of animals in culture, however, one cannot help but note the fixedness of the animal subject in mid-nineteenth-century paintings. Animals are frozen, in effect, by normative social ideals.

John Ruskin's opinions on the proper use of the animal subject in painting confirm the point. In the third part (1856) of his four-part study *Modern Painters,* Ruskin has little trouble in distinguishing those physical features in animals which exemplify virtues from those which exemplify evils; nor does he hesitate to attach aesthetic value to the former: 'The beauty of the animal form is in exact proportion to the amount of moral or intellectual virtue expressed by it' (p 249). He also has a definite idea of the nature of those virtues: they are the virtues of the Victorian Age:

wherever beauty exists at all, there is some kind of virtue to which it is owing as the majesty of the lion's eye is owing not to its ferocity, but to its seriousness and seeming intellect, and of the lion's mouth to its strength and sensibility, and not its gnashing of teeth, nor wrinkling in its wrath; and farther be it noted, that of the intellectual or moral virtues, the moral are those which are attended with most beauty, so that the gentle eye of the gazelle is fairer to look upon than the more keen glance of men, if it be unkind. (pp 249–50)

Humankind can look to animals to learn valuable lessons about moral conduct: 'There is not any organic creature, but in its history and habits will exemplify or illustrate to us some moral excellence or deficiency, or some point of God's providential government, which it is necessary for us to know' (p 247). Thus, certain animal eyes, like those of cats and owls, have a 'corpselike stare' which is the ultimate in ugliness (p 248); other eyes, like those of the serpent and alligator, are raised aesthetically one stage above those of the cat and owl but are still ugly because of the malignancy that is in them; the 'fair eye of the herbivorous tribes' of gazelles, camels, and oxen begins to approximate beauty; while the human eye, assuming the requisite virtues stand behind it,

exists at the summit of the hierarchy of the beautiful. The very
nicety of Ruskin's discrimination would bear a certain cogency to
Victorian sensibilities, but the linkage of aesthetic value to moral
assessments that are by no means given is clearly pernicious to
human relations with animals. Ruskin's appeal for some high aim
in art is reminiscent of Schopenhauer's hierarchy of aesthetic values, though Schopenhauer of course finds animals inherently
wanting as artistic subjects.

Ruskin's aversion to the anti-human features in animals may
be judged from his advice to Landseer to give up offering the
public realistic paintings of the hunt:

I would have Mr. Landseer, before he gives us any more writhing otters,
or yelping packs, reflect whether that which is best worthy of contemplation in a hound be its ferocity, or in an otter its agony, or in a human
being its victory, hardly achieved even with the aid of its more sagacious
brutal allies, over a poor little fish-catching creature, a foot long. (p 242n)

To be fair to Ruskin, an ethical motive informs this piece of advice:
he does not like to see animals tormented and evidently wishes
that humankind would abandon such practices as otter-hunts.
His hope seems to be that if members of the public have before
them nothing but images of noble animals, they themselves will
eventually acquire the virtues represented in those images. The
desire to suppress representations of pain and ferocity clearly
testifies, nevertheless, to exclusion from the aspirations of art
much of what is true in nature. Animals kill each other even in
the absence of humankind, and sea otters are sometimes made to
writhe in mortal distress by carnivorous orca whales. According
to Ruskin's theory of art, then, artists have to sanitize nature for
the moral improvement of the recipient of their images. Advocate
of compassion towards animals though Ruskin is, he cannot find a
place in his view of civilization for the whole animal, pain, predation, and all.

The naturalism in animal paintings of this period, then, has a
disturbingly and paradoxically unreal quality to it. Arnold Hauser's
observations on naturalism in *The Social History of Art* are particularly true of this transitional phase in approaches to animals.
Naturalism, he says, is 'always aiming at a particular and immediate goal, always concerned with a concrete task and confining

its interpretation of life to particular phenomena.' In sum, he remarks, naturalism 'is not aimed at reality as a whole, not at "nature" or "life" in general, but at social life in particular' (4:25–6). Hauser's commentary provides a good explanation for the curious combination of near-perfect naturalism and unabashed anthropomorphism in paintings of animals to the mid-point of the nineteenth century. Animals have become the object of undisguised social programs.

'Breeding' is a word to keep in mind in the interpretation of animal painting of this period. In her commentary on the literal breeding of animals, Harriet Ritvo notes the rhetorical function of the living animal as a 'work of art' (p 55). Grossly overweight cattle reflected in their bodies the authority of their aristocratic owners. Of course, these animals were too large to move any great distance and suffered from shortness of breath (p 75), but at least their bloodlines were true. Similarly, in the visual arts, living animals are transformed into models of good breeding. Where commissioned portraits of prize cattle show the animals standing stolidly as an almost inanimate testimony to the power of their masters, the more imaginative paintings of animals imbue their subjects with virtues salutary to the moral character of the human audience. The wildness of the animal is virtually eliminated from the visual arts. In painting, the animal sits transfixed by whatever social ideal it is meant to illustrate.

William Holman Hunt's *The Scapegoat* (1855) epitomizes the paradox of naturalism and social import. The painting shows a long-haired goat, its head decorated with the red wool of the ritual sacrifice, panting under the heat of the Dead Sea climate. The sun and the red symbol seem equally to weigh the goat's head down towards the arid mud of the shoreline. Hunt travelled to the Dead Sea with this image in mind, purchased a goat and spent days in the heat reproducing on canvas the goat's manifest exhaustion. Despite such concern for realism, Hunt's aim is spiritual; if others missed the symbolism and saw only, in Kenneth Clark's phrasing, a 'silly old goat' (p 22), the whole experience was for Hunt an ecstatic one. Between the actual physical circumstances of the painting's origins and the burden of symbolism, the strain placed on the goat is immense. In his comments on *The Scapegoat,* Ruskin praises Hunt's motives and sentiments, but finds the painting 'a total failure' because of certain ill effects he perceives in the composition. Evidently the fact that the painting shows genuine animal suffering is not sufficient to impress either the public or the aesthetic theorists of the age.

Edwin Landseer's animal paintings, however, acquired an admiring audience. Those that found most favour bring naturalism into the service of the social good. His *Monarch of the Glen* (1851) is a stag of character, posed with pride to model the finest in human personality and bearing. The dog in his *Old Shepherd's Chief Mourner* (1837) suffers visibly; with its head resting on its master's plain wooden coffin and its ears pulled back in pain, the dog expresses grief more fully than most humans can. In both paintings, the animal is locked into the stylized sentiment; within the fixed terms of the painting, no possibility exists for the stag to flee in terror or the dog to go on its way in natural insouciance. If the spirits of those who came to see *Monarch of the Glen* were flagging under worldly burdens, they would receive hearty encouragement to brave the trials of life. The viewer wavering in his or her loyalty to family could come away from *The Old Shepherd's Chief Mourner* refreshed in belief in both the naturalness of pathos and the deep feeling of nature for humankind. The overt message is that humankind is lovable; the subtext speaks for the absoluteness of human control.

A phenomenon more openly telling than nature paintings is the popularity of lithographs (1829–42) by J.J. Grandeville (pseudonym of Jean Gerard), forerunner to other artists in the animal-fabulist line like John Tenniel, Edward Lear, and Beatrix Potter. The imposition of social values upon the animal is the *raison d'être* for Grandeville's works. Naturalism is still in force. The drawings show patient attention to accuracy; but for all the effort spent upon whiskers and beaks and antennae, the purpose remains wholly remote from animality. Grandeville's lithographs show a wide range of animals, birds, and insects dressed up in human costume and sitting at writing desks, delivering toasts at dinner, or – an owl; most offensively to the creature itself – hunting birds with a rifle. Grandeville's aim, of course, is to satirize humanity, not to insult animals; he gains permission to appeal to comic worries, such as excess weight, romantic complications, and the fondness of the master of the house for the hired maid, by the patent absurdity of his personification. The objects of his satire are largely conventional. Some of his cartoons have a levelling tendency: it seems absurd that well-dressed birds should seek to bar a monkey and a mouse dressed as peasants from riding with them on an omnibus: all are animals, no matter what apparel they happen to wear. One might argue, however, that on the whole Grandeville's animals soften the mockery of society by universalizing trivialities. The radically levelling vision which would truly recognize individuals riding on omnibuses or getting ready to go to parties as animals even when human heads are sitting atop the costume has not had its day even yet.

One of Grandeville's cartoons swerves close to the edge of true assault. In it, three crows are dissecting a cadaver composed of human legs and thorax and a crocodile head; the hands of the crows are buried in the intestines of the corpse. Human and animal skeleton parts are piled up beside the table. A parrot dressed as a woman peasant, with a loaf of bread under her arm, is making a gesture of decline. The caption, spoken by the crows, is: 'Won't you stay and have dinner with us, Mother Pilon?' Given that crows are scavenger birds often imagined pulling bits of flesh off human corpses, the lightly humorous suggestion has grim implications. The human dress very nearly drops away and the danger of the genuine animal to human complacency almost emerges. It remains an open question, though, whether gallows humour like this reminds us of situations we would rather not think about, or instead makes the unthinkable tolerable.

For the most part, Grandeville, like other artists of this period, uses the animal to reflect back to humankind a quaintly hygienic version of society. Realism in formal details is made consistent with a desire for control over the 'animal' in humans and the animal itself. Fur and feathers drawn with infinite care could also be artistically arranged and cleansed of the evidence of living in nature that tends to adhere to real animals. Groomed and posed, the animal reassured humanity of the sanctity of humanity's virtues and sentiments.

One might expect such civilized productions from European artists, in view of the long centuries European culture had to subordinate wilderness to human ideas. One would hope for something less confining from the American artist surrounded by scenes of untamed nature. In fact, American painters generally demonstrate, if anything, even greater tyranny over the animal subject than the Europeans. In *An American Bestiary,* Mary Sayre

Haverstock cites qualities in nineteenth-century American animal painting which are precisely the same as those of European animal paintings: 'American primal contests could readily be observed in the wild, but the academic artists tended rather perversely to concentrate on the more static animal characteristics: majesty, dignity, and serenity' (p 87). Later in her book, she quotes critic James Jackson Jarves' comment on Thomas Henry Hinckley's mid-century animal portraits: Jarves observes that Hinckley painted animals 'with the *animal* left out' (Jarves' italics, p 152). Even in the American context, with its fondness for encounters with the wild, Jarves could apparently intend this remark as praise of Hinckley's work.

Aside from the peculiarly decorative contributions of the usually unknown artists described as primitives, visual representations of animals in America in the first half of the nineteenth century suggest the triumph of humankind in several ways. American portraits of animals differ little from their British counterparts in manifesting a love of fine breeding. An urge simply to record the fauna of the New World produces numbers of paintings rivalling if not surpassing the output of European artists. Control of the animal is evident in the works, half-art, half-science, of American nature-illustrators like Charles Willson Peale and family and John James Audubon and sons. With the premise behind them of cataloguing wildlife for the non cognoscenti, these pictures do not stint on accuracy. Where they depress is in the unlivingness of the animal tableaux. Audubon is of course to be forgiven for working from dead animals and birds; one can hardly expect memory to rise to perfection in realism when the object it is asked to reproduce takes flight after an instant's glance. It must be granted, nonetheless, that the static animal of the taxidermist is a poor substitute for the living, moving original. Something is awry when the immobilized animal is hailed as true to life.

Given the apparent abundance of life in the New World, it is unlikely that a fear of losing animals informs the encyclopedic interest in capturing their likenesses. George Catlin appears to have been unique in his desire to preserve images of the way of life of North American Indians and in his alarm at the slaughter of native animals by Indians and fur-traders (Haverstock, p 63). One quality that is unusual about Catlin's animals is that they actually bleed. Perhaps not as perfect in execution as the works of other artists, Catlin's paintings have the virtue of depicting natural aspects of animals. *Buffalo Chase* (1832) shows bleeding buffalo in the foreground and the rest of the herd charging away into the distance pursued by Indians on horseback. The record Catlin creates comes from his reaction against the selfsame civilized ideals that other painters reinforced in their images of animals.

It is interesting to compare Catlin's *Buffalo Chase* with formally similar images of the hunt coming from Britain. The formal similarity is in the flow of animals and hunters across the landscape. But whereas Catlin gives visual equality to animals and hunters, British artists transfer animal energy from the victim to the hunters themselves, often relocating the idea of victimization too, in downed horses and riders tumbling over the ground or dropped into streams. In his etching *Easter Monday* (1817), Henry Alken could almost be mocking the pretence that humankind asserts its prowess against nature in the hunt. In his note on this work, David Coombs draws attention to the fact that the distant quarry is 'a carted (that is, domesticated) stag, whose benign spirit and undignified posture are suggested by the large bow tied around his neck' (p 147). Is this animal going to be dragged down by the hounds and killed? In fact, as the etching tacitly informs the viewer, carted stags often were not killed but captured and saved for another hunt. Nature may be 'red in tooth and claw, / With ravine,' but the British are not interested in killing animals, or so their images of the hunt reassure them.

American scenes of the hunt other than Catlin's tend to confirm stereotypic notions of national character. That tendency in the British print to dot the pageantry with a few human and horse victims is counterposed in the American print by a taste for the intrepid hunter looming large in the landscape evidently able to handle any danger that comes his way. Occasionally, slain birds or deer lie at the feet of these big men or tucked into the back of a canoe. Most frequently, the artist will suspend the action at the point at which the hunter is taking aim at a distant animal target. Arthur F. Tait's *Still Hunting on First Snow* (1855) is typical, showing two hunters in bright costume in the foreground firing their rifles at two alert deer in the background, made smaller than the hunters by perspectival realism and standing still despite the fact that a third deer is already dead on the ground.

Some American images of animals, however, reveal the importation of cultural ideals. In his famous painting *The Peaceable Kingdom* (c 1830), Edward Hicks actualizes a vision of universal love and harmony which conforms entirely with the hopes of European writers denouncing cruelty to animals. All of Hicks's animals are gentle animals; the eyes of even the wild felines and bears show that spirit of mildness which Ruskin perceived only in the eyes of the 'herbivore tribe.' The overt and conscious aim of this painting is to eliminate the wildness of the animal. The animals are a cooperative community held together by an innate desire for peace. In the background, Indians and settlers exchange gifts. Peace will reign in the New World. There are no victims here.

It will have been observed that discussion has shifted from literal animal victims to artistic representations in which animals appear not victimized but adored. The point, of course, is that the beautiful animals in pictures from the first half of the nineteenth century have been pressed into compliance with ideals that not only serve the human social project but also tacitly reinforce those attitudes which make for animal victims in the first place. By excluding wild, terrified, dirty, or suffering animals from orthodox culture, these pictures effectively license mistreatment and acts of aggression. Various political and philosophical forces were beginning to take heed of the animals discounted by art – the long-suffering working animal, the victims of blood-sports and vivisection. In the meantime, artists were discovering how useful animals could be in the socialization of the public.

CONCLUSION AND CODA

It was possible that the citizen duly civilized by sufficient exposure to virtuous animal models would lose any urge to harm or neglect living creatures. Perhaps it was the shock to such citizens of encountering graphic written descriptions of cruelties to animals that brought them in significant numbers to the protest movements later in the century. In one form or another, animals were at least coming to public attention. When Darwin's *Origin of Species* arrived on the scene, people were willing to puzzle over his theory of continuity between humans and animals. Cultural history had prepared the ground for Darwinian theory to that extent. What is more, the animal victim had become a source of distress, whether that distress arose from tender feelings towards animals or attachment to the moral ideals of civilization.

The theory of evolution does not, of course, resolve the conflict between Enlightenment and Romantic attitudes towards animal victims. In modern Western culture, the animal victim is still held suspended between Enlightenment rationality and Romantic myth. One of the changes effected by the theory of evolution, however, is the negation of intellectual distance: abuses of animals, even institutionalized abuses, once disclosed, stir up deeper feelings of discomfort and deeper intellectual insecurities than reason, sentiment, or Romantic idealism would incite. Animal victims have become living, breathing, suffering fellow-beings. Carried through into the post-Darwinian age, pre-Darwinian controversies have become correspondingly alive, correspondingly meaningful, and, as the following chapter seeks to demonstrate, correspondingly immune to resolution.

Before moving on to a theoretical discussion of the modern animal victim, however, I must mention one work from the mid-nineteenth century which does do justice to the animal. Herman Melville's *Moby Dick* anticipates by eight years the effect that Darwinism will produce in cultural thought on animals. Like Darwin, Melville compels anthropocentric culture to attend to the animal as it exists beyond the pale of civilization. He creates a total world in which the energy of the wild animal can exist. Matter-of-fact to the point of un-novelistic reportage where the ordinary whale is concerned, Melville enfolds the anomalous white whale in myth. Yet the aura of myth serves paradoxically to give force to the generalized animality of the leviathan, in outright antagonism to culture-bound distortions of the elemental beast. With Moby Dick, Melville sums up the polarized aspects of nature that will plague modern representations of animals. Until the last three chapters of the novel, Moby Dick exists in theory and anecdote alone. He exists in the doubloon nailed to the mast, in Ahab's wooden leg, in Ahab's obsession and his bitterness. For Ahab, Moby Dick exists profoundly. The captain and the whale form a unity; the mind of Ahab, in the magnitude of its workings, has been shaped by Moby Dick. By means of Ahab's mania, Melville brings the Romanticism of the animal to actually endanger civilization, to shake the faith of humanity in the reality of its supposed virtues. The long absence of the white whale from the narrative is constitutive; it is an absence around which primitive cultures built myths, and which the accretions of civilization had hidden from consciousness. Until the whale is sighted, 'Moby Dick' is a name for all the inexplicable potency of the wild animal. Following Darwin, when humanity attempts to subdue nature, it attempts to subdue all the patient, resistant energy Moby Dick embodies. Following Darwin, as Melville implicitly predicts, humanity will not be able to destroy the Moby Dicks of the world without psychic and actual damage to itself. Moby Dick is no victim. Compassion, humanitarian sentiment, cannot contain the modern animal victim. Indeed, the inability of culture to rationalize animal reality is the reason animal victims gain ground in serious literature for adults. The modern animal does not make an easy victim, hence the power of the post-Darwinian animal victim to subvert conventional belief and disclose unacknowledged cultural material.

2 The Animal Victim in Its Cultural Context: *Some Theoretical Considerations*

INTRODUCTION

The power of the animal to resist victimization is of critical importance to any theoretical consideration of the animal victim in culture. In a material sense, human dominance of the animal kingdom seems absolute, from control of numbers in any species right down to the matter of genetic manipulation to produce different animals. In domains of thought, too, humanity seems to possess absolute freedom to conceive of animals in ways that either acknowledge or discount victimization. It could well be argued that current ethical concern for animals is merely a cultural phenomenon, a fashionable piety now, perhaps, but one that can easily evaporate with the vicissitudes of cultural need and desire. Ethics which include animals have, of course, a great weight of long-standing cultural resistance to dislodge. Indeed, ethical systems alone may not have sufficient force to counter human aggression, since the victimization of animals is in all likelihood foundational to culture and civilization. Keith Tester says of the early modern period that 'aggressive behaviour towards animals was an active way for humans to define themselves as the centre of the universe and the zenith of God's work' (p 51). The persistence of aggressive behaviour suggests that humans have not transcended the need to prove their distinctiveness by means of the domination of animals. In *Dominance and Affection: The Making of Pets*, Yi-Fu Tuan goes beyond the historical context to suggest that 'Cruelty to animals is deeply embedded in human nature' (p 89). This observation can be true only in so far as human nature has been altered by culture, for it is difficult to imagine how the animal ancestors of our species came to distinguish themselves from other animals in wholesale enmity without some rudimentary cultural assistance, perhaps in the form of weapons. If eons of actual power over animals have determined our ways of thinking about them, then other ways of thinking about animals can disturb humanity's confidence in its self-assumed entitlement to use other animals at will.

To grant this point is not to agree that the whole question of ethical treatment comes under the absolute authority of culture. The position that culture is all-in-all is itself part of the larger issue of humanity's victimization of nonhuman animals. That position depends, moreover, upon the convention which imagines a schism between the human animal and other species. Today's ethical debate takes place in a very different context from that which presupposes essential dissimilarities between the human species and others. The conception of culture which would have it that human dominance over other animals falls within the power of cultural vagaries runs into a philosophical hornets' nest with the Darwinian notion of continuity between humans and animals. Although the theory of evolution might seem to license human supremacy, it also places the animal in a position to challenge culture.

It has become apparent that culture does not possess final authority over all regions of thought. In view of the pervasiveness of human uses of animals, the implementation of ethical practices is difficult enough, but the acknowledgment of animal reality in cultural consciousness is shot through with complications. Darwinism calls attention not only to the animals living at large all around humankind but also to the animal that resides in the human being. Cultural alienation from animals therefore infiltrates the sense of being of each individual person. Having assumed and acted upon the belief that culture separates humans and animals, people now scramble to retrieve vital connectedness with animal reality, if only because something essential in human nature depends upon rightful interpretation of the nonhuman animal. Products of modern culture are trying to realize the animal in both its cultural and anti-cultural dispositions and are encountering formidable areas of confusion in the process. Culture is being edged out of its position as sole arbitrator of human perplexities. Owing in part to Darwin's influence, the natural animal now lays claim to significant aspects of life over which cultural expression tends to falter.

For one reason or another, Western culture has chosen to plague itself with the idea that the human species is interconnected with animals existing outside of culture. Culture may indeed represent an insuperable barrier to human understanding of the animal's reality. Yet the idea of continuity situates some of that extra-cultural reality inside of the human individual. The very least that can be said, then, is that culture has created a grave problem for itself in generating the idea of continuity. The possibly unreachable meaning of the animal has become integral to comprehension of the human being. Animals have an epistemological claim upon us, and victimized animals have a moral claim upon culture. Conversely, cultural arguments are not confined to culture alone when they deal with humanity's trespass upon the lives of other animals. Granted, attempts in the last three centuries philosophically to cross the conceptual abyss between humans and animals have had little effect on our habitual practices. We are fortunate in the modern era at least to be confused over the right way to think about animals.

I shall return to the issue of the effect animals have upon culture in the last part of this discussion. It is, of course, a crucial issue, and one that makes for a persistent undercurrent of disquiet in the contemplation of less sweeping subjects. Taking Darwinism as a point of departure for theorizing generates its own problems, the dimensions of which need to be delineated even if resolution cannot be achieved. One way or another, Darwinism removes the basis of human arrogance, but whether it does so by landing us in an entirely amoral universe or by sanctifying all living beings is an open question. These two poles of Darwinian theory establish the framework for subsequent inquiry into various aspects of the problem of animal victims.

Philosophical tangles occur at almost any point of entry into consideration of animal victims. Following the discussion of Darwinism proper, the first problem to be addressed is that of the individual identity of the animal as opposed to the collectivity of the animal's ontological status. This problem has particular implications for the means by which cruelty is discerned and invalidated, as is suggested by the highly useful insights into the subject found in Philip P. Hallie's book *Cruelty* (1969; 1982). The question

Antoine-Louis Barye's *Tiger Searching for Prey* displays Romanticism's capacity to honour the self-contained power of the lone, predatory animal. (Musée Louvre – Dépt des Arts Graphiques; © photo R.M.N.)

Human and animal are tumbled together in Eugène Delacroix's *Lion Hunt*. Delacroix concedes true aesthetic power to the hunted animal's rage. (Mr and Mrs Potter Palmer Collection; photograph © 1992 The Art Institute of Chicago. All Rights Reserved)

Combining naturalism with religious symbolism, William Holman Hunt's *The Scapegoat* almost inadvertently conveys animal suffering directly to the Victorian public. (Walker Art Gallery, Liverpool. With the kind permission of the Board of Trustees of the National Museums and Galleries on Merseyside)

Edwin Landseer's stag in *Monarch of the Glen* exemplifies sterling qualities of character admired by the Victorians. (By kind permission of United Distillers)

Also a model for human conduct, Landseer's dog in *The Old Shepherd's Chief Mourner* shows how love, fidelity, and grief should be expressed. (Courtesy of the Board of Trustees of the Victoria and Albert Museum, London)

"Won't you stay and have dinner with us, Mother Pilon?"

Grandeville goes overboard in the 'socialization' of the animal. He uses animals in human dress to satirize the superficially civilized. In this cartoon, however, he elicits the threatening quality of the animal with a curiously objectless black humour.

Perhaps it is because George Catlin's heart is in the right place – he was an early conservationist – that he equalizes humans and animals. In *Buffalo Chase, Mouth of Yellowstone* (1832–3), his buffaloes actually bleed from their wounds. (National Museum of American Art, Smithsonian Institution, Gift of Mrs Joseph Harrison, Jr)

British images of the hunt typically depict panoramic views of the chase; they also shift the idea of victimization from the hunted animal to the hunter. Henry Alken's hunters in *Easter Monday* (1817) are described as 'Men of determined Courage Riding Hard.' There is a tacit reassurance in this painting that the stag will not be killed. (By the kind permission of the Trustees of the British Museum)

American images of the hunt, by contrast, typically depict large, individual hunters in the foreground aiming at distant animals, as is shown in Arthur F. Tait's *Still Hunting on First Snow* (1855). (Courtesy of The Adirondack Museum, Blue Mountain Lake, NY)

Edward Hicks's *Peaceable Kingdom* (this version was painted c 1834) eliminates all the wildness from animals. To nineteenth-century sensibilities,
the ways of natural animals were incompatible with utopian ideals. (National
Gallery of Art, Washington; Gift of Edgar William and Bernice Chrysler
Garbisch)

William Hogarth's engravings *The Four Stages of Cruelty* (1751) offer the
typical Enlightenment thesis that cruelty to animals leads to cruelty to
human beings. Hogarth depicts, nonetheless, the animal's resistance to victimization in the first stage (above), and allows a victory to the animal at
stage four (opposite), in which a dog feeds upon the hanged criminal's heart.
(By the kind permission of the Trustees of the British Museum)

In the context of the painting as a whole, Hogarth's cat comments wryly upon the seeming innocence of the children. (Reproduced by courtesy of the Trustees, The National Gallery, London)

By itself, the cat (detail) in William Hogarth's *The Graham Children* illustrates Hogarth's vivid appreciation of the alertness of the natural predator. (Reproduced by courtesy of the Trustees, The National Gallery, London)

of individuality versus collectivity stands at the core of two approaches to animals which rationalize victimization: behaviouristic science and the ethos of the hunt. The contrary methods used to disguise victimization in the hunt and behaviourism will be examined and challenged. Analysis of hunting and behaviourism leads naturally into the broad issues of domestication and wildness, which are foundational to interpretation of the way in which culture came to distinguish itself from nature. Working hypotheses for this part of the discussion will be drawn from Freud's observations on animal sacrifice in *Totem and Taboo* and René Girard's exploration of the subject in *Things Hidden since the Foundation of the World*. With the global paradoxes arising from cultural anthropology in hand, discussion closes with the specific dilemmas confronted by modern fiction as it seeks to assimilate animal victims.

The overall aim of these theoretical speculations is to establish that animals are no longer passive recipients of human tyrannies. It has been a long-standing habit of philosophy to define human nature and human status in contradistinction to the rest of the animals. Humans are human, the argument runs and has run for centuries, because they possess language while other animals do not, because they exercise reason while other animals do not, because they are self-conscious while other animals are not, because they are aware of their own impending death while other animals remain blissfully unaware that they will die. One by one, these bastions of human supremacy are falling. Ultimately, the whole exercise of judging ourselves against other animals will fall into disrepute. As the props to human distinctiveness collapse, the excuses for victimizing animals lose materiality. Animal resistance to human domination elevates our victimization of them to the level of real significance. It is all to the good, therefore, that Darwin does not reify the meaning of animals. The upshot of his theory is that culture cannot establish itself upon the back of the animal, that animals are subjects whose existence and interests not only warrant but demand critical attention.

THE POLARITIES OF DARWINISM AND THE STATUS OF ANIMALS

Darwinism is, of course, a scientific theory. From one point of view, Darwinism has appeared to foster reductionism in subsuming culture under the blind workings of an indifferent nature. Change from this point of view is either adaptive or maladaptive and survives or disappears accordingly. The few thousand years of cultural development mean little in the grand unfolding of natural events, and should civilization and the human species vanish, nature will quietly grow over the gap as if nothing of moment had occurred. Accepting continuity between humans and animals appears to involve accepting this vision of human effort as expendable in the great scheme of nature. It seems to entail conservatism on a scale larger than political conservatism and infinitely more impersonal.

Political theories based on hierarchies of dominance, like social Darwinism and eugenics, are mistaken, however, when they seek support in Darwinian evolution. James Rachels offers the necessary reminder that, within Darwin's system,

adaptations are not 'directed' to any particular end. There is no 'more evolved' or 'less evolved' in Darwinian theory; there are only the different paths taken by different species, largely, but not entirely, in response to different environmental pressures. Natural selection is a process that, in principle, goes on forever, moving in no particular direction; it moves this way and that, eliminating some species and altering others, as environmental conditions change. (pp 64–5)

From this perspective, human beings are not only not different in kind from other animals; they are also not sitting at the top of the evolutionary chain of being. There is no chain of being, and all living entities are in a state of equality within the indifferent workings of nature. Detaching the notion of final causes from nature appears at first to put culture in a position of absolute authority over moral issues.

George C. Williams has used an amoral vision like that described by Rachels to call the evolutionary process 'abysmally stupid' (p 400). Nature, Williams argues, is 'morally unacceptable'; only with the 'blindness of romanticism' can we ignore the objectionable phenomena of predation and parasitism in nature (p 398). Williams is using evidence from sociobiology to take the argument made by Thomas Henry Huxley in *Evolution and Ethics* (1894) even further: where Huxley cast nature as the enemy of culture, Williams sets out to prove that 'the enemy is worse than Huxley thought' (p 399). From Huxley's point of view 'the state of art,' which may be loosely interpreted as culture in general, 'can be maintained only by constant counteraction of the hostile influence of the state of nature' (*Evolution and Ethics,* p 33). The 'ethical process,' he asserts, 'is in opposition to the principle of the cosmic process' (p 31). Harking back to an eighteenth-century preoccupation, Huxley uses the image of a garden to advance his argument. Only by applying the powers of art can humankind prevent the garden from sliding back into natural chaos. It is the garden as a whole, metaphorically speaking, that humankind must bear in mind. Within Huxley's argument, the teleological garden resurrects a hierarchical vision. An organized 'polity' props up civilization and opposes both the amorality of nature and the ethic that would emerge out of an anti-hierarchical apperception of life. Ridiculing the ethic of a 'golden rule,' Huxley asks rhetorically: 'What would become of the garden if the gardener treated all the weeds and slugs and birds and trespassers as he would like to be treated, if he were in their place?' (p 33) 'Darwin's bulldog' – as Huxley was known during the debates that followed publication of *The Origin of Species* – apparently began to strain at the leash, for although it is clear that Darwinian evolution is not ethical philosophy, it is equally clear that the theory supersedes the belief that nature is the enemy and that artificial gardens are for some reason preferable to natural wilderness. It is only from an anthropocentric position, which seeks to preserve the special value of human culture, that evolution appears to render nature 'stupid' and immoral. Value persists in evolutionary theory, in part through the salvaging of natural acts like predation and parasitism from human condemnation, and in part through the methodological presupposition of deference to the values nature makes for itself. If it is Romanticism to cease from reviling nature because it does not conform to a particular set of moral codes, then Darwin's theory unquestionably inclines towards such Romanticism. The naturalist of a Darwinian persuasion would not oust those slugs and birds sandwiched neatly between the weeds and trespassers in Huxley's garden, but would observe, take notes, and probably find some strangely human correspondences among their ways. Darwinism, that is to say, does not divorce humankind from nature, and value can survive the collapse of hierarchies. I would argue, furthermore, that animals give the lie to many post-Darwinian philosophies, and especially to those that expel nature from the moral community and then conclude that there is nothing of value out there to encroach upon human dominion.

It should be apparent that animals as we know them in our daily lives do not support a vision of universal obliviousness. When we look at other animals, the equalization described by Rachels has a different complexion from that indifference which alarms thinkers like Huxley and Williams. It can, in Tom Regan's fine phrasing, indicate that nonhuman animals 'are the experiencing subjects of lives that matter to them as individuals, independently of their usefulness to others' ('Honey Dribbles Down Your Fur,' p 105). The latter part of Regan's statement corresponds to Rachels' description of the evolutionary process in so far as it breaks the human hold upon value and posits numerous independent and equally important ways of living within nature. Although human beings may have difficulty in following Darwinism to the point of experiencing themselves as animals, it is more likely than not that they feel a living and immediate affinity with the animals they know, however few in number those animals might be. That sense of attachment with another 'subject of a life' argues against conceiving of nature as inhumanly abstract design.

There are indications in Darwin's work itself that his understanding of animals is not predicated upon reductionist belief, but relies upon a vision of animals nearing that which Regan describes. Empiricism might indeed find Romantic tendencies in some of Darwin's observations about animals. In answer to those who protested that evolutionary theory stripped humankind of its special significance, Darwin gave the pointed reply: 'When I view all beings not as special creations but as the lineal descendants of some few beings which lived long before the first bed of the Cambrian system was deposited, they seem to me to become ennobled' (*Origin of Species,* p 373). He finds awe in the seemingly mundane evidence of inheritance; for him inheritance is 'a deep organic bond' uniting species across widely disparate regions of the earth (p 280). Along with occasionally investing the fabric of life with a Romantic spirit, his writing sometimes departs radically from empirical discourse to instil poetic value in the individual animal. Of, for example, some ants whose nest has been destroyed, he observes that 'two or three individuals of F. fusca were rushing about in the greatest agitation, and one was perched motionless with its own pupa in its mouth on the top of a spray of heath, an image of despair over its ravaged home' (p 195). In *The Descent of Man,* he says that 'the brain of an ant is one of the most marvellous atoms of matter in the world, perhaps more so than the brain of a man' (p 436). Also in *The Descent,* Darwin reports and does not criticize a charming anecdote about affection between a couple of snails:

[A]n accurate observer Mr Lonsdale informs me that he placed a pair of land snails (*Helix pomatia*), one of which was weakly, into a small and ill-provided garden. After a short time the strong and healthy individual disappeared, and was traced by its track of slime over a wall into an adjacent well-stocked garden. Mr Lonsdale concluded that it had deserted its sickly mate; but after an absence of twenty-four hours it returned, and apparently communicated the result of its successful exploration, for both then started along the same track and disappeared over the wall. (p 614)

Anecdotes like this occur frequently throughout *The Descent of Man.*

It is not in anecdotes alone, however, that Darwin expresses anti-reductionist belief. The qualities he finds in animals when he presents evidence for the idea of continuity are tinged with a Romanticism which subsequent empirical judgment would reject. He devotes the third chapter of *The Descent of Man* to demonstration that 'there is no fundamental difference between man and the higher animals in their mental faculties' (p 446). Many of his assertions about animals would be questioned by current scientists, but from his perspective they are self-evident. He notes, for example, that the 'fact that the lower animals are excited by the same emotions as ourselves is so well established that it will not be necessary to weary the reader with many details' (p 448). 'It is almost superfluous,' he remarks, 'to state that animals have excellent *Memories* for persons and places' (p 452). It is also obvious to him that animals exercise reason: he says that 'only a few persons now dispute that animals possess some power of reasoning. Animals may constantly be seen to pause, deliberate and resolve' (p 453). 'All animals feel *Wonder,* and many exhibit *Curiosity*' (p 450), he states. Where males of any given species of birds display brilliantly coloured plumage, he says of the female bird that 'it is impossible to doubt that she admires the beauty of her male partner' (p 467). Within his world-view, animals not only emote and reason, but recall events, wonder at unusual occurrences, and respond to aesthetic dimensions of their experience. All of these points seemed to Darwin to be plain common sense.

In *The Expression of the Emotions in Man and Animals* (1872), Darwin will back up these claims with a mass of detailed obser-vation of the physiology of emotion in humans and animals. The universality of emotional expression, and the similarity of the physical signs of emotion in humans and animals, confirm his previous assumption of a common ancestry for all species. In this book, one finds animals esteemed not in words so much as in the care with which Darwin attends to their behaviour and his pre-supposition that their behaviour manifests underlying feelings of an order equalling that of human beings. That the approach in *The Expression of the Emotions* goes beyond the post-Darwinian behaviourist's methods may be seen in an assertion about insects: 'Even insects,' Darwin writes, 'express anger, terror, jealousy, and love by their stridulation' (p 349). In the first half of the twenti-eth century, it would be the rare scientist who would grant this much feeling to nonhuman animals, much less to insects. Most would reject a great deal of Darwin's comments on animals as anthropomorphic.

Two points Darwin makes in the third chapter of *The Descent* are crucial to understanding the difference between the perspective that generated evolutionary theory and the reductionism that purports to take its cue from Darwinism. The vision of life that legitimates the kind of appeal he makes in the anecdote about the snails and the tragic image of the homeless ants can be discerned in his simple assertion that the fact that 'animals retain their mental individuality is unquestionable' (*Descent*, p 460). For Dar-win, animals do not exist in some neutrally collective state, as both human use and empirical evaluation assume. Animals know themselves as individuals. Furthermore, 'animals not only love, but have desire to be loved' (p 450). Following up on this point, Darwin will later mention signs of affection among social animals and altruistic acts performed by animals (pp 475–8). At the time that he first notes love in animals, he cites an incident that has moral implications decidedly out of step with any value-free no-tion of science:

In the agony of death a dog has been known to caress his master, and every one has heard of the dog suffering under vivisection, who licked the hand of the operator; this man, unless the operation was fully justified by an increase of our knowledge, or unless he had a heart of stone, must have felt remorse to the last hour of his life. (p 449)

In view of testimony like this it is not surprising that Stanley Edgar Hyman derives from Darwin's writings the Blakean message that 'Everything that lives is holy' (p 78). Perhaps Mary Midgley's quotation of the Bible at the end of *Beast and Man* to illustrate the 'sort of way Charles Darwin looked at the physical universe' (p 363) will come as a bit of a surprise, but the passages from the deity's words to Job which she cites – 'Hast thou given the horse strength?'; 'Doth the hawk fly by thy wisdom?' and so on (Job 38:41) – are an uncharacteristic reminder to humankind that other animals live by their own powers. Remove the idea that a distant god has bypassed human dominion to lend animals their individual traits and we do have a vision of animals that humbles humankind in somewhat the same fashion as Darwin's theory does.

Darwin's vivid apprehension of animal subjectivity validates the grand theory he presents to culture. In its original state, the idea of evolution does not neutralize the world; it depends upon the recognition of qualities in other animals that philosophy and religion have treated as the exclusive preserve of the human individual. Describing this aspect of Darwinism as Romantic might seem to discredit at least this one feature of his theory as unscientific. Nevertheless, aspects of Darwin's thought that may be discounted as Romantic or even sentimental from an empirical point of view are neither anomalous nor decorative but a substantial part of his theory as a whole. If a distinction in kinds of discourse must be assumed, then the least that can be said is that the two ways of interpreting life – Romantic and empirical – inform each other in Darwin's work. Despite scientific resistance, moreover, culture has not remained oblivious to the Romanticism in evolutionary theory. The inherent Romanticism in the idea of continuity between humans and animals is working itself out at present in the animal rights controversy and in attempts to establish environmental and ecological ethics.

One way or another, then, it is obvious that Darwin has problematized the world in a new way for modern culture. It is equally obvious that the nonhuman animal resides at the heart of the dilemmas that Darwin has left to us. We have become aware that the haecceity of the animal stands in conflict with the global schemes under which the animal has been philosophically subsumed. Where science was busily neutralizing nature, converting nature into mechanical process opposing culture's ethical and aesthetic values, animal reality now intervenes to confound the tidy separation of nature and culture. With the animal at the crux of the problem, Darwinism is dialectically disposed either to infuse nature with an objectivity so supreme that it is immune to culture or conversely to endow nature with subjectivity (or 'holiness') so pervasive that anthropocentric culture begins to looks woefully solipsistic. In either case products of culture are left conscious of their own ineptitude and insufficiency. The living presence of the individual animal has turned nature into a genuine obstacle for human belief.

ANTHROPOMORPHISM AND ANIMAL INDIVIDUALITY: RESTORING POWER TO THE ANIMAL VICTIM

There are weak ways of defending animals and denouncing cruelty against them. In certain guises, the anthropomorphism licensed by Darwin constitutes an equivocal method of rescuing animals. It would appear, for example, that a carter beating his horse represents a clear-cut instance of cruelty. In our age, the total innocence of the animal, and indeed its patient submission, arouse the anger which defines the act as cruel. But would the beating be cruel if the animal were assumed to be simply a tool requiring force, an object like a car or lawn mower on which frustrations could be vented without the question of ethics arising? No philosophy, one hopes, would condone beating animals. At a certain point (though not normally at the point at which the horse is harnessed to the cart in the first place), emotional equipment engages and informs us that this act violates some ill-determined line between use and abuse. It remains odd, nevertheless, that the animal can be an instrument for human use at one moment and a being with pains and rights at the next. If this contradiction in attitudes were not troubling enough, the sentimental anthropomorphism which might set restraints upon the carter's violence represents another kind of violation. When a mystic like Margery Kempe sees 'Christ being beaten' when she is in fact looking at a suffering horse, she is doing a disservice to the animal. With sentimental anthropomorphism, what suffers is not the animal *per se* but a phantom person standing in for the animal. The approach may well prevent abuse, and that is a fine thing, but animal autonomy has evaporated in the process.

In his book *Cruelty,* Philip P. Hallie stresses that cruelty is a flexible concept contingent upon issues of power and identity. Before he added a postscript to his book in 1982, Hallie had concluded that the only method for rectifying cruelty is retaliation from the victim. In order to make headway with this idea, it must be granted first of all that speaking of victimization in the abstract is faulty both politically and emotionally. Real bodies are hurt, genuine rights violated, when one being is cruel to others, and recognition of this fact is essential. As an experiential phenomenon, power itself requires a materialized rather than an abstract victim. Yi-Fu Tuan delivers an observation to this effect when remarking upon some people's relations with their dogs: 'Power over another being is demonstrably firm and perversely delicious when it is exercised for no particular purpose and when submission to it goes against the victim's own strong desires and nature' (p 107). Perhaps pity can be blamed for the belief that abject passivity is a necessary aspect of the victim's role in any act of cruelty. Sentiment and morality seem to favour helplessness in victims. Compassion merely repeats, however, the power relationship instituted by maltreatment. Revenge re-establishes what Hallie describes as the victim's 'particularity and force' (p 44) against the oppressor's desire that the victim become a faceless abstraction.

As an example of a true depiction of the dynamic of abuse, Hallie cites William Hogarth's *The Four Stages of Cruelty.* Even in the first engraving where the boys torturing the animals seem most powerful and secure against retribution, Hogarth depicts the animals' pain and thereby impresses the viewer with their individuality. As Hallie observes, the dog tormented by Tom Nero is 'a strong dog ... accustomed to his own way of moving, his own way of satisfying his needs' (p 28). The cruelty in Hogarth's series attains full ugliness because Hogarth is acutely aware of the victim's identity. It is no accident, either, that Hogarth has created, in Kenneth Clark's words, 'possibly the best cat in art' (p 187) in his painting *The Graham Children,* or that that cat achieves its stature because of its open-mouthed and open-clawed attention to a caged bird. Although Hogarth's point in *The Four Stages of Cruelty* is to show that cruelty to animals leads to crimes against people, the strength of his case may be seen at the first 'stage,' where nature forcefully condemns acts of cruelty by means of the animal's struggle for freedom. Hogarth is not afraid of animal identity and seems even to enjoy the animal's less-than-civilized urges. That is why he is one of the few of his age to see cruelty to animals truly: his cats and dogs are fully cats and dogs, with their own lovable individuality.

There seems, however, to be a paradox at the outer edge of the process of cruelty where the generalized animal victim resides. Hallie speaks of the 'innocence' of cruelty in the Marquis de Sade's works. Because Sade's victims are stylized out of existence, 'the cruel ones seem to be maiming or killing no one' (p 53). If the aim of cruelty is to deprive the victim of identity, then what abuse remains once this purpose is accomplished? 'No one,' in effect, is being hurt. It will be apparent how crucial this paradox is to the legitimization of animal victims. Total victimization, to which animals have been subject, tends to negate itself. Bind the conception of the animal fully to human devices and what is victimized is an idea rather than an animal. By Hallie's paradigm, therefore, the resistance of the victim is at once an obstacle and a requisite to cruelty proper.

The nature of animal resistance is clearly peculiar. Biting and clawing under abuse may qualify as assertions of animal freedom because such actions are anti-human not only in the obvious sense that they express opposition but also in the sense that they are instinctive rather than reflective. Viewed as instinctive, however, these reactions seem to lose particularity, to revert to being an abstract property unrelated to animal identity. Objectively, perhaps, human beings cannot be transformed into the complete 'zero,' the total abstraction, that apparently negates cruelty. We ascribe to ourselves ontologically a personal self, a 'soul' as this quality is sometimes designated, and thus human suffering always has emotional and moral force. The necessary, defiant 'self' of the animal is hardly as secure as that of each human being. Between primitive and modern times, objective opinion held that animals have no identity, and certainly are devoid of soul (or else what would distinguish the human being?). In circles claiming the highest of objectivity even now, the attribution of identity to animals is regarded as sentimental foolishness.

Since souls have fallen into decline, language is often asserted as the primary point of demarcation between humans and animals and the *sine qua non* of identity. In their discussion of abuses of animals, Horkheimer and Adorno use the argument of language to deny to animals that power which by Hallie's account actualizes cruelty: 'Escape from the dismal emptiness of existence [they note] calls for resistance, and for this speech is essential. Even the strongest of animals is infinitely weak' (p 247). It is this premise that undermines Adorno and Horkheimer's attempted defence of animals against particular ills in human attitudes. They are perceptive in their critique of bourgeois substitutes for recognition of animal identity. Their analysis, to be sure, highlights the obvious point that animals cannot enact revenge upon their oppressors. Nonhuman animals cannot organize revolutions, or write letters of protest to politicians, or bring criminal charges against scientists, farmers, and hunters. But in light of this truism, Adorno and Horkheimer seem to find it necessary to capitulate to the traditional refusal of identity to animals. They assume that language is an essential attribute, not only for communication of personal subjectivity, but also for the existence of that subjectivity in the first place. Having assumed that, they must also assume that animals have no persuasive power to counteract the selfsame ills in human attitudes the writers denounce. Divested of internal experience all its own, the individual animal cannot be the subject of cruelty because it is not a subject. Its pain is denied reality. It falls into sameness with every other animal, and the whole issue of victimization is thereby neutralized.

Treating animals as a collectivity is the standard approach to suppressing the sentiments that are aroused by cruelty. In many people's minds, the issue of primary importance in killing animals is whether or not another animal is still available to be killed and used. The conversion of animals into products for human use or into anonymous entities for scientific manipulation could continue endlessly without disturbance to human peace of mind were it not for the idea of continuity between humans and animals. However much personal feeling might disconfirm such continuity, modern humanity is obliged to confront the problem of a more intimate fellowship with animals than orthodox thinking of the past had allowed. Whether continuity implies that human-like identity must be granted to animals, or conversely that animal-like non-identity (as the customary contrast has it) must be accepted as the true human state, the very existence of this dilemma represents a threat to human self-possession. Each animal embodies this threat, particularly (as will be seen) in the arts. In a generalized way, the possibility that culture itself came into being not in some divinely mysterious way but by determinable evolutionary principles challenges the presumption of distinction for the human species. Since human distinctiveness has collapsed to that extent, does it also follow that the human species should be viewed as a collective, as we have viewed animals, and treated accordingly? Most people would find this proposition offensive to any idea of morality or humanity. But if the human person is to preserve his or her claim to moral consideration under the authority of the idea of continuity, then the individual animal attains moral status of a greater than sentimental variety. Once the locus of the disowned demons of humanity's moral structures, each particular post-Darwinian animal now compels moral attention, if not, at present, moral rights. We may have no precise idea of the nature of animal identity, but we are required nonetheless to give animals a legitimate place among our thoughts. Indeed the indeterminacy of animal being renders the animal all the more unsettling to a culture wondering about its own animal origins. By this roundabout and somewhat grandiose route, the modern animal attains the power of resistance, the freedom, that makes its victimization important.

Thus far, I have been extrapolating from Hallie's original conclusions about cruelty. In the 1982 postscript to his book, he recants on his earlier feeling that the potential for counter-aggression on the victim's part is the only way to dismantle the structure of dominance and subordination established by cruelty. As an example of an alternate method of rectification, he cites the protection given to refugees from the Nazi occupation by the entire French village of Le Chambon. The attitude of the villagers, he notes, was one of welcome rather than compassion. He proposes that hospitality gives the necessary recognition of the victim's identity, and replaces the 'I-it' power relation with 'I-you' equality.

Hallie's new solution is, of course, a highly civilized one. That is what makes it so difficult to apply to animals. By convention, social graces like hospitality have been developed in opposition to animality; such graces would seem thus to be inherently hostile to the animal way of life. Hospitality coming from humankind to other species would likely imply to most people treating all animals as pets. The image of the friendly pet represents its own kind of trespass against animals. As to actual pets, we welcome into our homes the smaller animals we have domesticated but could not tolerate having an untamed hyena or wild boar rushing about the house. Our mental houses are much the same: wild, or dirty, or slimy creatures throw into disarray the tidy, rational world we like to establish in our minds. Hostile animality may well have residence in subconscious hinterlands and jungles, but the civilized mind by definition wants its animals under control.

The actualization of this figurative process may be seen in qualities desired in companion animals. Companion animals are trained to be obedient to our commands. They are curbed, leashed, and penned. They are neutered ('fixed'), except when propagation of their physical traits has market value. Actual, physical deformities, like the squashed noses in pug dogs, are bred into them. These acts of violence are signs of a fundamental aversion to the natural animal. When it takes the form of aesthetically motivated pruning and impairing of animal bodies, that aversion is clearly condemnable. Such aversion has become reprehensible, too, when it leads to wanton destruction of wild animals. How, though, are we to express hospitable intentions to animals we have not first made into pets, if only in our minds? The wild animal will not likely respond with gratitude to human gestures of friendship, despite what children's stories may say. Friendly feeling towards the wild animal, moreover, seems to alter the animal's essential identity in human consciousness. Part of our understanding of the wild animal's identity, that is to say, depends upon the fruitlessness of humanity's sociable designs. Current conventions of hospitality will not work with wild animals. Before inviting animals into our homes and lives, we have compelled them to relinquish definitive qualities of free and natural growth, movement, and mating. The true animal 'you' (if the inherent anthropomorphism of 'you-ness' may be temporarily forgiven) has been outcast from such civilized attitudes as hospitality.

However wrong it is to think of sexuality, appetite, ferocity, and the like as animal qualities, and to reserve love, altruism, and strategy for humankind alone, the idea of culture itself depends upon this distinction. Culture is formed out of suppression of traits associated with the wild animal. We tend to think that cruelty in general originates with animality. When we wish to describe the people who commit appalling acts of violence, the most extreme expression we can find is that they are 'animals.' Our word 'bestial' carries the same insult to animal nature. The morality and righteousness which counters cruelty we call 'humanitarianism' and thereby perpetuate the long-standing belief that in overcoming violence, humanity conquers the beast in itself. To become good and kind, the traditional distinction says, people must suppress their animality, from which flow such crudities as selfishness and aggression. When the aim is to rectify violence towards animals, this paradigm would have it that that aim is satisfied by anti-animal aspects of human nature. The paradox arises that a kind of arrogance is inherent in programs that advise transcendence of nature. This is clearly evident in lines from Tennyson quoted earlier: 'Move upward working out the beast, / And let the ape and tiger die' (*In Memoriam,* cxviii). Tennyson may have intended the ape and tiger to be metaphors for human qualities, and the suggestion that these qualities be eliminated is malevolent enough. But the worse effect of such thinking is the death of real apes and tigers. In 1875, John Colam, secretary for the RSPCA and thus an individual who should have had the finest of feelings for animals, supported the idea of exterminating tigers because he could not see 'why the noxious, ferocious and deadly enemies of mankind should not be destroyed' (Turner, p 128). It would appear that virtue has had little trouble with the destruction of undomesticated animals. It is even possible that virtue has licensed such destruction. In real terms, the assumption that human life has superior spiritual value over that of other species leads both to negligence with the resources that sustain the lives of other animals and to outright killing of those animals whose death satisfies whatever caprice people choose. Animals suffer for our rejection of what we consider to be the animal aspects of human nature.

Clearly, anthropomorphism crosses back and forth across the issue of cruelty to animals, sometimes rationalizing victimization by depicting animals as wicked, sometimes countering victimization by depicting animals as all too human. Despite the fact that Darwinian continuity validates a certain amount of anthropomorphizing, the ideal would be a conception of animals as animals which finds ethical significance in their own state of being. We turn now to two conceptions of nature which purport to establish the animal identity of nonhuman animals and to remove the hindrance of anthropomorphism. Unfortunately, both approaches not only sanction actual abuse but seem to be founded upon a systemically victimized animal.

BEHAVIOURAL SCIENCE AND THE HUNTING ETHOS: BLAMING THE VICTIM

Tennyson notwithstanding, a crusading spirit has never honestly motivated the victimization of animals. One does not find hunters believing that they are on a moral mission to sweep the world clean of the animal enemy for the sake of civilization. If the rationalization for hunting were victory over nature, the restocking of dwindling supplies of wild animals to hunt would make nonsense of that claim. This is not to say that moral fervour does not enter into this ritual killing of animals. Notions of nobility, manliness, and heroism unfailingly attach themselves to philosophies of the hunt. The hunter cannot seek to weaken nature; he has an ideological investment in a powerfully resistant victim. In fact, people who hunt animals claim for themselves a mystical sympathy with the beast which is incomprehensible to non-hunters and urban people. Randall L. Eaton makes this claim when he remarks that the 'hunter is the animal he hunts and the environment in which it lives' (p 10). He goes on to cite Buddhism as the archetypal opposition to his philosophy:

Though the Buddha forbade the killing of sentient life ... the *skilled hunter,* a true hunter, knows something the Buddha does not know. The gray fox ... is a true hunter, and the ground squirrel it [kills and eats is] also a hunter of grasses and seeds, and as one works back from stomach to stomach there is a secret and a secret hidden deep in that. The gray fox and the skilled hunter have no need of what is forbidden by the civilized prophet, precisely because they have not been corrupted by civilization in the first place. Only civilized people need prophets ... because only civilized people have lost the transcendence, humility and oneness with Nature. (Eaton's italics, pp 17–18)

The critique of civilization seems fair enough: it is true that, as Ortega y Gasset puts it in his *Meditations on Hunting,* the 'urbanized and cultivated man has always felt a funny snobbery towards anything wild, man or animal' (p 80). Distaste for what is perceived as the vitiation of nature by civilization informs Ortega's position that *'There is ... in the hunt as a sport a supremely free renunciation by man of the supremacy of his humanity'* (Ortega's italics, p 59). Conquest of nature is at issue in blood sports, but the nature participants claim to confront is one that they also claim to vivify by their acts. Unlike the urban person, the hunter is alert to nature and to the ways of the natural animal. The argument in a nutshell is that civilization elevates humanity to the enfeeblement of its conception of animals, while in blood sports people voluntarily abandon their prestige to become one with animals, stalking as they stalk, killing as they kill. Note, though, that this argument relies totally upon the conventional dichotomy; the animal, actually and psychologically, is still viewed as the source of traits opposing culture. Conversely, whether viewed as the source of corruption or the source of virtue, civilization is still set up as the antagonist of animality. The moral scheme is the same as that with which Tennyson was operating, only inverted.

One might have greater faith in such claims, too, if hunters did not arm themselves with the tools of civilization for their sport. But as Konrad Lorenz observes in *On Aggression,* 'No sane man would even go rabbit-hunting for pleasure if the necessity of killing his prey with his natural weapons brought home to him the full emotional realization of what he is actually doing' (p 208). If Lorenz is right, the actual distance that separates the person with the gun from the animal he or she shoots runs parallel to a psychic distance that alone enables the pulling of the trigger. Both the overall morality and the technology of the hunt, therefore, manifest the traditional abyss dividing humans and animals. And despite the hunter's presumed humility and mystical union with nature, the animal is nonetheless dead at the end of all the philosophizing. One doubts very much whether the big-horned sheep or grizzly bears who become the object of the sport appreciate being so honoured by the hunter's renunciation of his or her humanity.

The question arises, then, whether an amoral or even antimoral approach to animals counteracts humanity's proclivity to victimize them. The promising aspect of anti-moral approaches is that they take away from natural animal acts the negative morality that humanity falsely applies to them. The wolf's attack on the lamb can be viewed with equanimity as behaviour appropriate to the predator and necessary for its survival. The whole machinery of symbolism which converts the wolf into the slavering beast of horror stories instantly disintegrates into ludicrousness. Traditional ideas of morality have not been particularly kind to animals.

Behaviourism is one example of an epistemology doing its best to adopt an amoral stance for its program of explanation. It professes to adapt Darwinian principles to the field of human psychology, replacing purpose, in B.F. Skinner's formulation, with 'contingencies of reinforcement' as evolutionary theory replaced 'antecedent design' with 'contingencies of survival' (p 224). The only useful information for the behaviourist is that which can be seen and measured. Moralizing may be interesting as something that human beings do, but it has little relevance to what can be truly known. With the behaviourist approach, there should be no excitement from giving pain to animals, since the connection that links the behaviourist with his or her subject is scientific rather than personal.

The following sample of the language of animal experimentation illustrates the effort to overcome the personal connection. The quotation pertains to John Garcia's discovery of the 'stimulus fittingness principle' and describes the experimenters' application of painful or noxious conditions to a rat as it drinks water:

An audiovisual stimulus was made contingent upon the rat's licking at the water spout, thus making it analogous with a gustatory stimulus. When the audiovisual stimulus and the gustatory stimulus were paired with electric shock the avoidance reaction transferred to the audiovisual stimulus, but not the gustatory stimulus. Conversely, when both stimuli were paired with toxin or x-ray the avoidance reactions transferred to the gustatory stimulus, but not the audiovisual stimulus. Apparently stimuli are selected as cues dependent upon the nature of the subsequent reinforcer. (Garcia in Sahakian, ed, p 360)

First of all, the use of the passive voice ensures that the experimenters never appear in this description. An objection to the use of personal pronouns as immodest is one explanation for this peculiar style. That style also has the side benefit of absolving the experimenter of blame in the matter of hurting animals. By the second sentence of this description, the rat has also disappeared; it becomes an 'avoidance reaction'; its need for water has become a 'gustatory stimulus.' Although this particular experiment gives the animal more credit than ever before in the behaviourist tradition, inasmuch as animals are assumed to respond to injury intelligently rather than by simple association, the language shows no comparable advance in recognizing that greater animal intelligence. The passive voice moves from the acts of the experimenter to those of the rat, so that the rat is not credited with choosing well between harmful circumstances or understanding that its nausea likely resulted from consuming something toxic rather than hearing or seeing something. Linguistically and hermeneutically, responses are taking place quite independent of the rat who is giving them.

Furthermore, the elimination of the rat from the final sentence serves the purpose of generalizing from rats to humans. It is that kind of generalization that lends zeal to the behaviourist's activities. As John B. Watson explains, 'The interest of the behaviorist is more than the interest of the spectator – he wants to control man's reactions as physical scientists want to control and manipulate other natural phenomena' (p 11). Behaviourism employs animals analogically, and persistently, as a step towards the goal of predicting and controlling human conduct. In her study of attitudes towards our closest animal relations entitled *Primate Visions,* Donna Haraway detects an idealistic aim behind work in the laboratory: 'Both the symbolic and utilitarian aspects of people's use of other primates have been bound up in the project of imagining and producing the ideal human being in the ideal society' (p 64). The irony, of course, is that whatever ideal in human character experimenters hope to produce from their investigations of animal behaviour presupposes a virtually non-existent subject. The view of the animal in the above quotation implies a view of the human being as likewise vacant.

Morris Berman points out the mutual depersonalization which occurs from scientific experimentation on animals in his book *Coming to Our Senses.* In an echo of the I-you relationship that Hallie applies to the issue of cruelty, Berman examines the cultural history of Self and Other. In modern times, Berman points out, animals are now regarded as laboratory tools, experimental 'equipment,' no more significant on an invoice or order sheet than test tubes or graduated cylinders. They are literally 'stuff,' and this is the nadir of the Self/Other relationship ... Whereas the animal Other was once sacred, it is now literally garbage, waste material, and this seems to spill over into the human realm. Assembly line genocide and the treatment of the human body as a medical specimen are two obvious expressions of this. If Other is nothing more than scratch paper, so to speak, Self is finally going to be regarded in the same way. (p 83)

It is, of course, not just the human and animal objects of behavioural observation that are divested of subjectivity, but the experimenters themselves. The use of the passive voice subsumes the experimenters, and thus all beings, animal and human, subject and operator, disappear.

The demystified animal of pure behaviourism is also a fundamentally devitalized animal. Because animals and their visible acts are taken to be one and the same, no residue of animality escapes human explanation. The animal is thoroughly conquered; it is simply a system of behaviours to be isolated, manipulated, and tabulated. What does victimization of the behaviourist's animal matter? All that has value are its responses to applied stimuli, the benignity or harm of the stimuli entering into the project only as properties to be recorded – and recorded without reference to the person committing these acts, as if they originated not with people but with some grand anonymous design. Behaviourism coalesces with hunting philosophy in the claim to cast off human evaluation. There is in fact a unity between human and animal in behaviourism in that the anonymous animal, the animal without identity, meets the anonymous human being, the human being without identity. Unfeeling as it is, such disownment of values represents an honest attempt to arrive at truth, and truth of a highly modern character, that is, stripped bare of what is taken to be cultural distortion.

Yet a certain irrationality pervades the multiplication of facts. The futility of a purely objective approach was discovered by D.O. Hebb in his studies of chimpanzees at the Yerkes Laboratories of Primate Biology. He found that when anthropomorphism was prohibited, researchers could not make meaningful assessments of chimpanzee behaviour:

All that resulted was an almost endless series of specific acts in which no order or meaning could be found. On the other hand, by the use of frankly anthropomorphic concepts of emotion and attitude one could quickly and easily describe the peculiarities of the individual animals, and with this information a newcomer to the staff could handle the animals as he could not safely otherwise. Whatever the anthropomorphic terminology may seem to imply about conscious states in the chimpanzee, it provides an *intelligible and practical guide to behavior*. The objective characterization therefore missed something in the behavior of the chimpanzee that the ill-defined category of emotion and the like did not – some order, or relationship between isolated acts that is essential to comprehension of the behavior. (Hebb's italics, p 88)

Hebb should have taken heed of Darwin. Had he done so, he and his colleagues might not have wasted time trying to efface themselves. His reference to safety in the handling of animals is a gesture of defence against the scepticism of fellow behaviourists. To the non-behaviourist lay person, the idea that animal acts become meaningful only when the animal is granted internal purpose and emotion is simple common sense. Hebb allows that anthropomorphism leads researchers out of the realm of the strictly measurable and into qualitative questions where agreement and control are less assured. For meaning to exist at all, however, it seems that the observer must come out from behind the veil of impersonal detachment and relinquish total explanatory control. From this concession follows the return of import to the matter of victimization.

In several significant ways, behaviourism and the philosophy of the hunt stand at polar extremes with respect to the animal victim. Between them, they delineate a crucial conflict that inheres with the animal victim in modern culture. With the hunt, victimization counts for too much; it is elevated to a spiritual level, to a mystical fatedness which is presumed to invalidate whatever mercies civilization dictates. The nature of the animal is imprisoned in predation; the whole of nature becomes an endless round of pursuit and conquest or, which is more likely, an endless game. The hunter requires each individual animal killed to embody a value system hostile to culture. With behaviourism, victimization counts for too little; the collectivized animal becomes an abstraction unamenable to moral import. The world explained by the behaviourist's animal is a neutralized world, full of facts but cut off from moral consciousness. The victimization of the animal in the hunt is of the character of biological mandate; in behaviourism, it is of the character of biological accident. In effect, both behaviourism and the philosophy of the hunt blame the victim for its own suffering or death. In asserting unity with the animal and relinquishment of cultural significance as the virtue of their projects, the behaviourist and the hunter seek licence for their activities from the animal itself. The hunter transfers responsibility to the animal's own natural appetite and predatory characteristics; the behaviourist transfers responsibility to the animal's indifferent relation to cultural construction. Previously the victim of the conceptual rift between humans and animals, the animal now becomes a sacrifice to the theoretical sacrifice of human distinctiveness. What remains stable in this reversal in perspective is the victimization of animals.

One detects a certain sense of guilt in rationalizations for hunting and scientific experimentation on animals. Hunters like Eaton and Ortega are aware that the assertion of human prowess in conquest of nature has fallen into disrepute. Though it survives among a few, usually wealthy and usually male persons, the safari mentality which sees the individual heroically conquering the wilderness with his virility and his arsenal of weapons has become an absurd anachronism. Now the killing of animals must express deep humility before nature. More than this, if Ortega is to be believed, the hunter willingly assumes the guilt and repugnance associated with the spilling of blood. Noting that a 'white rag stained with blood is not only repugnant, it seems violated, its humble textile material dishonoured' (p 105), he insists that a hunter makes a great sacrifice in confronting the bloodshed which the non-hunter cravenly avoids. His reaction to blood on a cloth is as markedly peculiar and jittery as the argument he is making. That he must aspire to martyrdom manifests the shakiness of his position. Likewise, the relinquishment of self in behaviourist language is a response to growing societal hostility towards practices that give harm to animals. Post-Darwinian vivisection controversies elicited from physiologists claims of mystical prowess similar to those coming from contemporaneous devotees of wilderness hunting expeditions. A perceptive analyst of the far-reaching implications of the late nineteenth-century vivisection uproar, Coral

Lansbury quotes a statement made by the harassed physiologist, Claude Bernard:

The physiologist [Bernard writes] is no ordinary man: he is a scientist, possessed and absorbed by the scientific idea he pursues. He does not hear the cries of animals, he does not see their flowing blood, he sees nothing but his idea, and is aware of nothing but an organism that conceals from him the problem he is seeking to resolve. (Lansbury, p 132)

Lansbury also cites a phrase from John Davidson's *The Testament of a Vivisector* (1901): the vivisector is, according to Davidson, a person 'sublime and terrible in martyrdom' (p 169). The naïvety of such overblown bids for heroism reveals the depth of discomfort produced by victimization of animals in modern culture. Causing pain to animals found little favour with respectable society, hence the invention of mystic dramas among physiologists who strove to justify their work. Surprisingly, that investment of the laboratory with holy significance could still occur not so long ago. In an article in *Look* magazine in 1967 (28 November), writer Oriana Fallaci attributes super-human grace to a professor removing and dismantling the head of a living rhesus monkey named Libby – named not by the researchers but by the reporter herself. Fallaci observes surgeon Professor White's fingers as he strips the facial features from the anaesthetized monkey to reach the still-working brain:

There is always a moment when they seem to be the fingers of a priest celebrating a Mass. And because of this, perhaps, you didn't cry for Libby. Not even now that those fingers were stealing her nose, her left eye, her right eye, and her features no longer existed. In their place was a smell of burnt flesh. Professor White looked tired. Perspiration clouded his glasses. (pp 100–1)

Apparently, even Professor White's glasses are holy. They appear to possess as much significance as the monkey whose life and identity the professor is destroying. The monkey's brain, it seems, is to go on living and thinking all the while, and that is the object of the experiment. In spite of the repellent reverence of the reporter, the article does at least have the virtue of bringing to light the ugliness of laboratory research upon animals.

Where once they had to defend their practice by pronouncing themselves martyrs, vivisectionists ultimately found it more effective simply to shut and bolt the doors on their laboratories. At the end of the nineteenth century, during the anti-vivisectionist debates, the conquest of the wilderness could still assume heroic proportions for itself because the wilderness was a place beyond the reach of culture. Ethics and reservations about assaulting animals simply did not by definition apply to regions where civilization did not hold sway. Thus the defensiveness of the modern hunter shows the expansion of culture into the once alien territory of the wilderness.

There is, it will be observed, a kind of see-saw action between the hunt and scientific experimentation on animals. Where the hunt was at one time self-evidently noble, science was having to protest loudly as to the nobility of its victimization of animals. As laboratory science found the linguistic and epistemological tricks which conceal animal suffering from cultural attention, the hunt lost ground as a respectable activity. The wilderness has been naturalized in this century; acts of violence against wild animals continue unrelentingly, but they are no longer morally tolerable. At the same time, though society may not have been sold on the vision of the scientist heroically suppressing tender-hearted impulses, it has tacitly acknowledged the sanctity of the laboratory by conceding that moral judgments do not apply there. The willingness of present-day society to turn a blind eye to the often pointless torment of animals in the laboratory suggests how deeply entrenched in culture is the victimization of animals. The transfer of sanctity from the wilderness to the laboratory has proceeded so smoothly and subtly that one almost suspects an intransigent need in humanity to go on subjecting animals to pain.

DOMESTICATION AND THE SACRIFICE OF ANIMALS:
CULTURE COMES UNDER THREAT

Victimization is more than a matter of ethics. Modern theories tend towards locating victimization at the root of culture itself. In *Totem and Taboo,* Freud speaks of the deliberate shedding of blood as a mechanism for uniting members of primitive tribes. Freud's interest is primarily to indicate the importance of the father, and the killing of the father, as a point of contact between anthropological and personal psychological history. When he does discuss the sacrifice of animals, he does so to stress the significance of the animal as a substitute for the father (p 141). How else, he implies, can one explain the intensity of emotional ambivalence surrounding the ritual killing of animals? Freud relies upon the anthropological work of William Robertson Smith for his comments on animal sacrifice. At one time, by Smith's account, the tribal killing of all animals was attended by ceremony and every member of the tribe was required to eat the flesh so that all would be responsible for the deed. All sacrificed animals, by virtue of being sacrificed it seems, linked the tribe with its gods. Later, distinctions were made between ordinary animals and those that were unclean or taboo. Only the killing of taboo animals required ceremony and the sharing of the flesh, and only the blood of those animals held the sacred bond between gods and tribal members. The widespread domestication of animals for slaughter gradually put an end to the guilt associated with the shedding of animal blood – or so runs Freud's summary of Smith's findings. For Freud's purposes, the primitive link between totem animals and the gods remains in personal psychology where the child associates particular animals with the father. The object of his comments is not animals *per se,* and yet it is interesting that he should choose to note the sacrifice of animals as a mechanism deeply embedded in the development of culture. It is interesting, too, that Freud finds cultural progress occurring alongside the isolation of sacred animals for sacrifice from ordinary animals who could be killed without a tribal need for collective atonement. The normalization of the killing of animals apparently goes hand-in-hand with the rationalization of moral stricture. With the domestication of animals, emotional intensity surrounding the shedding of animal blood shrinks from a collective to a personal level. This, at any rate, is the process implied in *Totem and Taboo.*

René Girard has recently espoused a much different view of the issue of domestication and sacrifice of animals. In *Things Hidden since the Foundation of the World,* he argues that domestication proceeds out of the urge to sacrifice animals. Domestication is not a separate, economic process which precedes and eventually overtakes primal violence towards animals. Rather, it is a necessary stage in the culturally formative sacrificial motive. To satisfy the point of ritual killing, he says, the victim had to be different from and yet similar to members of the tribe. Thus animals destined for sacrifice had to stay with the tribe for a time and seem to assimilate tribal habits before they became legitimate objects of the ritual. This idea seems credible, since it is difficult to imagine an animal brought in fresh from the wild making a suitable sacrifice. In a way, although Girard does not make this point, the sacrifice of a wild animal would mean challenging powers too great for the mechanism of sacrifice to bear. Freudian interpretation lends such magnitude to the sacrifice of animals in equating the animal victim with the father. That is to say, the wildness of the animal would have equivalent alienness and potency to the father; equal psychic force would have to be mustered to assault either the father or the undomesticated animal. But by Girard's analysis, sacrifice is a kind of culmination of the process of 'hominization.' He notes that imitation is an impulse evident in all higher mammals, and that acquisitive imitation – in simplest terms, an impulse to reach for the same object as another animal has reached out to appropriate – is prohibited among all animals because of the rivalries it creates. By a theory of mimesis too abstruse to tackle here, Girard suggests that the origins of human culture reside in the ritual human beings discovered for overcoming the prohibition against acquisitive imitation. Since the bonding together of the community inherently creates conflicts associated with imitation, the sacrifice of a scapegoat works to discharge those conflicts and reinforce community cohesiveness. Instead of going after each other in violence, tribal members single out a victim to crystallize and take responsibility for a diffuse tension. The victim of sacrifice, Girard says, 'is even believed to have brought about its own death' (p 27) and is taken to be sacred because its death really does defuse community tensions. Thus the 'victimage mechanism' is foundational to culture.

Girard is aiming towards establishing the essential and even anthropological truth of the Gospels. Victimization is indeed at the heart of culture, he notes, but to make this finding is also to think in Christian terms (p 276); hence, tautologically, the truth of Christianity. Yet Girard wants simultaneously to claim that he has 'gone further than [his] predecessors in [his] rejection of anthropocentrism, since [his] anthropology is rooted in the animal kingdom' (p 443). This desire to have it both ways, to invoke the authority of both religion and science, is puzzling and to a degree annoying. Just when one thinks one has found an interpretation which makes sense of the persistence in culture of victimization of animals, that interpretation launches off into ideology and departs from the solid ground given by attention to animals. It is an even greater irritation then to find this specifically Christian belief justified by recourse to animal ways, when religion is a phenomenon at the furthest extreme from animal existence and has rationalized indifference, at best, and, at worst, aggression towards animals.

With the animal, instead of Christianity, as the aim, Girard's theory works well to account for the totality of cultural victimization of animals; it removes complacency from the process of domestication and thus restores to the domestication of animals the dynamic of victimization. It is also pleasing to find what could be an abstract totality grounded in a psychologically plausible mechanism of defusion of conflict. Extrapolating from Girard towards rather than away from the animal, one can see that the entrenchment in culture of victimization of animals is humanity's response to its own tendency to subsume the world. Instead of falling victim directly to human appropriation, animals are the scapegoats for humanity's legitimate revulsion against its own proclivity to anthropomorphize, to 'hominize,' the whole of nature. Clearly humankind cannot endlessly impose its own myths upon nature without cost. At some point in time or in the chain of reasoning, the difference of nature from human constructions asserts itself and generates fear and anger in the collective mind. The animal makes a perfect object for the need to sacrifice which arises from that fear and anger, for it represents that difference which has caused the fear and anger in the first place and, at the same time, it sustains the anthropomorphism which has become so excessive as to call attention to itself. Rather than assaulting nature wildly in an explosion of emotion, the community reinforces the sanctity of its myths through controlled sacrifice. Ritual anthropomorphizes killing, where killing is an act most hostile to culture. By means of animal sacrifice, the community can mollify nature without risking internal disintegration.

Between Freud's theory and Girard's, we have an anthropological conflict similar to the philosophical conflict defined by the hunt and behaviourism. For Freud, victimization is primal; for Girard it is global. Culture represses the connection between humanity and its animal victims for Freud; for Girard, culture embodies that connection. With the Freudian account, culture naturalizes the animal so that culture itself can exist; that is to say, culture separates itself by breaking primitive attachments to the animal. The sacrifice of taboo animals may have represented a sublimated murder of the father, but civilization relies on the energy that comes from repression of violence. For this reason, the ritual sacrifice of animals has ceased with the evolution of culture. With Girard's account, culture naturalizes the victimization of animals; culture *is* violence in that it sanctions the acquisitive mimesis prohibited among animals. The concentration in a surrogate victim of tensions arising from the exercise of acquisitive mimesis permits culture's ever-expanding subordination of all that is alien to human purposes. Since acquisitive mimesis is itself a kind of violence in its intolerance of difference, the disappearance of animal sacrifice speaks less of the kindness of culture and more of its imperialism. The actual domestication of animals, the expansion of humanity into wild regions of the earth, and the symbolic domestication of wild animals by means of empirical objectivity may well negate the need for sacrifice but only because these processes supersede the natural prohibition against appropriation.

In the conflict which pits culture against the animal, domestication is clearly a pivotal phenomenon. It is pivotal because it expresses in one process radically opposed relations between humans and animals. Nowhere is the double-sided nature of domestication better illustrated than in the difference between the death of a pet and that of a farm animal. The companion animal will go to its grave attended by grief often equal to that which follows the death of a human being. The farm animal is dispatched and dismantled with as little feeling as that which attends a car to the scrap heap. Where ethical practice is concerned, the logic established by pets leads to full moral status for animals within strictly anthropocentric moral codes. The logic of the farm animal argues for the total absence of moral status for animals. That is why, when arguments against cruelty to animals arise, farm animals represent the most contentious issue: farm animals are so profoundly entrenched in society as economic units that the attempt to find moral significance in their situation seems foolish. If farm animals do not merit activation of conscience, then why should any other animal? Even with this line of reasoning, however, pets stand as an unanswerable obstacle. Pets may well be bought and sold; they may be used to lighten the lives and improve the health of prisoners or senior citizens in extended care homes. Yet there is no doubt that conscience is aroused when pets are subjected to harm. Acts of sadism against pets can in fact generate greater horror than acts of sadism against adult humans, since pets, like children, do not have such psychological defences as martyrdom at their disposal. The emotional content, in modern Western culture, of a cat's being hung up by its back paws and having its throat slashed is utterly different from, and even antipathetic, to that which is elicited from the quantities of pigs and chickens subjected to exactly the same treatment. The pet and the farm animal express such highly polarized relations with animals that one might be tempted to posit two attitudes rather than one as the genesis of these creatures. On the one hand, human beings project human identity onto the animal, with all the moral and emotional value that attends regard for another person. On the other, human beings reduce the animal to materiality, setting at nothing whatever claims it might have upon conscience. From the animal's point of view, the diametrically opposed results springing from the single drive for domestication would have to be puzzling.

A third kind of animal, the wild animal, has destroyed the unity of the domesticating urge. Both the pet and the farm animal are achievements of past culture; at one time, both the dog and the cow represented the triumph of culture over the wild beast. Human morality could cope with contradiction because human morality, whether aimed at technological control or at befriending the natural world, was absolute. Subjugation of the wild animal, actual or metaphorical, was so crucial that culture could bear any contradiction to accomplish that aim. As long as the animal manifested human ideas of order, humankind did not feel the need to examine its conceptions of animals closely. Since Darwin, the wild animal has intervened in the cultural narrative written by domestication; animals untainted by human contact are demanding their place in the story of what is right and wrong, true or untrue, in life. Because culture and domestication are deeply interlinked, the disruption caused by the legitimization of wildness is profound.

Attention to the problem of domestication and wildness turns the modern moral relationship with animals on its head. If it is true that only the uncivilized human being is alarmed at the killing of animals and requires mechanisms for assuaging conscience, then current concern for the lives of animals does not necessarily indicate urban squeamishness over the shedding of blood. Instead of signalling an extension of pre-established ethics to accommodate animals, the present effort to find grounds for the rights of animals might originate in the subversion of known culture by as yet unarticulated and long-buried forces in the collective mind. All animals are wild animals for the pre-civilized person; all are his or her equals or superiors and demand atonement for trespass upon the sanctity of their lives. Domestication may well teach humanity to kill dispassionately by seeming to transform the cows herded off to the slaughterhouse into commodities, but the cows are living beings nonetheless, with all the potential for awakening the ancient guilt obscured by domestication. Unlike people of different ethnic backgrounds, animals will not truly come over to the side of those who conquer them. Domestication is a cognitive trick which blinds humanity to animal resistance. A herd of cows grazing placidly in a field may not seem to be withholding much from humanity's purposes, but their apparent blankness originates with human perspective. If the cows come when called or gather without much protest for the journey to the butcher, their conformity is a matter of indifference to their nature. The artificiality of animal conformity is manifest most clearly in performing animals, where the imitation of human tricks which so delights some spectators is clearly a travesty occurring outside of the essential animality that remains beyond the reach of human interference. Culture eclipses animal identity but cannot eliminate it. Animal identity abides, waiting only for cultural recognition. Primitive animal sacrifice, rather than calculated collectivization and slaughter, articulates the gravity of aggression against animals. Why we have needed to kill animals (apart from mundane self-interest) is an open question. If we are to go on killing animals, it would seem better that there at least be some guilt accruing from the act than that the slaughter pass as an unremarkable event congruent with the steady progress of civilization. Guilt at least honours the difference of the animal from ourselves, even if it does not prevent killing.

We have travelled a great distance from the carter beating his horse. A reader would be justified in thinking that such high-flown remarks on culture have little to do with any given instance of abuse of animals. Perhaps the animal victim in art cannot bear as much meaning as is expressed in centuries of cultural development. Yet art is, of course, a product of culture, and that is, naturally, how theories of culture enter into determination of the status of the animal victim in modern art. In addition to the internal theoretical dilemmas delineated above, modern art has the overarching dilemma that it must violate its own terms to cope with the post-Darwinian animal. Civilization may not seem to be as much of a blessing now as it once seemed, especially when theories like Freud's and Girard's speak of repression and victimization as generative drives. Modern culture is having doubts about itself. Accurate or inaccurate, theories like Girard's and Freud's express cultural misgivings about the previously self-evident value of culture itself. The demand upon modern culture to wrestle with the reality of the animal is a crucial aspect of its current self-doubt. If the products of culture are now beginning to express the feeling that culture itself is under attack and cannot stride confidently forward to expropriate every phenomenon in the natural world, it is largely because the lives of animals are threatening the authority of culture. Indeed, animals have become the source of current uneasiness in culture because they provide a stance outside of culture from which culture may look at itself.

Thus it is valid in our century to effect the kind of reversal Margaret Atwood makes in her discussion of what she sees as a particularly vivid Canadian attachment to animal victims: 'it is likely that Canadians feel threatened and nearly extinct as a nation, and suffer also from life-denying experience as individuals – the culture threatens the "animal" within them – and that their identification with animals is the expression of a deep-seated cultural fear' (p 79). The logical awkwardness at the heart of this statement is useful. Within the bounds of the conventional dichotomy of culture and animality, it is impossible for the feeling that one's culture is under threat to translate into the polar opposite feeling that one's animality is under threat from culture. This apparent illogicality works, however, because Atwood is positing an especially strong bond with the animal in Canadian culture. Canadians identify with the animal victim, she proposes, because their own culture is closer than others to being itself 'animal.'

This idea goes wrong only in confining the 'deep-seated cultural fear' to Canadians alone. Modern Western culture in general is under threat – and under threat as specifically and directly as Atwood's remark suggests – from the animal. When modern culture reaches out to victimize the animal, it wounds itself. Each animal victim is a revelation. Each animal victim opens a path to modern culture's insecurity.

From the range and variety of dilemmas touched upon thus far, it will be apparent that the animal victim is the locus of much meaning and little resolution in modern culture. Argue for kindness to animals and one is immediately entangled in paradoxes and conflicts unknown amongst pre-Darwinian habits of thought. What if humanity in fact serves its own feeling of superiority by taking pity on animals? What if gentleness to nonhuman creatures is the ultimate expression of humankind's pretensions to moral dominance over nature? Animals are not kind to one another, and human beings are, after all, animals themselves. If the law of survival of the fittest applies, then human animals violate nature in countermanding the scheme that has set them up as masters of other animals. Continuity from animal to human, it seems, licenses the free exercise of the power nature has given to humankind. Humanity debilitates its own animal nature with its moral strictures. Only by casting off those moral strictures can humanity view aggression among animals fairly, not as the source of evil but as a part of life. The best approach, by this line of argument, is to learn coolness in killing from the animals, to cease from suffering pangs of conscience in the business of death because pangs of conscience spring from a false view of life that the human animal has imposed on itself. Instead of demonstrating human superiority, then, morality would seem paradoxically to signal humanity's failure to live in the world as the world is. The animal who kills without regret is as one with the world, while humankind neurotically denies life with its moral structures. At any rate, these are the conclusions that appear to arise from humankind's statement, 'We are like them.'

What conclusions, then, come from the opposite assertion, 'They are like us'? Continuity from human to animal would expand the progressively widening sphere of moral concern into the animal domain. Just as morality has advanced to embrace previously outcast groups of people, so too does it follow logically that morality could eventually acknowledge animals as autonomous beings with the right to be left in peace. Since the direction of this expansion of moral concern – what we think of as 'humanitarianism' – has been ideally to avoid bestowing an alien morality upon nonconforming cultures and to accept the ontological moral status of those cultures independent of specific codes, viewing animals as subjects of morality need not represent a threat to animality in general. The problem resides in the utopian vision projected by such moral ideals. The hope for a universal 'Peaceable Kingdom' in which killing has ceased and no being persecutes another certainly does exclude the habits of the natural animal. Humanitarian acceptance of animal predation would appear culturally to entail the establishment of two moral communities, one for a population of gentle, vegetarian human beings, and another for the amoral, carnivorous animal – a kind of moral 'game preserve,' as it were. In terms of ethics, there is nothing especially wrong with this vision of two worlds, except in so far as it divides species even more thoroughly than they are currently divided.

One way to cross this divide may be to argue that humans are biologically vegetarian (as Shelley does), that their animal nature is therefore violated by exploitation of other animals. Another may be the assertion that animals in fact demonstrate rudimentary acts of moral conscience such as self-sacrifice. That arguments like these are appearing in modern thought on the rights of animals testifies to the need in culture to encompass animality in its moral sphere. It must be admitted, however, that at present these arguments are not very compelling against the global victimization founded upon the setting of a moral cut-off point where humankind ends and animals begin. Given the totality of victimization of animals, ending cruelty towards them requires a more profound reading of animal life than philosophy and science have produced thus far. In the meantime, the indeterminacy of the animal's reality can only help to enhance the animal's portentousness in modern culture.

THE ARTICULATE ANIMAL AND MODERN FICTION

Up to this point, I have been ranging freely over large ideas which simultaneously locate and complicate the matter of the animal victim. The time comes now to attempt to apply some of those ideas to fiction in which the animal victim plays a significant role. In literature the victimized animal cannot be a statistical entity whose performances are charted; nor can it be a mere commodity destined for the market-place. By its very nature, literature cannot help but grant some degree of autonomous identity to animals. At the same time, however, the author cannot cast off the legacy of culture and create the pure animal, the animal without reference to human constructions of the world. The need to make literary meaning out of the animal requires anthropomorphism, however tentative that anthropomorphism has become with the tension placed upon culture by the new demand to acknowledge animality. How that demand enters into literature is a significant problem for literary theory.

In *Beasts of the Modern Imagination,* Margot Norris takes one approach to the incorporation of the animal into literature and literary theory. Norris perceives greater than theoretical import in Darwinism. She takes Darwin as the founder of what she calls the 'biocentric tradition' in which writers write 'with their animality speaking' (p 1). In view of the disparate meanings that attach to the idea of animality, Norris' assertion is extraordinarily difficult to prove. She means more than that authors like Darwin, Nietzsche, Kafka, and Lawrence respect animals or place animals in the forefront of their philosophies. She means, as she says in her conclusion, that somehow in these authors' works 'thought "acts" as life does' (p 238). Life acts in ways that are quite different from the normal workings of the intellect. In order to cause thought to act as life does, in Norris' analysis, these writers build hostility to art and philosophy into the form of their works in ways that approximate the program of deconstructionism. In clearing away cultural and intellectual impositions, these writers introduce animality as a positive force, as an end-in-itself released from subjection to interpretation and evaluation. Nietzsche, for example, executes 'the bestial gesture' in his 'need to erase the anthropomorphic interventions of pedagogy, mimesis and intellectual influence itself' (p 2); in *Ecce Homo,* he strips away all the authorial masks that represent concessions to 'the other,' the reader, and 'reveals himself behind them all' (p 98). In this fashion, his demythification of cultural constructs enters the form of his works and he confronts the reader 'organism to organism' (p 88). The animal becomes important to Kafka, Norris argues, 'because the radicalness of his ontological vision required a negative site of narration, the site of animal being' (p 133); his narration 'constitutes a bestial gesture that marks the trajectory from signification to its obliteration, from remembering to forgetting. Becoming the beast is remembering to forget, as being the beast is forgetting to remember' (p 119). Similarly, the animal in Lawrence's works exists as an absence which art cannot represent: the 'biocentric universe Lawrence substitutes for the anthropocentric one is, finally, silent and unconscious, an ontology founded on the negation of the self-conscious subject and therefore inaccessible to literary inscription' (p 171). Norris proposes that Darwin initiates this tradition of discovering the creatural through self-repudiating texts by removing the idea of an Author from Nature. Darwin's theories challenge the most fundamental of the oppositions on which Western culture depends, oppositions, Norris notes, of human and animal, male and female, nature and culture:

With the disappearance of the Author from Darwin's universe these oppositions, which have been elevated virtually to the status of logical categories or necessary ways of thinking about the world, collapsed into a kind of Derridean freeplay. In reading the traces of natural life, the interplay of presence and absence in the fossil record or in the vestigial or rudimentary organs in living creatures, Darwin discovered form as linked not to the eternal action of mind or the intelligence of a Creator, but to the absent action of force: force extinguished and obliterated, or deferred in its effects, by time. (pp 37–8)

It is alarming to think that any genuine introduction of the animal into culture has to take negative form, the form of forgetting, of erasure, of absence, of deconstruction. Norris does demonstrate convincingly, however, that Darwinian theory is not just one cultural phenomenon among others and that Darwin has originated the demand to break out of culture and pointed the way towards doing so. Her book also warns tacitly against premature syntheses of the deep oppositions questioned by the autonomy of animals.

Norris' analysis makes it clear that language is a major difficulty in the effort to clear a place for the natural animal in the products of culture. Communication is no longer a one-way proposition whereby the human mind has free and absolute authority to explain what nature is all about. A natural being, the nonhuman animal responds meaningfully to nature in ways humankind would like to know. Indeed, the animal's ways of living in nature exist in the human mind and the human body, regardless of the difficulties consciousness has in grasping the animal in the person. The point is not that there is now no difference between humans and animals; the important historical change hinges rather upon the fact that animal distinctiveness now bears authority of its own. The reality of other minds, other experiences, or simply other eyes watching us places the demand upon culture to comprehend the language of nature. We have believed that language separates humankind from the rest of the animals. Language shapes thought and presents the human mind with a world quite different from that which animals occupy. Now that animals have assumed importance in our ways of knowing the world, doubts arise as to the power of language to escape culture and address nature.

When culture seeks language appropriate to the eloquence of the natural animal, it suffers discomfort. As soon as language begins to articulate the vital inner experience of animals, the suspicion arises that culture is learning more about itself than about animals *per se*. Anthropomorphism has become one of the great anxieties of the modern age, which is strange considering the licence evolutionary theory gives to finding correspondences between humans and animals. Fear of anthropomorphism does attest, however, to the intensity of the modern desire to know the animal directly. It also attests to the dominance of the neutralizing language of science. Where language tries to go beyond formulaic description of animals, it risks the charge that it is anthropomorphizing animal experience. Since it is obvious, now, that the world does have meaning for animals, meaning which may correspond to human meaning at some points and may not at others, the need to bring language into line with animal reality is not a trivial matter. In view of the sense of holism that marks the apperception of animals, radical divisions in language that attempts to cope with animals promote the fear that language isolates humankind from nature. Because animal life expresses important aspects of human reality, the failure of language to convey the totality of human understanding of animals suggests that crucial regions of the human psyche stand beyond the reach of language. Dependent on culture, language appears to be incapable of criticizing culture fundamentally enough to convey the essential connections between humans and animals. We know that human individuals are not made wholly by culture and animals certainly are not. Since human 'being' and cultural 'being' are not identical, culture evidently does not subsume the totality of realizable life. If language operates only upon human projection, when the external world in the form of animals is clearly communicating nonhuman meaning, then language truly divorces humans from nature – and in a fashion that hardly feeds the pride of our species in its own intelligence.

According to Gillian Beer, all major scientific theories like Darwin's 'disturb assumed relationships and shift what has been substantial into metaphor' (p 3). Until Darwin's time, culture sustained what seemed to be a substantial connection with the animal in the form of anthropomorphic metaphor. Indeed, animals lent life to the metaphors of the cultural imagination. It 'is not unreasonable to suppose,' John Berger notes in 'Animals as Metaphor,' 'that the first metaphor was animal' (p 504). One of the great ironies of the theory of evolution is that it arrives at a time when humankind is losing touch with nonhuman animals, when animal species are vanishing with frightening rapidity and day-to-day existence involves little contact with natural animals. Loss occurs across the whole spectrum of human experience. The physical loss of other animals leaves the human species lonely and isolated. Just when we need to know animals in some substantial and meaningful way, moreover, previous linguistic attachments to the animal collapse into metaphor. Berger concludes his observations on the metaphoric use of animals with this distressing comment:

Until the 19th century ... anthropomorphism was integral to the relation between man and animal and was an expression of their proximity. Anthropomorphism was the residue of the continuous use of animal metaphor. In the last two centuries, animals have gradually disappeared. Today we live without them. And in this new solitude, anthropomorphism makes us doubly uneasy. (p 505)

Although it is a moot point that metaphor had expressed the proximity of humans and animals, the contrary language of science speaks primarily of human alienation from animals. Neither anthropomorphic metaphor nor scientific discourse can grasp that paradoxical fusion of felt affinity and appreciation of difference which enfolds animals. In a way, however, scepticism about the power of language to encompass the full significance of animals has contributed to the liberation of the animal.

Naturally enough, modern fiction reflects current upheavals in relations between humans and animals. Fiction wrestles with the historical conditions in which it finds itself, and animals possess exceptionally pressing significance in the modern age. Where other kinds of discourse – scientific, philosophical, and even poetic – are attempting to lay the animal to rest, fiction recognizes the singular difficulties animals bring to culture. In modern fiction animals take an active part in human conflicts. Animality represents one of the problems faced by humankind in fiction as in life. Because the animal state of being has concrete presence in human existence, and because language is having trouble encompassing the nonhuman and yet vital meaning of animals, animals lead fiction into territories where disputes between nature and culture emerge. Modern fiction is acutely aware of the great difficulty of knowing the real animal through culturally defined methods of representation. The problematic character of the real animal in its location beyond the bounds of realization throws the depiction of human reality into question. Margot Norris argues that in the biocentric tradition she explores, mimesis 'is the negative mark, the mark of absence, castration, and death, an insight that required artists to reevaluate the ontological status of their media as negative being, as mere simulacra of life' (p 5). But since fiction does not close off the world, it is in a unique position to give material representation to the inadequacies of language and thus to sustain without finality the multi-sided and conflicted being of the animal. Fiction elicits the reality of the animal by revealing the fragmentariness of human responses. The impenetrability of the natural animal in turn discloses that culture presents humankind only with 'simulacra of life.' Mimesis, then, does not arise solely from describing animals directly, but also from revealing those places in culture and the human psyche that distort, abbreviate, or obliterate animal being. Conscious of the estrangement of culture from nature, modern fiction restores value and meaning to the total animal which other modes of discourse disavow. Modern fiction works with the animal's resistance to assimilation into culture. The victimized animal in fiction is, therefore, the source of profound discomfort, as one hopes it is, or will be, in life.

CONCLUSION

If animals had remained silent, discourse could have remained contentedly self-enclosed. Philosophy and science could have continued unchallenged to makes assertions about what animals are and are not. With the stirring of the once dormant animal in the human psyche, the natural animal now has something to address. Contrary to recent attempts to teach chimpanzees to use human signs and grammatical forms, the point is not that animals can communicate our own meaning back to us. Rather, humankind is obliged to seek out significations in itself which may meet up with the animal state of being. *What* the animal means – the obsession of past and present thinkers – is secondary. *That* the animal *means* in our century is crucial.

Culture knows animals best in their role as victims. In no other role is the animal so well prepared for anthropomorphism. It would appear, then, that the animal victim should give little trouble to a product of culture like fiction, since products of culture have both tradition and sentiment to draw upon. A curious thing happens in much modern fiction, however, and that is that the animal victim refuses to be assimilated. In response, fiction elevates the issue of acts of aggression against animals to the level of a genuine problem. The power of the animal victim to splinter human certainties reveals the extent to which animals even in this role defy human authority.

Under these conditions, the animal victim in fiction reverts to the state of the sacrificial animal of the premodern past. The destructive act recognizes itself for what it is, and mechanisms of justification must be deployed. Just as sacrifice of animals occurred in defiance of larger forces, either natural or deistic, that militated against the sacrifice, so too does the sacrifice of the animal in post-Darwinian fiction occur in defiance of ethical and theoretical values demanding reconciliation between humans and animals. Within the bounds of civilization, animal sacrifice is one way of restoring wildness to the animal. In contrast to the pathetic victim, subsumed by pity, the sacrificial animal threatens civilization. It threatens civilization, on the one hand, by pointing to a region in life where civilization does not have dominion. On the other hand, the sacrificed animal informs us that we are not as civilized as we like to believe. In view of the conflicts adhering to domestication and wildness, it is appropriate to begin examination of the animal victim in modern fiction with stories that attempt to introduce the wild animal to readers grown accustomed to domesticity in animals and in themselves.

3 Home Turf:
Animal Victims in the Wild

INTRODUCTION

Stories about animals in the wild enjoyed a vogue in the late
years of the nineteenth century and the early years of the twentieth. In North America, these stories capitalized upon and pro-
moted the wilderness cult which gave rise to the scouting movement and a fondness for camping in the wild. They emerged from
the combined strains of hunting legend and natural history.
Charles G.D. Roberts notes this double heritage in 'The Animal
Story,' the introduction to his collection of stories *The Kindred of
the Wild*. The two sources, Roberts suggests, retrieve the animal
from long years of neglect and darkness under a Christian regime
(p 21). The combination of science and hunting lore, however, results in a certain uneasiness. At times content to observe the wild
animal and its ways, the early writers of this type of story cannot
resist the rousing tale of the hunt, the thrill of menace and pursuit
and final victory or defeat. While seeming to honour wild animals
for themselves alone, these writers simultaneously romanticize
the wild. The first part of this chapter examines the peculiarly
waffling conception of animal victims produced out of this composite
of romantic adventure and natural history using stories by Jack
London, Ernest Thompson Seton, and Charles G.D. Roberts.
   As the century progressed, writers began to realize how thoroughly humankind victimizes wild animals. A clearer and, paradoxically, more powerful image of the animal victim emerged from
outrage at human assaults upon wild animals. Anger informs the

works of fiction examined in second part of this chapter. Notably, these works by Henry Williamson, Fred Bodsworth, and Allan W. Eckert do not hesitate to condemn the hunt, even when, as in Eckert's *The Great Auk,* hunting has the excuse of commercial trade to back it up. A willingness to denounce the exploitation of wild animals is a pivotal distinction between the narrative approaches to animal victims of the early tales and those of the later works. Both tacitly and directly, Williamson, Bodsworth, and Eckert attack the idea that humans are entitled to exercise their taste for adventure in the wild and upon the body of the wild animal.

Writers who tell tales about wild animals invariably aspire to realism. They aspire to realism not just as a mode but as an ideal. At times, one suspects that these writers find the wild animal's life more 'real' than the fabricated life of civilized human beings. Desiring realism, however, writers face polarized difficulties. On the one hand, they cannot write natural histories pure and simple, since natural histories are not narratives as narratives are commonly understood. Narrative elements may exist in natural histories, certainly more so than in strictly empirical accounts of animal behaviour. But the fiction-writer needs to construct a whole narrative, with a beginning and a conclusion and adventures along the way, an obligation which natural histories seldom observe. The writer of the wild animal's story does more than inform; he or she adds dramatic qualities to the animal's life to make it amenable to narrative.

The second difficulty, then, is anthropomorphism. However amenable anthropomorphism makes wild animals to narrative, authors must be extremely cautious about the human qualities they project onto nonhuman animals. Part of the work of stories about animals in the wild, after all, is to convey the alienness of the wild animal's life. Many human constructions are misplaced when applied to nonhuman animals, and to animals living in the wilderness in particular. The early writers of wild animal stories felt that they were fighting the humanization of animals in fiction. The dynamics of the later stories depend less upon the anti-anthropomorphic urge. Where wild animals are concerned, then, realism is caught somewhere between undramatic empirical fact and the distortions of anthropomorphism.

The particular mode addressed in this chapter is what Alec Lucas calls the 'fictional animal biography,' as opposed to the 'true animal life-history' ('Nature Writing in English,' p 544). Fictional animal biographies purport to be 'true,' but as we are well aware the idea of what constitutes truth in literature is fraught with problems. An observation may be true in literature without conforming to facts. Indeed, literature may tell us how far removed from truth facts are. This line of argument is especially pertinent to literary depictions of animals, given the flatness of empirically presented facts about animals. Writers of the fictional animal biography may well go wrong as to facts but still manage to tell the truth about the wild.

The early stories came in for the criticism that they told lies about nature. In *The Nature Fakers,* Ralph H. Lutts delivers a fascinating account of the history of the 'nature-faking' controversy between John Burroughs and Theodore Roosevelt on one side, and Ernest Thompson Seton, William J. Long, Jack London, and, to a lesser extent, Charles G.D. Roberts on the other. Roosevelt, an avid hunter, and Burroughs, the famous naturalist, cited various inaccuracies in stories about the wild. A protracted argument occurred, for example, over whether or not a wolf could bite through a caribou's chest to the heart, an incident described in Long's *Northern Trails* (see Lutts, pp 90–2, and passim). Roosevelt declared that this act was impossible, while Long mustered the anecdotes of an Indian guide to support his report. Vigorous as this and other debates over fact were, the argument does seem to trivialize the issue of realism. While an error of this sort (if it is an error) might well detract from *Northern Trails* as a work of natural history, it need not disqualify the book as a realistic narrative about wild animals. William J. Long raises a good point in the course of this debate: how can Roosevelt claim to know animals when his purpose in entering into the woods is to kill them (Lutts, p 113)?

A general criticism raised by Burroughs and Roosevelt, however, might disqualify *Northern Trails* and others as realistic narratives. Above all, Burroughs and Roosevelt objected to depictions of animal thought in these stories. Animals do not reason, they protested. Sometimes, the narrative in these early works does rely upon animals making complex calculations. Seton insisted, for instance, that foxes had learned to lead hunting dogs onto high trestles just before a train came (see 'The Springfield Fox'). Incidents like this aroused the ire of the scientifically minded

Burroughs and Roosevelt. Perhaps foxes have indeed learned to lead hunting dogs into the path of oncoming trains: underestimation of animal abilities is chronic amongst conventional scientists. The point in this context, however, is not the truth or falsity of Seton's assertion, but what that assertion reveals about his understanding of the wild in general. How far does his belief about foxes take his narrative towards a vision of a wilderness populated with little people? Is Seton's fox the Reynard of the beast fable, a human rogue with a bushy tail and all covered with fur? Factual errors may indicate the kind of distortion that reshapes wild animals once again for human interests. It is nevertheless revealing of the spirit of the times that the faction represented by Burroughs and Roosevelt believed that they could condemn the first stories about wild animals by picking upon scientific inaccuracies and not upon the general romanticization of the wild.

Leaving aside the intermediate question of reason, anthropomorphism at its most obvious involves the imposition of moral conflicts that nature does not acknowledge. Nature, we are justified in assuming, does not distinguish morally between predator and prey, as human ideology has done for long centuries. Nature is the arch-democrat: she does not favour the sweet, harmless animals over the carnivores, or the courageous over the cunning, or the tall and graceful over the low and wriggling. Moral partiality stops at the boundary dividing the human from the natural world.

Wild animals, however, have been particularly susceptible to moral judgments. This susceptibility stems in part from that very alienness that writers of the wild animal's story need to address: wild animals have been used to symbolize the human ignorance and savagery that civilization strives to transcend. Some have been represented as the moral antithesis of civilized ideals. Wolves are wicked, and the shark is a veritable metaphor for rapaciousness. Apes are stupid and loutish. The hawk's success in killing small creatures has made it into a symbol of humanity's warlike spirit. Even the metaphoric innocence of fawns and rabbits feeds into the moral biases of civilized humankind, in so far as that innocence highlights the wickedness of those animals, not 'us,' who kill them. Susceptibility to moral judgments arises, I would guess, from the fact that wild animals do not work for human beings. They are, that is, useless to us; or rather, they resist being used by us as domesticated animals do not. It would be typical of our species to find a way to use an animal conceptually when it resists all our efforts to use it materially. In view of the anthropocentric disposition that has determined moral values, the defiance of the predatory animal would naturally appear evil.

Deprived of conventional moral judgments, an author is hard put to create a story. With the removal of moral conflict the wild animal's life seems to have little narrative potential. The death of the animal victim seems no tragedy and the evasion of death no victory. Strict empiricism converts the animal's life into a series of events barely distinguishable from accident. All events resolve into plain undifferentiated fact. How is a writer to make a story if there is nothing to choose between the fox and the pheasant that it catches, or the pheasant and the grub that the pheasant scratches up out of the earth?

Identification of the polarized dilemmas of empiricism and anthropomorphism serves a purpose. They help to distinguish early narratives from modern ones. Neither the early nor the modern narrative stints on moral drama. The modern stories are, if anything, more blatant in their moral tone than the early ones. The irony is that they also adhere more closely than the early stories to natural history. What occurs between the first phase of this interest and the subsequent efforts is the recognition of the menace that human beings are to wild animals. A cultural shift has taken place, more obviously by Bodsworth and Eckert's time, but also in nascent form in Williamson's (*Tarka the Otter* was published in 1927). This shift turns the pre-Darwinian assumption of human distinctiveness on its head, morally speaking. Human beings *are* different from other animals: they are much more destructive. Initial cultural complacency over the plight of the wild animal led to the freedom to use wild animals narratively to serve human ends. The kind of sanction which permitted the hunt also permitted the manipulation of wild animals to promote moral ideals. Probably unwittingly, the early writers used the wild animal as a moral and spiritual commodity.

In sum, then, stories about animals in the wild encounter many of the theoretical problems discussed in the previous chapter. At base, these stories attempt to bring the wild animal into the human sphere. They juggle this aim with the demands of the wild animal's difference from anything or any being that civilization produces. Occupying a world that is not man-made, living a complete life that resists human interpretation, the wild animal tests the story-teller's power to overcome culture and allow nature to speak. In 'The Animal Story,' Roberts describes the kind of story he and others write as 'a potent emancipator.' The animal story, he writes, 'frees us for a little from the world of shop-worn utilities, and from the mean tenement of self of which we do well to grow weary' (p 29). We have good reason to be tired of our world. But is the request for emancipation, one has to wonder, yet another demand that the wild animal confirm our spiritual desires?

PART ONE:
AMBIVALENCE, IDEOLOGY, AND EARLY NARRATIVES

The use of animals to strengthen ideals does have its advocates. In his article 'The Revolt against Instinct' (1980), Robert H. MacDonald admires the overriding concern with morality he finds determining the narratives of Seton and Roberts; for them, he argues, the animal story is:

an affirmation of man's need for moral and spiritual values. The animal world provides models of virtue and exemplifies the order of nature. The works of Seton and Roberts are thus celebrations of rational, ethical animals, who, as they rise above instinct, reach towards the spiritual. This theme, inspired as it is by a vision of a better world, provides a mythic structure for what is at first sight, realistic fiction. (p 18)

This imposition of moral and spiritual values upon animals may be all very well when the object is revitalization of the human psyche, but it does little to foster a realistic appraisal of the ways of the wild animal. The particular qualities MacDonald identifies, the exercise of reason and ethics, the transcendence of instinct, are clearly those that civilized humankind would wish to cultivate in the human animal. The combination of 'models of virtue' and 'the order of nature' in this statement should arouse reservations. Are these writers really being true to the animal? No doubt, Seton, Roberts, and the others who wrote stories about wild animals in this period felt that they were revealing the order of nature primarily. That their stories do in fact convert animals into models of virtue suggests that there is something odd about their particular view of the wilderness.

Evidently, the order of nature for London, Seton, and Roberts is 'eat or be eaten,' 'kill or be killed.' The earliest writers of tales of the wild confronted readers with what they took to be the true mercilessness of nature. For the most part they set anthropomorphism down to the sentimental and lachrymose, the efforts to wring pathos out of all animal victims. Surely, nature disbarred effusions of sentiment over animal victims in the wild. These writers find, with some justice, that sentimentalism distorts the alien character of the wild animal. If nature extends no special care to the morally appealing animal, to the good, patient, long-suffering animal, then neither would the writer who aimed for realism in the wild animal's story.

In conformity with attitudes of the late nineteenth century, tales by London, Seton, and Roberts manifest a direct Darwinian influence in their efforts to illustrate that popular code for Darwinian theory, survival of the fittest. This attitude is deceptively neutral. In their divergent ways, London, Seton and Roberts confound Darwinism with the conception of nature as red in tooth and claw. For them, realism means bravely facing the struggle for survival in the wild. They display to readers the gashed throats, crushed skulls, and torn bellies which, in their reading of the wild, figure persistently in the drama of the natural animal's life. Their aim is to supplant Victorian neurosis over bloodshed among animals with assent to the ongoing battle in the wild. In depicting the state of nature as radically contrary to the generalized ideal of love, they hope to undermine that anthropomorphism which allows wild animals to be assimilated by the tender sentiments of the reader. Certainly the high drama of battle makes for vigorous narratives, and certainly the 'soft,' civilized reader, then and now, needs to overcome aversion to the killing among animals that is part of truth of nature, but London, Roberts, and Seton conflate human moral evaluation with the normal workings of animal life. They raise a rival morality to the sentimental variety and show virtue residing in strength. Narrative is motivated by power, and we are well aware of the *frisson* associated with power at the turn of the century. Might is indeed right in these early animal narratives – right empirically, according to popular woodlore, and right morally. The codes of the wild, as represented in these tales, would show readers how to liberate themselves from the artificial moral constraints of civilization. In ways that are both devious and vacillating, these early stories reveal an ideological motive almost as strong as that of the sentimental tales they critique.

Animal victims are therefore the source of much awkwardness in the spiritual quests of London, Seton, and Roberts. Although victimization is constitutive to the philosophy of heroism through strength, it is not wise to be honest about the victims scattered along the path of the hero, even when those victims are animals and not humans. Honest regard for the animal victim might rouse the indignation of civilized readers. Thus, according to the specific needs of the narrative at the time, pathos continues to envelop some animal victims, while sensationalism, that emotional harmonic to pathos, envelops others. Vacillation over animal victims discloses the insecurity of the moral vision imposed upon the wild. Ruthlessness is fine in fantasy, and such fantasies do, no doubt, emancipate the imagination from suffocating moral strictures. But when fantasy arrives at actual aggression against actual bodies, fictional mechanisms become necessary in order to prohibit revolt in the witness to violence. The devices used by London, Seton, and Roberts to mystify the victimization of animals expose the peculiarly slippery form of anthropomorphism they apply to the wild animal. The feelings they seek to elicit in readers serve human rather than animal ends. These writers persist in trying to draw messages to humankind out of a wilderness that is equally determined to remain silent.

Jack London and the Überhund

When Jack London felt compelled to defend his faith in animal reasoning against the disbelief of John Burroughs, he appealed to the analogy likening evolutionary theory to the Copernican revolution. Both scientific discoveries ousted humankind from its presumed pre-eminence. Addressing 'Mr. Burroughs,' he closes 'The Other Animals' with a recommendation for humility:

By [the other animals] you stand or fall. What you repudiate in them you repudiate in yourself – a pretty spectacle, truly, of an exalted animal striving to disown the stuff of life out of which it is made, striving to use the very reason that was developed by evolution to deny the processes of evolution that developed it. This may be good egotism, but it is not good science. (p 266)

These remarks have the levelling tendency that one would hope for from any post-Darwinian observer of animals and humans. Jack London, however, is a volatile character, confronting an unsettled cultural situation. His dog stories wander in and out of moral hierarchies.

In this respect, the most embarrassing of his dog stories are the last he wrote. Both *Jerry of the Islands* and *Michael, Brother of Jerry,* novels about the adventures of terrier siblings, invoke truly appalling hierarchies of dominance. Good fun is made out of the dogs' habit of 'nigger chasing,' for example, and their adventures are steered towards linking up finally with the 'white gods': evidently London himself and his wife, barely disguised. The demotion of people of colour below the level of animals is bad enough, but the elevation of any members of humanity to the status of gods in relation to other animals speaks for an expanded hierarchical arrangement that even an anthropocentric thinker like Burroughs could not have tolerated. The excuse that it is the dogs themselves that confer divine status upon London and his wife does not eliminate the impression that London concurs with the assessment.

There are, however, good white gods in London's stories and bad white gods, a distinction which his dogs are well able to discern. What makes this particular distinction suspect, as one seeks to understand London's attitudes towards the wild, is the association of the good white gods with love. Granted, the regime of love is much to be preferred over mere dominance and force. The questionable element is the moral opposition of the regime of love to the primitive and to the untame. The wild and primitive is apparently morally inferior to the love that emanates from the white gods. With London's stories, we are still in the domain of moral hierarchies: the elevation of human love affects his judgment of the wilderness and what it means.

London's reputation stems, in part, from the contrast he draws between the soft, civilized life in California and the rigorous, hard-scrabble existence of the North. He is unusual among writers of the wild animal story in making use of this contrast. His best-known animal stories, *The Call of the Wild* (1903) and *White Fang* (1906), share a narrative scheme based on the contrast between these domains of domesticity and wildness. The distinctions he draws between California, 'the Southland,' and the Arctic, 'the

Northland,' are so unambiguous that the formula he applies is
easily reversed from the first novel to the second. In California,
dogs are pets; or, to put it in terms appropriate to London's scheme,
they are wimps enjoying a life of ease. In the Arctic, dogs work
hard or they die; their life is a constant battle against cold, hunger,
and brutality. If, from sheer physical strength, Southland dogs
survive in the North, London will grant them the advantage of
superior intelligence over their less civilized cohorts. The Northland
dog, transported to the South, distinguishes himself (the formula
would not work with female dogs) in his instinctive courage and
will to survive. Moral formulas are already evident in this schematic of qualities and locations. Before one accuses London of
operating upon moral clichés, however, the defence can be made
that with this simplistic dichotomy he is striving for the
elementality of the wild animal's existence. If nature is a battle-
ground, it is fairly logical to view the world in terms of clear
divisions, in terms of good places and bad places, friends and
enemies, heroes and adversaries. London's romanticization of the
North and of the animals that live there falls in line with the
cultishness of the period. He presumes, like others of his time,
that the spiritual and moral ideals he writes about have actual
existence in nature, the crucial exception being love. It may well
be anthropomorphic to impose moral distinctions upon wild animals, but London imposes rudimentary moral distinctions in the
hope of capturing the essential quality of wild animal life. Thus
the dichotomy of Southland and Northland fits in with the general
simplification of the meaning of wilderness.

In *Call of the Wild*, Buck, a domestic but unusually powerful
dog from the 'Southland,' is stolen for work as a sled-dog in the
Arctic. Numerous adventures toughen his character and prepare
him to embrace the harsh spirit of the North. His last ties with
civilization are severed when Indians kill his master, a wise old
prospector and one of London's 'love-gods.' To this point, Buck has
lived by his moral credo never to attack human beings. Returned
fully to the wild with his master's death, Buck is freed from the
obstacle of conscience and the fear of humankind; he is empowered
to kill humans. He exercises this new freedom liberally, and for
several years after the event, upon the Indians who killed his
beloved white master.

The fact that Buck sheds human blood marks for London the

dog's total reversion to the wild animal state. That state, however, is hardly amoral. London's attraction to Nietzschean transcendence of small and fearful morality inspires the following paean to the wild spirit in Buck: 'Life streamed through him in splendid flood, glad and rampant, until it seemed that it would burst him asunder in sheer ecstasy and pour forth generously over the world' (p 93). The ecstatic life-force in Buck is inextricable from his power and pride as a killer: 'He was a killer, a thing that preyed, living on the things that lived, unaided, alone, by virtue of his own strength and prowess, surviving triumphantly in a hostile environment where only the strong survive' (p 92). After he has 'killed man, the noblest game of all' (p 98), he goes on to prove himself worthy to run with a wolf-pack by defeating several dominant wolves in unequal battle. Although it takes a hermeneutic shift to view this super-dog as a victim, the kind of moralization of the wild which London instantiates in Buck clearly serves human rather than animal interests. Indeed, the whole exercise is a cultural one, exploiting wildness in animals to celebrate a moral code that would be offensive if translated into the human and social sphere.

White Fang, the half-canine, half-lupine hero of the story named for him, follows a reverse course in life to that of Buck. The offspring of a wolf and a sled-dog, White Fang consciously abandons the freedom of the wilderness in obedience to the canine instinct for submission to human 'gods' (p 177). Passed down a succession of increasingly civilized owners, he is finally rescued by Weedon Scott, who transports White Fang to his estate in 'the Southland.' London describes Weedon Scott directly as a 'love-god,' because Scott earns White Fang's total loyalty with kindness: 'He had gone to the roots of White Fang's nature, and with kindness touched the life potencies that had languished and well-nigh perished. One such potency was *love*' (p 251). Love does not convert White Fang into a weakling, however; nor is he denied the benefits of his wild nature in his new state of domesticity in the Southland. His ultimate triumph is to kill, with the high approbation of the civilized world, 'a human beast' (p 286), an escaped murderer, who threatens his master.

Some confusion of values is evident even from these simple plot outlines. London writes animal romances, using any convenient occasion to enhance the heroism of his animal champions, whether that means endorsing natural robustness or favouring alternately the virtues of civilized morality. Although he depicts the benefits of these conflicting spheres as wholly opposed, it seems to matter very little which one is drawn upon so long as Buck and White Fang come out charged afresh with superhuman strengths. Even their responses to victimization are superhuman; both dogs survive beatings and injuries that would have killed any normal animal, including the human animal. While London does not condone cruelty to animals, he is nonetheless pleased to provide such hardships to prove the courage of his canine heroes.

The flexibility of London's ethics is evident also in his judgment about the dog-fights in which White Fang is forced to engage. While he is well aware that the sport exploits and victimizes the dogs, he is also free to admire White Fang as the virtually indomitable victor in these contests. Only when it becomes necessary to introduce the love-god from the South does London bring his noble animal to the point of death and allow the alien Southland voice to condemn the spectators as 'cowards' and 'beasts' (p 237). The other dogs, victims of White Fang's superior intelligence and tenacity, subside before the conqueror without much complaint from the author. When White Fang is dispatching fellow dogs, London is reserved on the score of blood and injury. When the fight is equal (equal, that is, with respect to the powers London has invested in the wolf-dog), when, say, the whole pack of sled-dogs gang up on White Fang, London does not stint on graphic detail of slashed flesh and gleaming fangs. Under attack from all sides, White Fang becomes 'a lightning flash of slaughter' (p 213), an incarnation which London esteems.

Because killing is an essential element of London's celebration of the wild, he finds it necessary to elevate predation into a philosophy of life. Heroes, of course, should not slay weak beings, and yet it is apparent that wild animals kill and eat other, weaker animals. London copes with the contradiction by introducing ponderous metaphysics. When the cub White Fang experiences the elation of killing and eating a ptarmigan and her chicks, London fends off sentimentalism with the assertion that White Fang 'was justifying his existence, than which life can do no greater; for life achieves its summit when it does to the uttermost that which it was equipped to do' (p 158).

A similar, but more complex, invocation of imponderables occurs in *Call of the Wild* on the occasion of Buck's first experience of the urge to 'kill with his own teeth and wash his muzzle to the eyes in warm blood.' This urge comes over Buck as he leads a pack of sled-dogs in the pursuit of a snowshoe rabbit. Among the pack is Spitz, enemy of Buck and the current leader of the dogs. Spitz takes a shortcut to catch the snowshoe rabbit: 'The rabbit could not turn, and as the white teeth broke its back in mid air it shrieked loudly as a stricken man may shriek. At the sound of this, the cry of Life plunging down from Life's apex in the grip of Death, the full pack at Buck's heels raised a hell's chorus of delight' (p 49). Elevating the death of this snowshoe rabbit to an illustration of the ineffables of Life and Death constitutes dramatic preparation for the inevitable fight to the death between Spitz and Buck. But it is not Buck who has killed the innocent victim and brought the forces of Life and Death into play. Spitz has invoked the dreadful powers, and done so, it is hinted, by cheating. Buck could almost be avenging the death of the rabbit when he first tackles his enemy. Thus, when Buck does 'wash his muzzle up to the eyes in warm blood,' he does so with the sanction of moral provocation, and not out of simple appetite or predatory impulse. The blood is the blood of an deserving and formidable enemy, not that of the rabbit, the only real victim in the episode. Furthermore, he wins the battle because he possesses 'a quality that made for greatness – imagination' (p 51), a quality for which he may thank, presumably, his life as a domestic pet in California. As with contests between White Fang and his canine rivals, that between Buck and Spitz is delivered in full, bloody, and bone-crunching detail. What makes it possible for London to present these naturalistic specifics is his having cast the situation in moral terms.

London makes bold moves against the soft sentiments. Buck's vitality and virility emerge from the rough life of the Northland dog. It pleases London to write that:

Mercy did not exist in the primordial life. It was misunderstood for fear, and such misunderstanding made for death. Kill or be killed, eat or be eaten, was the law; and this mandate, down out of the depths of Time, [Buck] obeyed. (p 76).

London's 'primordial code,' however, is an act of bravado which moralizes the wild for the benefit of readers feeling repressed by civilized codes of conduct. The sensationalism surrounding the fights with animal foes highlights the blood and disguises pain of the animal enemy. Metaphysics block sympathy for the weak animals slain by the heroic dogs. Using animals to explore the assertion of personal power has a dual function. First, it is an inoffensive way to advocate hierarchies of dominance and self-serving behaviour; second, it excuses such behaviour by locating it in primeval ways of being. The urban reader is tacitly encouraged to muscle ahead in the struggle for life, leaving behind a trail of 'enemies.' It could be argued that London's animal heroes gave him temporary relief from the socialist views he championed outside of his animal adventures. The canine hero discharges the contradictory fondness in him for Nietzschean power. The wild allows London to imagine the exercise of sheer muscular power as a moral force. Instead of confronting the wild, he reverses conventional social values and creates a competing myth. Buck and White Fang are models for human conduct; yet, as dogs, they allow London to evade the consequences of his philosophy.

Ernest Thompson Seton's Aspirations to Tragedy

Critics examining stories about animals in the wild frequently cite a statement from Seton's 'Note to the Reader' in *Wild Animals I Have Known*. In a two-sentence paragraph, Seton makes this defence of his work: 'The fact that these stories are true is the reason why all are tragic. The life of a wild animal *always has a tragic end*' (p 11). Robert MacDonald links Seton's statement to the 'natural law' of 'kill or be killed' (p 19). James Polk locates the tragic sensibility in Seton's depiction of animals who 'struggle to survive and heroically accept a defeat which is inevitable' (p 53). Margaret Atwood finds in Seton's assertion the Canadian psyche's identification with victims (pp 74–5), though she proposes that 'pathetic' would better describe the fates of Seton's animals. Seton himself interprets his observation in a 'Note to the Reader' for the subsequent collection of stories *Lives of the Hunted*:

For the wild animal there is no such thing as a gentle decline in peaceful old age. Its life is spent at the front, in the line of battle, and as soon as its powers begin to wane in the least, its enemies become too strong for it; it falls.

There is only one way to make an animal's history un-tragic, and that
is to stop before the last chapter. (p 11)

Polk's battle imagery is evidently appropriate, as are the references to survival of the fittest. Clearly Seton's idea of tragedy
presupposes a life spent in valorous struggle against adversaries,
and then the termination of that life through no fault of the animal but because of failing strength alone. Since one could hardly
call the death of a wild animal from a struggle with another wild
animal 'unnatural,' one looks for the ideological belief that would
lead to Seton's feeling that their deaths are tragic.

Despite the appeal to tragedy, Seton sought the cachet of natural history for his animal stories. He worked as a naturalist and
did illustrations of animals and birds. He claimed that his stories
told the truth about wild animals, that he had seen animals perform the various acts of cunning or sacrifice that they perform in
his stories. He is not embarrassed about the spiritual values he
asserts in his tales. What did annoy him were suggestions that he
invented the incredible feats of love and sagacity out of which his
animal adventures are spun. 'These stories are true,' he announces
at the beginning of his 'Note to the Reader' in *Wild Animals I Have
Known.* He has, he says, personal knowledge of every one of the
animals named in the stories, although he admits that three of
the animals are composite portraits. He also tacitly defends the
assignment of personalities to animals.

Natural history, Seton remarks in his 'Note,' 'has lost much by
the vague general treatment that is so common' (p 7). Regardless of
the slight defensiveness, there is justice in his statement. He even
has good reason for discerning (p 8) hostility in the generalizing
approach. What else could explain the irrational denial to animals
of internal experience? He offers a corrective to the anonymity of
natural history's animal by telling the story of individual animals.
Perhaps Seton oversteps the confines of credibility in translating
animal 'language' into English, but his program for story-telling
is not quite as insistently human as London's. While much of
London's narrative scheme depends upon humanized places – the
Northland versus the Southland – and human hierarchies extending from 'love-gods' to human 'beasts' with animal heroes sandwiched in between, Seton does try to present the wild animal's life
as it appears to him. To his credit, though he denies an ideological

motive, he also seeks to increase the reader's sensitivity to animal suffering.

When Seton complains, while his Don Valley partridge 'Redruff' hangs dying in a snare, 'Have the wild things no moral or legal rights? What right has man to inflict such long and fearful agony on a fellow creature, simply because that creature does not speak his language?' (*Wild Animals,* p 297), he is appealing to the plight of the animal as animal, not as a model for human virtue. He makes a large leap from the one pheasant caught in the snare to the abstract generality of animal creation, but the personified Redruff stands for him as a representative of the whole kingdom of personified and victimized animals. Granted the human who has set the snare is an especially vile example of our species, a man who hates work and hunts partridges out of season, a man who has shot Redruff's mate while she lay before him on the ground moaning 'as though begging for mercy' (p 285), and who has trampled Redruff's chicks underfoot. Granted, too, a kindly, honest man could not have been the one to cause such suffering to a partridge in a Seton story, even though Seton himself is not averse to shooting down anonymous squirrels and rabbits, or to collecting specimens of larger creatures. Nevertheless, by its very simplicity, Seton's ethic strives for compassion for the wild animals. He believes that nature licenses humanization, where science would cut off any move to attribute character and purpose to animals. It is clear, nonetheless, that he has felt it necessary to impose moral interpretations upon animal acts in order to win empathy for his animal protagonists.

Pathos abounds in his stories. Convinced that the fate of wild animals is always tragic, he steers each tale towards victimization. Unfortunately, as Margaret Atwood says, his stories never really do rise above pathos, partly because Seton tends to fudge the issue of victimization for literary and emotional effects. In 'Lobo, the King of Currumpaw,' for example, he describes the death of the king-wolf Lobo's mate, Blanca, as a tragedy, and even as an 'inevitable tragedy' (p 36), somehow overlooking the fact that blood is bursting from Blanca's mouth and her eyes are glazing over because men are strangling her with lassoes drawn tight by their horses. One is inclined to protest that there is nothing 'inevitable' about this death, that the idea of tragedy is artificially applied to this circumstance. This equivocal striving after tragedy is evident also in the last line of 'The Pacing Mustang' (*Wild Animals*), a story which describes the capture of a wild horse and then his escape as he leaps off a cliff to his death; the Mustang lands on the rocks, 'a lifeless wreck – but free' (p 222).

The fates of mother animals reveal that sentimental promiscuity in Seton which stands in the way of a full sense of the tragic in the animal victim's story. In 'Raggylug, the Story of a Cottontail Rabbit' (*Wild Animals*), pathos surrounds the death of the mother rabbit, Molly, whose life has been devoted to the training and protection of her son. A 'thoroughly bad and unscrupulous fox' (p 77) from Springfield chases Molly out amongst some icy weeds where she freezes to death: 'In a little while the cold, weak limbs ceased to move, the furry nose-tip of the little mother Cottontail wobbled no more, and the soft brown eyes were closed in death' (p 112). Seton is aiming for deeper feelings than pathos; the furry, wobbly nose and large brown eyes are meant to contribute to an impression of her courage in living the difficult life of the wild animal, and to the courage of all like her: 'Poor little Molly Cottontail! She was a true heroine, yet only one of unnumbered millions that without a thought of heroism have lived and done their best in their little world, and died' (p 113). Molly's littleness, her status as a victim within the animal kingdom, elicits from Seton a tragic vision held above the natural animal in the realm of theory.

Seton has to shuffle emotive terms to locate the theoretical tragic in the life of the mother predator. 'The Springfield Fox' relates the tale of a mother fox and her son. The mother fox could indeed be the selfsame animal that drives Mother Cottontail to her death, since the fox holds to her predatory ways simultaneously as she demonstrates a deep attachment to her cubs: 'Some animals have so much mother-love that it overflows and benefits outsiders. Not so old Vixen it would seem. Her pleasure in the cubs led to most refined cruelty' (p 158). Her 'cruelty' takes the form of the torture of mice and woodchucks for the purpose of training her cubs to kill. These representations of viciousness have an air of naturalism, but one that is rarified by Seton's underlying moral aversion to such habits. Since the animal personalities in his tale are foxes, Seton does not call them 'thoroughly bad and unscrupulous,' but their savagery complicates the moral condemnation that Seton applies freely when the animal protagonist is a cuddly and conventionally innocent rabbit.

Seton uses Vixen, nonetheless, to exemplify a form of love, a 'tough love,' as it were, which he links with the moral qualities of the wild animal. The people in the story, the 'guilty ones' (p 171), find Vixen's earth and kill all but one of her cubs. To free the last, now captive, cub, she 'quenche[s] the mother in her breast' (p 180) and feeds him a poisoned chicken head. Vixen, like Molly Cottontail, is a heroine. She employs the exceptional insight she has demonstrated all along to free her cub from an unbearable existence as a captive. Her act illustrates simultaneously the sagacity of which Seton wants to inform his readers, and the high moral spirit of the wild. As in 'The Pacing Mustang' (and, in fact, in London's stories), the wild means freedom. Seton finds nobility and tragedy in Vixen's story only because he has transferred to her the idealization of freedom he himself needs to value predatory animals.

Let a predatory animal dare to threaten good human beings, however, and Seton's attitude shifts completely. Though 'The Boy and the Lynx' (*Animal Heroes*) ends with the discovery of the desiccated corpses of the mother lynx and her two cubs, and though it is 'a year of hard times for lynxes' (p 125), Seton shows little sympathy for the lynx. Because, ultimately, she will menace a human family weakened by illness and starvation, Seton execrates her natural need to kill for food. He absolves the human beings of blame in this matter; they do not practice 'mere killing for killing's sake' (p 131), and the boy, Thor, regrets shooting a harmless porcupine (p 133). But the fact that the lynx does not kill for killing's sake either and, in fact, does not kill wantonly, as Thor does, evidently does not impress Seton. The moral mechanism of victimization is reversed in this story, so that the humans must appear innocent while the lynx must appear cruel. Casting the mother lynx as the enemy, Seton concurs with Thor's revulsion at the sight of the lynx with a chicken in her mouth: 'How fierce and cruel the brute looked! How Thor hated it! and fairly gnashed his teeth with disgust' (p 133). Thus it is a moral victory, and not a mere matter of survival, when Thor musters the last of his failing strength to plunge a fishing spear into the body of the vicious, snarling 'beast' (p 143). Whether this tale reveals Seton's true feelings towards predatory animals, hidden by a defensive naturalism in other stories, or whether narrative needs have superseded his customary appreciation of the wild animal's courage, his lapse into the language and morality of Victorian horror at the wild suggests his ultimate allegiance to humankind. Morally and spiritually, his vision is anthropocentric.

Confirmation that Seton's vision of the wild ultimately serves human rather than animal interests comes in his essay 'The Natural History of the Ten Commandments.' Interestingly enough, this confirmation involves animal victims. As its title suggests, the essay finds evidence among animals of the operation of the biblical code. Seton finds animals abiding by six of the ten commandments, though he has considerable difficulty in proving their commitment to monogamy. For this one commandment, Seton argues that the animals highest on the evolutionary scale are monogamous, but will mate again with the death of a spouse. Inherently absurd creatures, geese go overboard with the dictate and will not re-mate after the death of their first companion (p 26). Thus nature supports moral aversion to promiscuity but permits remarriage, says Seton, begging the question in rather obvious fashion.

Fortunately, Seton does not attempt such contortions with the commandments relating to God. He admits that he 'could find nothing in the animal world that seemed to suggest any relation to a Supreme Being' (p 31), and that therefore nature does not at first appear to manifest adherence to the four biblical commandments relating to the deity. He proceeds, however, to list anecdotes, in all of which an animal hunted or injured by another animal takes refuge with human beings. The conclusion to be drawn from this evidence is obvious:

when [animals] have done all that they can do, and are face to face with despair and death, there is revealed in them an instinct, deep-laid – and deeper laid as the animal is higher [on the evolutionary scale] – which prompts them in their dire extremity to throw themselves on the mercy of some other power, not knowing, indeed, whether it be friendly or not, but very sure that it is superior. (p 33)

It must be clear how flattering this image of humankind is: not only are we superior to animals, as imagined deities are to us, but they take us to be their gentle saviours, expecting succour from us in their times of despair. It is an irony not to be missed that in one of Seton's anecdotes, an injured moose, presumed by Seton to be seeking aid from humankind, is shot to death.

Unlike London, Seton does not represent human beings as gods in his animal stories. 'The Natural History of the Ten Commandments' indicates, however, that he comes to the wild convinced of the reality of moral codes that have always favoured the human species over nonhuman animals. The specificity of the ideology he applies accounts for the failure of his stories to rise to tragedy. As long as the writer asks the wild animal to affirm civilization's values, its story is not its own. The animal's death is not the animal's tragedy but that of a moral being who acts within a moral system that is imposed upon the wilderness. How can there be any kind of tragedy in these stories when they send the reader away with renewed faith in the reality of human ideologies? Seton must be granted several points: that empiricism is hostile to the individuality of animals, that animals do have experiences, that there is what we now call 'bonding' between individual animals, and that bonds are not broken without some pain or at least puzzlement to the animal. Nevertheless, he has a spiritual design uppermost in his mind. He misses the robustness of animal resistance to the kind of humanization he effects.

Charles G.D. Roberts and Theoretical Realism

Charles G.D. Roberts' first animal story, 'Do Seek Their Meat from God' (reprinted in *Earth's Enigmas*), was published in 1892. It makes an appropriate starting place for discussion, since its theme parallels that of Seton's 'The Boy and the Lynx' in that suspense hangs upon the hungry, powerful animal preying upon a helpless human being. 'Do Seek Their Meat from God' exemplifies Roberts' restraint and the sympathy he holds, in theory, for wild and predatory animals. The two panthers in Roberts' story, parents of two cubs, hear the cry of a little boy and head off with the intention of making a meal of the child:

It would be thoughtless superstition to say the beasts were cruel. They were simply keen with hunger, and alive with the eager passion of the chase. They were not ferocious with any anticipation of battle, for they knew the voice was the voice of a child, and something in the voice told them the child was solitary. Theirs was no hideous or unnatural rage, as is the custom to describe it. They were but seeking with the strength, the cunning, the deadly swiftness given to them to that end, the food convenient for them. (pp 22–3)

As the expression goes, Roberts talks a good game. He is fair-minded enough, as well, to make a link between animal and human: the child's father saves the child by shooting the two panthers, but at the end of the story we are shown 'the dead bodies, now rapidly decaying, of two small panther cubs' (p 27). A human family avoids grief at the expense of the animal family. We live, they die – the observation is accurate. I cannot agree with James Polk's assessment, however, that Roberts' 'stark conclusion reminds us of the animals' rights' (p 55). Having capitalized upon the threat to the child and thrill of the rescue, Roberts seems, rather, to cap the emotional action with the sight of the dead cubs. When one compares consistent acknowledgment of animal rights in narrative with Roberts' approach, it becomes apparent that drama is uppermost in Roberts' mind. Human flesh is sacrosanct for Roberts as it is for Seton, not so much because technology assures the human victory over animals, but because human beings are the keepers of moral and spiritual value.

In 'The Ambivalent Beast,' Joseph Gold points out rightly that among Roberts' stories, those that are 'free of human interference are the most aesthetically pleasing' (p 84). If the reason for this is, as Gold indicates, Roberts' ambivalence as to the place of human-kind in nature, then that ambivalence bears the additional fault of hubris: the belief that our dilemmas count more than those of other animals. The moral value Roberts invests in the human species brings the usual human conceit into existence. That conceit, in turn, reduces the narrative to melodrama and action adventure. Action adventure of the most simplistic variety occurs in 'King of Beasts' (*The Feet of the Furtive*), in which a naked man kills a tiger and proves himself master to all the other animals in the jungle. Melodrama is evident in his novel *The Heart of the Ancient Wood*, in which a pure and virtuous, and vegetarian, girl finds the strength to kill her own pet bear when it menaces the man she loves. Both Johns, hero of 'King of Beasts,' and Miranda, the animal-loving heroine of *The Heart of the Ancient Wood*, prove that they have the 'right stuff' in this moralized version of the wild. These stories quite clearly aim at character-building.

Whether Roberts is aware of it or not, he evidently finds it necessary to deploy, as London does, the extremes of sensationalism and mysticism to justify sparing the life of the wild animal in its confrontation with the more powerful human species. One of his many stories about bears, reprinted in *Thirteen Bears,* illustrates his dilemma. He establishes two plot-lines in 'With His Back to the Wall,' the one belonging to a black bear who becomes the object of a pack of wolves' hunger, and the other belonging to Job Thatch, a trapper who is slowly starving in the desolation of winter and who has broken his leg as an additional hardship. The pronoun in the title, then, is ambiguous; the bear is driven to a rock-face by the wolves and Job Thatch is driven to desperation by 'the White Death' (p 63) closing in on him. The wolves are the mutual enemy of both bear and trapper; their cry, as they approach the bear, has 'a ring of hate in it' (p 58). As the story-lines converge, Job Thatch too hungers for bear-meat, but witnessing the black bear's courage as it defends itself against the wolves, he joins in the fray, killing wolves right and left with his rifle and his axe.

With the requirement upon him to conjoin the efforts of human and bear, Roberts yields to sensationalism. One mighty swipe of the bear's paw 'smashed [a wolf's] head and hurled a lifeless mass clear over the backs of the pack' (p 71). One blow from Job Thatch's axe is followed by a 'fountain of scarlet' (p 73). As the battle subsides, the wolf victims drop in 'kicking and writhing paroxysms' (p 74). The remainder retreat ignobly, with 'grey, feathered tails curled down beneath their haunches' (p 74). Now comes the time when Job can get his bear-meat, but he has a change of heart when the bear raises its 'gaunt and bleeding head' to defy the rifle as it had defied the wolves. Addressing the bear as 'old pardner,' as he has throughout the battle, Job foregoes the temptation to assure his own life with the death of the bear. A less perceptive writer might now have had the bear and the man become fast friends. Roberts, however, lets the bear revert to its animal state and leave the scene without gratitude. But with his act of charity, Job Thatch has scored a victory, over the 'White Death,' the 'Silent Adversary,' of the wild: 'In his mystical imagination he could perceive the vast, silent unseen powers of the wild, which had so treacherously conspired against him, drawing back in grave defeat' (p 76). Chivalry triumphs over the inherent hostility of the wild, both the hostility that Roberts concentrates in the wolves, forgetting that they too are starving creatures, and that holistic (for Roberts) hostility of wild nature which slowly erodes the moral defences of the civilized person.

Roberts' value system can shift radically between affirmation of Victorian pride in civilization and its opposite, the affirmation of might and mercilessness. He places high value upon power because that is how human beings become one with the wild – by partaking in the struggle for dominance that the wild means to him. It is interesting, though, that the wild means this to Roberts primarily when human beings are around in his stories. Sensationalistic physical contests, with flying blood and crunching bones, form the drama in the presence of human individuals. When there are no human beings present, Roberts takes a consciously unemotional approach to the animal victim. In the strictly animal stories, he builds a narrative out of a neutral chain of events that leaves some animals dead and others fed.

Typical among these stories is 'In the Year of No Rabbits' (in *The Feet of the Furtive*). 'In the Year of No Rabbits' brings together a mother lynx, a mother moose, a bear, and a fox. The mother lynx kills the cow moose's new-born calf. The moose in turn tramples the lynx to death. A bear whom the lynx had previously attacked now feasts upon the moose calf, and the fox eats the mother lynx's abandoned young. The rabbits, whose disappearance had caused all this tension among the larger animals, return, and one of them hops about through the pile of bleaching bones left behind by the past season's struggle. There are emotions in this story. The lynx feels alarm at the threat of the fox and bear to her kittens. The moose feels 'tender ecstasy' (p 62) for her calf, seeks vengeance on the lynx and mourns over the dead calf, 'muttering thickly in her shaggy throat' (p 66). But the rapid and matter-of-fact sequence of deaths forestalls sentimentality. The human element here is Roberts himself: he braves the unpleasant scene of mothers and infants being killed. He sets the facts down bluntly for the improvement of the squeamish. In this story and similar ones, Roberts grounds the alienness of the wild animal upon its immunity to sentiment.

It is primarily in the scenic effects that Roberts manages to escape anthropomorphism. He impresses upon readers the alienness of animal life by devoting time and art to the animal's environment. 'Black Swamp' (in *Thirteen Bears*) demonstrates the emotional complexities arising from his concentration on the landscape. The swamp has an identity of its own. Nature takes bizarre form before Roberts' fascinated gaze. Then, suddenly, 'it seemed as if the spirit of the monstrous solitude had taken substance' (p 3). This 'spirit' is the bear, emanating out of the swamp in search of grubs and small fish. No human beings appear in this story. A raccoon determines the plot by knocking a hornets' nest down into the arms of the sleeping bear, which in turn causes the bear to seek relief in a treacherous mud pond and then to drown when he cannot recover a stable footing: his 'gaping muzzle, strained straight upward, [emitting] hideous gasps and groans' (p 15).

The bear hovers uncertainly between seeming a monstrous beast, 'a portion of the swamp come alive' (p 11), and metamorphosing into a simple shambling creature browsing for maggots in whimsical unselfconsciousness. The raccoon, for contrast and conflict, is 'a gay little figure that seemed an embodied protest against all the dark and enormous formlessness of the swamp' (p 8). The two animals are symbolic adversaries, not merely formal ones. And yet empathy does not seem to fix itself anywhere; empathy is elicited but is given no secure hold for its gratification. In the end a nightmare element attaches to both the pathos of the bear's drowning and the 'untriumphant curiosity' (p 15) of the raccoon as it observes the bear's agony. The strangeness that Roberts has written into the landscape discomposes assessment of the event, so that the victim's death defies author and reader to find the appropriate tenor of feeling for the occasion. The confusion of compassion is not an ill effect, especially given the entanglement of reason in the swamp setting. In a sense, Roberts produces an accurate reflection of modern perplexity over the correct way to respond to animal victims. That he has to reach past the living animal and into the landscape to enkindle objectivity with art and thus to confound conventional emotive responses indicates his ambivalence towards the wild animal.

Two narrative effects, then, bring Roberts close to evocation of the inherent value of wildness in animals: detailed description of the specific landscape and the somewhat unnaturally rapid chain-reaction. With both effects, Roberts consciously defies anthropomorphism in the matter of animal victims. A story which illustrates the empathy Roberts can achieve when he relaxes his guard and allows himself to humanize an animal victim is 'The Homesickness of Kehonka' (*The Kindred of the Wild*). Kehonka is a wild goose, hatched on a farm and kept prisoner there by the farmer's clipping of one of his wings. Unlike his brother who accepts this state,

Kehonka yearns for the wild. Standing exiled in the farmyard, Kehonka calls to the migrating flocks of geese that pass overhead, but he is left 'to call and call unanswered' (p 129). The flock's freedom, the totality of their lives, should by rights be Kehonka's as well: 'It was his, it belonged to himself – that strong, free flight, that calling through the sky, that voyaging northward to secret nesting places' (p 130). By heroic effort and against the terrible imbalance that his clipped wing causes to his flight, Kehonka manages to join a passing flock. As he feeds amongst them, his 'very soul trembled with desire achieved' (p 131). A female goose finds him attractive and they begin courting rituals. When the flock leaves, however, he cannot keep up with them and drops to earth, alone again: 'In his sick heart glowed still the vision of the nest in the far-off solitudes, and he felt that he would find there, waiting for him, the strong-winged mate who had left him behind' (pp 135–6). All these features make for tragedy: the exile, the injury, the desperate but futile struggle to satisfy yearning, the loss of a mate. Roberts speaks of Kehonka's soul, of his 'sick heart,' of visions of the full life from which the goose is disbarred. I would guess that it is precisely this deep empathy with the wildness in the animal that Roberts represses in other stories. His defences against this empathy rise up again when he reports Kehonka's death in the jaws of a fox, but by allowing himself to break with empirical objectivity, to imagine desires, visions, and a soul in this goose, he escapes both the theoretical harshness and the theoretical spirituality that mar other of his stories.

Perhaps this successful transcendence of theory brings into focus a failing characteristic of these early stories: they seem to manifest the instability and self-consciousness of theory deliberately applied. In 'The Homesickness of Kehonka,' Roberts gives in to a desire to humanize, to respond humanly to the unhappiness of the wild animal. Perhaps narrative would have honoured the wild animal more fully, in these times, if writers had abandoned the bravado of theoretical neutrality or sensationalism in favour of honest sentimentality over animal victims. Roberts' choice of subject is also informative, for in this story, he allies his emotive and aesthetic forces with the wounded wildness of the animal. Where the wild spirit is masterful in London's stories, virtuous in Seton's, and generally merciless in Roberts', 'The Homesickness of Kehonka' shows that the wild can be injured, and injured deeply, in humanly intelligible ways.

I am suggesting, then, that these early writers really want to sentimentalize over the wild animal victim, that they would like nothing better than to be allowed the luxury of pity. Sometimes they do allow themselves the luxury, but more often they take flight from what they would consider weak emotionality into forced neutrality or celebrations of heroism. Signs of ideological imposition, mistaken for realism, abound in their stories. Clearly, the spectacle of the animal victim in the wild elicits emotional responses that require discharge in narratives. The imposition of moral structures, ideas of virtue and images of battle, helps to account for pre-existing emotional response to the suffering animal. Writers who take up the wild animal's story after its first flourishing in the decades around the turn of the century find an enemy on which to focus hostility and distress over animal victims, and that enemy is humankind.

PART TWO:
TRAGEDY AND THE ANIMAL VICTIM

The actual content of the ethics espoused by Henry Williamson, Fred Bodsworth, and Allan W. Eckert is not the critical factor in the success of their representations of animals in the wild, although I must confess to favouring their unqualified condemnation of human interference in the animal's life. The critical factor is the effect that their ethics have upon the conception of the wild. Where the early writers struggled and failed to integrate what they saw as human superiority into the wild, the three writers examined now build the estrangement of humankind from the wild into their narratives. Human beings come as invaders and destroyers into the wild animal's domain. The ethic divides our species radically from the wild, as culture has divided us from nature. Thus animals are indeed left to their own ways and conceived of as subjects of dramas for themselves and not for us. The animals Williamson, Bodsworth, and Eckert write about have inherent value, and their natural ways are sufficient to establish that value. These three authors write against their own species. Estranged from their own kind, they honour the animals they write about as animals and not as moral exemplars or heroes. As a material upshot, the actual content of the ethics on which these stories operate, as opposed to their conceptual effect, directly serves the animals' need to survive by pricking the consciences of those who harm them.

The shift to the world-view that legitimates this approach can be seen most vividly in the divergent conceptions of what constitutes realism when it comes to animal victims in the wild. While the fates of the animals in these stories may not fit standard definitions of tragedy, the idea of tragedy best covers the distinction that is to be made between the pathos of the early tales and the weightier emotional impact achieved by the later ones. The adventure element disappears from the later works along with the romanticization of the wild which has always served our cultural needs instead of the interests of nonhuman animals. In these stories we find not a forced pseudo-neutrality which attempts to imitate scientific objectivity, but fondness for natural animals *per se*. Truth and fact are less in conflict in these stories than they were in the early ones. Since the ways of the wild animal are honoured in their own right, the animal's natural behaviour becomes part and parcel of narrative truth. Art gives up trying to straddle the world of culture and the world of nature and allies itself with the natural animal. Thus one finds Fred Bodsworth incorporating actual journal descriptions of the slaughter of the Eskimo curlews into his story, as a way of remaining narratively with the last curlew while still revealing the human history that has determined its plight. *The Great Auk* is likewise historically accurate, as its Epilogue informs us. In these two cases, there was no need to invent the animal's tragedy.

Of the three writers, Williamson is a transitional figure, not only because his work emerges at the beginning of the cultural shift to animal-centred thinking but also because he is British. The British 'wild' is not as intimidating as the North American wild. The British wild offers only rare predatory animals that can be represented as bloodthirsty and ferocious, and not very large predatory animals at that. In addition, for the past two centuries, British culture has led the way in increasing sensitivity towards animal victims. The sentimentalism and humanization opposed by the early North American writers is largely a product of British culture. In a certain respect, the tameness of the landscape and the proclivity to sentimentalize is a disadvantage to Williamson. It is all the more remarkable, then, that he manages to inject a typical British outrage at cruelty to animals into his stories while still conveying the alienness of the wild animal. Like the other writers representing this phenomenon, he reserves moral judgment for the human animal.

Natural Victims and Victims of the Hunt in Williamson's *Tarka the Otter*

Henry Williamson is something of an oddity among the writers assembled here. *Tarka the Otter* anticipates the ethics of stories that will be written some thirty years later, but Williamson's prescience is not entirely due to political acumen. Indeed, to the discomfort of anyone who wishes to praise him, he was attracted to fascism. An excellent account of his political and ecological views can be found in Anna Bramwell's *Ecology in the Twentieth Century: A History*. Williamson's political extremism provided him with a way of critiquing the malaise of civilization, the pollution, the unhealthy food, the shoddy education that civilization substitutes for integrity with nature. A wholesale dislike of most of what human beings do, then, fuels his attraction to fascism. His animal narratives receive the benefit of the misanthropy underlying his political heresies. Perhaps it is fortunate, nevertheless, that *Tarka the Otter* pre-dates the most radical phase of his political attractions. Where *Salar the Salmon* (1935) barely pulls free of natural history (fish evidently defeat even Williamson's powers of empathy), and his war-novel, *The Phasian Bird* (1948), seeks spiritual links between a solitary golden pheasant and a deeply embittered, politically outcast man, *Tarka the Otter* reveres the fullness of the wild animal's life by means of uncompromised, anti-human identification with the animal. The world of which Williamson writes is Tarka's world; in this world, the voice of humankind is, if not wholly repulsive – for there is one brief appearance by a loving soul – then wholly alien.

It is particularly apt to speak of the voice of humankind when analysing Williamson's *Tarka the Otter*. The actual voice is the most salient and most deadly announcement of the intrusion of the human being into the animals' world. In this story, the presence of human beings is confined mainly to what an otter would experience, with the crude *'Tally-Ho!'* of the otter-hunters signalling the arrival of people into the otters' peaceful domain and emblematizing humanity as a whole. The otter-hunters cannot be

entirely excluded from the text; they are, after all, of crucial importance to the drama, since they cause Tarka's death. But their
appearance as fragments, as harsh cries and as rubber boots in
the water or as glimpses of distant crowds, negates identification
at the same time as it imitates the otter's point of view. Holism
exists in the otter's world; the upper world of the human being is
grotesque.

There are no bad animals in *Tarka the Otter*. There are no good
animals either, for that matter. The owl that attacks Tarka when
he is a cub is not a marauder; he is a predatory bird who has
mistaken the otter for a rabbit and is therefore unprepared for
the counter-attack from both Tarka and Tarka's mother. The owl
dies, with half its feathers torn from its breast by the mother
otter, not because it is a wicked owl for menacing our hero but
because of misjudgment, unfortunate timing, and the roused
strength of the otter (p 34). Williamson clearly seeks to overcome
his readers' prejudices about animal victims of other animals.
More than once in the novel, he collapses events to give the 'feel'
of the food chain. On one of those occasions, the otters have made
a meal of some frogs:

[The otters] left some of the frogs uneaten, for there were eels in the
ditch. Iggiwick, the vuz-peg [hedgehog] ... found the remains and was
gleefully chewing when a badger grunted near. With a squeak of terror
the vuz-peg rolled himself in a ball, but the badger bit through the spines
as though they were marram grasses. Iggiwick squealed like marram
grass in flame. Later in the night nothing was left except the trotters,
teeth, and spiny coat of poor Iggiwick. (p 49)

Despite Williamson's assignment of a name to the hedgehog, and
the pitying adjective 'poor,' the animal is introduced and killed too
swiftly for sympathy to concentrate upon it. One would be justified
in suspecting that Williamson has given the baby name Iggiwick
to the hedgehog for the very purpose of disabusing readers of
their juvenile sentiments for animals. The hedgehog and whatever
personality it might possess are subsumed under the pressures of
the natural system of eating and being eaten (not, as London has
it, 'kill or be killed'). Even the simile likening the cry of the dying
hedgehog to marram grass in flame tends to obstruct compassion,
for while the reader might gain a vivid auditory impression of the

sound and its piercing shrillness, grass is insentient and does not suffer. The sound is inhuman, as is the import of the animal's death. The hedgehog's remains, furthermore, have a quality of absurdity about them, although they can easily be envisioned as pathetic as well.

Since the 'anti-story' effect of these evocations of the food chain is foundational, another instance merits examination. This time, Tarka has brought to his mate, White-tip, a lamprey which had been attached to the side of a trout before Tarka happened along. White-tip is not much interested in the gift, but Tarka persists:

He dropped it before her again and again, pretending to have caught it anew each time. She swung away from his offering as though she had caught the lamprey and Tarka would seize it from her. The sickly trout, which had been dying for days with the lamprey fastened to it, floated down the stream; it had been a cannibal trout and had eaten more than fifty times its own weight of smaller trout. Tar from the road, after rain, had poisoned it. A rat ate the body the next day, and Old Nog [a heron] speared and swallowed the rat three nights later. The rat had lived a jolly and murderous life, and died before it could fear.

The lamprey escaped alive ... (p 87)

It will be observed here that characterization marks off the trout and the rat in this sequence. This flourish, however, works less to humanize the natural cycle than to demonstrate that animals can have individual lives and still be impersonal objects of natural processes. The 'cannibal' trout might seem to be subject to just retribution for its evil ways, but because its apparent punishment is accidental, its moral status is a non-issue. The trout could just as likely have been the most upright trout-citizen ever created, a fond husband and father, and a born leader. Probably perfectly innocent fish were also poisoned by the tar. In fact, given the impartiality of the event, the cannibal trout is absolved of guilt: it is an innocent fish like any other. Likewise the rat, that much reviled object of human antipathy, briefly attains the flair of pirates before it is speared by Old Nog. Its life is filled out only to be immediately extinguished, and thus it too sustains the quality of innocence. The only creature that survives this particular series of events is the lamprey, which has had no attributed personality whatsoever. It starts out as the flaccid object pure and simple of

Tarka and White-tip's exchange, and then fate ironically selects it over the other, personified animals for escape. Although one can discern here some uneasiness between literary playfulness and scientific neutrality, the two drives are at least able to coexist.

The logic and temperateness of the natural chain of victimization, the undramatic cycle as Williamson presents it, disclose the illogicality of the otter-hunters' activities. Because Williamson focuses intently on animal experience, and because he disallows sentimentality as he chronicles the daily and seasonal habits of animals, the hunters' determined assault upon the otters is incomprehensible. The meaninglessness of the hunt in comparison with the orderliness of natural proceedings renders the hunt condemnable, and cruel. The natural system has a totality of its own; the humans are barbaric invaders. The *Tally-hos* break insolently into the animals' peace; the hound dogs churn up the water. In the otters' view, human beings are monstrous, not morally (for them) but physically. White-tip experiences a crowd of hunters and spectators as 'cries and tongues and legs' pursuing her from pool to pool; watchers on a bridge are to her 'faces and waving arms' (p 143). Later, as he glides silently through the pack of dogs, Tarka sees the legs of the hounds 'joined to their broken surface-images. From underwater he saw men and women, pointing with hand and pole, as palsied and distorted shapes on the bank' (p 231). Undoubtedly a troop of happy, harmless bathers would appear equally nightmarish. Yet the human world's lack of organic coherence from the otter's perspective points up the unintelligibility of the purpose of the hunt. Happy bathers might well look bizarre to an otter but at least they keep their peculiarities to themselves. Thus animal consciousness determines the moral reading, not spiritual values imposed from without.

The death of Tarka's cub Tarquol does approach tragedy. All through the novel, Tarka has lost family – siblings, cubs, a mate – to humanity's strange hatred of his kind. Tarquol is singled out from the rest as most like Tarka himself. The loss of fellow-otters has been so unrelenting that the reader is acutely aware of the vulnerability and likely brevity of the life of Tarka's beloved cub. The animals play together, but Williamson wisely resists the urge to invoke a father-son bond between the two. He swerves from strict realism only to allow a dream to Tarka 'of a journey with Tarquol down to a strange sea, where they were never hungry, and never hunted' (p 205) – a slight departure which rationality forgives, for surely one can imagine that dreams of peace, perhaps without specifics, come to animals. Realizing Tarquol's inevitable fate, the reader begins to hope for acts of heroism and impossible cunning, for Tarquol to elude the hunters and find a place of ultimate safety, for Tarka to rush in as his cub is being mauled and rescue him. In an earlier animal story, narrative could stretch to implausibilities like these. Williamson's story, however, rules out the incredible escape. Nature, naturalism, forces the reader along the implacable course of events.

The description of Tarquol's death holds a curious place in the paradigm of pathos and gore. It would not be correct to say that the cub's death has the same neutrality as that of Iggiwick the hedgehog. Nor would such neutrality be appropriate, since the cub's death occurs not in nature but in the nightmare world of the human being. That is where tragedy enters the scene. Only the subtlest manipulation is required to create grief over Tarquol's death; there is no need for jets of blood to splash or Life and Death to obtrude into the action. Neither, and more importantly, is there any need to humanize Tarquol:

Deadlock [an otter-hound] seized [Tarquol] and shook him and threw him into the air. Tarquol sprang up as soon as he could feel, snapping and writhing as more jaws bit on his body, crushed his head, cracked his ribs, his paws, his rudder. Among the brilliant hawkbits – little sunflowers of the meadow – he was picked up and dropped again, trodden on and wrenched and broken, while the screaming cheers and whoops of sports-men mingled with the growling rumble of hounds at worry. Tarquol fought them until he was blinded, and his jaws were smashed. (p 227)

This description marks the end of a chapter. The suspension of the obvious conclusion to the conflict tends, from one perspective, to establish Tarquol's heroism: he fights until his power to fight is exhausted. Nevertheless, the smashing of the jaws and all the other injuries are simply truthful aspects of what happens when a pack of dogs worries an otter. With effort, the reader can step back from the scene and view each dreadful injury as straightfor-ward reportage on Williamson's part. The death of Tarquol, an otter with a name and a history for the reader, is no different from the death of any other otter caught by hounds. Emotional impact may be greatest at the level of the individual otter, but empathy at this level extends also to the whole world of otters persecuted by the alien world of humanity. Readers are confronted, then, with a cruel injury to nature itself; revulsion arises from the spectacle of so peaceful and steady a life being wrenched and riven for no purpose. The wholeness of the otters' lives is destroyed with the progressive rending of Tarquol's body. The grotesque fragmentariness of humanity inflicts itself upon the otter's body. Animal harmony, therefore, is as much the victim in the death of Tarquol as the otter cub itself.

Tarka disappears at the novel's conclusion also in a state of suspension – literally, in that the last of his life is given to the reader in the form of bubbles suspended on the surface of the water, bubbles cast up by Tarka's final exhalations. Williamson does not present to the reader Tarka's experience as the otter drowns, only the signs of the drowning. The collapse of the body to the bottom of the pool, the bursting lungs and fading consciousness, are left to the reader's imagination. Perhaps Williamson himself could not quite face the death of the otter whose history he had filled out with his literary craft and perspective. The suppression of somatic detail, however, is emotionally effective. Presentation of Tarka's experience as he drowns might have produced pathos; the anonymity of the death creates the effect of tragedy. Williamson generates sadness for the animal way of dying. In his final struggle, Tarka has managed to kill the otter-hound Deadlock, but such heroism as that feat might imply is repressed. The final paragraph of *Tarka the Otter* runs thus:

They [the otter-hunters] pulled [Deadlock's] body out of the river and carried it to the bank, laying it on the grass, and looking down at the hound in sad wonder. And while they stood there silently, a great bubble rose out of the depths, and broke, and as they watched, another bubble shook the surface, and broke; and there was a third bubble in the sea-going waters, and nothing more.

Oddly, the 'sad wonder' experienced by the otter-hunters at the death of their hound transfers to Tarka; and 'sad wonder' is indeed the appropriate response. The last two words of Tarka's story collapse the two dimensions of animal death in fiction. For that natural impartiality given by the scientific perspective, the death of any individual animal is 'nothing more' than yet another disappearance from the collective. It is an event unmarked and unmeaning. On one side of the dialectic, the 'nothing-more' of Tarka's death implies a shrug of the shoulders, a noncommittal reaction. From the perspective of literature on the other side of the dialectic, however, the fact that there is 'nothing more' to come after the last bubble has the cathartic impact of tragedy. One does not need to apply human distortions to Tarka to explain the tragic effect; Tarka is not our little animal friend, or a plucky little hero, or a survivor (in the modern jargon) of many hardships. That which is alien and animal in Tarka has become real. The fact that there can be an empirical 'nothing-more' only serves to heighten the emotional devastation of Tarka's death.

Relating tales of extinction, Bodsworth and Eckert almost have an easier time of it than Williamson, for the degree to which humankind has separated itself from nature is readily apparent in its power to eliminate a thriving species of animal and its ignorance in having done so. The tragedy of the animal victim is inherently personalized by its being the last of its kind. The rift between worlds, articulated by Williamson, comes sharply into focus as the world of the dwindling species grows increasingly vulnerable to human aggression.

Nonhuman Tragedy in Bodsworth's *Last of the Curlews*

John Stevens' introduction to the 1963 New Canadian Library edition of *Last of the Curlews* addresses the question of tragedy:

If Bodsworth is to win us over to his conviction that the passing of this species is in some sense tragic, then he must succeed in making us accept his two curlews as complex and beautiful individuals, distinctly inferior to us in conscious reasoning, but akin to us in some other way. Highly developed self-awareness, usually a necessary condition in tragedy, is not possible here. (p ix)

Stevens then goes on to speak of the fable-like, or even laughable, quality of stories that humanize animals. He has, however, touched upon a pivotal issue in the tragedy of the extinction of species of animals. If the disappearance of the Eskimo curlews is tragic because they are 'complex and beautiful individuals,' then the tragedy is a human one: we have lost a marvellous species of bird. In order for the extinction of his species to be judged a tragedy for the curlew himself, it might indeed appear at first that Bodsworth must find in the curlew sensibilities and experiences that correspond with those of the human being. This dichotomy, however, is not so much false as narrow and dated. Granted, the sense of the tragic in *Last of the Curlews* is held somewhere between the vision of a whole world in which there will be no more curlews and the experiences of the lone remaining individual bird. But the attempt to locate a human element in the tragic underestimates the effectiveness with which Bodsworth excludes the human from the curlew's story.

In the context of Stevens' remarks, it is interesting to note how easily tragedy bypasses self-awareness, assuming this characteristic to be a standard prerequisite. In the case of Bodsworth's curlew, the tragic element is associated not with consciousness but the reverse: with the curlew's utter mistakenness as to the true circumstances that determine his fate. The narrative hinges upon the curlew's instinctive faith that he will find a female curlew, despite the many years in which he has seen no other members of his species at all. This note, that the female is coming, recurs throughout *Last of the Curlews,* each time with the same definiteness. From the curlew's perspective, the female is coming, and he performs repeatedly the annual rituals of returning to and defending his territory in the confident expectation of her arrival. Almost immediately after the death of the female curlew he has encountered by sheer luck, the same confidence returns, and it is that confidence with which the story ends. His unerring migratory instinct brings him each year to the territory he defends for the female of his species, a distinctive S-twist in the Arctic river. The last sentence in the story finds him back at this territory, which 'must be held in readiness for the female his instinct told him would soon come.' The simplicity of this statement concentrates the vast tragedy of which the curlew is the focal point. In all the wide world, there may well be no more female Eskimo curlews. One thinks of the wide world and of the loneliness of the curlew, even if these thoughts are beyond the sensibility of the curlew himself. The tragedy for the individual bird is that the forces of nature in him continue to assume that all is right with the world when humankind has laid waste that world. Perhaps even in human tragedies, a crucial element is that the individual is caught in circumstances he or she cannot grasp intellectually.

Taking Bodsworth's curlew as an example, it appears that animal innocence is a large part of the tragedy of animal victims. As a wild animal, the Eskimo curlew bears with him a natural world which should operate by the cycles for which his instinct prepares him. The destructiveness of humankind is incomprehensible to him. His instincts do not and cannot account for human violence. In *Last of the Curlews,* the curlew's world is not so much subsumed by the larger and more powerful world of humankind as it is wrecked by the incursions of an inexplicable animal. The biological instincts within the lone, last curlew remain proof against the trespasses of humankind. This wholeness places him in a different category from that of the pathetic victim.

The curlew's way of life testifies to the power of this bird: the plain muscular power involved in migrating nine thousand miles in a matter of weeks, the power of the knowledge that guides him faultlessly from place to place across that distance, and the power of the drives in him that would have assured species survival had humankind not interfered. The curlew is right in all that he does; there is no fatal flaw here. A large part of the tragedy is that those very powers which make the curlew a marvellous creature have been rendered futile by a being who should know better. Since the curlew's powers are fully intact, he is not pitiable. Nevertheless, from the perspective of worlds, the world the curlew trusts in versus the actual state of affairs, he is utterly helpless. This synthesis of natural integrity and ultimate exposure to the irrationality of humankind reflects back upon the typical pathos of the early stories: most of the wild animals in the early stories are too much in control of their situations for their suffering to rise to tragedy.

One irritant in *Last of the Curlews* is Bodsworth's repeated concessions to behavioural reductionism which denies intelligence to animals. He speaks of the curlew's 'rudimentary' (p 55) and even 'meagre' (p 52) brain. He asserts that the curlew's 'behaviour was not controlled by mental decisions but by instinctive responses to the stimuli around him' (p 36). Aside from these jarringly non-literary gestures of defensiveness, Bodsworth finds a good location for the empirical facts of the curlew's plight. He intersplices the story with passages of historical and scientific fact under the rubric *The Gantlet*. These passages outline the first sighting of the Eskimo curlew, the naming, the massive slaughter in the nineteenth century, the dwindling of once vast numbers, and then the incredible last sighting of a mating pair of curlews, the very pair whose story Bodsworth is telling. All the details are historically and scientifically accurate, with the exception of the hope that the last mating pair of curlews could save the species as a whole. The effect of this isolation of data is the reverse of that which poeticizes the long view at the expense of the curlew: the ugliness of the slaughter and the reduction of this species of bird to piles of corpses 'as large as a couple of tons of coal' (p 106) are acts performed by our species. The curlew is reduced, not inherently, but by us. The facts speak for themselves; as presented, they disallow authorial condemnation, but nevertheless illustrate human culpability on a vast scale. They prepare the way for the otherwise incomprehensible act of the only human being who appears in the curlew's story.

Last of the Curlews follows the migration of the curlew over one year, from the Arctic tundra to the mudflats of Patagonia and back again, a total distance of some eighteen thousand miles. Parts of the story are informative, describing the various stopping places, the reasons for the V-formation of the birds' flight, the intricacies of the curlew's wing structure. Bodsworth does not represent the trials of storm and cold during the migration as adventures but as simple hazards of a long journey. It is difficult to imagine the emotional effect that might have attached to the curlew had the bird's fate been to die with snow-clogged wings in the open ocean. No doubt some such natural death does await the curlew beyond the confines of the narrative. Within the narrative, empathy for the curlew grows when chance brings him together with a female of his own kind. The hope that this lone curlew at least might be able to resume a natural life elevates his situation beyond the anonymity of death in nature. Since it hinges upon the consummation of biological drives, however, that hope does not humanize the curlew.

The female repairs the curlew's broken life. Her arrival is 'strangely drab and undramatic' (p 83), but the recognition between the two birds of the same species is 'sure and immediate' (p 85). We like to portray human love as rare and beautiful and full of trials. Bodsworth himself practises this romanticism in his novel *The Strange One,* which likens the difficult love between a Scottish man and an Indian woman to the fidelity between a barnacle goose and its anomalous mate, a Canada goose. The love that develops between the two curlews is literally rare, since they are the last of their species and have found each other in a world that stretches right across two continents. Though the mating rituals of the curlews follow the instinctive biological pattern of their species, the fact that they are able to satisfy these mating urges at all is almost a miracle. Certain features of their courtship are reminiscent of human love: the offer of a gift, which in the curlews' case is a snail; the strutting and protectiveness of the male; the soft *quirking* sound they make to each other; and the terrible distress when the two are separated during a snowstorm, then their huddling together, neck to neck, when they find each other again. Despite these similarities, however, it is in this part of the story that Bodsworth's resistance to anthropomorphism, an irritant elsewhere, proves its narrative worth. Sympathy goes out to the pair of curlews in part because they love each other as human beings sometimes do, but also because the pair-bond, as animal behaviourists call it, completes the long-unfulfilled biological cycle. Emotional responses to the graces of natural courtship between mating birds are enhanced by the realization that in this case the chance to mate has come about against incredible odds. These qualities, then, win consent to Bodsworth's seemingly anthropomorphic statement that the male 'felt as if he had been reborn and was starting another life' (p 86).

They also strengthen the impact of the death of the female curlew. The death is tragic, as I have suggested, not because it means the extinction of the species, but because of its effect upon the lone individual curlew left behind. As is the case with the death of Tarka and that of the great auk in Eckert's story, the description is painful to read. That the death occurs at the peak of the curlews' mating fervour, at the very moment that the male treads the female for the first time, stresses the innocence of the curlews and the boorishness of the farmer who shoots the female. The eagerness of the man is repulsive: he jumps off his tractor and runs to get his gun – for the wanton pleasure of shooting a bird.

The events turn suddenly from the curlew's mating ecstasy to his frantic bewilderment over the thunderous sound of the gun, the blow to one of his wings, and the female's failure to follow him into the air. In content, the effort of the female to join her mate, the *keering* call of alarm that they send out to each other, the struggle to remain together and then the preening that the male gives her as she dies might all seem melodramatic. Replace these curlews with human beings and such a judgment would probably be legitimate. The judgment would also have been legitimate had Bodsworth shown the male curlew pining away, or lingering beside his mate's body, or remaining faithful to her ever after, although these actions would not have strained credibility greatly. Instead, as would be consistent with the instincts of most species, the curlew's mating urge reasserts itself and he flies off alone towards the S-twist in the river to seek the female that he knows will come. His memory is short, but this does not reduce for the reader the impact of the difference between the joys of nesting with the female that should have been the curlew's and futility of his hope at the end of the story. We know that the species is doomed in either case, and thus empathy goes to the individual curlew.

Bodsworth's description of the suffering of these curlews never steps out of line with natural behaviour. The curlews' inability to understand why their mating has been so cruelly checked is mirrored in the reader, for there was no reason for this killing. It is no consolation for the reader that the individual curlew's anguish is brief, that he quickly forgets his mate and proceeds with his instinctive pattern of life. In this respect, the curlew is not akin to us at all. We do not have here an Oedipus who puts out his eyes for the monstrousness of his fate. Yet the curlew's unaltered faith that his world continues on normally does not distance the sense of the tragic from him. It is not appropriate to apply human measures to the curlew's misfortune, to say that the curlew is the unconscious dupe of forces larger than himself, or that he occupies a special kind of hell in which his desire will never diminish and never be satisfied. Such evaluations posit simple identification disbarred by both the alienness of the curlew from ourselves and by the narrative structure. *Last of the Curlews* is ultimately a simple story, having the simplicity of nature itself. The moral divide is likewise simple. Though it is wrong to speak of villains and heroes in this situation, human guilt is plain enough. *Last of the Curlews* achieves tragic complexity, nevertheless, in compelling readers to yield the fullness of feeling to a nonhuman being.

The Inadequacy of Moral Outrage and Eckert's *The Great Auk*

Tarka the Otter ends with the words 'nothing more' to indicate the death of one animal of a still-surviving species. When we arrive at the absolute 'nothing more' of Eckert's description of the death of the last great auk, empirical and historical realities are compelled to align themselves with literature. Eckert reports the actual circumstances of the death of the last great auk, just as he remains true to the natural experiences of this sea-bird and his flock. He combines the techniques of Williamson and Bodsworth, showing us directly the effects of incessant human violence, as does Williamson, while simultaneously segregating the natural world from the human one, as does Bodsworth. Instead of being protected from the magnitude of human guilt, as one is by the journalistic reporting of Bodsworth's text, the reader of *The Great Auk* is confronted with assaults that do not stop even when they reach the very last of a species. None of these stories forgive human beings for their aggression against animals, but *The Great Auk* disallows even the forgiveness that might be forced externally upon these events. Williamson's otter hunters do not annihilate the otters, and one might be inclined to argue that there are other Tarkas whose stories can be told. Bodsworth's farmer in all likelihood shoots the last female curlew unwittingly, thinking it is a different kind of bird or simply not thinking at all. The hunters who killed the last great auk killed it precisely because it was a rare animal. Their act was not wanton but deliberate. In narrative form, with the peaceable life of the great auk fully and lovingly described, the historical events produce a depth of feeling not assuaged by the freedom of moral condemnation.

The factualness of the events could well grant Eckert considerable liberty in the matter of anthropomorphism. That he resists descent into personification attests to the faithfulness of his art to the animal and its cause. He does not name any of the birds in the story. If the last great auk is one of the finest of his kind, larger by inches than others and empowered by the flock to lead them, these qualities are aimed not so much at impressing the reader as at indicting humanity. The most distinguished of the species (and the last) is still only an economic proposition to the men who kill the great auks. In fact, of course, the best of any animal species is the object of hunters; economics has little to do with the hunt *per se*. The rationale of economics completely fails to justify the slaughter in *The Great Auk,* since, as with *Tarka the Otter,* the animal's perspective has narrative omnipotence. Eckert does not attempt, however, to enter the great auk's mind and translate its thoughts into human language. By 1963, when *The Great Auk* was published, the public might tentatively be trusted to find at least as much interest in natural history as in the self-flattery of anthropomorphism.

Nothing says that natural history has to be flat and unliterary to be accurate. The amusement Eckert gets out of describing the 'ludicrous and awkward' movements of the great auks on land does not distort the reality of the birds. He describes vividly the 'grossly exaggerated wobble' and related aspects of their gait:

Far, far to the left they'd lean as the right foot shuffled forward several inches, then equally far to the right as the weight shifted to this foot and the left shuffled forward. Their stubby flipper wings thrashed the air constantly and futilely for purchase. Frequently they slipped and fell onto the hard rocky surface in a tangle of swinging wings and frantically pumping feet, but always they scrambled up unhurt, cushioned by the thick down of their breasts. Their progress toward the higher portions of the island was for all the world like the extravagantly awkward bumblings of a troupe of circus clowns. (p 13)

These, and other amiable particulars of the great auks' habits, increase delight in the natural bird without eliciting the luxurious sentiment of compassion. The reader is convinced of the authenticity of detail, not pressured to identify with birds. Yet the invocation of the great auks' happy clumsiness on land turns out to have been keenly purposive when the time comes to give the circumstances of the last great auk's death. Struck by a man with a club, the great auk 'rolled over, scrambled back to his feet and continued his pitiful wobbling run to the cliff edge' (p 125); the futility of the bird's attempt at escape is achingly obvious. What was a sweet absurdity in the great auk, and should have guaranteed the friendliness of humankind, fatally betrays the last great auk to human aggression. Our pleasure is betrayed as well, for art has drawn us to this creature to show us that humanity will never again enjoy in life the quaint, determined solemnity of so simple an attribute of the great auk as its comical gait.

Eckert's power to enkindle empirical fact with literary meaning springs from his uncompromised faithfulness to the great auk. In an italicized section of the story, Eckert lends poetry to the hatching of the great auk chick. The italics do not stress the action so much as they encapsulate it from the rest of the story. The reader sinks into the inside of the egg, away from the daylight world of normal print. The passage opens biblically with *'In the beginning ...'* and yet what follows is not the least bit mystical. Poetry emerges from the physical, from the hardening of the spine, the first flexing of the muscles, the somatic complaint against confinement. When the chick's egg tooth finally breaks a hole in the shell, it is not 'Life' that rushes in but fresh air: *'two pea-sized lungs were inflated for the first time'* (p 20). From this micro-level, one can reach outward and find empirical fact informing the drama of the narrative itself. As the novel pursues the great auk's growth and migration, Eckert offers periodic counts of the numbers in the flock. There appears to be cause for elation when the great auk's pathetic flock of one hundred and twenty-six meets up with an armada of over four thousand birds (p 60). As our hopes rise with the increase in numbers, we temporarily forget the novel's view of humankind. The larger numbers only foreshadow a more terrible catastrophe when people discover the flock.

There has been a 'harvest' of Eldey Island birds early in the novel. The fishermen drive the clumsy fowl along planks into waiting dinghies, smacking them on the head with clubs as they witlessly follow the flock. In another encounter with humankind, the cluster of great auks making their migration southward become the victims of a hail of shrapnel blown into their midst by men firing from boats for no discernible reason, no doubt for no reason whatsoever. The leader of the flock is struck; he 'flopped spasmodically as a jagged chunk of metal tore away most of his skull' (p 64). Clearly it is better to die by natural causes than from the attack of this terrible animal, the human being. When the inevitable carnage does take place, upon the increased flock of nearly five thousand birds, we anticipate learning nothing pleasant about our species. Compassion for animals is too puny an emotion to cope with the scene of the slaughter of over forty-eight hundred birds. The hours of clubbing, the endless swish-thump as the great auks' heads are broken, the boats piled full with carcasses – these elements rudely shake the reader out of any illusion that pity for the animal can do battle against such aggression.

If we are inclined to excuse the massacre as a tragic mistake caused by economic necessity, Eckert will not allow us this illusion either. As the day wears down, some of the men begin to play a horrifying game with the great auk fledglings, useless as meat but a too easy target for play. The game begins with one man throwing a fledgling at another:

The throwing game rapidly degenerated into a kicking game and now the men turned into overgrown boys delightedly kicking at the animated black lumps of fuzz on the ground, seeing who could kick them highest or farthest. The best ones to kick, of course, were those which were still able to stand up on their hindquarters, because those would loft high into the air and plop to the ground dozens of feet away in a broken heap. After all, the men had worked hard. All day they had worked hard. Let them have this little bit of fun. What could it possibly matter to anyone? (p 95)

Literature cannot produce an uglier scene than this one – or at least not that I have found. Eckert's scene is not properly defined as gory, or as tragic. The reader can and will grieve over the final seconds of the last great auk's life. But grief over the terrible waste of the fledglings and the fact that the kicking game dooms the species to extinction is overwhelmed by hatred of humanity. A more powerful connection with nature than the tender heart is necessary to combat the ingrained beliefs that allow anyone to kick a helpless baby bird. The ugliness of the slaughter is bad enough. The kicking game divides us forcibly from our attachment to the human species. Even a confirmed misanthropist would find it difficult to put a philosophical cast upon the aversion this scene provokes.

Polemics arise naturally from this event in the story; outrage plays havoc with the critical stance and needs to be discharged. And yet polemics, like compassion, fail to do justice to the effect Eckert has produced. Moral fury is gratifying, but it does not free us from our constitutional and definitive sense of entitlement over nature. Eckert has accomplished as much as art can accomplish towards upsetting human sanctities and tangling up both reason and sentiment. That he himself feels the need to relieve anger in open sarcasm – 'Let them have this little bit of fun' – is understandable.

But let us step back from the story and see what has occurred with this development. Convinced of the truth of this representation of humanity, the reader struggles to divorce herself or himself from the prevailing value that allows people to victimize animals in this way. That value is culturally all in all; nothing besides belief in human primacy rationalizes the playful destruction of the fledglings. If readers are moved, then, to any emotion, value has come from a successful literary evocation of the lives of animals in their natural state. Efforts to reach into humanitarian sentiments to repudiate the fishermen's act are headed off by undeniable realism. Although the episode is shocking, the cruelty has emerged naturally from the exigencies of the narrative. In fact, as one realizes afterward, Eckert's story would have been inconsistent if it did not offend convention and sentiment with some revelation of this kind. Only naïve optimism about both the ultimate goodness of humankind and the willingness of authors to spare us from truth leaves readers unprepared for this display of absolute recklessness. Recklessness with the species as a whole, we learn, originates in the attitude exhibited by the fishermen. Remaining insensitive to the episode is a near impossibility. If passionate denunciation of human cruelty eases conscience, however, it cannot obscure the factuality of this scene behind an overlay of spiritual value. Nothing soothing can come out of this event.

So let us try the argument that all we have before us is conservationist propaganda and that those who are moved by the story have been duped. The charge of practising shallow propaganda could be laid against any of the stories that defend the rights of nonhuman animals, and it is especially important to test this charge when, as with *The Great Auk*, the description of the victimization of animals shatters critical distance. That the annihilation of the great auks did occur is indisputable, yet this line of defence does not get at the essence of the objection. A critique like this is aimed at the warping of life to convert it into art, and not very good art, since its purpose is moralistic. This complaint arises normally when the moral is obvious and rather simplistic. For an answer, it must be granted first of all that Eckert does not preach; didacticism is most evident not in instruction to the reader on how to behave but in explanation of the great auk's habits and migratory routes. These details cannot, I believe, be faulted as imaginary; nor can they be dismissed as aesthetically unnecessary.

As to moralism, the earlier wild animal stories generate more obviously than Eckert's the simple instruction to 'be kind to animals.' The early works, moreover, are not even remotely capable of stretching to as grim a scene as that of the fishermen's game with the great auk fledglings. They are held back by a desire to impart wholesome values to the reader. These values demonstrate ultimately that nature speaks with a human voice, and that animal victims reconfirm culturally based ways of knowing and feeling. They cannot touch upon the totally inhuman, either in animals or in acts of cruelty.

Eckert does not let us off the hook for the death of the last great auk. Pathos and sensationalism are close at hand, but are held back by consciousness that in truth, at some point in the mid-nineteenth century, the very last of the great auks did close its eyes upon the world. As with *Last of the Curlews,* the final acts of violence by human beings are committed against a mating pair of birds. Hunting, the collection of specimens, and then a hurricane reduce the flock to a scant seven birds. Specimen collectors kill three of the seven, including the old one-eyed female who has been a kind of touchstone throughout the narrative and whom Eckert describes as 'the binding thread, the vital spirit that linked them all and willed them to carry on' (p 115). Of the four now remaining, two are caught by killer whales, leaving only 'our' great auk and his mate to return to the Eldey Island nesting ground. Eckert pauses to admire the 'incredibly strong-shelled egg' the auks produce, its 'rich creamy white' colour and the dappled shades of brown on its surface. The pause is a warning, of course, and yet the smashing of this egg by a hunter is again a historical fact and not artistic licence.

The massacre on a large scale is hateful, but the image of six men with clubs bearing down upon these two precious, and utterly vulnerable, birds and their egg – again, a historically accurate image – encapsulates the hideousness of our species from the animal perspective. The six men approach the great auks and the male gives the female the signal to flee from the egg they have been guarding:

As the female darted between two of them and headed for the cliff edge a bloody club streaked down in a vicious arc and crushed her skull. She was dead before her body stopped rolling.

The great auk managed to elude the swings of two men and then was hit a glancing blow by the third. He rolled over, scrambled back to his feet and continued his pitiful wobbling run toward the cliff edge. The men rushed in pursuit – and one of them, intent only upon the great auk's fleeing form, stepped on the single large egg and crushed it into an obscene yellow stain on the gray rock.

Only a dozen feet separated the great auk from the edge now, but it was too much. A whistling blow from a club slammed into his neck and shoulders, shattering bones and stopping him permanently. (pp 125–6)

As with the early stories, hard language marks this description. No doubt, Eckert has a motive akin to that of London, Seton, and Roberts in giving us graphic violence: he will not protect us from the shedding of blood and crushing of bone. Still, there is none of the thrill of sensationalism in this scene; there is no appeal to that attraction to violence with which some people approach the wilderness. The bloodshed does not operate as a corrective to sentimentalism, but as a corrective to anthropocentrism as a whole.

Hard words pair up with what seems like the standard fare of pathos in death; the great auk's 'final wheezing breath' could almost represent a parody of pathos, had Eckert not been so careful with sounds all along. It could not have been easy for Eckert to imagine this scene, let alone put in words the magnitude of its meaning. He achieves some distance from sentiment by compelling the reader to see with the great auk, in his last moments of life, humanity laying waste to the island's sea-birds, smashing every murre egg for that season and loading up boats with carcasses. Pathos might have represented the fading vision of the great auk looking out upon a happy, sunny world that it would know no more. We can be grateful that Eckert allows us the luxury of grief and anger when his narrative reaches this pitch. Far from being propagandistic, *The Great Auk* conveys the truth of human aggression against animals too powerfully for simple moralism to bear.

CONCLUSION

This chapter has been a long one. I have dwelt on stories about wild animals for this length of time because wild animals demand representation as they are, without human interference. All animals require us to get out of our skins and recognize the autonomy of beings different from ourselves and worlds different from the one we have created. With animals in the wild, this requirement is the more pressing because these animals really do live full lives in a complete world, all in the absence of human contact. Human imagination needs to stretch itself to invoke the wild animal's manifest resistance to being incorporated into art. Given the magnitude of this difficulty, it is little wonder that authors resort to some fairly obvious narrative ploys: the romance of the hunt, the thrill of battle, the pathos or sensationalism potential in animal death, and the contrary strategies associated with deliberate empirical neutrality. Before Darwin, no one really cared about the wild animal's story, and one can therefore excuse blatant narrative devices or emotional manipulations. These writers are, after all, striving to translate into the familiar that which is alien and inaccessible to civilized readers. As we have seen, a degree of humanization of wild animals is legitimate on certain occasions, but the ever-present danger in narrative is using the animal to serve human needs and desires. The early narratives slide constantly into this habit. From the methods applied by the later writers, it appears that direct assault upon anthropocentrism is at present a requisite to freeing the wild animal from aesthetic exploitation. Freed from conceptual service to humankind, the animal victim can deliver a considerable emotional impact.

One way or another, all of the stories discussed thus far have engaged fundamental moral issues, whether through the request that animals affirm human moral codes or the isolation of human from animal to demonstrate either human superiority or human guilt. Morality in these stories clearly falls on either side of the continuity/discontinuity dilemma that Darwinism has left us with. While the first animal stories tackle continuity, they fail to honour the animal victim as a subject of its own narrative. The next wave of stories, of course, acknowledges the rift that manifestly exists between our species and others, but leaves the issue of continuity up in the air. When the object is to tell the wild animal's story, the impetus to tap human animality does not arise. In the broader cultural domain enfolding modern fiction, however, the difficult task of broaching the elusive animal in humankind confronts the author. As we move now to fiction in which the animal victim, domestic or otherwise, is involved in human dilemmas, it turns out that what is alien and inaccessible in the animal upsets the very moralism it has been asked to articulate in the wild animal story. The questions raised by the presence of animal victims become more cerebral than those raised in the wild animal story, as is consistent with the intellectual quality of human animality. From this point forward, the animal victim preys less upon emotion and more upon the cultural safeguards to human distinctiveness.

4 The Urban Context: *Dispossessed People and Victimized Animals*

INTRODUCTION

Urban existence and cruelty to animals are strangely interlinked. It is no accident that William Hogarth sets his landmark *Four Stages of Cruelty* in the city. Nor is it arbitrary that the worst torments suffered by Anna Sewell's Black Beauty occur in the city and that peace returns to the horse when he is retired to rural life. As far as the imagination is concerned, city life subjects animals to the most unnatural and most reprehensible mistreatment, while pains inflicted upon animals in the country appear to blend in with the general trials of natural existence. That is probably why organized protest against cruelty to animals originated in cities and current animal rights campaigns are still viewed as an urban phenomenon, and resented as such by nonurban people who believe that inhabitants of cities simply do not understand animals. Of course, there is no reason to think that cruelty to animals in the city is any worse or more frequent than cruelty to animals in the country. Suffering is suffering, wherever it occurs. Nevertheless, qualities hover about urban cruelty to animals which arouse particular indignation. Two of those qualities, I believe, are salience and dissonance – salience because animals are scarce in cities and their nature marks them out conspicuously from the background of city ways, and dissonance because cruelty to animals jars with the civilized ideals maintained by urban people.

For writers of fiction, the dissonance which enters into basic concepts of animals and cities is particularly fruitful. In the realm of ideas, a fundamental disharmony exists between animals and cities. Animals really do not belong in cities, either physically or conceptually. The difficulty presented by the effort to imagine cities and animals in conjunction might well explain the scarcity of urban stories containing significant animals. The animal does not fit naturally into narratives about cities. If the urban stories that do contain significant animals are indicative, however, animals can serve an important function for city dwellers. Their lack of fittingness is useful, for they address the dispossessed spirit of the urban person. That dissonance which marks the animal as a stranger to the urban setting permits writers to express the substantialness of the human sense of being likewise disowned by city life.

That animals do not truly belong in cities, then, has both psychic and literary value because some vital aspect of human nature does not really belong in cities either. Though the whole idea of animality is problematic, it is reasonable to argue, in this post-Darwinian age, that animals embody the reality in the human being which city life strives to negate, that it is in fact the animal in the urban person which feels, rightly, dispossessed. The relationship between human and animal is no longer metaphoric: the discordant reality incarnate in animals is a human reality as well. This is not to say that urban stories operate upon the cliché that human aggression denotes the assertion of the 'beast' in humankind and that aggression in itself therefore represents the anti-urban reality. Indeed, in these stories it is generally the peaceableness of the victimized animal which serves to unhinge the individual's defences against the truth of his or her existence. The uncivilized animal, it seems, has a capacity to live directly, without neurosis, while the city person struggles to hold on to a sense of identity against forces too large and ill defined to assail. Sorting out the meaning of the urban animal victim entails coming to terms with the convoluted and paradoxical ways in which large issues of civilization penetrate and perplex the familiar ground of personal existence.

Animal victims in the urban setting allow the expression of antipathy to the civilizing process. The cities we have built to shut out the natural world seem not to free but to oppress us. Likewise, the urban state of mind subjects human nature to constraints which threaten to overbalance the burden that civilization puts upon the psyche. Unable to dismantle cities, caught up, in fact, in the compulsion to magnify to the point of grotesqueness concrete symbols of the triumph of civilization, humanity begins to complain about the enfeeblement of its personal will. We take pleasure from calling our cities jungles, since that metaphor restores the thrill of conquest to activities which seem meaningless at the level of the individual person. In addition to the actual pressures of city living, there is the pressure to manifest a corresponding degree of enlightenment – a near impossibility given the distance by which technological prowess has outstripped the capacity of the psyche to advance beyond crudity. Moral nature is at a loss as to how it can measure up to the might of civilization expressed in cities. Human lives are therefore squeezed in ever tighter yet unconceptualized strictures upon will and desire. The city asks of the human being that he or she become fully domesticated, yet removes content from the idea of domestication. How can the individual be 'naturalized' to the urban environment? Erected in opposition to nature, cities undermine the feeling of at-homeness in the world.

With a vision of the city before us, it becomes a great irony that humankind has upon it the intellectual demand to think of itself as fundamentally animal. What kind of animal produces structures and societies like those we have created? At a cultural level, the rationale for the power enfigured in cities has been removed with the disintegration of the idea of human supremacy and the interjection of the idea that human beings are simply animals after all. Monuments to human distinctiveness have lost their import and their solidity. The Darwinian controversy has had a greater than ideological effect where technological testaments to pre-Darwinian mentality are concerned. Asked to compare city life, emblem and flower of civilization, with how animals act and what they construct, people are confronted with a blatant absurdity. It is to humanity's credit that it has not instantly rejected the theory of evolution to overcome the ridiculousness of its own posture as it tries to regard its works as essentially animal in origin. Indeed, it may be that the selfsame feeling of the growing irrationality of the products of civilization has contributed to the appeal to the animal for stability. In stories taking up the theme of the animal victim in an urban setting, therefore, the animal is not simply a fictional device used to make a statement about human psychology.

The violation, first of all, of the urban prohibition upon any hint of the creatural and, secondly, of the sanctity of the rare animal visitor to the inhospitable (even to people) urban scene has as much bearing upon culture as upon personal neuroses.

The ultimate in human domination of nature, it turns out, escapes human control and puts in exile vital aspects of the psyche. Identity scrambles to find a foothold in the city. Many people, it seems, feel like outcasts in the city. In fiction, the animal victim serves to articulate a deeply experienced feeling of dislocation in the urban person. Urban stories tend to pair animal victims directly with social outcasts and misfits. In so doing, they touch upon the alienation experienced by even the most normal of city inhabitants. In turn, by means of a deeply felt personal isolation on the part of the individual character, these stories achieve an intense and complex reading of the import of animals within urban culture.

If city life excludes animals, its ideals certainly exclude tormenting them. Animals are not victimized casually by those who live in the city. Nor do the few writers who attempt to pull together the polarized realities of animals and cities depict the victimization of animals as an indifferent event. Narratively speaking, the conceptual dissonance between animal nature and city mores is almost bound to manifest itself in violence. What other kind of narrative effect would serve to place animals realistically in cities? The source of the violence against animals in modern urban fiction, however, is not the deficiency cited by rural and backwoods people to claim superior knowledge of animals. In fact, the very dilemma that fiction writers face in uniting animals and cities draws out a highly complex appreciation of the animal. In a strange way, acts of violence in these stories acknowledge the reality of animals. The moment of enlightenment, for the reader if not obviously for the character, comes with recognition of the similarity between the victimized person and the victimized animal. It appears paradoxically that, by means of aggressive acts, urban people can reach across the chasm separating urban and animal life. Indeed – and this is a most terrifying feature of urbanism – cruelty to animals in the urban setting muddles up sanity with madness. In the fiction that brings the urban person to the point of cruelty to animals, that cruelty can even signal the individual's genuine contact with his or her own humanity.

Of course, the 'humanity' of the urban person is a tangled and contradictory entity and genuine contact cannot truthfully be depicted as unambiguous. Not surprisingly, therefore, acts of violence against animals represent both opposition and acquiescence to urban values. The descent from the civilized ideal of moral probity into the killing of animals has a quality of perverseness quite distinct from other kinds of aggression practised in cities. On the one hand, doing harm to animals clearly violates urban and civilized values. In an admittedly mean and repulsive fashion, the morally repressed can express genuine defiance of the burden of civilization through cruelty to animals. On the other hand, with animals representing the human reality repressed by the city, aggression against them is also a symbolic annihilation of resistance to those values. Violence towards animals is a demonstration of acquiescence in so far as it acts out hatred of the restless animal within the human being. Granted, the feelings of power achieved by the small and weak through tyranny over beings who are smaller and weaker and even more marginalized than themselves are hardly admirable, and yet the dramatic self-realization that these social outcasts, and readers, achieve acts as a new force of liberation against the tendency of city life to negate individual identity. It is not simply through enhanced feelings of power that the marginalized individual seeks existential self-confirmation in victimizing animals. Rather, the move to break the resistance of animals borders on attempted theft: theft of the animal's self-possession. The animal victim holds out against personal disintegration in a way that the human victim cannot. Issues of power are intertwined with existential issues. Animals stand absolutely and ontologically clear of urban life, while the human characters portrayed in these stories are half in and half out and decidedly in need of enlightenment.

In some ways, it should be said, the city has been a great boon to animals conceptually. Outcast, the animal is under no symbolic or emotional obligation to humanity. It can be its vital, sane self and not excite humankind's lust to find itself everywhere reflected. The city already reflects humankind so obsessively that the thought that the nonhuman lives and breathes in some genuine world is a balm to the soul. As to the terrors of chaos and brutality which animals once represented, these have been put back where they belong, on civilization's doorstep. Outside of the thrill that mutant or supernatural beasts give to fans of the horror movie, the terror elicited by the modern, natural animal is for the unknown in the human species. Acceptance of the autonomy of the animal from human symbolization thus renders the intrusion of animality into city consciousness all the more meaningful. The substantialness of the natural animal throws human nature into ontological doubt. Painful as it is, that doubt is good for urban people, surrounded as they are by ultimately vacant symbols of the triumph of humankind.

The observations I have been making here are derived from four of the works of fiction which I will be discussing in this chapter. These stories do the most intense work with animal victims and offer the most profound and complex insights into the problematic relations between urban people and animals. As is consistent throughout this book, I am looking for stories which value animals in their own right and not simply as they are useful to analysis of human dilemmas. In fact, in Roald Dahl's 'Pig,' Thomas Mann's 'Tobias Mindernickel,' Katherine Mansfield's 'Fly,' and Giorgio Bassani's *The Heron,* the human image suffers depreciation as the authors invoke the fullness of animal being. The claims I am making are analytic, then, rather than statistical. Other urban stories involving animal victims, like *Black Beauty,* Doris Lessing's 'An Old Woman and Her Cat,' and Yashar Kewal's *The Birds Have Also Gone,* might well elicit compassion for the animal, but they fail, I would argue, to reveal the degree to which the animal outsider to cities perplexes the human condition.

The opening section, 'Tales of the Slaughterhouse,' does touch upon a work of fiction which also fails to reveal the full extent of the problems animal victims address in the urban setting. Upton Sinclair's *The Jungle* contrasts sharply with the other four stories discussed in this chapter, and yet it is useful here as illustrative of the kind of imagined victimization which does not have a sufficiently profound appreciation of animals to achieve the social critique this novel purports to make. The failure is useful because, at first thought, the cool, impersonal victimization practised in slaughterhouses might seem to epitomize the kind of trespass against animals that springs from a civilized and technologically oriented society. City people, it might at first appear, would more readily convert animals into commodities than their rural counterparts, and attempt to deflect the charge of cruelty by the disinterest of the killing. Given the depersonalization to which cities subject the human animal, it would follow that the conversion of sentient farm animals into live*stock* and pounds of meat represents the ultimate in urban victimization. Assessment of *The Jungle* suggests, however, that a purely social reading of the analogy falls short of deep analysis.

It might still be the case, of course, that slaughterhouse methods denote the ultimate in urban negation of individual meaning, but as far as fiction is concerned, the intimate interconnection between one animal and one person yields the strongest critique of urban values. What looks at first like a paradox – the marginalized world of one person and one animal reproaching the vast, indifferent city – represents in fact a direct attack upon the fundamental disorder of urban existence: the dispossession of the individual. The paradox resides in the effect upon the person of the victimization of the individual animal. The protagonists in the four stories that do do justice to the animal remain troubled, confused, and marginalized, even more so than before their encounter with animals. Indeed, if one is looking for heroism, these characters fail so badly on the score of personal integrity as to be contemptible. Nevertheless, shaken, broken, and even despicable as they are, these characters have come face to face with the animal; they have seen and dared to touch the reality that city life strives to repress. The last of the stories covered in the following discussion, Giorgio Bassani's *The Heron,* rises to the final paradox, whereby personal disintegration comes around to a kind of heroic acceptance of the anti-animal, anti-human mandate of the city. Before we arrive at that final paradox, however, we will trace several stages in fictional accounts of the urban animal victim.

TALES OF THE SLAUGHTERHOUSE

Slaughterhouses are a deeply hidden secret in modern society. The conceptual abyss that culture has created between humans and nonhuman animals is in the case of meat most vividly and eerily apparent. There exists a great well of secrecy between the hamburger hidden under lettuce, tomatoes, pickles, and a slice of bun and the business of butchering the cow which brings that hamburger into existence. In her feminist-vegetarian study, *The Sexual Politics of Meat,* Carol Adams refers to the live animal from which the meat comes as 'the absent referent' (p 47), with the emphasis on the idea of absence. It is here that the city person's lack of contact with animals becomes a critical factor, for those acts which isolate meat from the live animal are, conceptually at least, an urban phenomenon. Like much of the food that comes to urban people, most meat (with the exception, perhaps, of hearts and tongues) is carefully cleaned up, packaged and sold with the purpose of preventing consumers from thinking about the source.

Adams makes astute observations upon labourers and animals under capitalism and the metaphoric correspondence between the 'disassembly line' in the slaughterhouse and the disintegration of the worker's sense of self:

One of the basic things that must happen on the disassembly line is that the animal must be treated as an inert object, not as a living, breathing being. Similarly the worker on the assembly line becomes treated as an inert, unthinking object, whose creative, bodily, emotional needs are ignored. For those people who work in the disassembly line of slaughterhouses, they, more than anyone, must accept on the grand scale the double annihilation of self: they are not only going to have to deny themselves, but they are going to have to accept the cultural absent referencing of animals as well. (pp 52–3)

The loss of a sense of self, brought into focus by the scene in the slaughterhouse, has relevance not only to capitalism but also to urban life. A distinction Barbara Noske draws between the roles of humans and animals under capitalism brings in the theme of dispossession associated with life in cities. Noske observes that, unlike human workers, 'animal "workers" cannot "go home" at all. The modern animal industry does not allow them to "go home" – they are exploited 24 hours a day' (p 17). On both counts – the fragmentation of personal identity and the sense of homelessness – the butchered animal articulates profundities in the psychic state of the urban individual. Indeed, the apparent differences yielded by a social critique of capitalism's exploitation of animals and workers become similarities when raised to the level of urban culture. Of course, as a general rule, neither cities nor capitalism kills human beings outright, whereas the whole purpose of the meat-producing industry is to take the life of animals. Urban stories propose, nonetheless, that the urban person's loss of identity has a violence to it that might pass unnoticed were it not for the potential analogy with the actual, physical violence done to animals. That violence, furthermore, is connected with the point that Noske makes: some fundamental life essence in human beings, intimately associated with the animal, finds no home in the city, and is, like the animal 'worker,' permanently estranged and held captive in alien circumstances which negate it. The legitimacy of such an analogy notwithstanding, it takes a consistent respect for the animal victim on the author's part to avoid diminishing animal suffering in the process of likening animals' fate in slaughterhouses to the condition of the human being under any social system which does not kill him or her.

Upton Sinclair's *The Jungle* is vulnerable to the criticism that it merely exploits the real and terrible suffering of animals to deliver a social message about human misery. Sinclair examines human social issues first and foremost. He chooses the meat-packing industry to show how poor people get trapped in ugly circumstances. He is worried about the humanity in humankind and sees good, loving, healthy people becoming desperate and hateful under the tyranny of urban capitalism. *The Jungle* thus shares with the nineteenth-century British hunting prints mentioned in the first chapter of this book a kind of slippery displacement: that is, it steals the idea of victimization from animals and transfers that idea to the human victim. While much can be made of the coolness with which animals are slaughtered and the coolness with which cities dismantle human lives, Sinclair does not have the scope of vision or sensitivity to the animal's plight to use the analogy to deepen his argument. His novel does have the virtue, however, of actually calling attention to the ugly business of animal slaughter, whether its aim is to improve the lot of animals or not.

In the last analysis, of course, Sinclair's argument leads logically to vegetarianism, a regimen he does advocate at the climax of *The Jungle*. A charismatic professor of philosophy who converts the novel's protagonist to the honourable fight for socialism notes that 'meat is unnecessary as food' and that the habit of eating meat would stop if people had to kill the animals with their own hands (p 408). The argument is specious in that people who live on farms do kill the animals that provide them with meat; but it is valid if applied to stereotypic urban squeamishness over animal death. Philosophically, then, Sinclair recognizes the implications of his use of animal victims. Dramatically, however, *The Jungle* suffers from the same flaw as the wild animal stories written at this time (*The Jungle* was published in 1906): the theory is all very well, but the narrative itself fails to acknowledge the inherent value of animals. The metaphoric use of animals vacillates because it is not grounded in narrative allegiance with the animal.

To give Sinclair credit, he does note animal suffering directly as he records the impressions of the immigrant family on their first visit to the slaughterhouse in Chicago. Jurgis, the hero of the novel, thinks about the innocence and trustingness of the hogs and of the 'cold-blooded, impersonal way' in which they are killed, hooked by their back legs and hauled upside down on a trolley to have their throats slit (p 44). Jurgis also thinks of the individuality of the hogs and of the indifference of the machinery to their squealing anguish (p 45). Had Sinclair carried through with these kinds of observations, his novel might have transcended social propaganda and made a deep critique of urban capitalism. But these true revelations early in the novel descend to metaphors as Jurgis undergoes his conversion to socialism. Jurgis recalls his pity for the hogs and learns that 'a hog was just what he [Jurgis] had been – one of the packers' hogs' (p 376). The Beef Trust, he learns, is the 'Great Butcher' which rules the city of Chicago and consumes the innocent labourers' lives.

The analogy has utility. An indictment of capitalism or of any system could not find a much more compelling instrument than comparison with the butchering of animals. The description of big city corruption, of the slum life to which that corruption condemns the poor, and of the resulting disintegration of families supports the message that human beings are victimized almost as fully as slaughtered animals. If one compares the potential for healthy and happy social accord among the immigrants with the anger, neglect, and disease that poverty brings them, the violence done to human nature is arguably of a degree similar to the killing of animals, were one to discount the value life itself has to animals. Because Sinclair does lose his grip on the animal victim's reality, his social critique is not as deep as it could be.

An aspect of *The Jungle* which raises suspicions is its highly conventional, almost clichéd, use of the metaphor of the beast. Sinclair resorts to this metaphor persistently as he describes the increasing desperation of his characters. When Jurgis is imprisoned for biting a man on the face, Sinclair likens him several times to a wild beast (pp 185, 191, 192, 193). His fellow prisoner is also a wild beast (p 202). When Jurgis has sexual intercourse with a prostitute, 'the wild beast rose up within him and screamed, as it had screamed in the jungle from the dawn of time' (p 262). People driven mad by poverty and slum living have 'hideous, beastly faces' (p 277). The unemployed men who assemble in the yard of the meat-packing plant are 'an army of fifteen or twenty thousand human beasts' (p 328). Since Sinclair does not really care about animal identity, his conceptual use of the beast metaphor is loose in the extreme. It can denote pent-up rage in the prison, or mindless obeisance in the stockyard. He uses it to describe sexual passion and insanity, without caring much that the image both sensationalizes perfectly manageable human phenomena and denigrates animals. Flexible as they are, all of these metaphors are meant to indicate degeneration of one sort or another.

The most telling use of such metaphors, however, comes in Sinclair's description of the forces that oppress the labourer as 'wild-beast powers of nature' (p 140) and 'wild-beast powers of life' (p 361). The muddle surrounding this extension of animal imagery to social corruption is best indicated in the context for the first of these quotations. At this point in the novel, Jurgis realizes that 'it was true – that here in this huge city, with its stores of heaped-up wealth, human creatures might be hunted down and destroyed by the wild-beast powers of nature just as truly as they ever were in the days of the cavemen!' Sinclair is at least consistent: the metaphor of the beast in this context is supposed to suggest the ultimate in degeneration, the disintegration of urban social congress by the predatory forces of brute nature. Capitalism, the metaphor indicates, thrusts the city down from the position of civilized eminence and back into savagery. One winces at the mention of cavemen, though the analogy was possibly not quite as trite in 1906 as it is now. Perhaps the best that can be said about these kinds of metaphors is that Sinclair simply perpetuates the conventional distinction between domestic animals and wild ones: domestic animals brought to slaughter are pitiable, much as are workers whose lives are eaten up by the capitalist system, while predatory animals are of such ferocity as to permit the kind of use Sinclair makes of them. Beyond that distinction, however, one thinks of the whole of animalkind and realizes that the promiscuous use of animal imagery is part and parcel of Sinclair's capitalization upon the victimized animals. Human beings might die by accident in slaughterhouses, but animals are brought there deliberately for the sole purpose of dying there. Animals are by far the most persecuted victims of the meat-producing industry.

As a further critique, the idea of the city as a jungle performs the same double disservice as the use of the beast metaphor: it mistakes the nature of social oppression simultaneously as it mistakes the nature of jungles. The jungle metaphor is not explanatory but conventional in the worst sense. Indeed, it would be good if cities worked as well as jungles work. The exposure of insufferable working conditions does produce outrage, but it would be difficult to change the system if one were looking for the wild beasts that caused the damage in the first place. On the surface of his argument, Sinclair confounds the idea of dehumanization with a return to the animal state of being. At the same time, he wishes to draw upon the innocence of animal victims to explain capitalism's effect upon humanity. The confusion may not matter ideologically, but it does matter conceptually. The recognition of that fundamental similarity between capitalism, cities, and slaughterhouses, that all three are human constructions and human constructions only, might have led to a better grasp of what, precisely, is damaged by these systems and where to lay the blame. Sincere and consistent regard for animal victims would have made the problem of cities and human suffering less amenable to solution, but the irony is that such regard would have produced a deeper revelation of the effect of urban capitalism upon humanity than the anthropocentric vision.

It is ironic that, with a storyline that includes animals only at its climax and no social message, 'Pig' performs a more troubling critique of the slaughterhouse and a more profound questioning of the human state than does *The Jungle*. As a macabre story, driven by the sinisterly humorous vision of its author, Roald Dahl's 'Pig' certainly puts the problem of cities, animals, and people beyond resolution. Interestingly enough, the primary victim of the meat-producing industry in 'Pig' is a human being. 'Our hero,' Lexington, is actually butchered at the end of the story, in the same dispassionate manner as pigs are butchered. He is, however, first 'animalized' in a sense. He is raised nearly from birth, in complete isolation from civilization, by an eccentric vegetarian aunt in her home in the Blue Ridge Mountains. After Aunt Glosspan's death,

Lexington comes to New York City with all the innocence of an animal brought to slaughter. He knows nothing at all of the wicked ways of the urban world, and neither he nor the reader could anticipate that those wicked ways extend to the butchering of human beings for meat. Dahl thus puts the reader in the same position as Lexington: the surprise ending repeats, in an admittedly minor and safe fashion, the violent shock suffered by Lexington and, not incidentally, by the pigs who are also dragged to slaughter on the same conveyer belt carrying our hero to his death.

The reader has been subjected to a surprise earlier in the story during the circumstances that render Lexington an orphan. Those circumstances hint at the bizarre nature of that archetype of cities, New York. The events with which 'Pig' opens are set in Manhattan. Lexington's parents come straight out of a screwball comedy. They are a charming, light-headed couple, returning home tipsy from a night on the town, when some policemen, virtual Keystone cops, mistake them for burglars and fire upon them, 'scoring several direct hits on each body – sufficient anyway to prove fatal in both cases' (p 186). The hilarity surrounding this episode puts readers in a puzzling position, for we are required to cope with the jarring contradiction of a happy, screwball couple receiving the impact of a hail of bullets when such delightful figures rarely become physical bodies in any sense, let alone in the sense of being wounded. Unquestionably, New York City entails both of these images: of the frivolous night on the town enjoyed by superficial people and of gritty assaults upon human bodies. Normally, such images are mutually exclusive and a gulf exists between the narratives that work with one or the other of them.

In combining narrative visions that usually exclude one another at the beginning of 'Pig,' Dahl anticipates the deadly fusion of clashing ideas at the end of his tale: the fusion of slaughterhouse practices with sacrosanct human flesh. Cannibalism, of course, is not unusual in works of horror. Nor is it unusual that violation of the taboo against cannibalism be tinged with humour, as it is in 'Pig.' The films *Eating Raoul* and *Parents* are recent examples of sinister amusement being drawn from the idea of people eating other people. 'Pig' distinguishes itself from other humorous renditions of cannibalism in centring upon the human victim and raising important existential questions about the actual difference between humans and animals. I have already mentioned the utter innocence in Lexington which establishes his kinship with the pigs brought to the slaughterhouse. It is another quality in Lexington, however, that perplexes the whole issue of pigs and humans, and that is his wholly undiscriminating taste in food.

In his isolated life with his Aunt Glosspan, Lexington discovers a talent for preparing wonderful dishes out of vegetarian ingredients. His palate is highly sensitive and he becomes a truly creative gourmet. As a small boy, Lexington expresses incredulity at his aunt's report that other people actually kill cows 'like Daisy and Snowdrop and Lily' (p 190) to eat them. Yet for one reason or another, he does not acquire his aunt's moral aversion to meat-eating. He is, indeed, morally unequipped to cope with any kind of immoral behaviour. His innocence is absolute, not only in that he does not commit the sin of killing and eating animals before his aunt dies, but also in that he has no notions of morality whatsoever. Thus, when his aunt dies and he comes to New York City, he has no defences against the corrupt habits of urban people. In fact, he is grateful to the unscrupulous lawyer managing his aunt's estate for the fifteen thousand dollars that the lawyer ultimately gives him out of his half-million-dollar inheritance. Blissfully naïve, Lexington goes directly from the lawyer's office to an extremely dirty cafeteria, there to taste meat, a 'greyish-white slab' (p 198) of roast pork, for the first time in his life.

His ecstasy at finding this wholly new and eminently tasty food suggests an association with the conventional view of pigs: he is living by his taste buds alone and will consume anything that satisfies his sensual needs. One has to bear in mind that the conventional view of pigs as undiscriminating feeders is unfair. Nevertheless, Lexington's pure sensual delight at the taste of meat does put a different complexion on the title 'Pig.' Has Lexington sinned, then? Has he proved himself a 'pig' in the conventional sense and thus become susceptible to slaughter? Or has he not sinned, since he cannot balk morally at the slab of meat, and thus proved himself an innocent animal ready for butchering?

At the slaughterhouse, his response to the sight of a pig being hooked up to the pulley and dragged upside down into the secret regions of the building only deepens the dilemma of his moral state. Unlike the immigrants in *The Jungle,* Lexington experiences no sympathy for the pigs. The struggles and squealing of a particularly 'nimble' pig as it hops along on three legs and fights the pull of the chain elicit from Lexington only the observation that this is 'Truly a fascinating process' (p 203). He is curious about the 'funny cracking noise,' which is the sound of the pig's leg or pelvis breaking, but is ultimately more concerned that the recipe for this strange new meat stuff is extremely complicated than that the pig is suffering.

Lexington is not the only human victim of Dahl's macabre slaughterhouse. Evidently, all the human visitors to the place end up travelling along the conveyer belt with the pigs towards the man who slits throats. The attendants do not single out Lexington for any special reason. His oddities are interesting to us, but really any question of Lexington having brought down this fate upon himself for some reason, either because of the 'sin' of enjoying meat or the animal-like innocence of his nature, becomes nugatory with the undiscriminating nature of the slaughterhouse. The expression 'it's all meat to me' comes to mind. All flesh is meat to this slaughterhouse. This random killing truly resembles the ways of the meat industry. Ultimately, it does not matter whether Lexington is a good human being or a bad one, an innocent animal or an amoral one: the slaughterhouse is after flesh alone. In this respect, Dahl equalizes humans and animals in a way that Sinclair does not.

Since the story is bizarre, one cannot derive a moral or social message from this literal slaughter of humans, except possibly to observe wryly that the wicked urban world from which Aunt Glosspan has protected Lexington is more wicked than we realize. Dahl does put us inside the butcher's victim by following Lexington on his upside-down course towards death. He does not, however, depict this death as cruel and shocking. Lexington is alarmed but not panicked. He does not seem to be in a great deal of pain after his throat is slit. The blood pours into his eyes and he grows sleepy, but that is about all we learn of the physical effects of butchering. Perhaps the insidious gentleness of the slaughter might lead someone to opt out of a meat diet. Yet 'Pig' is not obviously an argument against meat-eating. Nor is it clearly an argument, made metaphorically, about the inhumane treatment of even the most innocent of sentient beings, human or otherwise. The effect of the story, rather, is to raise the existential question of what quality in humanity keeps us out of slaughterhouses. Why should Lexington, or the anxious woman with the long white gloves who precedes him up the conveyer belt, be exempt from slaughter when pigs or 'Daisy and Snowdrop and Lily' the cows are not?

An interesting aspect of 'Pig' for comparison with the upcoming stories is the way in which Lexington is an outsider like other urban characters associated with animals. I have suggested that Lexington is animal-like in his innocence and sensuality and deviates thus from the norm. In this sense, Lexington represents directly the animal disowned by urban circumstances. To some extent, he also represents the good in humankind: the naïvety, the appreciation of simple existence, the brightness and beauty – for he is a beautiful being, and young. One would expect, then, that he would be a special case, a figure of the kind of being specifically disowned by urban worldliness. His death, however, is not a sacrifice, not a moral event in the sense that it symbolizes the destruction of the good. It is not the pain and moral significance of his death that reveal the misery produced by slaughterhouses, but the absence of meaning.

The three tales to be discussed next, 'Tobias Mindernickel,' 'The Fly,' and *The Heron,* also deal with the impersonal nature of cities and with the feeling of individuals that they personally have been rejected by some quality peculiar to urban existence. 'Pig' is distinct from these stories in showing at its climax that the urban state treats humanity in general with indifference, that there is nothing personal in the violence cities perform upon human nature. This is a good point to take with us into interpretation of the next three works: that the intense feeling of being personally outcast experienced by the protagonists of 'Tobias Mindernickel,' 'The Fly,' and *The Heron* springs paradoxically from the absence of interest in the person that is atmospheric to cities. Indeed, the absence of personal interest felt by the urban individual accounts for the feeling of being personally outcast. If there were an enemy to confront, the urban person would not feel as thoroughly effaced as these stories suggest. This is where the animal victim enters the scene: when it comes to being personally dispossessed by cities, animals are unsurpassed.

TOBIAS MINDERNICKEL, URBAN MISFIT

At the onset of the age of psychoanalysis, Thomas Mann gave expression to 'civilization and its discontents' in a remarkable little story entitled 'Tobias Mindernickel' (1897). With extreme economy, Mann articulates the violence done to the human psyche by urban living. Mann may have been lucky to have detected dislocation to humanity before slums and misery were themselves dispossessed by the unearthly elevation and cleanliness of city-scapes. Persona non grata in 1897, Tobias Mindernickel would now be a virtual untouchable among the bright folks going about their business on city streets. To argue that this twisted, tormented character has some connection with the general run of humanity might seem to strain credibility. Our private lives, one might protest, do not drift into the kind of pathology that Mindernickel practises; nor do we maintain as bizarre a relationship with the natural animal as Mindernickel does. Perhaps the argument must rely on possibilities: on taking some of the standard neurotic tendencies of the civilized and driving them into collision with the amoral, uncivilized animal. There is, that is to say, a kind of logic behind the psychological developments in 'Tobias Mindernickel,' and that logic takes Mindernickel's relationship with his dog beyond a metaphor for abstract urban dealings with similarly abstract animals.

The argument that 'Tobias Mindernickel' deals with realities and not with metaphors hinges in large part upon the emphatic presence of the dog in this story. Twenty years after he wrote 'Tobias Mindernickel,' Thomas Mann published a long, affectionate essay, 'A Man and His Dog' (1918). In this essay, Mann describes his dog Bashan's physical features, habits, and demeanour with loving particularity:

I get an odd, intimate, and amusing sensation from having him sit on my foot and warm it with the blood-heat of his body. A pervasive feeling of sympathy and good cheer fills me, as almost invariably when in his company and looking at things from his angle. He has a rather rustic slouch when he sits down; his shoulder-blades stick out and his paws turn negligently in. He looks smaller and squatter than he really is, and the little white boss on his chest is advanced with comic effect. But these faults are atoned for by the lofty and dignified carriage of the head, so full of concentration. All is quiet and we too sit there absolutely still in our turn. (p 443)

One quality to note about this passage is the familiarity of the relationship Mann describes. Anyone who has kept companion animals must know the pleasures of feeling the animal's body weight and warmth. Mann's power to experience and then relate his intensely personal connection with Bashan stems from his willingness to set aside his own concerns and turn his mind fully to the dog.

Another comment Mann makes in 'A Man and His Dog' is directly pertinent to analysis of 'Tobias Mindernickel' as an urban story. Mann speaks of his return home from an evening's carousing in the city. He comes home, he says, with his head 'in a whirl of ideas and wine and smoke':

And then the embodiment of that other, truer, soberer life of mine, my own hearthstone, in person, as it were, may come to meet me; not wounded, not reproachful, but on the contrary giving me joyous welcome and bringing me back to my own. I mean, of course, Bashan. (p 454)

It would be difficult to find a more direct or more vivid expression of the at-homeness summed up in a companion animal. This passage is a reminder of the living reality of the animal which is made to suffer in all of these urban stories, for one can extend the idea of 'at-homeness' in the world to any animal. The simple truth Mann articulates suggests the extremity of the act of hurting a trusting animal. Indeed, I would imagine that the idea of injuring that animal which greets one at the door, which does embody home and one's 'truer' life, is inconceivable for most people. A person would have to depart a long distance from his or her truer life to hurt an animal, when that animal holds in trust the familiar affiliations of human existence. The fullness of Mann's appreciation for dogs is active behind 'Tobias Mindernickel,' active and familiar to readers. By violating that appreciation, the story reveals the extremity of the contortions to which urban life can subject human nature.

Tobias Mindernickel preserves enough humanity to suffer agonies when he becomes the object of public scrutiny. As happens so frequently to fringe people, his demeanour in the street earns him the jeers and contempt of the neighbourhood children, who pursue him, yelling 'Ho, ho, Tobias!' Adults gather in the doorways to laugh at the spectacle. A spectacle is the last thing Mindernickel wants to be; in public he seems to want to shrink into nothingness.

In representing Mindernickel thus, Mann appeals to the timid private self in every reader, that self which feels like a caricature out in public. The idea that everyone in the anonymous crowd but oneself possesses a native sense of superiority undoubtedly afflicts most people. No doubt, too, the feeling of being wounded by the public gaze causes many people to respond as Mindernickel does, with exaggeratedly self-deprecating politeness. Mindernickel is unquestionably an oddity. Nevertheless, the city does tend to make people feel that their humanity is grotesque. Mann has not failed to draw empathy to his character.

He does not, however, stop with plain identification; he goes on to have Mindernickel enact the fantasy which attaches itself to the posture of humility. If they only knew, this fantasy runs, they would realize that this clownish exterior hides the soul of a saint. An opportunity arises for Mindernickel to express the nobility of his soul, to display the true Christian virtue of loving one's enemy: when one of the jeering children falls to the pavement, Mindernickel binds the child's wound with his handkerchief, uttering words of compassion. The automatic nature of this reaction, its total conformity to convention, should lead us to suspect inauthenticity or at least compulsiveness. For the moment, however, the character seems a gravely misunderstood man, a saint no less in capacity for forgiveness than in suffering persecution.

Mindernickel's physical circumstances are of equal importance to his personality in establishing that interposing an animal into this life is either hopeless or outright dangerous. Mann's brief description invokes the typical urban experience of enclosure and dreary sameness. Mindernickel's 'mean and shabby' rooms are as cramped as his personal existence. An adjacent building blocks the view out of his window. His single contact with nature is a pathetic one: on his windowsill stands a flowerpot filled with soil but growing nothing at all; once in a while, he sniffs the earth in the flowerpot. This occasional whiff of the odour of dirt constitutes the sum total of the character's nonurban experience prior to purchasing a dog. In fact, given the establishing descriptions of Mindernickel's surroundings and psychology, it would be difficult for a reader to predict the appearance of an animal as a motivational element in the narrative. The impression of constriction is so great as to preclude even the thought of animality. The narrative itself imitates the impossible contortion expected of a conceptual union between the man's life and the dog's.

Any reader anticipating some elderly and urban variation upon 'lad-and-dog' friendship when Mindernickel buys the dog has allowed optimism and fantasy to obscure the deadliness of the setting. The simple fact that the dog is described on its introduction into the story as 'a muscular little animal' presages disaster. This healthy creature will struggle against the oppressive confinement in which Mindernickel expects him to live. Still, there is Mindernickel's unrecognized saintliness to tempt readers into imagining other outcomes than that which takes place. This is, we have been told, a 'sinister' story: perhaps the creature will turn out to have rabies and will cause the death of this unwitting but well-intentioned man; perhaps the nasty street children will kill the kindly man's beloved pet – anything to enhance the impression of Mindernickel's martyrdom. Mindernickel's martyrdom is, of course, of a very different character than these, actually wholesome, turns of event would indicate. He is a martyr to the need to be a saint in order to justify the pain of existing corporeally in the world. The muscular energy of the dog shames Mindernickel.

Esau, as Mindernickel calls the dog, expresses sheer biological exuberance, a joy in bodily existence wholly alien to the man. The dog is an affront to Mindernickel's way of life. Esau has no symbolic import; the animal will not even conform to the, albeit clumsy, training Mindernickel attempts to impose upon him. Animal symbols do not nose potatoes around the room; nor do they use their freedom, as Esau does on his one escape from confinement, to chase cats and eat dung in the street. The contrast between Mindernickel's public behaviour and the dog's could hardly be greater; Esau has no conception of 'the public.' Outdoors simply means freedom to him. On the score of symbolism, the public character Mindernickel adopts is self-consciously symbolic, while the dog's performance manifests total disregard for even the most obvious human construction of public and private domains. Clearly, then, the dog is immune to the abstract fabrications of vice and virtue. If Mann were aiming for the pathos of Mindernickel's condition, he would not have had Esau, 'frantic with joy,' greeting the character's juvenile tormentors when he meets them during his flight from incarceration in Mindernickel's rooms. The dog does not discriminate between good and bad people; there is no evil in his world, and that too is offensive to the structure Mindernickel has unconsciously imposed upon life. One is compelled to contemplate the possibility that the cruel street urchins manifest a healthy physicality attractive to canine innocence. And although Esau falls victim to civilization, in the form of Mindernickel's delusions of being super-civilized, he is only the Universal Animal in so far as he epitomizes ardent particularity. He is a dog all unto himself, and he cares for and knows nothing about the woes and virtues invented by civilization. As such, Esau is an unexpectedly cheerful presence in what was promising to be a gloomy tale gratifying only to dour moralism. That he is a natural animal, without symbolic dimension, intensifies rather than detracts from his significance to feeling. Esau's freedom and energy actualize the reader's escape from what could otherwise turn out to be a ponderous, ideologically orthodox story about the urban nightmare and its oppression of the poor and marginal.

The dog epitomizes the animal vitality Mindernickel wants to extinguish in himself. The man's obsession with forcing Esau to *obey* reveals how imperfectly he has repressed his own native impulses. With his public humility and ready supply of altruistic sentiment, he has succeeded only in torturing the animal in himself and diverting it towards viciousness. He forces his animality to serve the delusion of compassion, as is evident in the joy he experiences when he first accidentally wounds his dog with a kitchen knife. The accident discloses to him the perfect mechanism for placating the polarized drives in his personality. He can victimize the intractable animal simultaneously as he creates a focus for his voracious desire to manifest tenderness. Emotional response moves in the reverse direction as well: the melancholic outlook on life, which sees injury everywhere, caters to the need for pleasure. Mindernickel discovers that he can manufacture misery to delight his soul's longing for hatred of life.

Stabbing a dog is obviously not the act of a sane person. Nor can the miseries of Mindernickel's environment be blamed entirely for this development. Mindernickel's part in the conflict between his environment and the animal is to cooperate so far with urban values as to wish to annihilate the animal in himself. At the same time, he rebels against the pressures to which urban life subjects his personal sense of being. The logic of his act is that, in outdoing the city's inherent denial of animality, he establishes his personal distinctiveness; he acquires a personality. Mann indicates that Mindernickel's pathology has some relationship to city existence with typical economy. He briefly elicits the larger urban scene just prior to Mindernickel's ultimate act of tyranny over the dog. He notes again the sterile flowerpot, and has Mindernickel's figure stand out 'black and uncanny against the grey wall of the next building' (p 57). These emblems indicate the poverty of the man's life and the degree to which his madness is a product of the unnatural circumstances of the city.

The repulsive features of Mindernickel's act stem not from the rage underlying it, but from his use of the dog's pain to reinforce the artificial saintliness he upholds. As Esau lies dying, Mindernickel attempts the usual expressions of pity:

'My poor brute, my poor dog! How sad everything is! How sad it is for both of us! You suffer – yes, yes, I know. You lie there so pathetic – but I am with you, I will console you – here is my best handkerchief –'

This time, of course, the handkerchief, even if it is Mindernickel's best one, is inadequate to rectify the situation. Equally and more saliently inadequate are the verbal utterances of woe and empathy. Esau dies as cleanly as he has lived, without fuss beyond a look of 'complaining, innocence, and incomprehension.' The absence of pathos leaves the moment free for the man's response, which is to lay his face against Esau's body and weep 'bitter tears.'

That is all the description that Mann gives, and all that is required to raise the crucial question in the reader's mind. These tears Tobias Mindernickel is weeping, are they genuine tears or are they the ultimate in fraudulent sentimentality? Since Mann does not say whether there is joy or remorse in Mindernickel's heart, the reader is confronted with an existential dilemma. If the tears are authentic, then the whole shocking episode speaks of the greater availability to Mindernickel than to his tough-souled neighbours of healthy appreciation of the animal. Mindernickel has seen what this animal represents more clearly than most people ever see animals. Mindernickel realizes fully and intensely the extent to which Esau defies his, Mindernickel's, very existence. He may hate Esau's defiance, but he does see it. It is hard to face a conclusion like this because the stabbing of the dog is decidedly abhorrent and Mindernickel's behaviour with Esau prior to the stabbing displays no understanding of the animal's needs. Nevertheless, it could be argued that this misfit has an active relation with his own animality, albeit a hostile one. Authentic tears would indicate a love of the animal underlying delusional hatred.

If the tears do represent false consciousness so abandoned that it cannot recognize itself, however, then the conclusion must be that the urban psyche can sustain an inconceivable degree of delusion. The mind capable of carrying through on faked compassion in the face of indisputable cruelty must be warped beyond salvaging away from animal stability. Thus the story encapsulates the conflict to the urban mind that the animal creates, pitting forced sensitivity against hapless loathing, and authentic empathy against the cultural neurosis of hostility towards animality. Socially outcast, Tobias Mindernickel is certainly mad, but mad in a way that either epitomizes the depravity of the city or pushes that depravity towards a nakedness which gives access to reconciliation with the animal. However one interprets Mindernickel's state of mind, the story that contains him accomplishes the latter effect, that of stripping away the guise of authority from civilization's notions of virtue. Thomas Mann achieves this effect, moreover, quite simply because he loves and understands the dog Esau.

SHOWN UP BY A FLY: KATHERINE MANSFIELD'S EXCURSION INTO URBAN SENTIMENTALITY

The idea of virtue in sentiment is likewise the target of Katherine Mansfield's 'The Fly' (1923). The dynamic of the narrative is similar to that of 'Tobias Mindernickel,' though with significant reversals. The most evident among these reversals is the title, which makes the animal victim the centrepiece of the story and simultaneously suggests analogies between the fly and the man. Empathy for Mindernickel attaches at first to the man's misunderstood humanity. Empathy must then tolerate the appearance of indefensible cruelty in this urban victim who is like ourselves. 'The boss,' in contrast, is not a likeable character. Presumably, he wields considerable power over other people. Mansfield uses the fly to compel readers to confront their antipathy to her archetypal 'boss.' Initial hostility to the boss must suffer the prospect that this obese, wealthy, vulgar man is as much a victim as the fly he himself torments.

However much power the boss may be assumed to have, his identity is of less consequence than Mindernickel's. Whereas the name of Mann's character denotes inferiority, Mansfield's has no name. He is one anonymous boss among others; his business, also undefined, is like every other business operation in the city. Less successful persons have names: the office messenger is named Macey; a retired, virtually senile friend, five years younger than the boss, possesses the ironic name 'Woodifield.' Even 'the City' earns the importance of capitalization, while the boss remains devoid of a personal marker. It will turn out, as one comes to expect of these urban stories, that the fly which also lacks a name holds steadier ownership of its individuality than the man, despite its depending for its life upon human caprice.

As in 'Tobias Mindernickel,' place is of signal importance in 'The Fly.' The opening line of the story is Woodifield's observation to the boss, 'Y'are very snug in here' – a comment which should instantly arouse suspicion that 'snug' is not quite the right adjective for the boss's room. Although its furnishings are finer, the boss's office has the same sense of crampedness and isolation as Mindernickel's apartment. One has the impression, too, that the boss does not do much more there than Mindernickel does in his rooms, which is to stare vacantly into space until chance or necessity provides some stimulant to action. There is no mention of a home or domestic situation for the boss. He appears to be entirely ungrounded in the world yet nevertheless confined to one place. Woodifield introduces a sense of spaciousness, though at several removes from the locale of the story. He speaks of his daughters', not his own, trip to Belgium and of their happening upon the grave of the boss's son, who has been killed in the Great War. In ironic contrast to the office, the cemetery, by the daughters' report, expresses amplitude in space: the graves stretch for 'miles,' and 'nice broad paths' extend through the beautifully landscaped scene. Even though Mansfield invokes these antithetical places with utmost simplicity, one is justified in sensing reproach to the kind of civilization which treats its dead to the luxury of space but pens up the living in tight little rooms and allows them only third-hand or symbolic ('Woodifield') contact with physical freedom. That restriction to close quarters should correlate with the lack of a true home is typical of the strain to which urban life subjects the human spirit.

The boss has in the past achieved some sort of identity and enfranchisement with his sorrow over the death of his son. He has even bragged about his grief to people, declaring that he for one will never recover from the loss. For six years, he has managed to focus the sense that he exists as a person upon spells of weeping over his son's death. After Woodifield's departure, he intends to enjoy another such session in the privacy of his office but finds that he cannot generate the appropriate feelings. Reality is setting in: the photograph of his son, once a cue to sentiment, now seems a particularly unattractive representation of the lad. Perhaps genuine feeling has for months been sliding unnoticed towards contrivance.

A fly comes to the boss's rescue. The fly is company and distraction; the boss is not alone. The reader, too, is thankful for this new presence, because the fly is the breakthrough which necessitates analysis. A greater boon: this fly is drowning in the boss's inkwell and requires aid, which the boss abstractedly supplies leaving the drenched creature on a piece of blotting-paper on his desk.

Becoming engrossed in insect activities must be a recognizable phenomenon to all readers, even if they have left behind that particular fascination along with their childhood. One common response to the fly which Mansfield completely disbars is that which sees it automatically as repugnant and dirty, as a 'hideous little bat, the size of snot,' to quote Karl Shapiro's poem 'The Fly.' Nevertheless, one has to stand back and notice that this is only a fly, that we are witnessing a powerful and wealthy man fooling about with a fly on his desk. The detached perspective does not deny the fascination of insects, or endorse that casual response which causes people to swat at an insect before it touches upon conscious senses. There is, however, a certain absurdity which should not be missed as the situation gathers importance. Emotional significance does rely upon the reader's becoming as absorbed as the boss in the fly's recuperation. The dimensions of that interest imitate the broader conflict of ludicrousness versus emotional intensity: pathos hovers close to empirical appeal. The manner in which the 'struggling legs' of the fly in the inkwell have cried out 'Help! help!' is only in part an encouragement to sentimentality; the words work also as a simple concretization of abstract distress. Likewise, the clean-up operations of the fly demonstrate painstaking effort and total intentionality. Except to the boss's vulnerable sensitivities, the fly's action does not denote manly perseverance in the face of adversity. The simplicity of the now clean fly's relief mutes the potential anthropomorphism of Mansfield's observation: 'Now one could imagine that the little front legs rubbed against each other lightly, joyfully. The horrible danger was over; it had escaped; it was ready for life again.' The 'horrible danger' is of course the dreadful black fluid in the inkwell, truly horrible from the fly's perspective but tending towards absurdity from ours. One can certainly pity flies and project oneself imaginatively into their tiny crises; even so, the reader realizes as the boss does not that the fly proceeds with life instinctually and not from moral inspiration.

The provocation of the fly's natural recovery to the man who looms above should not be strange to readers. The boss is not deviant; the idea of dropping another blot of ink on the fly simply occurs to him, without rationale, without malice. Herein lies the cleverness of Mansfield's use of a fly instead of a more obviously sentient creature: moral protest must contend with empirical interest. Of course no animal more vital than a fly is likely to turn up in the boss's office, and that too is part of the irony. Should the boss's spirit yearn for communion with the animal, he has only a fly to go upon. No wonder, then, that meaning is subject to maximum stress; meaning wants profundity and has a mere fly on which to exercise itself. One can anthropomorphize the fly and endure the sense of absurdity, or dismiss the fly as simply an insect and put up with the accusatory voice of conscience which calls that attitude cruel. One can indict the boss for obliviousness to another being's suffering, or view the destruction of the fly as an inadvertent by-product of absent-minded experiment. The antinomy resides in the boss himself. His remarks to the fly as it struggles to recuperate imply empathy; he thinks of the fly as a 'plucky little devil' and admires its courage, noting that 'That was the way to tackle things; that was the right spirit. Never say die.' On the third dousing with ink, the boss 'actually had the brilliant notion of breathing on [the fly] to help the drying process.' At the same time as he esteems and even helps the fly, however, he is systematically killing it. He reads a program for living into the fly's persistence, and yet consciously or unconsciously obliterates the life he is supposedly cherishing. If there were consistency in the illustrated disposition towards animals, the voice of moral zeal and apparent encouragement should correspond to the contradictory feeling of hatred, and not to a neutral empirical interest.

Either that neutral interest does reflect hatred, then, or the moral zeal occurs neutrally without true connection to its declared object. As in 'Tobias Mindernickel,' resolution of revealed contradiction is less important than the annulment of faith in formulas for living.

Several other deaths accompany the death of the fly, and these deaths are the source of the 'grinding wretchedness' the boss feels as he flicks the corpse of the fly into his waste-paper basket. The boss's effort to sustain uncontrolled grief (an oxymoronic activity in itself) over the death of his son dies; in effect, the son himself truly dies at this point, for the boss cannot remember that he had been thinking about his son before he became absorbed in the fly's predicament. By a twisted form of logic, the gung-ho approach to life also dies. The boss's seeming capitulation to grief had all along hidden a belief in forging ahead manfully against despair. The fact that the fly cannot symbolize the power of life to triumph over the severest obstacle extinguishes simultaneously the luxuriance in pathos and the hope of a moral cure. With the annihilation of the moral consequence he had tried to invest in the fly, the boss is left with a blank life, a life as idle and unmotivated as the act of dripping ink upon a fly. Thus the spiritual value and distinction the boss had attributed to himself in his feeling for his son evaporates; he falls back into neutrality. He becomes one boss indistinguishable from the others, just as flies are interchangeable one with another from an objective point of view. For this reason, one comes to feel sorry for this normally unpitiable man.

Between 'Tobias Mindernickel' and 'The Fly,' then, polarized views of the animal assault human claims to moral status. Esau the dog embodies the natural animal's superior joy in life; the wounded animality inside Mindernickel strikes out at this joy. The fly represents that animal blankness on which anthropomorphism founders; the boss's attempt to drag out of that blankness some pseudo-hearty moral value succeeds only in killing the fly and his own illusions of significance. What unites the two stories and distinguishes these urban dramas is the existential nature of the encounter with the animal. It is beside the point whether authenticity consists in the ecstatic bodily freedom displayed by the dog or the amoral submission to anonymous fate demonstrated by the fly. Although they are polar opposites, both aspects of the animal disillusion the human protagonist. Since the animal is already an alien being in the urban setting, it is not surprising that the extreme in victimization disables belief in moral sanctities. Those moral sanctities have themselves depended upon suppression of animality within the urban person. Mindernickel's tears and the boss's 'grinding wretchedness' signal the pain of entry into urban anonymity.

RECLAIMING VICTIMIZATION IN THE CRUMBLING CITY: GIORGIO BASSANI'S *THE HERON*

The ultimate in existential encounters is, of course, earnest contemplation of suicide. Given the depths of unhappiness tapped by animal victims in the urban story, it was inevitable that some work of fiction should cause the animal victim to combine with urban decay in a way that initiates thoughts of suicide in the protagonist. Giorgio Bassani brings these elements together in *The Heron*. Perhaps it comes as no surprise that, because the narrative moves towards the resolution of suicide, tensions that have inhered with the animal victim in the three previous stories are dispelled in *The Heron*. While Mindernickel and the boss, and even Jurgis of *The Jungle* struggle to fortify aspects of their personal lives against victimization, Edgardo Limentani of *The Heron* eventually concedes in total to the condition of the victim. The effect of this complete submission is to release the animal from the kinds of conflict and pressure sustained in the slaughterhouse tales, 'Tobias Mindernickel,' and 'The Fly.' The heron, of course, is no less dead by the end of the tale than the dog Esau, the fly, or the many animals that come to the slaughterhouse. Nevertheless, *The Heron* relinquishes the cruelty of circumstance and the cruelty of assault upon the animal, simultaneously as it gives up rationalization of urban existence. Indeed, if one were looking for analogies with the slaughterhouse, the disintegration of the city which Bassani notes in *The Heron* seems unconsciously to imitate the nightmarish dismantling of bodies and of meaning in the slaughterhouse.

Another factor determines the fragmentation of place and personality in *The Heron* and that is the location in history. The setting is northern Italy in 1947. The anti-Semitism suffered by Limentani during the war is supposedly at an end. The communist agitation that has recently raised hostility against him as a landowner has received a political blow with the exclusion from cabinet

of members of the communist party. Understandably, Limentani
has little faith in the apparent change of heart of those who supported the Fascists during the war, and takes little comfort from
official strictures upon resentment against the wealthy. At this
precise time in political history, therefore, Limentani lives in a
permanent state of mistrust.

That mistrust is so deep that it has bodily effects. The heart of
trouble is revealed when, 'with a curiosity, a surprise, and a bitterness never experienced before,' Limentani observes his penis
as he urinates: 'Grey, wretched, pathetic: with that mark of his
circumcision, so familiar and, at the same time, so absurd ... It
was no more than an object, a mere object like so many others'
(p 110). Later, he dreams of unbuttoning his trousers in front of a
prostitute who notes that, where his penis should be, he has
'nothing at all' (p 124).

The act of eating disgusts Limentani; he suffers chronic consti-
pation. At one point, he fills himself with food beyond repletion
and then has to put up with the resulting pain in his stomach and
bowels. The description of his approach to the meal reveals the
impairment of Limentani's relationship with his own body:

He filled his mouth with the sweet-sour pulp of the shellfish, and swallowed: draining then long gulps of wine, or stuffing himself with bread.
Nevertheless, he soon felt disgusted with the food and with himself.
What was the use? he thought. His head bowed, in his corner – in that
heat, in that stink, in that greasy and promiscuous semidarkness – it
was useless for him to chew, to swallow, suck, spit, gulp. (p 103)

Limentani is a victim corporeally at every point that life is sustained. He suffers revulsion both at the source of creation, the
penis, and at the dissolution of physical integrity symbolized by
the elimination of wastes.

Complete alienation from his own physical existence informs
his epiphanic experience, at the novel's climax, in front of the
taxidermist's shop window. He has looked at images of himself in
reflecting surfaces previously; he is as estranged from his own face
as he is from his penis. In the mirror, his face looks as if it 'didn't
belong to him': 'How base and disagreeable his face was, too, he said
to himself, how absurd it was!' (p 6). And just as his penis disappears
in a dream, so too does his reflected image threaten to fade. He sees

himself in a mirror on a wardrobe; it is 'a distant image, barely hinted at, as if it were about to dissolve' (p 117). When he sees his reflection in the window of the taxidermist's shop, he at first tries visually to penetrate the glass, to get rid of his image which is 'barely a shadow, true, but still irksome' (p 157); he wants to 'give himself the illusion that the glass itself didn't exist' (p 157). In fact, he wants to join the animals, who seem to exist in a 'little theater,' speaking to him of immutable beauty in death. There they are, immobilized in postures imitating animal vitality. They have solidity; they are imperishable. They will not disintegrate, but they do not have to struggle with recalcitrant bodies either. The idea of killing himself comes to him. He scans his face again, and sees every feature plainly: 'the bald forehead, the three horizontal lines that crossed it from temple to temple, the long and fleshy nose, the heavy, weary eyelids, the flabby and almost womanish lips, the hole in the chin, the wan cheeks, smudged by his beard' (p 159). His face is not losing its clarity as much as it is reverting to geological ambiguity. His idea, the idea of committing suicide, founds itself in the unequivocal beauty of the stuffed animals.

As his body suffers from heavy meaninglessness, so too is Limentani's life characterized by inertia: it takes him a mighty effort of will to go on the hunting trip which is the core event of the single day in Limentani's life covered by the novel. The start of his trip has the quality of nightmare: time passes on the morning of the hunt, but Limentani makes no progress. He is at last underway when a need to defecate diverts him to the town of Codigoro, to find bathroom facilities. Once there, he is held up by conversation with the café owner, the erstwhile Fascist Bellagamba; it takes him ages in narrative time to ask to use the bathroom, and then further ages to climb the three flights of stairs to the best of the lavatories.

Having finally arrived at the toilet, he sits there straining away and reading old newspaper clippings while his bowels refuse to give him relief. Snipped into a jumble of words and half-words, the newspaper clippings are impenetrable to his desire for meaning. He finds one meaningful headline, and then struggles to recall the date of the event. He searches randomly through the other fragments for help:

[H]e was unable to establish the origin of any of them, but not all were cut from the pages of the same paper, and not all were of the same date.

IGHT TO REBELLI – ATED BY CONSTI, another headline said, in letters even bigger than the first. And another: OGLIATTI AND NENNI – ATTACK GOVERNME; and another still: VE JEWISH BLOOD–IN TODAY'S POLAND. (p 39)

In this manner, the fragmentation of the historical period spirals downward to delay one man, on a toilet, desperately trying to make sense out of his world – or only to enjoy a bowel movement. As he looks out the window, too, he finds the scene of Codigoro and environs incomprehensible: 'Like a surveyor without his necessary instruments, he tried to measure distances and proportions with his naked eye' (p 40). Points, like the Monument of the Dead, a ruined watchtower, and barges' masts, stand out, but how these are related to one another in terms of distances escapes Limentani.

Later in the day, the meaning of the structures brought together under the name 'Codigoro' defies Limentani, just as the newspaper clippings have defied him. Marking this novel as an urban tale most importantly is not the establishment of buildings oppressively fixed on the landscape but the disintegration of place. A lucid instance of this disintegration is the changing of street names in the ancient part of Codigoro. Three years earlier, at the time of the Liberation, the street names had been replaced with the names of heroes of socialism. The old ceramic signs had simply been whitewashed over, and now the hand-painted letters of the streets' new identities are already dissolving away. Limentani spells out 'LO MAR ['Carlo Marx']; ANTON GRAMSCI; E. CURIEL; IUSEPPE TALIN; C E IA ROTTI,' and then mentally fills in the missing letters (p 148). As much as this dissolution symbolizes the fortunes of communism, it also encapsulates the general unhinging of location. Names of places will not stick, any more than the character of the town will remain stable. The central square in Codigoro is a jumble of disparate purposes. The cafes where the aged male residents gather to smoke and drink are located amidst churches, government buildings, and shops, the most telling of which is an agricultural machinery shop whose window displays an American tractor described as 'Something blind and formless, destitute of any function whatever' (p 141). Like the history given in the newspaper clippings, and like the dissolving features of Limentani's own face, the town is losing its identity. Late in the evening, a fog falls over the discongruous structures of Codigoro. With obvious symbolism, Bassani has Limentani wandering through this fog before the character sees his own face in the taxidermist's window and decides that suicide is the one clear and definite course of action available to him.

Limentani finds himself wholly dispossessed. History and place have abandoned him. The hunting trip is his last bid to establish a place for himself in the fragmented post-war reality of northern Italy. But since the hunting trips of gentlemen from the city have become an offensive anachronism in the eyes of the valley folk, and since he has no real inclination to shoot birds in any case, the plan is absurd at its inception. If he knew of the lives of those who affix their identities to urban values, he might have considered it fortunate that he has been expelled psychologically from the neuroses of modern existence. He might have framed a philosophy out of his alienation, a philosophy of self-sacrifice or of rebellion. Instead, he experiences his life as groundless, materially and ontologically. Only the thought of suicide can consolidate this sensation of utter lostness.

There is nothing secure in Limentani on which to base aggression against the birds he is supposed to be killing on his day's hunting. He takes this lack of desire as a failure of virility, but in truth what he lacks are the artificial constructions culture puts upon life. Disabused of philosophies of life, divested of cultural preconception, Limentani is able to see the waterfowl of the marsh with total clarity. In fact, the coots that approach his blind and of course the heron itself are visually the clearest and most coherent elements in the novella as a whole. While Limentani cannot fathom the layout and import of Codigoro and environs, he can see and record minute details of colouring on the coot flying past him: 'slate-black feathers, lightly tinged, on the back, with an olive-yellow; head, neck, tail, and crupper black; the lower parts just a shade lighter; the wingtips white; the beak, flat, bluish; the legs green, shading into orange in the upper part; the red iris, wide, glassy' (pp 84–5). He observes these particulars, as in a dream, all in the instant before the coot is shot down by his hunting guide. Although this perfect image of the coot is followed up by his feeling that 'Nothing, any longer, appeared real' (p 85), the visual immediacy of the bird with its life in threat contradicts, not reality *per se,* but the unreality of modern urbanism.

The heron and its injuries assume an intense presence in Limentani's mind. That is to say, he sees the heron with complete lucidity and also makes meaning out of its suffering. He comes up with a simile for the heron: it is 'like an old Caproni plane' (p 85), like 'the kind of plane they used in the First World War, all canvas, wires and wood' (p 87). He observes the heron so closely that he notes that on its 'perfectly smooth' head 'something fragile stood up, from the back: a kind of wire, an antenna, who knows?' (p 86). The 'antenna,' of course, is the fine, slicked-back crest of the heron. The machine analogy that Limentani initially conceives gives way before appreciation of the creatural particulars of the bird. As it comes face-to-face with him in his hunter's blind, Limentani observes that it is brown 'all over, except for the feathers of the neck and breast, a delicate beige tone, and except for the legs, the yellow-brown of fleshless bone, or relics' (p 89). He imagines, also, what the wounded bird is thinking as it paces around the marsh:

[I]t still tried to get its bearings, to recognize, if not the places, at least the nature of the objects surrounding it. A few steps away, for example, it noticed the punt, half on land and half in the water. What was that? A boat, or perhaps the body of a great sleeping animal? Best to keep out of its way, anyhow. (pp 87–8)

It is no wonder that Limentani identifies with the heron 'completely' (p 88). The injured bird cannot find its bearings, just as he cannot. It too is bewildered; it too is a victim.

The thoughts Limentani ascribes to the wounded heron could well be his own as he moves uncertainly through the post-war landscape: 'Where am I? ... And what's happened to me' (p 87), he imagines the heron thinking. He can't shoot at the heron to put it out of its misery because that would be 'shooting in a sense at himself' (p 91). Despite this identification, Limentani has in fact very little identity to project onto the animal. The process seems, rather, to work in the reverse, with the heron giving a voice, briefly, and a body to the man's diffuse distress. Later, when he is cast adrift in Codigoro, with no plans and the prospect of nothing but more inertia in the future, he hangs on to the heron's experience to understand his own. What should he do? he wonders: 'Stay here, then? But to what end? Before its eyes, from loss of blood, had become hooded, the heron must have felt much as he felt now: hemmed in on all sides, without the slightest possibility of escape' (p 145). Limentani's predicament is so profoundly without resolution that his state of mind approximates animal perplexity. Just as the heron finds nothing in its store of knowledge to determine how it was wounded, why it cannot fly any more, and what it is supposed to do now, so too is Limentani divested of an explanation for his circumstances and of the power to change them.

The artlessness of the pain shared by the heron and the man prohibits sentimental anthropomorphism. There is a tender moment during the period of the heron's bewilderment: still preserving its slow-stepping grace, the heron comes right up to the hogshead where Limentani is hiding; it 'huddle[s] against the hogshead ... just like a shivering old man, seeking the sun' (p 89). From his position inside the blind, Limentani can no longer see the heron; yet he senses its movements by sound and, virtually, by touch through the side of hogshead. The potential for benevolent condescension is great in this instant, but Limentani's lack of ego and the author's existential aim combine to uphold the creatural dignity of the heron in its confusion. Where drama could infuse the analogy of animal and human, we find instead that the human is reduced to the simple yet profound act of seeking the warmth of the sun. Limentani's empathy with the heron is based not on pre-existing directives of conscience or cultural acquisition but on the plain physical proximity of the injured animal.

There is, therefore, a noticeable absence of ideology or self-congratulation in Limentani's thought of rescuing the heron and taking it to a veterinarian in the city. The plan originates *ex nihilo,* simply as procedural rectification of misfortune, and not as moral or sentimental mandate. In a cultural setting where a desire to shoot birds is one of the norms of masculinity, the impulse to pay a veterinarian to heal a conventionally worthless heron is truly incredible. A person more secure than Limentani in his or her alienation from social norms would perhaps have carried through with the plan of saving the heron. It is a pity that he does not follow the impulse to rescue the heron; the creativeness of the plan, in contradistinction to the decomposition of the cultural context, makes it a reasonable alternative to suicide as a solution to the victim mentality. Standing in outright opposition to convention, the plan has a quality of existential authenticity similar to that which has arisen from the deaths of animals in the previously discussed urban stories. It is a revelation, if not dramatically as the point of climax, then at least in its qualitative distinctiveness from any other type of thought represented in the story. To every person of his acquaintance, from any perspective available in the culture as given, Limentani would have appeared a lunatic had he reached out of his blind, taken hold of the heron, wrapped it in a blanket and bundled it into his car, then driven this wild creature to the urban centre and requested of city mentality and technology that it muster itself on behalf of a being whose value and even existence are wholly unrecognized in that setting. The effect would have been much the same as if Katherine Mansfield's 'boss' had rushed his ink-clogged fly into a laboratory for cleaning under a microscope. In Limentani's situation, nothing legitimates his desire to rescue the heron apart from that socially illegitimate object, the heron's suffering.

There is no hope, then, for the heron. The faint thought that would have become Limentani's existential breakthrough into healthy eccentricity is instead converted into its opposite, an equally existential submission to victimization in its fullest meaning. Instead of temporizing with victimization, accepting some of it and pretending that the rest does not truly imply what it implies, Limentani manages to fuse the bodily, hence animal, will to persist with what is in fact a physical sensation that he is a victim right down to the substance of his identity.

The death of the heron enters into Limentani's deliberations in front of the taxidermist's window display. The collection of stuffed animals appears to him to have achieved physical stability, to have arrived at a state of corporeal perfection no longer menaced by pain or time. They stand in *tableau vivant,* alongside an assortment of hunting equipment. The fox posed between a pair of rubber boots expresses 'an overwhelming, almost insolent health, saved as if by enchantment from any possible harm, of today or tomorrow' (p 158). The life of the fox has become immune to the kind of offence given to the heron. In its frozen posture the fox exemplifies life, but this is life beyond questioning, life not subject to interpretation and misinterpretation, distortion and injury. To Limentani's wounded imagination, the stuffed animals represent life in a state of totality, and identity in a state of completion. The exhibited unity of death and physical integrity comes to Limentani as a revelation: by means of suicide, he can seize control of the victimization his society has inflicted upon him; the question of his existence falls into his own power instead of other people's.

The personalized correspondence between human and animal in *The Heron* has significant benefits for the heron – for the heron, that is to say, both as a literary object with meaning, and as a natural animal such as one might encounter in a local marsh. The quality of relatedness between Limentani and the heron in fact stands as a revolutionary novelty against the backdrop of cultural insensitivity. In contrast to the depersonalization effected by cities, there is a concrete expression of attention to the individual in Limentani's feeling for the heron. Without the prodding of doctrine or gratification of conceit, Limentani simply experiences the heron as an individual creature in pain. He understands the animal integrity of the single bird. It is this fundamental integrity that urban society puts in exile. At base, amidst the clamour and ostentation of urbanism, the life of the individual animal, and the animal life that individual humans share with that individual animal, suffers the supreme and totally irrational offence of being set at nothing.

No wonder, then, that when Limentani takes heed of his own body, in the utter absence of kindliness well-grounded in the world, he mistakes cultural disownment for an authentic discovery. In the sense that urban culture conceals its contempt for the individual, Limentani has indeed encountered truth. Where he goes wrong, and completely wrong, is in imagining that the suicide solution originates with his own psyche, that in killing himself he will act upon his personal, elemental will in opposition to cultural imperatives. The irony is that his culture whispers to him that he is worthless and he has misheard the insidious voice as his own. He thinks he can at last assert his genuine, free decision against social values, but he is instead accepting, bodily, social and cultural rejection of identity. After this paradoxically true and erroneous insight, living on would mean tolerating constant awareness of dissimulation. At this point, the heron takes on critical relevance. The heron gives secure creaturely grounds for living under such conditions. Limentani has truly betrayed himself and his reason for living in allowing the heron to die.

CONCLUSION

From Mindernickel to Limentani, we have reached the place at which polarized tensions invoked by the animal victim stand face to face with each other. The bogus sentimentality underpinned by authentic viciousness in Mindernickel looks across at the authentic friendliness in Limentani which is undermined by habitual and hence inauthentic aggression. Materialized contradiction has run to general dematerialization, and all with the animal as a steady point of reference. It becomes apparent that, despite its grimness, Thomas Mann's vision contains an element of optimism for urban culture which is simply washed away in the seventy years separating his story and Bassani's. We can cope with civilization and its discontents; we cannot make headway with civilization minus contents – if such obvious word play is not too offensive. We can be at home in contradiction; we cannot be at home in unreality. We can live with disturbed identities; we cannot live with no identity. For the urban person, domestication and victimization become one and the same thing.

The Heron takes the relationship between urban disintegration and the individual's disownment of his or her own animal corpus as far as that relationship can go. Were the animals destined for the slaughterhouse subject to existential despair, they too might find it useless 'to chew, to swallow, suck, spit, gulp' as Limentani does, and might find suicide the means by which they could retrieve their personal integrity from the complete disregard they suffer in their particular circumstances. I raise the image of suicidal farm animals for two reasons: to indicate, on the one hand, the degree to which human constructions like slaughterhouses and, I would argue, cities can negate individual identity, and on the other hand to suggest the distance Limentani, the boss, and Mindernickel have put between their identity and the patient immediacy of creatural existence. Of the slaughterhouse tales covered at the beginning of this chapter, only the surreal satire of Roald Dahl's 'Pig' comes close to expressing the full meaning of urban victimization of animal and human. One simple conclusion that may be drawn from all these urban stories is that the animal victim invokes both the varieties and depth of dispossession experienced by city-dwellers. In the process, these stories express extreme distrust of such forces of civilization as the city represents. The comprehensiveness of the critique relies, furthermore, upon narrative recognition of the animal victim's particularity. It is this quality in the animal which brings the issue of victimization home to the human individual, making victimization an intimate rather than a social dilemma. From such existential puzzles, we turn next to works of fiction which implicate the animal victim in the even more intimate realm of human sexuality.

5 Animal Victims and Human Sexuality: *Body Trouble*

INTRODUCTION

It might have been appropriate to follow the pattern of the foregoing chapters and title this one 'Animal Victims in a Pastoral Setting.' Certainly the dynamics of the stories to be discussed in this chapter are significantly affected by the authors' choice of a rural scene. City-dwellers appeal to the rural environment to correct many of the neuroses caused by harried urban existence. The rural environment supplies a manageable dose of nature, just enough to produce the appropriate contemplative mood, but not so much that the aching urban soul will be overwhelmed with the antipathy of nature to human construction. In modern stories, however, the choice of a rural setting enables the expression of another vast confusion in culture which generates animal victims. If the stories about animals in the wild raise issues of morality and stories involving animals in urban circumstances induce existential dilemmas, stories that work with animals in pastoral circumstances unearth peculiarities in human attitudes towards sexuality. Not surprisingly, the domain situated between the wilderness, with its defiance of human control, and the city, with its obsessive celebration of civilization, invokes that similarly troubled region of the human psyche, that sexual wilderness which human culture seeks most fervently to prune and transform. We know of the ambivalences and paradoxes that invade cultural responses to sexual activity. The strains upon what should be one of the more natural acts of the human animal are brought forcefully into consciousness with acts of aggression against nonhuman animals.

Now, one would expect to find animals here and there on the landscape in any pastoral story. Part of what makes orthodox pastoralism pastoral is its deployment of comfortable animals, the domestic beasts of the farms and fields, or cheerful little birds and rodents which pose no threat to human control. One would expect, too, that the modern pastoral story would address problems in sexuality, since sexual expression should, in theory, be safe in this semi-human, semi-natural environment. In theory, the pastoral setting should be sufficiently natural and yet sufficiently civilized to allow for wholesome sexual expression. When the happy theoretical arrangement, of animals on the landscape and human couples amiably retiring to the fields or woods for sexual intimacies, breaks down, as it inevitably does, sexual conflict reaches across to those placid animals off in the distance and victimizes them. Apparently, the pastoral mode does not overcome sexual tension; if the animal victims in these stories tell us anything, they indicate the exacerbation of culture's deeply repressed feelings about sexual intercourse.

It is, of course, wholesome in itself merely to look at sexual activity, since our culture has been so overwrought about sexuality that it has had to pretend that men and women do not copulate – like animals. It is at the time of 'making love' that the human being wishes most ardently to declare: 'I am not an animal.' Psychological mechanisms and social institutions have arisen to lend cultural significance to unceremonious coupling. What would otherwise be plain mating is decorated with romance, erotica, and bawdiness. Religious and legal rituals convert sexual union into a fundamental social bond. Society and culture cannot bear to have men and women coming together freely to mate and then going on their ways with equal insouciance. The morality that condemns sexual promiscuity protects basic social structures and imposes cultural structures upon consciousness. By means of embellishment for disguise and conceptual apparatus for sublimation, humanity has attempted to transform its sexual union into an act utterly different from that in which animals engage. If biology offends our cultural selves, it seems to offend us most intensely at a genital level. We can pride ourselves on having outstripped animals in social development and technological power. But however much mystification we practise, at some point human individuals of opposite sexes are going to have to concede to making genital contact in much the same way as animals do.

Given the importance of sexual neurosis to culture, it is significant that the theory of evolution emerges at a time when sexual repression is in its most tyrannical phase. In an age when people are most vigorously disavowing their creatural sexual acts, they are suddenly required to conceive of themselves as fundamentally interlinked with the rest of animal creation. The ideological and religious arguments that followed upon Darwin's theory have philosophical importance, but one would expect that the site of deepest disturbance would have been the erogenous zones. The secrecy already surrounding sexuality apparently prohibited conscious realization of the implications of the idea of evolution for procreative intimacies. But while there may be no direct expression of outrage at the revolution to the perception of sexuality implicit in Darwinism, agitation of pre-Darwinian sanctities manifests itself in efforts to preserve those sanctities. The insecurity of post-Darwinian observations on human sexual habits, that is to say, reveals at least subconscious unhinging of over-constructed elaborations upon natural copulation. When copulation enters the picture, it becomes clear that acknowledgment of the human species' connection with animals threatens a massive amount of cultural material. It can hardly be surprising, then, that modern authors wrestling with sexuality generate animal victims in the process of undermining cultural categorizations of sexual experience.

Sexual intercourse and the killing of animals are linked by a similar problem: Can we commit these acts in innocence? The myth of Eden combines these two dilemmas by positing the innocence of nakedness along with the absence of at least human death. In the Edenic myth, the body is evidently inviolate to both shame and suffering. Many questions are left unanswered by the biblical account of this myth. It is unclear whether the first man and woman need to engage in sexual intercourse before the fall; and it is equally unclear whether or not the human or animal diet requires the death of nonhuman animals. Nevertheless, a state of innocence apparently presides over all natural acts, even if those include sexual intercourse and eating other animals. In an indirect and necessarily unsuccessful fashion, the modern pastoral story attempts to cobble together that ideal state of guiltless sex and reconciliation with mortality.

From a modern ethical perspective, of course, anxieties over the killing of animals are entirely legitimate. Similar anxieties over sexual intercourse are less well founded than those which adhere to causing the death of another living being, and yet the association of guilt with sexual intercourse has rarely been denounced or even questioned over the centuries prior to the modern age. Fairly arbitrary conventions determine whether sexual intercourse is wicked or merely naughty, or consummates the purest of loves. The crux of the problem is that the innocent coupling of nonhuman animals has been treated with disgust, particularly by religious doctrines. Human sexuality is also treated as unwholesome to the extent that it imitates the habits of animals. Unflattering comparisons with pigs, dogs, and rabbits are made. Humankind submits to its base, bestial instincts in following through on sexual desire without some intervening cultural transformation. Innocent biological drives, then, are landed with a heavy burden of guilt. Even the wholly unassuming body becomes an object of sin, with certain parts provoking secrecy so grave as to magnify those parts monstrously or cause them to vanish, depending upon the kind of authority which attends to them. In view of the thicket of moral judgments that surrounds plain animal mating in humankind, much more is going on in the association of sexuality and the victimization of animals than the simple discharge of psychological frustration.

One dimension of sexual existence and animal victims has been touched upon already in the previous chapter. It could be argued that part of what is wrong with Thomas Mann's Tobias Mindernickel and Katherine Mansfield's 'boss' is a fundamental obstruction of sexual need. Both men seem to suffer from psychic castration. Objectless sexual tension could be the source of their violence against animals. There is no need to speculate upon the protagonist of *The Heron:* he is overtly afflicted with sexual debilities. Unlike the other characters, Edgardo Limentani recognizes and accepts sexual dysfunction. He also evinces unambivalent empathy with the nonhuman animal; sexual impairment does not run underground in him, creating havoc and hostility. He looks squarely at his penis and finds it pathetic; he dreams that he has no penis at all. He takes ingrained cultural aggression against animals and turns it on himself. His story illustrates, in effect, a culturally based association of sexlessness with compassion for animals.

In the stories to be discussed in this chapter, the converse of this association also comes into play. If those who are sexually naïve or neutered in one way or another display fondness for animals, those who are sexually alert kill or torment animals as a mark of their passion. Although complicated by various permutations, the simple dichotomy constitutes a starting place for thought on the subject. What is remarkable about this dichotomy is that it is the complete reverse of what one would expect would follow from the Darwinian assertion of continuity between humans and animals. The idea of continuity should validate empathy with animals simultaneously as it promotes calm assent to such fundamental animal functions as sexual intercourse. One should find in post-Darwinian stories that persons in tune with sexual passion are also in tune with animal life, with the result that they leave animals alone. Ignorance or prudishness on the score of sexuality should be the qualities that lead to cruelty to animals. Instead, authors who deal with sexuality in the climate of Darwinian thought tend to revert to a pre-modern connection of sexuality with bestiality, of lust for sex with a lust to kill.

In *The Tender Carnivore and the Sacred Game,* Paul Shepard asserts that there is a 'primal' link between hunting and sexual intercourse:

The symbiotic interplay of the hunt and love, of predation and copulation, is a primal motif, surely preliterate, and older than the agricultural theme of the cycle of birth and death ... The spear's interpenetration of the body and the flesh as the source of all new life are the iconography of venery – at once the pursuit of love and game. (p 169)

He speaks of 'the most profound of life's passions, the demonic moment of the kill and of orgasm' as 'related' moments (p 170). He says that the human hunter is distinct from the animal predator because of 'hundreds of centuries of treating the woman-prey with love, which he turns back into the hunt proper'; and he adds that the 'ecstatic consummation of this love is the killing itself' (p 173). I quote Shepard here to illustrate the extreme form that association of sexual intercourse and hunting can take. Shepard is, of course, offering his views as truths of the human condition. It is perhaps more accurate to observe that he articulates a long-standing belief in the correspondence of male sexual prowess with prowess as a hunter. A subconscious attitude like that which Shepard exemplifies could perhaps explain some of the stranger passions and sources of trouble among the writers trying to deal with sexuality.

It seems true that human beings do confound the actual, physical motions of sexual intercourse with some idea of aggression, perhaps because of the deviation into turbulence from normal, erect self-control. Guilt and extreme privacy also enhance the feeling that we are doing something wrong, hence aggressive, when we have sexual intercourse. The spill-over of these intense feelings into impressions of the nature of hunting and killing animals is strange but common enough to plague conceptions of sexuality. In any event, some modern writers evidently believe that they are regenerating human sexuality by distancing ideas of romantic love from sexual desire and interjecting an element of aggression. At base, the introduction of aggressivity might be an attempt to explain, simply, why sexual intercourse is something out of the ordinary in spite of its being almost as regular a practice as washing one's hair. If the introduction of the idea of aggression is meant to explain the thrill which tinges human sexuality, it also gives new life to the old-fashioned impression that sexual intimacies are sinful.

While a regression to outmoded belief may be rationalized on the grounds that sexual intercourse pure and simple has been a taboo subject for centuries, and that quantities of subterranean material have not been dealt with and require articulation, it remains odd that permission to address sexuality elicits the stereotype of nature as 'red in tooth and claw.' Maturity on the matter of sexual desire is difficult to achieve. Writers are, after all, struggling against deep-seated adversity to the whole subject of human sexual encounters. The irritation that arises from the effort apparently finds a target in the animals that happen to be present on the scene. With the deepest of ironies, animals are sacrificed to human search for healthy genital intercourse.

What healthy genital intercourse would look or feel like has become entirely unclear in modern culture. The vast reservoir of yet to be realized material precludes the establishment of ideals, despite strenuous efforts on the part of authors like Mary Webb and D.H. Lawrence to break down orthodoxies and hint at a better way of being. If there is some hidden ideal at work in the pastoral story, it is certainly not the blithe gratification of desire, the casual coming and going, that characterizes animal mating. Authors cling to the idea of elaborations upon ordinary sexual congress, even though they may object to the particular romantic or prurient elaborations that culture has enshrined. This inability to conceptualize explicit ideals does have merit. Ideals tend to produce further repression, as current demands for orgasmic performance in our supposedly liberal era attest. Nevertheless, the remoteness of any idea of healthy sexuality has left authors floundering about amongst clichés and neuroses. Since animality appears to be the reason for the struggle in the first place, the animal falls victim to narrative hostility. Authors are not separating themselves from the violence their characters practise upon animals. An unacknowledged assumption seems to be that if the narrative of human sexuality will not come out cleanly, the animal must be to blame.

In the first three stories to be discussed in this chapter, the authors attempt to reduce the confusion in attitudes towards sexuality by offering their protagonists two clear and antithetical choices of person. One of these persons represents, roughly speaking, asexual love; the other represents, again roughly speaking, unlicensed sexual passion. The sexual being of the protagonist vacillates painfully between alternatives, producing considerable unsteadiness in narrative progress. The narrative of Mary Webb's *Gone to Earth,* for example, swerves between the decision of the protagonist Hazel Woodus first to accept the advances of the squire Jack Reddin who appeals to her sexual desire, then to marry the minister who offers her respectability, then to escape from respectability to the squire's mansion and erotic appeal, then to return to the love of her minister husband, and finally to plunge with her pet fox into death at the bottom of an abandoned quarry. Niels Lindstedt, of Frederick Philip Grove's *Settlers of the Marsh,* delays proposing to the prudish woman he loves for so long that he is tricked by his own naïvety into marriage with the local prostitute. In Lawrence's *The Fox,* Nell March is caught between a mystic attachment to the boyish killer of the fox of the title and loyalty to her fussy, repressed, near-lesbian comrade Jill. Despite the clarity of the choices available to Niels, Hazel, and Nell, then, the whole issue of sexuality radically disrupts narrative cause and effect. The consequent strain upon the human need for resolution is evidenced by the fact that all three stories end effectively in murder.

A virtual parody of murder closes John Steinbeck's 'The White Quail,' as well. Indeed the 'murder' has behind it the theme of virility and the hunt addressed in other of the stories. In addition, 'The White Quail' brings into focus a phenomenon evident in the other three stories: in the modern story, marriage does not guarantee happiness. Marriage, in other words, does not set the seal of perfection upon sexual relations. Only a rather unthinking modern comedy could posit marriage as a passage into fulfilment. If the implication of all the old tales which end joyously in marriage is that the couple will now go off and experience complete and guiltless sexual accord, modern tales clearly put the value of sexual harmony ahead of the benefits of marriage. The grim, joyless marriage of the Tellers in 'The White Quail' brings one to realize that none of the marriages in the other stories are successful either.

Sexual passion remains unresolved. Unresolved, sexual passion in turn creates havoc in relations between men and women. Narratively speaking, the explosion into violence against animals allows authors to show how much havoc sexual tensions produce, and how vitally sexuality opposes the normal social order of human relations. Animals are scapegoated, certainly, but the complication is that authors are also attempting to retrieve a conception of sexual health by breaking down pious notions of compassion. Conversely, by injecting the idea of sexual passion into the subject of feelings about animals, these authors are also reaching for a full-bodied, as opposed to a purely mental, appreciation of the animal, to use Lawrencean terminology. A troubling aspect of this dynamic is that, like rationalizations for the hunt, it approves of the killing of animals as part and parcel of the lusty way of life. We begin, then, with *Settlers in the Marsh,* in which a man achieves sexual maturity by shooting both his wife and his horse.

THE CREEPINESS OF ADULT INNOCENCE: UNSETTLING OF THE MARSH

Niels Lindstedt murders a great deal more than his wife and horse at the climax of *Settlers of the Marsh.* He murders, also, his sexual innocence and the related illusion of personal power that had permitted him to create a prosperous farm upon the stark Canadian prairie. Frederick Philip Grove is a master at planting

large men upon the barren prairie landscape. His particular genius was for conveying the slow struggle of these men to compel
more and more land to produce greater and greater yields against
the reluctance of the soil and the vagaries of climate. While the
raw work of originating a homestead appeals to his imagination,
however, he is sensitive to the point at which mastery of the land
overbalances and becomes ostentation. The fortunes of Abe
Spalding in Grove's *Fruits of the Earth,* for example, begin to collapse once Abe constructs a mansion and barn complete with the
most modern technological gadgetry. Likewise, Grove puts Niels's
ambition in increasing peril simultaneously as Niels distinguishes
himself from his less successful neighbours in building a large
and neatly appointed house which he thinks of as 'a palace in the
wilderness' (p 70). The prairie, it seems, is easily offended. The
settler's place in the landscape is highly tenuous; should he over-
step the point at which hardship ends, he wins only bitter disillusionment. As disillusionment deepens within Grove's victorious
settler, it connects up with the sexual continuum. The uncultivated
prairie appears literally to be virgin at the start of a Grove novel.
The chaste male patiently romances the prairie, receiving love
offerings of acreage and hay in return. Grove does not, however,
perpetuate the idea of the land as symbolic earth mother bearing
fruit under human cultivation. No doubt the barrenness of the
prairie itself thwarts notions of natural fecundity; the land rules
out any sense of harmonious propagation. Farms are established
against the will of the prairie.

Foreboding punctuates Niels Lindstedt's rise to mastery over
the prairie in *Settlers of the Marsh.* With his prosperity confirmed
in the construction of his 'palace in the wilderness,' he still post-
pones asking the chaste Ellen Amundsen to marry him. The
chapter concluding the ascent of his fortunes ends with the words,
'Something dreadful was coming, coming ...' (p 85). That 'something dreadful' appears immediately in the next chapter in the
form of Clara Vogel, local prostitute and female predator. Clara
Vogel is certainly a recognizable stereotype among culture's representations of the sexual woman. She also ends up as a scapegoat to cultural hostility to sexuality. She inveigles a ride from
town in Niels's wagon. She admires his horses: 'Why Niels ...
what a team!' (p 90), she observes, almost as if she were remarking upon Niels's virility, and 'she smiled at him from her black,

beady eyes when the horses bent into their collars and stretched the traces.' The description of her eyes as black and beady enhances the association of this woman with animals. The straining of the horses has an undeniable hint of sexual tumescence about it.

With the introduction of sexual connotations, the straightforward economic wisdom of Niels's decision to buy magnificent Percheron horses gives way to what are for him impure implications. Instead of looking at those implications directly, Niels experiences disquiet at the level of his relationship with the prairie. The heady atmosphere of illicit sensuality emanating from the woman causes Niels to doubt the power he had seemed to effect in his victory over the land:

He felt as if he were thrown back into chaos ...

He had thought that he had fought all this down years ago. His conquest had been a specious one. He had conquered by the aid of a fickle ally: circumstances ... Something was still stirred in him by this woman, something low, disgraceful ... (p 90)

The suppression of sexual interest evidently represents a foundational element of Niels's triumph over the prairie, or at least that is what his interpretation of events tells him. He had thought, subconsciously, that his pristine, non-sexual nature had somehow elicited approval and prosperity from the prairie. Evidence of uncontrol in nature and in his own being shakes his faith in personalized mastery.

The third chapter of *Settlers of the Marsh* is not, however, Clara Vogel's chapter; it belongs, instead, to Ellen Amundsen, as its title informs us. Within Grove's peculiar conception of sexuality, Ellen Amundsen, too, is 'something dreadful': a woman with a deep loathing for sexual intercourse. Her loathing has sprung from witnessing her father essentially kill her mother with his demand to exercise his conjugal rights upon her ailing and exhausted body. As her mother dies in her arms, Ellen resolves never to put herself in a man's power, and to become as competent as any man in farm work so that she will never have to submit to a man's sexual needs.

This horror of sexuality is not Ellen's alone. It is evident, of course, in Niels's feeling that his response to Mrs Vogel is 'low' and 'disgraceful.' It is evident, more pertinently, in the author's preclusion of a conceptual middle ground for Niels between the sensible but sexually unapproachable woman and the opulent, lascivious temptress. A peculiarly coy episode occurs at the centre of the 'Ellen' chapter, an episode which is apparently meant to denote paradisiacal sexual innocence. Ellen and Niels, it must be remembered, are people of about thirty years old, mature in most ways except for their immovable virginity. On the day that the issue of marriage is about to come to a head, the author suddenly starts calling them 'the boy and the girl.' If that affectation were not debilitating enough to any notion of sexual maturity, Grove slides into the present tense in the middle of the episode. The dalliance of 'the boy and the girl' remains comfortably in the past tense while the couple stray happily through the rustic scene, observing birds and rabbits and picking berries. But for some reason, Grove wants to be in the present tense when Nature, in the role of a rain-storm, takes up the burden of the sexual tension in the narrative. The circumstance which instigates the shift from past to present tense involves horses.

The pivotal incident occurs when the happiness of these innocents is about to be interrupted by contact with a man and a woman driving a buggy along the road. The impulse of Niels and Ellen to flee from the social responsibility of conversation is certainly understandable. Nevertheless, their flight turns also upon a strangely ambiguous statement concerning the horses pulling the democrat. Horses, Grove explains, 'are scary in the bush' (p 96). Horses, that is to say, are *nervous* in the bush; but the meaning of 'scary' that comes automatically to mind marks the horses as frightening creatures prompting the reflex to escape. Obvious sexual symbolism attaches itself to horses, symbolism which might indeed prove ominous to 'a boy and a girl.' Niels and Ellen run away from the snorting animals to hide in the 'virgin bush.' In so doing, they temporarily forestall the conscious awareness of the sexuality that would unite them as two mature people and situate them in time and nature. They enter the idyllic present, where they can remain innocent.

Just as the horses have symbolically isolated and carried away with them implications of sexual passion, so too does nature perform the task of sexual expression for the boy and the girl. There is overt sexual energy in Grove's description of the coming storm:

The air is breathless: even the slight wafting flow from the east has ceased. Nature lies prostrate in expectation of the scourge that is coming, coming. The wall of cloud has differentiated: there are two, three waves of almost black; in front a circling festoon of loose, white, flocculent manes, seething, whirling ... A winking of light runs through the first wave of black. A distant rumbling heralds the storm ... (p 98)

Note that Grove again invokes the imagery of horses in likening the first wave of clouds to horses' manes. Straightforward details of sexual ardour inhere with the breathlessness of the air and the reference to nature lying 'prostrate in expectation.' Much Freudian innuendo could be taken from the fact that Niels and Ellen conceal themselves from the storm in a cavern Niels has made in the side of a haystack: perhaps the boy and the girl have regressed even farther from adulthood in a symbolic return to the womb. In any event, the decidedly unpastoral storm relieves the virginal couple of the necessity to act upon sexual pressures. At the end of the chapter, Ellen tells Niels the story of her sexual repression and Niels, disturbed and disillusioned, heads off to his fateful liaison with Mrs Vogel.

Clara Vogel virtually rapes Niels. Given the novel's preconceptions, forcible seduction seems to be the only way Niels will ever have any sexual experience. Niels is not grateful, and Grove himself does not challenge Niels's censure of the woman. After giving Clara only one brief kiss of passion in the park, Niels 'almost hated the woman for what she had done to him' (p 121). Subsequent events confirm his extreme and almost laughable reaction. When Clara comes to his hotel room that same night and, to use a suitably old-fashioned phrase, has her way with him, Niels is so naïve that he believes he is now obliged to marry her.

The marriage is a disaster. As their marriage degenerates, Niels wonders what brought them together in the first place. The line that follows immediately upon this question is delivered with authorial conviction: 'Lust was the defiling of an instinct of nature: it was sin' (p 138). This novel may well posit that remaining chaste is an instinct of human nature; it is difficult to comprehend, however, how nature may be said to repudiate lust when horses and storms manifestly articulate an amoral version of sexual passion.

Clara Vogel is the author's scapegoat to his own ambivalence over sexuality. Her charge that Niels has committed a crime in marrying her and then refusing to 'reconquer [her] from day to day' (p 155) falls into the same category as the awkward melodrama which would have the virginal Niels overcome by the temptress. Statements that defend desire for sexual intercourse, in other words, descend to a level of implausible and artificial theatricality. The attitudinal dynamic of the novel requires Clara to lapse into vengeful promiscuity. The adulterous liaisons she takes up to punish Niels for his innocence strain credibility. Eventually, she invites strange men to Niels's 'palace in the wilderness.' At one point, she lies in the arms of a lover, kissing him and gazing mockingly at Niels, who has accidentally stumbled upon the scene (p 174). Niels discharges whatever anger he might feel in hard work and long hours of Bible-reading.

As in all tragedy, the crisis that breaks this stasis is precipitated by knowledge. Finally, one of Niels's neighbours supplies him with the information he had not known before: his wife, as the entire district was aware, was the local prostitute. For some reason, this piece of information affects Niels more deeply than all of his wife's blatant infidelities. The news kindles suppressed rage in him and sends him off to shoot his wife and to shoot also, not incidentally, his favourite Percheron, Jock. It should be noted, here, that there is no plausible reason for Niels to shoot the horse, outside of the author's frustration with natural sexuality. Niels is overwrought, certainly; but an equally and perhaps more credible psychological response in him might have been the destruction of his palace in the wilderness. Surely, Clara has ruined his dream and not his affection for his horses. Appropriate as the shooting of the horse is to the problem of virility, Niels has thus far been so puritanical – with authorial approval – that he seems devoid of the sexual knowingness that would cause him to select Jock as a target of his rage. Grove, on the other hand, does possess the requisite ambivalence.

It would be pleasant to believe that Grove knew the vulgar meaning of the word 'jock.' Throughout *Settlers of the Marsh*, he has adopted so coy and moralistic an attitude towards sexual matters that an off-colour in-joke would go a long way towards redeeming him as a commentator. In addition to being a jaunty sort of name for a horse, 'Jock,' of course, is a slang term for the penis. It is already fairly obvious that in shooting Jock, Niels is symbolically annihilating some aspect of his sexual being; but if one could determine that Grove was aiming for a direct correspondence between the horse and the male organ, the relation between the animal and sexuality would then rise to a complexity that would in turn lend much needed ambiguity to the moral scheme of the novel as a whole.

The Percherons are a likeable, if peripheral, presence in the novel. They have appeared on the scene as a sign of Niels's success; they are indispensable in his only sphere of power, the farm work. The horses befriend Niels unguardedly; they nicker at him when he appears. He is more comfortable with Jock than he is with the people in the novel, and the horse is kinder to him than the people are. To say this is not to argue for misanthropy. Rather, if one translates the friendly intercourse between man and horse into the symbolic value implied by the pun on the name 'jock,' the conclusion one comes to is that Niels does express phallic knowledge, although in sublimated form. Grove cannot, therefore, be as prudish as he seems when only surface values are taken into consideration. Nor is his novel communicating nothing but aversion to sexuality. Whether Grove is conscious of it or not, the horses do sustain a natural energy of a kind that is nowhere else in evidence in the novel. That energy is pointedly transmuted into sexual energy all in the instant that Niels shoots Jock.

There is, however, a significant complication to the interpretation of the horse as the traditional embodiment of phallic power, and that is the fact that Jock is a gelding. Indeed, when he is first introduced into the novel, Jock is described as an 'enormous gelding' (p 82), which might seem to be something of a contradiction in terms. The shooting of the horse is so important that Grove goes over it twice in the novel, once when the farmhand discovers Niels with the gun in his hand and Jock 'convulsively kicking his last at [Niels's] feet' (p 182), and again later when the entire sequence of events is explained in detail. It is on the second telling of the incident that the word 'gelding' becomes crucial. In fact, so that we do not miss the point, Grove repeats the word 'gelding' twice in the brief description of Niels's entry into the barn:

Niels, swaying again, came very near to the rump of the gelding.

Jock, as the door was opened, had turned his head. When his master swayed near him, he, expecting a blow, kicked out.

Niels raised his gun and shot the gelding through the head ... (p 187)

Niels could be symbolically abolishing his emasculated self in killing his castrated horse. It could be said, then, that recognition of the true nature of his marriage has launched Niels forcibly into sexual maturity.

Supporting this interpretation of Niels's act is the achievement of the traditional sexual order at the end of the novel. When Niels comes home from prison several years after these events, he takes on the role of 'the man' to Ellen's long-protracted girlhood. Where Niels once played, in effect, 'the girl' to Clara's sexual assertiveness, he now assumes the position of the experienced male beside the properly inexperienced female. The 'man' and 'the girl' take another walk through the bush. It is spring; the birds are fluttering about and the leaves rustle gently in the breeze. There is not a hint of a storm on the horizon; no horses appear on the road to disturb the couple. Pastoral innocence has returned, and in keeping with this bucolic tranquillity is the romance Niels and Ellen are to share: 'It is not passion that will unite them; what will unite them is love' (p 216). Accepting this new relationship as a happy ending is difficult when one recalls that it has depended upon the scapegoating of Clara Vogel and all that she represents. The antithetical meanings which can be taken from the shooting of the horse also contribute to an unnervingly sinister undertone to the superficially harmonious resolution of the narrative.

It is apparent, therefore, that entirely conflicting messages may be drawn from Jock and from Niels's act of shooting the animal. The ambivalence surrounding Jock yields, in turn, wholly contradictory readings of the novel. Grove may want to wrest healthy sexuality from the cumulation of events. But if Niels is supposed to have won his virility from killing Jock the 'gelding,' why is passion denied at the end of the story? The moralist in Grove would have it that Niels has annihilated that 'beast' in himself which was attracted to Clara Vogel. Having abandoned sexual desire, Niels has become a loving, patient mate for the sexually timid woman. Following this line, however, love comes to depend upon neurotic asexuality. Work in the other direction – have Niels and Ellen's relationship be properly and fully sexual at the end of the story – and the novel ends up linking mature sexual expression with the victimization of the animal. Given that, as per convention, the horses have been the locus of phallic potence throughout the novel, the conclusion that the elimination of, symbolically, 'the horse' leads to sexual maturity seems a logical impossibility. This confusion of meaning is a sign of the loosening of culture's hold upon the animal. The attempt to coordinate human sexuality with response to the animal has led Grove to produce not only confusion of meaning but totally polarized meanings. Because sexual implication will not attach securely to the horse in *Settlers of the Marsh,* the horse instead discloses the radically ambivalent nature of attitudes towards sexuality. It is a toss-up whether Niels's derangement or the author's equivocation is most responsible for the killing of Jock. The docile, nickering animal comes in for aggression because of its steadfast refusal, culturally speaking, to regulate the sexual significance it is asked to sustain.

GONE TO EARTH: BRINGING THE DILEMMA OF
COMPASSION TO THE SURFACE

Distinguishing Mary Webb's *Gone to Earth* from *Settlers of the Marsh* is Webb's attention to hunting. She complicates the issue of sexuality by making her protagonist Hazel Woodus' sexual lover an avid hunter, particularly of foxes. Because sympathy for the wild creatures is a theme of Hazel's life, she should have a long way to go to submit to Squire Reddin's amorous advances. An additional complication is that Hazel is not so much innocent about sexual matters as downright ignorant. She is four months pregnant before she learns that she is going to have Reddin's child, but she has to be told she is pregnant by another woman. Even then, she fails to make the connection between sexual intercourse and pregnancy, complaining that Reddin has pulled 'a sneak's trick' on her to 'make [her] have a little 'un unbeknown' (p 250). Webb's view of sexuality is not intellectualized; she builds into her novel cultural dilemmas so profound that the only possible resolution is the elimination of Hazel and her fox, the paired source of the trouble both to the novel and to the human community which cannot assimilate these two beings. The lack of resolution is also cosmological: *Gone to Earth* alternates between frankly naturalistic observations and superstitious moral outbursts as indiscriminately as its heroine wanders between Jack Reddin's estate and the cottage Edward Marston, the minister, keeps with his mother.

Christopher Nash, who uses *Gone to Earth* as a model for his discussion of animal motifs in the modern novel, asserts that 'Hazel *is* an animal, [and] does perhaps represent the first instance in modern literature in which a true protagonist is more animal than human in the customary sense' (Nash's italics, p 43). Nash's argument must be taken seriously: he is almost alone among literary critics in attempting to develop a theory from the presence of animals in modern novels. Nevertheless, his contention that Hazel Woodus is an animal is curious, because *every* post-Darwinian human being is an animal. Erika Duncan's introduction to the novel tells us that Webb had read *The Origin of Species,* among other books, with 'great eagerness' (p 7). Despite never having read Darwin, Hazel herself makes the point about humanity and the animals in response to Mrs Marston's assertion that Foxy is 'only an animal': 'So're you and me animals,' Hazel declares (p 100). This premise, along with methods of denial and attempts at understanding, is precisely what gives the animal power in modern fiction.

It is interesting to contemplate, nonetheless, how Nash's observation illuminates what Mary Webb is trying to establish with Hazel. Hazel appears to be an animal to Nash because of her Romantic connection with the woods, her empathy with weaker animals, and her persecution by the righteous of the community. Nash centres upon Webb's comment that Hazel possesses 'the divine egoism that is genius' (p 44 in Nash; p 88 in the novel). Much of his analysis is directed towards defining this 'genius of egoism.' He finds himself forced to approach the problem of Hazel's status as an animal through contrasts, with the two men she is attracted to, and with humanity as a whole. In describing Hazel's misanthropy, Nash offers the following remarks:

'Humanity' is men [the species, not the people of that gender] in their abstract, organized cultural state – *men seeing themselves as beings,* rather than men *being.* Hazel *is* frighteningly misanthropic – if we insist on translating *anthropos* as a rational concept rather than as a living thing. So long as man insists on being a concept, a product of an elaborate *system,* rather than something living, there can be no contact between man and what is quintessentially living, the 'principle of life itself.' (Nash's italics, p 64)

Hazel is an 'animal,' then, in part because she does not exist for herself as a concept. Her 'egoism' is meant to denote the seamless integrity of her 'self' and her 'being' in both the physical and spiritual sense. The 'principle of life' Nash cites is from Webb's description of Undern, Jack Reddin's estate, where 'the very principle of life seemed to slumber' (p 29). Undern has an ill effect upon nature. Not only is the atmosphere of the place gloomy, but both its residents engage in unrestrained acts of aggression against animals. Jack Reddin, of course, hunts animals, but his dour manservant Vessons is subject to more dangerous outbursts of crazed violence against small creatures. Maddened by the possibility that Hazel is to be established as mistress of Undern, Vessons spends a whole day pointlessly shooting robins, swallows, wrens, goldfinches, and sparrows. Undern, represents, therefore, the essence of human malevolence against the 'animal' Hazel is supposed to be.

It is difficult, however, for Nash to state directly what Hazel's animality consists of as a positive state of being. He notes Webb's observation that Hazel 'seemed to be an incarnation of the secret woods' (*Gone to Earth*, p 54), and asks what that secret might be (Nash, p 49). Unfortunately, the novel only provides mysteries in answer to Nash's question. Hazel reaches out to 'something,' something 'vast, solitary, and silent,' which people 'stammer of ... in words such as Eternity, Fate, God' (*Gone to Earth*, p 53). Of crucial significance to Nash's reading of Hazel is Webb's comment that 'the creeds of men are so many keys that do not fit the lock' – the 'lock,' presumably, which bars the way to culture's attempt to know and state specifically how the mystery of Nature is embodied in the animal. The best that Nash can say is that Hazel contains 'a purpose, a place between the dark past and the dark future, *to which no purely human concept gives a key. The key lies else-where, somewhere in the secret wood*' (Nash's italics, p 50).

Romantic mysticism manifests itself plainly in Nash's exploration of his definite assertion that Hazel is an animal. Whatever he means to designate with the term 'animal,' it is a wholesome alternative to human mores and dogmas. The novel, however, is not nearly as certain as Nash that the animal affirms everything that is good in nature. Undern attracts Hazel, after all; it locates some of the darker aspects of Hazel's character and itself speaks of mysteries remote from the creeds of righteous people. By an unromantic reading of the novel, Hazel could also be described as an animal in her ignorance, superstitiousness, and inconstancy. Webb has been wise enough to add these culturally negative qualities into the mix that separates Hazel from the human state as culture defines it. Sexuality lies at the heart of conflicting interpretations of Hazel's affinity to animals. Hazel is, at seventeen, as 'sexless as a leaf' and in need of the 'spiritualization of sex' (p 16); Hazel has, not blood, but 'volatile sap' in her veins (p 163), which makes her a singular sort of animal indeed.

Whether her sexlessness and bloodlessness put her in a category somewhat lower than animals, and the spiritualization of sex will lift her into the human condition, is a problem the novel tends not to reduce but to magnify. It is a serious problem, too, because neither sexlessness nor spiritualization represents the animal way of being. The tension within the novel's view of sexuality is part and parcel of its attempt to exclude violence from the habits of the natural animal. Because Webb has lent to the sexually attractive Reddin a lust to hunt, the elision of predatory drives and death in the natural and the good is more noticeable in this novel than in the others. All the same, Webb has chosen a notorious (to British sensibilities) predator, the fox, as Hazel's totem animal.

Hazel's beloved Foxy does kill chickens, but only off stage. She never appears with blood on her teeth, or in attitudes of menace towards a weaker animal. Webb avoids the sensationalism of crunching bones and flying feathers, but she does so at a cost. After Foxy has stolen some chickens, Hazel remonstrates with her, 'sadly but sympathetically':

'You was made bad ... You was made a fox, and you be a fox, and its queer-like to me, Foxy, as folk canna see that. They expect you to be what you wanna made to be. You'm made to be a fox; and when you'm busy being a fox they say you'm a sinner!' (p 47)

It is only because Foxy's slaughter of the chickens occurs behind the scenes that Webb and Hazel can show this gentle tolerance of the fox's predatory ways. Hazel is supposed to be sensitized to the victimization of defenceless animals; she is supposed to have 'a never-broken pact with all creatures defeated' (p 229). The author cannot, therefore, confront her heroine with the mortal defeat of the chickens Foxy attacks. To do so would be to undermine further an already shaky ethical philosophy. Webb attempts to justify

Hazel's terror of the hunting hounds, what Hazel calls the 'death-pack': 'It was not the killing that gives horror to the death pack so much as the lack of the impulse not to kill. One flicker of merciful intention amid relentless action would redeem it' (p 185). Were Webb looking at Foxy closely, she would find also a 'lack of an impulse not to kill.' For the novel's purposes, however, Foxy herself must be amenable to pitiable victimization. She must bear an 'air of martyrdom' (p 14), and must not evince a thirst for blood. For all the meaning Foxy is meant to convey, she is thus something of a disembodied animal, reflecting quaintness and beauty but not natural instinct. It is little wonder, therefore, that the novel equates wildness with the spirit of poetry.

Webb is frequently more sensible than her heroine, however, on the score of natural events. Although she is already married to Edward Marston, Hazel enacts a magical ritual which determines that her dreams about Jack Reddin signify that this man, not her husband, is her destined lover. The decisive factor for Hazel amidst these portents is the simultaneously hopeful and wary conclusion that 'Foxy wants [her] to go' to Reddin (p 187). Webb interposes a naturalistic explanations for the magical signs; and of course Hazel's mind is full of Reddin, so it is little wonder that she dreams about him. Foxy's participation in Hazel's decision is less easily explained. If Foxy were a natural animal, with the full complement of animal attributes, an instinct for mating in the fox might correspond to a similar instinct in Hazel and truly inform Hazel's attraction to Reddin. It does seem clear that, in spite of the fuss about portents and the later moralizing over the 'crime' that Reddin has committed against Hazel, Hazel really wants to make love to the man. He excites her sexually in a way that her husband does not. While not wanting to deny Hazel's sexual desire entirely, Webb still needs to contend that Reddin has taken ad-vantage of the young woman's innocence. Because Hazel must be a victimized creature of the wild wood, Reddin must, for contrast, be 'the embodiment of the destructive principle' (p 169). On this score, Hazel's association with Foxy would confirm the link between sexual conquest and the hunt: Hazel wants Reddin because he will ravage her animal innocence. Neither superstition, nor natu-ralism, can cope with the contradictions in Hazel's passions.

The novel's implicit claim to speak for the wild founders upon carnal intimacies. Strong in condemning the Christian commu-

nity that in turn condemns Hazel's promiscuity, the novel equivocates over what might constitute healthy sexual expression. Webb
draws the conventional distinction between body and soul. Hazel
is spiritually drawn to Edward but physically drawn to Reddin
(p 232); Reddin's 'crime' is that 'he had made of a woman who
could not be his spiritual bride (since her spirit was unawaken-
ed, and his was to seek) his body's bride' (p 234). In castigating
Reddin, of course, Webb cannot help but castigate simultaneously
the physical longing for sex which reflects plain animal drive. As
the following passage illustrates, this dilemma makes for conspic-
uous omission and vagueness when the novelist aims to be most
candid:

That a woman should, in the evolution of life, cease to be a virgin and
become a mother is a thing so natural and so purely physical as hardly to
need comment; but that the immortal part of her should be robbed, that
she should cease to be part of an entity in a world where personality is
the only rare and precious thing – this is tragic. (p 256)

The process whereby a woman 'cease[s] to be a virgin and become[s]
a mother' *does* 'need comment' in this novel. Passing over that
process has led only to obscure contentions about immortality and
personality. Within Webb's romantic conception of the animal,
candour takes the form of aversion to copulation and procreation.
Any sort of candour on the issue of sexual intercourse takes courage, however, since intimacies kept deeply private leave those
who want to speak plainly in a lonely position.

Indeed, Mary Webb possesses a courage to address aspects of
sexuality more intimate than those addressed by the male writers
discussed in this context. For all its confusion, *Gone to Earth*
truly tackles doubts about sexuality from which discreet authors
usually withdraw. In this and other novels, Webb is less coy than
Thomas Hardy and D.H. Lawrence, recognized liberators of human sexuality. She does not shy away from the inexplicable in the
sexually aroused woman's choice of lover. She also broaches unpleasant aspects of the natural consequence of sexual experience
for women and that is motherhood. Evidently, the pain of childbirth
alarms Webb: 'a woman must have an amazing genius if she is
still a poet after childbirth' (p 205), she remarks. The poetic spirit,
as seen previously, is for Webb a definitive aspect of the wildness

that enfolds the animal. Thus it is because the 'ever-circling wheels of birth, mating and death' (p 257) are 'nothing' to Hazel that the character can sustain Webb's image of poeticized and morally pure Nature. By means of affection for victimized animals, Hazel overleaps the grim business of sex and birth to become a sex-free mother. She is Foxy's 'mam' (p 33); she has been 'mothering' some bees (p 244) before Reddin throws them in the fire. Finally, she offers to be Edward's mother (p 270) in place of Mrs Marston, who has left the home in disgust. The spiritual tenderness that legitimates Hazel's motherly relation to animals takes on an aspect of perversity when it extends to her mothering of her own husband, especially when she declines to have sexual relations with him. This unnatural development in the standing of husband and wife casts doubt upon the status of Hazel's mothering of the animals. Is that sentiment in her also unnatural? Motherhood, conventionally almost synonymous with nature, is highly unnatural in *Gone to Earth*. It is a great burden upon women; and Webb is frank enough to admit that.

Several of the novel's major themes are swept together in one episode involving animal victims. A common event in stories of country life, this scene finds all the rabbits in a field huddled in one small stand of wheat in the path of the oncoming reaping-machine. Waiting for the last stand to fall and the rabbits to make a break for freedom are a crowd of rural folk with heavy sticks in their hands. Hazel wants Jack Reddin to call the people off. She thinks about her sexual encounters with Reddin. The first time had been bad; there 'had been many times since, in the grey-tinted room, that had been nearly as bad. But for evoking a shuddering, startled horror in her mind, nothing came up to that Sunday night [the first time]' (p 253). Sexual intercourse, then, is explicitly associated with cruelty to animals, and specifically with the hunt.

This scene also occasions Webb's clearest synopsis of the dichotomous possibilities for the place of God with respect to animals and society. Among the delighted yells of the people pursuing the rabbits, Hazel's is the sole cry of opposition to the sport: 'Hazel stood alone – the single representative, in a callous world, of God. Or was the world His representative, and she something alien, a dissentient voice to be silenced?' (p 253). While this assemblage of concerns, of sex and death, nature and religion, is problematic enough, a higher pitch of difficulty is reached before the end of the episode. Hazel observes a single rabbit struck down in flight; she sees 'the look of its eye, white and staring, as it fled past her with insensate speed,' and then 'its convulsive roll over and recovery under the blow; and then the next blow' (p 254). The vision of the rabbit dying from wanton violence makes Hazel think about birth, and of the pain she has been told is ahead of her during childbirth. This interlinking of death with birth, of point-less violence with pain in the necessary continuance of life, puts the novel's themes beyond intellectual answers. By the logic of this scene, accepting as natural the process of mating and birth naturalizes also the ugliness of the hunt. Pain becomes part of Nature or God's plan for the world. Hazel's efforts to protect ani-mals from pain and death represent a denial of animal being.

Leave out the problem of sexuality and birth, and the novel is proof against the viciousness of Reddin and callousness of the God of the righteous. Hazel gives a cogent counter-argument to Edward's faith in the kindness of God. God does not free animals caught in spring traps and crying out in desperation: 'What for dun He give 'em mouths so's they can holla,' Hazel asks, 'and not listen at 'em. I listen when Foxy shouts out' (p 109). There may be no will to mercy in God, but there is a will to mercy in Hazel, and Hazel is attuned to nature, while Christian believers are not. Good Christians are prominent members of the fox-hunt that ends the story; a clergyman rides with the hunters, a 'large gold cross [bumping] up and down on his stomach' (p 286). He carries with him a Prayer-Book, the utter impotence of which is established with the violence of Hazel's death. With Foxy in her arms, Hazel is chased by the pack of dogs over the cliff-side of a quarry. At the level of philosophy, Hazel dies to point out the murderousness of the sport. Both the murder and the Christian element differentiate the fox-hunt from Foxy's appetite for blood. Foxy, at least, is not a hypocrite; the animal does not preach morality and practise evil. The violence of the fox-hunt is properly called cruelty; it highlights the potential for hatred of nature in religious creeds. The clergy-man, Reddin, and the rest are not behaving like animals. They are, in the novel's evaluation, behaving like Christians.

If Hazel's status as a natural being has wavered under the pressures of sexuality, she becomes a steadfast advocate of wild nature in the circumstances of her death. Her attempt to rescue

Foxy from being torn to pieces by the fox-hounds is unquestionably right. Tenderness is not out of step with nature when nature is threatened by human malevolence. The disembodied voice that cries 'Gone to Earth!' after Hazel and Foxy have fallen to their death articulates the return to materiality of two kindred souls of nature, killed by nature's enemies. Persecuted by the community, Hazel can remain the spirit of the wild driven back into a state of nature by violence. But add sexuality into the mix, and the agonized cry that closes the novel adopts a different irony. Incapable of tolerating the violence that attends the processes of life, Hazel has 'gone to earth' in the only home for her soul, which is death. Too sensitive to live on earth, she achieves spiritual harmony with Nature only in becoming a victim like the animals she loves.

Gone to Earth wanders thus towards a cosmology that incorporates sexuality and animals. Attempting to encompass both compassion for the animal and free sexual expression, the novel arrives at polarized cosmologies, one in which nature ravages the sensitive flesh, the other in which nature seeks to protect embodied beings from suffering. The aim of the novel is not philosophical; the novel is philosophical only incidentally to the unfolding of the narrative. But in the end, the tensions of narrative succumb to the need for cosmological explanation. The material, for all its apparent simplicity, will not rest comfortably in the narrative and cultural context. Webb has to look for reasons beyond culture to account for the difficulties sexuality and animal victims make for her. Finally, however, metaphysics cannot cope with the physical realities of sexual intercourse and ultimately breaks in two. Webb is a great deal more realistic about sexuality than most moderns, yet even in her candid vision, the hoped-for reconciliation of sexual passion and kindness towards animals remains a distant prospect.

D.H. LAWRENCE AND THE MYSTIC SEXUAL CONNECTION

As the inconsistencies within *Gone to Earth* suggest, making peace with the physical side of sexuality is interconnected with acknowledgment of the totality of animal nature. Pitying animals and viewing them as, in essence, victims imparts to sexuality the structure of victimization. *Settlers of the Marsh* in fact demonstrates the same phenomenon; like *Gone to Earth*, it steers sexual passion into the realm of tragedy. As we turn now to D.H.

Lawrence's *The Fox,* we would hope to find a less tragic vision of human sexuality. Lawrence has the reputation, after all, of being the 'priest of love.' From his poetry, he is also known as someone who has a particularly heightened consciousness of the richness of animal life. In Anthony Burgess' assessment, as a writer Lawrence is unique in his 'unpretentious sense of the sacredness of the world of beasts and reptiles, [and] willingness to give up his own raging ego ... in an almost desperate desire for identification with pure being untortured by thought and feeling' (p 119). With Lawrence's animals singly, one does see the passionate Romanticism which counters such spiritualized Romanticism as perplexes *Gone to Earth.* But even with Lawrence, the combination of animals and sexuality produces animal and human victims.

Violence against animals is not a preordained aspect of Lawrence's world-view. When such violence occurs in his novels, protest is usually somewhere in evidence. In *Women in Love,* for example, Ursula's rage at Gerald's brutal treatment of the horse at the railway crossing ('Coaldust') represents genuine feelings on Lawrence's part. In *The Plumed Serpent,* as another example, Lawrence condemns the bloodlust of a crowd witnessing a bullfight (chapter 1). He describes the goring to death of a mild-tempered horse by one of the bulls. When the bull nudges out of the horse a heap of steaming entrails, the crowd applauds as if it has seen a fine flourish in an equal battle. But Lawrence makes it plain, in the 'dumb incomprehension' of the dying horse, that the crowd's reaction is repulsive. As in *Women in Love,* a woman expresses opposition: Kate senses in the spectacle only 'human cowardice and beastliness, a smell of blood, a nauseous whiff of bursten bowels.'

Lawrence's first novel, however, offers an exception to his usual incorporation into his fiction of distaste for wanton aggression against animals. The main characters in *The White Peacock* are over-civilized. The novel as a whole reflects the influence of Victorian proprieties. Lawrence fights against those proprieties by means of several shocking scenes of violence against animals, in two of which people kill animals with their bare hands. These scenes intrude into the story with a clumsiness characteristic of fledgling writers. They articulate, nevertheless, a deep need to break away from the cultural snobbery of Victorian sensibilities. One aspect of those sensibilities Lawrence evidently wishes to overcome is the tender-hearted response to animals. As he goes on to locate terms of authority for his own vision, he grows less fearful of tenderness. The act of honouring the animal ceases to threaten his unique understanding of animal nature. In *The White Peacock,* he needs to utter indirectly, through the gamekeeper Annabel, the moral edict to 'Be a good animal' (part 2, chapter 1). By the time he writes *The Fox,* he has gained sufficient appreciation of what it means to 'be a good animal' to have become less defensive about the animal challenge to civilization.

Before moving on to *The Fox,* however, I wish to consider one instance of violence against animals perpetrated by Lawrence himself. He writes about this incident at length in the essay 'Reflections on the Death of a Porcupine' (1925). Though in this essay Lawrence struggles to justify having shot a porcupine, the guilt he feels is naked to see. He does protest too much, as Mary Webb does. It is almost unnecessary for Lawrence to inform us that he had never before in his life 'shot at any live thing.' Guilt leads him to self-revealing extravagance: the porcupine's tail is 'repulsive'; it waddles with a 'bestial, stupid motion' and makes 'squalor,' just as 'all savagery has a touch of squalor, that makes one a little sick at the stomach.' In sum, the porcupine is 'repugnant' (p 460). It is not the least bit like Lawrence to use the language of disgust on animals. Lawrence maligns the porcupine because he dislikes what he has done. He fears the porcupine, either in advance of or after the shooting, or both, because he wants to believe that the animal has forced him to kill its innocent, lumbering self. Although he does not say so outright, Lawrence's act is, to him, 'repulsive' and 'stupid'; he himself has brought on his own nausea. In fact, shortly after verbally abusing the porcupine, Lawrence bestows the self-same adjective, 'repugnant,' upon guns and his previous half-hearted experiences with them (p 464).

As if this blatant projection were not bad enough, Lawrence feels compelled to elevate the nasty incident to a fact of the cosmos. 'If the lower cycles of life are not *mastered,*' he says, 'there can be no higher cycle' (Lawrence's italics, p 467). Nature is based upon a hierarchy of dominance; tautologically, the 'lower' animals are those that are preyed upon by the 'higher' ones. A snake is 'higher' than a butterfly because the snake can devour a butterfly. Consequently, 'Life is more vivid in a snake than in a butterfly' (p 468). And, of course, it follows that because human beings can subjugate all the rest of creation, life is most vivid in human beings, or at least in those races of human beings that can subjugate other races. Lawrence hastily erects this entire crude and shaky cosmology all because he has done what others do without an instant's thought: shot an animal considered a pest. 'One must be able to shoot,' he remarks defensively, and furthermore 'I, myself, must be able to shoot, and to kill' (p 464). Lawrence is manifestly incapable of blithely shooting animals. The porcupine masters Lawrence; and Lawrence launches off into the metaphysics of superior vividness to recuperate from the blow to his self-possession.

In view of the vastly excessive denial Lawrence practises in 'Reflections on the Death of a Porcupine,' it will seem odd now to apply to him Richard Foster's praise of him as demonstrating a 'fierce integrity' (p 325). 'Fierce integrity,' nonetheless, is the right phrase for characterizing Lawrence's inability to conceal his true feelings behind a mask of objectivity. He may have been in a foul mood when he wrote the essay; he may have been fighting with his wife, or having a bout with his 'bronchials' that led him to doubt his virility. More likely he was simply suffering pangs of conscience over killing the porcupine. But whatever the explanation for this singularly uncalculated discourse, it is clear that there is a fully reacting person behind Lawrence's words. Lawrence does not adopt that intellectual distance which produces often speciously coherent philosophies. He says what he has to say unguardedly. Integrity, then, or guilelessness, is the quality that permits Lawrence to offer the following unadorned thoughts on a dead mountain lion as poetry:

> And I think in this empty world there was room for me and a mountain lion.
> And I think in the world beyond, how easily we might spare a million or two of humans
> And never miss them.
> Yet what a gap in the world, the missing white frost-face of that slim yellow mountain lion!
>> ('Mountain Lion')

Both the poem and the essay communicate authentic emotion, disparate as the expressed attitudes towards animal victims may be. No doubt it is to such plain, unromanticized regret over the death of a mountain lion that Burgess refers in his comment on Lawrence's appreciation for animals. Yet in backhand fashion, Lawrence also admits the potent effect the porcupine has upon his imagination. Despite himself, he honours the porcupine by appealing to the myth of dominance to camouflage his guilt.

Given the mess Lawrence makes of killing the porcupine – he aims badly and has to finish the job with a stick – it is ironic indeed to find him expounding upon the will of the hunter in *The Fox*. The hunt, he says, is 'like fate':

Your own soul, as a hunter, has gone out to fasten on the soul of the deer, even before you see any deer ... It is a subtle, profound battle of wills which takes place in the invisible ... It is your own *will* which carries the bullet into the heart of your quarry. The bullet's flight home is a sheer projection of your own fate into the fate of the deer. It happens as a supreme wish, a supreme act of volition, not as a dodge of cleverness. (pp 130–1)

It is ironic, further, that this talk of wills and fate is nowhere in evidence when Henry actually shoots the fox. There is, rather, a simple 'dodge of cleverness': Henry calculates where the fox will enter the chicken-house and shoots:

[T]here was the awful crash of a gun reverberating between the old buildings as if all the night had gone smash. But the boy watched keenly. He saw even the white belly of the fox as the beast beat his paws in death. (p 147)

The previous description of the hunt applies not to Henry and the fox, but to the sexual interplay between Henry, Nellie March, and Jill Banford. A different context causes the night to go 'smash' with the death of the fox, and that is the 'spirit of place' created by English civilization, comment on which precedes the actual shooting:

[S]uddenly it seemed to [Henry] England was little and tight, he felt the landscape was constricted even in the dark, and that there were too many dogs in the night, making a noise like a fence of sound, like the network of English hedges netting the view. He felt the fox didn't have a chance.

... He knew the fox would be coming. It seemed to him it would be the last of the foxes in this loudly-barking, thick-voiced England, tight with innumerable little houses. (p 146)

The will of the civilized has already negated the fox in the English landscape. The rural values Nellie and Jill attempt to uphold in their farming venture would necessitate the death of the fox. By those values, the fox is 'evil' and a 'demon' (p 115) for stealing chickens. The greater evil for Lawrence, however, is the tight civilization that eliminates foxes, in fact and in consciousness, without ever confronting either the sacredness of the fox or the blood from its death by violence. In *Gone to Earth,* the hypocrisy of the civilized is shown in the fox-hunt; in *The Fox,* the cruelty of civilization takes less dramatic and more insidious form. Civilization annihilates the animal bloodlessly, placidly maintaining the fiction of its transcendence of violence while steadily overrunning the physical and psychic territory belonging to the fox.

It is somewhat hypocritical of Lawrence to attempt to transplant the fox's significance to the sexual relations of Henry and Nellie March – and less hypocritical of him to show the failure of those relations once the pair is married. Nellie's submission to Henry has irritated feminist critics. Kate Millett suggests that *The Fox* depicts the typical male fantasy of 'anaesthetizing the bride' (p 265). Anne Smith charges Lawrence with reactionary belief: 'the semi-comatose acquiescent stupor of March at the end of *The Fox,*' she argues, 'presents woman as the 'gentle domestic beast' of the Victorians' (p 45). Due attention to the meaning of the fox undermines the premise that Nellie does finally surrender her being to Henry; and while feminists might still be angered at the association of the woman with the animal, from Lawrence's perspective the animal is a good deal wiser than the human male. Henry turns out in the end to be a whiny, self-important 'boy' (in fine contradistinction to Frederick Philip Grove's Niels, who becomes a 'man' at the end of *Settlers of the Marsh*). He does want from his wife the ego-submission that rightly incites women readers to rejection. Nellie's lethargy comes not from submission to the bumptious male, but from the death of 'the last of the foxes.' Her friendship with Jill had sustained her in the frisson of making a life on civilization's terms. She gained artificial energy from playing the man in society's threadbare understanding of gender roles.

The fox was teaching her an alertness that exists fully outside civilization's nervous vigilance. Henry proves not to be a substitute fox, and thus Nellie languishes for want of animal wakefulness in her world. She is not, then, a 'gentle domestic beast,' but a woman who has seen what it means to be untame and has not yet determined how she is supposed to live with that vision. Political critiques miss the point: dogma cannot lift Nellie out of apathy that has originated in civilization's suppression of values represented by the fox.

At the time of writing *The Fox,* Lawrence is honest enough to admit, by omission, that his conception of unromanticized sexual intercourse stands beyond his imaginative powers as an artist. Whereas Mary Webb peeks in upon Reddin and Hazel to find only horror, Lawrence has infused too much animal energy into his story for depiction of sexual relations between Henry and Nellie to be anything other than a disappointment. The preliminaries to sexual intercourse are already overcharged. On Henry's part, just the thought of Nellie's breasts beneath her clothes seems 'like some perilous secret' (p 155). To Nellie, one brief kiss from Henry seems to 'burn through her every fibre' (p 140). The 'deep, heavy, powerful stroke' of Henry's heart feels 'like something from beyond, something awful from outside, signalling to her' (p 160). From the start, she identifies Henry with the fox and feels at peace in his presence: 'she need not any more be divided in herself, trying to keep up two planes of consciousness. She could at last lapse into the odour of the fox' (p 125). The image of burning comes from a dream she has in which the fox sings to her outside the house, and then burns her mouth in brushing its tail across her face (p 126). The strange mastery Henry initially commands over her consciousness originates also with the fox. Intent upon shooting the fox, Nellie comes face to face with the animal in the woods: 'And he knew her. She was spellbound – she knew he knew her. So he looked into her eyes, and her soul failed her. He knew her, he was not daunted' (p 116). How Henry is to reproduce this wild animal knowingness in sexual intercourse is a question too strained for physical reality to bear. The fox must die to give Henry a chance of his own against Nellie's will. Unfortunately, Henry is unequal to the challenge, since, dead or alive, the fox instils in Nellie a knowledge unassailable by any male conceivable within the terms of the story. The fox is Lawrence's one clue to sexual power which exists outside of cultural disavowal. He successfully removes the emotional freight of victimization from the fox. But he cannot do the same for unromantic sexual intimacies between a man and a woman.

Victimization in *The Fox* does not seem to stem from Lawrence's frustration at failure to assimilate sexuality into a coherent world-view. What looks like victimization – the burning, the surrender of conscious self-control – is supposed to be part of a sexually charged vision of life. Sexually repressed and sexually repressing, Nellie's partner Jill Banford is almost an archetypal victim. She is pale, near-sighted, and physically incompetent; the others ignore her pathetic attempts at authority. She stands, nonetheless, for the despotism of English distaste for sexual expression. She must die, narratively speaking, to free Nellie's sexual being from the tyranny of civilized neurosis.

Pathos is Jill's domain; she is the one who pities the fox, who looks like 'a poor little sick bird' (p 141), whose crushed neck and head is 'a mass of blood, of horror' (p 174) after Henry has 'willed' her to stand in the path of a tree he fells. She is a victim as Frederick Philip Grove's Jock is a victim, as Webb's rabbits are victims, as, finally, Clara Vogel and Hazel Woodus are victims. The cultural repression of sexual passion that has produced all these other victims, Lawrence seeks to concentrate in the figure of Jill Banford. Jill's death calls attention to the fact that bodies have been dropping with fair regularity in these stories. The killing in *The Fox* stands out from the other deaths, however, in part because it seems as if, in Mark Spilka's words, Lawrence has 'sanctioned murder in defense of the life-morality' (p 199). It could be argued, contra Spilka, that the 'life-morality' is the very quality in *The Fox* that ensures that Jill Banford's death will be disquieting to conscience. That the human victims in these stories are women is not the telling point, although that is an issue that would certainly be worth pursuing. It is odd, rather, that the assault on bodies in the other novels passes by as somehow natural, while the virtual murder of Jill Banford is likely to excite indignation. One does not want to believe that the difference originates in approval of the killing of those who are sexually alive, for Clara Vogel and Hazel Woodus are clearly sexually responsive, where Jill Banford represents the forces in culture that associate sexual passion with guilt. She is not, however, a caricature or a symbol, any more than are the human victims representing sexual vitality. The difference resides, I think, in Lawrence's heightened sense of the body in general, for all the excess he builds into physical sensations. However self-enclosed and pathetic Jill Banford might be, she is not spiritualized as the other victims are. There is in *The Fox* no over-arching tragic vision to naturalize unnatural death.

What is disturbing is that Lawrence feels it no less necessary to incorporate violence against an animal into his amoral and unromantic vision of sexuality than do Grove and Webb for their tragic approaches to the subject. Like the others, Lawrence relies upon the affront to civilized mores that aggression against animals represents in order to address the possibilities for wholesome sexual expression. Indeed, it seems the more contradictory in Lawrence that he should kill the fox after having built the animal up into a symbol of sexual potence. The radical contradiction of assaulting an animal's body to prove sexual integrity is the more salient in Lawrence because of his maxim that we should 'be good animals.' With *The Fox*, he seems not to have had the courage to affirm that the living fox is indeed a 'good animal.' Perhaps the fear of appearing to fall into a Banford variety of anti-animal sentimentality drives him into the reactionary convention of linking the kill with mystic sexual prowess. At least he makes a retroactive apology to the fox by having Henry, the would-be virile hunter of women and animals, remain a fretful boy at the end of the story. For all that he lapses into a mystic enhancement of sexuality through the death of the fox, he resists the impulse to falsify his vision utterly with the sexual triumph of the man who did the killing.

THE EGOISM OF NATURE WORSHIP AND THE ABSURDITY
OF THE HUNT IN STEINBECK'S 'WHITE QUAIL'

John Steinbeck's stories are peppered with animal victims: the pony, pigs, and buzzard in *The Red Pony,* the cats and frogs in *Cannery Row,* the turtle, dog, and pigs in *Grapes of Wrath.* In her book *Animals in American Literature,* Mary Allen notes an 'absence of profundity' in Steinbeck's use of animals and says that this 'is a function of his detached realism: one may observe but not experience what they feel.' He will not, she says, 'take the literary license' to stir up compassion for animal victims (pp 117–18). Leaving aside objections to the position that it is 'literary license' to imagine the feelings of animals, one must also observe that Steinbeck, like Jack London before him, falls outside of the American stereotype when it comes to animals. Unlike Hemingway and Faulkner, he takes no pleasure in the death of animals; the 'absence of profundity' in this instance yields a good-natured (as opposed to strident) defence of animals, if not compassion for them. Since the hunt is at issue in 'The White Quail,' it is worth noting an anecdote from Steinbeck's *Log from the Sea of Cortez*. In this episode, Steinbeck evinces pride that an expedition to hunt big-horn sheep yields only a turd for a trophy (pp 163–7). Some of the hunting party go off in search of the game, while Steinbeck and his friend Ed Ricketts stay behind, sitting by a waterfall and chatting about animals and life in America. Those who have gone out to hunt return with nothing but sheep droppings. Steinbeck and Ricketts mount a sheep dropping:

And where another man can say: 'There was an animal, but because I am greater than he is, he is dead and I am alive, and there is his head to prove it,' we can say, 'There was an animal, and for all we know there still is and here is proof of it. He was very healthy when we last heard of him.' (p 167)

Steinbeck writes about ecological balance (*Sea of Cortez,* p 3) and the absurdity of hunting at a time when America still waxes nostalgic over the coonskin hat and Davy Crockett wood-lore, and great American writers are still working off literary energies on the myth of the hunt. His pleasure in the sheep dropping indicates that his opposition to bolstering virility through killing animals does not run to the sentimental response to nature. The 'absence of profundity' remarked by Mary Allen stems not from resistance to investigating the internal life of the animal, but from a willingness to let nature and animals be as they are.

Identification with an animal makes for both profundity and parody in 'The White Quail.' Mary Teller's antipathy to the natural animal is evident not only in her hysteria over the cat stalking 'her' white quail, but in her insistence that any significance the quail might have is focused upon Mary Teller alone:

'Why,' Mary cried to herself, 'she's like me!' ... 'She's like the essence of me, an essence boiled down to utter purity. She must be the queen of the quail. She makes every lovely thing that ever happened to me one thing.' ...

... The white quail stretched a wing backward and smoothed down the feathers with her beak. 'This is the me that was everything beautiful. This is the center of me, my heart.'

There are elements in Mary's response which correspond to modern methods of loving nature. From a Romantic perspective, such out-going of the human heart towards nature appears to be a genuine divestment of anthropocentric interests. To find, furthermore, the consummation of all loveliness in one beautiful creature seems the very peak of appreciation. In Mary's narcissism, however, Steinbeck represents a major failing of the Romantic response to the natural world. The animal can become 'profound' only when human beings project their own egos onto it. Steinbeck's critique becomes parody at the close of 'The White Quail,' when Harry Teller succeeds in symbolically shooting his wife by killing the quail.

'The White Quail' operates upon parallels between the Tellers' marriage and the perfectly landscaped garden which Mary keeps. Like the static garden Mary creates, the marriage is frozen in polite, mutual incomprehension. Like the slugs, little phallic symbols, which invade her garden and which Mary enjoys seeing squashed, Harry's penis (to be frank about it) threatens to destroy the artificial perfection of the marriage. Mary's tyrannical rule in the household manifests itself in the 'clean, quick, decisive answer' she gives to Harry's unspoken 'How about tonight?': she simply locks her bedroom door on him. She thinks it 'sweet and gentle' in her husband that he always tries the lock on her door silently, as if, she thinks, he were ashamed of his desire. The accumulated rage Harry evidently feels, furthermore, can be likened to the wooded hill which is, to Mary, 'the enemy,' the 'world that wants to get in, all rough and tangled and unkempt.' Just as the frozen beauty of the garden is precarious, the inhuman accord of the marriage is a flimsy barricade against natural, emotional chaos. Despite the fact that the Tellers will never have to deal with the wilderness of passion suppressed by their tacit pact to keep the peace, the animal victim opens up a glimpse upon passions as deep and uncontrolled as any of those tackled directly by characters in the other stories. One of the sources of the distinctiveness of 'The White Quail,' however, is Steinbeck's recognition of the falsity of the meanings his characters attribute to the quail, despite the genuineness of the passions that the bird's death exposes.

In keeping with the fragility of the state of affairs in both garden and marriage, the characters' conscious feelings are lightweight, almost absurd, as the feverishness of the slug-hunt suggests. Mary has headaches and hysterical outbursts, but these symptoms of neurosis are a different order of emotion from the strong passions of love and anger invoked by other writers who combine sexuality and animal victims. Harry is unfailingly subservient to his wife; he expresses deep feeling, prior to shooting the quail, only in the tightening of his grip upon the knob of the locked bedroom door. By keeping most of the emotion superficial, Steinbeck parodies some of the powerful forces that have determined human conflict in the other four works.

The title of the story suggests another parody. 'The White Quail' hints at Herman Melville's magnificent Moby Dick, the 'white whale.' On its small scale, Mary Teller's obsession reflects that of Captain Ahab. Hatred drives Ahab to pursue the white whale, hatred and that narcissism which finds personalized hostility in the wild creature's blind return of violence for violence inflicted upon it. Compelling the white whale to operate as a symbol has driven Ahab mad. Even so, the great whale endures symbolization better than the dainty white bird of Steinbeck's story because the whale fights back and asserts its creatureliness against human imposition. Whether there is or is not an intentional pun in Steinbeck's title, comparison of the white quail with the white whale says a great deal about the paucity of experience available to creators of gardens. Instead of the high seas and the leviathan, Mary has only a well-regulated landscape and charming little birds on which to build mental adventures. Her overwrought and virtually delusional interpretation of the white quail's meaning contains, metaphorically, the high seas and the leviathan, only in a domestic situation which ends up mocking the human impulse to make symbols out of animals.

Steinbeck pillories Mary Teller's ego-investment in the quail, but he does not necessarily condone Harry Teller's shooting of the bird either. Granted, Harry symbolically kills his wife in shooting the bird that she proclaims is herself. Yet the quail is a literal quail nonetheless; the authentic feeling of loneliness Harry derives from his act springs from the conjunction of that act's symbolic and its literal values. Narrative irony undermines the symbolism and affirms the reality: Harry would indeed like to murder his wife but has in fact shot a small, innocent, and entirely non-threatening animal. Irony establishes that Harry has not resurrected primitive animality against his wife's abhorrence of the ways of the natural animal. Even if Steinbeck were afflicted with belief in the virility of the hunter, Harry's little air rifle and the BB shot which scarcely damages the quail's body would make a mockery of Harry's manhood. Harry's foray into bush, following the shooting, has also its ironic quality: he does not brave the wild but crashes frantically up the slope, driven by fear of his wife's detection of his crime.

With the interplay of symbolism and reality, irony and authenticity, Steinbeck challenges the power of meaning that other writers have injected into their versions of the sexual struggle. He also challenges the human capacity for sexual liberation which other writers have brought about by means of animal victims. In 'The White Quail,' the domestic nightmare remains intact, its artificial perfection unshaken. Harry may have shot the symbol of his wife, but the woman is still locked in her bedroom upholding for both of them the pretence of decorum. Thus the sterile marriage rebuffs the heaving, oceanic forces of life and death which sweep through the lives of the characters in the other narratives. The entire symbolic equipment surrounding the quail lives on, though it is divested of even the slim plausibility it might have had while the white quail was alive.

CONCLUSION

The white quail is made a scapegoat to the sexual neuroses of both Mary and Harry Teller. In a sense, nevertheless, the sensibility Steinbeck cultivates is one that can aid in a critique of the other stories. Steinbeck's narrative does not license the victimization of the animal in quite the same way that Grove's, Webb's, and Lawrence's narratives do. This is not to say that the other narratives are deficient. Indeed, they carry greater weight aesthetically than Steinbeck's slight little story. Almost unwittingly,

they work with the ways in which culture co-opts nonhuman animals into the difficulties the human animal has with its own
sexuality. An undercurrent of fondness for animals exists in all of
these stories, and yet none of the authors refrains from victimizing
the animal to enhance the importance of what would otherwise be
quite bland human discord. Only Steinbeck seems consistently
aware of the animal's ultimate indifference to the ordeals that
culture builds into human sexuality. One would think that we
could keep our sexual neuroses to ourselves.

The thought of the animal living happily at large in the countryside, while human beings struggle to reconcile themselves to
the basic biological function of the sex drive, appears to be too
much of a temptation to writers. The benign setting, in contradistinction to the wilderness or the city, should guarantee narrative
friendliness towards animal life. But the selfsame failure to affirm
unromanticized sexuality results in failure also to sanctify animal
existence. The tendency, rather, is to sanctify the animal victim
as opposed to the living animal. The tenor of violence against
animals is, of course, muted relative to the cruelty we have seen
in, say, *Tarka the Otter, The Great Auk,* and 'Tobias Mindernickel.'
As discussion in the following two chapters will show, the violence
associated with sexuality is subdued on comparison, also, with
the cruelty which occurs under the authority of myth and aesthetics. As narrative strives for reconciliation with the animal
reality of the sexual act, it at least tempers aggression against
nonhuman animals. The modern attempt to overcome centuries of
disownment of sexuality runs parallel with the attempt to understand animals. Although the periodic meeting of these separate
paths leaves behind animal corpses, sympathy for the struggling
human being does extend to the point of laying the animal victim
to rest quietly.

6 Myth, Disillusionment, and Animal Victims: *Modern Variations upon Animal Sacrifice*

INTRODUCTION

Theories about myths, their purpose and meaning, have proliferated since the middle of the nineteenth century. As G.S. Kirk explains in *The Nature of Greek Myths* (see chapters 3 and 4), myths have been seen variously as rationalizations for ritual, as attempts to humanize nature, as proto-science, as charters for social conduct, as mechanisms for overcoming contradiction, and as transmogrifications of the infantile and irrational in the human psyche. Each theory strives to elucidate the quintessential features that will unite the great diversity of myths known to contemporary historians and anthropologists. All theories presume, at base, that current ways of knowing the world permit objective analysis of myth. Modern thought has it that while certain myths may survive, culture has intellectually transcended the myth-making habit of mind. According to Paul Ricoeur, culture has detached itself from myth by means of historical understanding; Ricoeur states that 'In one sense, [modern man] alone can recognize myth as myth, because he alone has reached the point where history and myth have become separate' (p 161). The theory of evolution also enters into the detection of myth as myth, since evolution generates a picture of the prehistorical past which supplants those pictures created by myth. The empirical attitude explicitly defines itself by its opposition to the metaphysical devices of myth: 'Happy is the man,' Mathew Tindal wrote in 1730, 'who is so far, at least, directed by the *Law of Reason,* and the *Religion of Nature,* as to suffer no Mysteries, or unintelligible Propositions, no Allegories, no Hyperboles, no Metaphors, Types, Parables or Phrases of an uncertain signification to confound his understanding' (in Harwood, p 124). 'Science is the critique of myths,' W.B. Yeats remarks, adding that 'There would be no Darwin, had there been no Book of Genesis' (in Levin, p 114). Whatever the analytical strategy for divorcing modern consciousness from myth, ours is an age that has greater faith in theories of myth than in myths themselves.

The assumption that the modern mind has outgrown mythic persuasions is critical to understanding the tensions inherent in post-Darwinian fiction that unites myth and the animal victim. Of all the phenomena that myth tackles, the animal is the most impervious to contrary imaginative approaches. When stories are told about animals, the residue of myth clings to the representation of those animals. For many centuries, the tale of the animal was relegated to that subordinate mythic form, the fable. The totemic animals of primitive myth devolved into the personified animals of moral tales, as are found in Aesop's fables, or of trickster stories like those generated around the figure of Reynard the fox. Natural history demotes fables to the status of tales for children, but natural history has also had difficulty in producing credible stories about animals, as we have seen in tales of the animal victim in the wild. Why do modern writers bother, then, to attempt the animal story? It looks as though empirical modes of thought encompass animals satisfactorily; empiricism appears, moreover, to render the animal immune to story-telling. The modern writer, however, is justifiably suspicious of the adequacy of empiricism's interpretation of animal life. To leave the animal in the hands of science, and continue to weave stories out of human situations, is to reinforce the outdated dichotomy of human and animal experiences. The idea of continuity between human and nonhuman animals demands the inclusion of animals in the creation of fiction. But whereas humans have history out of which to construct narratives, the natural animal seems to have only myth to legitimate its place and meaning in culture. Thus the author who incorporates animals into fiction is caught between two formidable sources of doubt: doubt as to the competence of natural history to articulate the significance of the animal, and doubt as to the value of myth in expressing the truth of the animal. Nowhere is it more obvious than in the study of myth and animals that the animal is a battle ground for nature and culture.

This chapter focuses upon three distinct ways in which modern authors have brought myth and the animal together in their stories. Gustave Flaubert's *Salammbo* illustrates the first way, which is to draw modern sensibilities back into the mythic mode. In fact, *Salammbo* pursues myth in so obsessive a manner as to produce nausea. Flaubert's representation of Roman times omits the objective point of view which detaches myth from history. He offers no avenue of intellectual escape from the suffocating decadence of his stories. He also produces quantities of animal victims in the process of reconstructing bygone mythic consciousness. For Timothy Findley, it is not myth but religion that is reckless with animal life. In *Not Wanted on the Voyage,* he condemns the Judaeo-Christian patriarchy which rationalizes violence against women and animals. Judaeo-Christian belief destroys the unity between humans and animals given by pagan animals; Findley employs the vibrancy of the mythic form to demonstrate what modern culture has lost with the disappearance of myth. This typically modern nostalgia for the potence of myth also informs William Faulkner's 'The Bear.' By spiralling backward through the history of one American family, Faulkner hopes to restore mythic qualities to the transitional phase in American life that saw the freeing of slaves. His history is framed, at the beginning, by the ahistorical myth of the bear hunt and, at the end, by the collapse of the hunting myth into a deeply embittered vision in which the hunter who slew the bear meanly stands guard over some squirrels he wants to shoot. These stories exemplify various stages along the spectrum of modern attitudes towards myth, from the sickening descent into myth in Flaubert to an almost equally sickening fall out of myth in Faulkner. Some preliminary remarks on myth in general are necessary to place the animal victims in these stories in the proper context.

The context for discussion of myth and the animal in this chapter is established by historical assumptions and attitudes rather than by definitions. Of course, definitions are helpful, and a general sense of definitional congruity does emerge from examination of attitudes. Whatever definition one employs, however, has a provisional quality arising from the multiplicity of dispositions informing the modern view of myth. The basic definition offered by the *Shorter Oxford English Dictionary,* for instance, reflects only one side of contemporary opinion. According to the dictionary, myth is 'a purely fictitious narrative usually involving supernatural persons, actions or events, and embodying some popular idea concerning natural or historical phenomena.' In this definition, one hears the voice of the scientist behind the words 'purely fictitious,' and the elitism of the scholar behind the words 'popular idea.' Other definitions are less sceptical. As a starting point for his discussion of myth, Jerome S. Bruner offers the elaborate definition proposed by Richard Chase: 'Myth is an esthetic device for bringing the imaginary but powerful world of preternatural forces into a manageable collaboration with the objective ... facts of life in such a way as to excite a sense of reality amenable to both the unconscious passions and the conscious mind' (Chase in Bruner, p 276). Typically modern reservations are still in evidence in Chase's definition. The 'world of preternatural forces' is 'imaginary,' and myths are seen merely to 'excite a sense of reality' instead of expressing reality. Nevertheless, this definition does touch upon neutral elements that occur in many attempts to understand myth. For one thing, myth is usually understood as an 'esthetic device,' most often as a 'story' of some sort. For another, the intention behind myth is generally conceived of as an effort to effect accord between world and mind. The idea of 'story' may be at odds with the harmony hoped for from mythic utterance, but these two components – narrative and an aim for unity – appear to be foundational to many definitions of myth. Unfortunately, these fundamental components leave most human constructions, from the aesthetic to the scientific, susceptible to being described as myth. The idea that myths are fanciful seems to be essential to modern culture as a means of distinguishing myths from its own ways of establishing truth.

With increasing frequency in modern times, of course, the word 'myth' is used to denote fallacies or even lies. The disbelief expressed by Mathew Tindal and other eighteenth-century scientists has percolated down into popular usage. Despite being informed time and again of the erroneousness of this use of the term, the modern person is likely to experience an ingrained and automatic mistrust of anything he or she hears described as myth. Indeed, the term 'myth' is often applied to destructive beliefs in modern life, as in Lewis Mumford's observations about the 'myth of the machine' or the pseudo-scientific 'myths' which Carl J. Friedrich and Zbigniew K. Brzezinski (pp 92–4) find propping up totalitarian ideologies. The hold that science and history have upon truth in modern culture is apparent in this designation of dangerous presuppositions as myth. If someone were now to use the phrase 'the myth of the animal,' it would be reasonable to assume that this person intended to point out harmful falsehoods in our beliefs about animals. It is much easier for the modern mind to condemn myth than to retrieve whatever benefits myth might have had for pre-modern culture.

At the same time as myth has become almost synonymous with 'lie,' certain modern thinkers like Carl Jung, Mircea Eliade, and Joseph Campbell have searched ancient myths for clues to an enkindled vision of life. Contemporary ecological movements in North America appeal to the myths of aboriginal peoples in the hope of establishing a deep ecology. Despite modern scepticism, myths appear to retain abstruse insights to which reason would like access. There is a strain in modern culture which has a liking for what Gillian Beer describes as the *explanation-resisting* quality of myth' (p 121). Alienated from the selfsame epistemologies that enable analysis of myth, people yearn for the holistic integrity of mythic consciousness. At times, modern life feels over-explained, and some people mourn the loss of the mythic capacity to penetrate through rational discourse to the underlying connectedness of nature and culture. From the alienated perspective, current problem-solving strategies, such as those based upon economics or technology, seem to have only an abstract connection with actual experience. The mythic spirit challenges reason, disclosing the ways in which historical and scientific approaches to life have resulted in fabrications of truth rather than substantial realities. Myth could help to overcome that terrible doubt that our conceptions of life are manufactured, and return us to the sources of reality beneath language and theorizing. Granted, the initial Romantic enthusiasm for a 'new mythology' has become jaded in the course of time and suffered the sobering effect of Fascist cultism. But hope remains for the power of myth to supersede rational epistemologies which have themselves become jaded. Faith in myth relies on the power of myth to invoke pre-explanatory primordial realities.

Science, religion, and myth compete over the epistemological territory which explains human relations with nature. In the nineteenth century, myths were seen as irrational, as the clumsy attempts of the primitive mind to comprehend and communicate facts of life that are lucidly intelligible to modern philosophers and scientists. Some thinkers, like Andrew Lang (see *The Making of Religion* p 291), denounced animistic myths in a vain attempt to salvage Christianity from being relegated to the status of one myth among others. Anthropological studies of myth were discovering events and figures in primitive narratives uncomfortably akin to features of Christian stories. Since science was the modern thinker's instrument for isolating myth from truth, religion was clearly in danger of becoming a story rather than a system of true belief. The attempt to rescue specific religious belief was largely unsuccessful, but myth did receive better treatment as post-Darwinian hypotheses were challenged and further explored. Serious anthropological investigation of myths has led by now to the use of myths to criticize religion, rather than the reverse. Where religion divides humans from nature, one segment of current opinion has it that the mythic sensibility knits us all into a natural whole again. Instead of being a frivolous entertainment and a wicked distraction from the probities of religion, animism holds the key to ecological and cultural unity.

For this faith to exist, however, a feeling of the isolation of humanity from nature must obtain. Faith in myth does not instantly create the experiential unity that recent appeals to animism strive for. Indeed, efforts to find the idea of unity with nature in myth reinforce the impression that humankind comes at the idea of unity from a broken world, whether that unity is the spiritual oneness of myth or the biological continuity of evolution. Paul Ricoeur puts it well in *The Symbolism of Evil*. Arguing that myth takes and even naturalizes a seminal impression of the imperfection of life, he says that myth 'makes the experience of fault the center of a whole, the center of a world: the world of fault' (p 163). Furthermore, he writes, 'If myth-making is an antidote to distress, that is because the man of myths is already an unhappy consciousness; for him unity, conciliation, and reconciliation are things to be *spoken of* and *acted out,* precisely because they are not *given'* (Ricoeur's italics, pp 167–8). Ricoeur sees myth stemming from an original division between humans and nature.

The idea that there is a rift between culture and nature is critical to speculation about the standing of animals in myth. It could be argued that myths are the initial attempts of primitive humankind to insert explanation between human experience and the ubiquitous powers of chaos. Chaos, as G.S. Kirk notes (p 46),

means 'gap' in ancient Greek, and not 'disorder,' as we have come
to use the term. Myth in its animistic phase, therefore, expresses
the desire to anneal the gap between nascent culture and indomitable nature. But as myth evolves into polytheism and then
monotheism, it widens the gap and comes to serve the interests of
culture by isolating the human species as the focus of the creative
spirit in the world. The history of myth follows the growth of
human power over the rest of nature. The sense of the sacred
withdraws from nature to concentrate upon human beings and
their acts. Thus Judaeo-Christian myth has all the elements in
the universe created in a few days, with a few flourishes on the
part of one omnipotent deity, and then quickly turns to the story
of humankind's initiation into moral understanding. While the
myths produced by animism frequently lend creative power to
pre-existing animals, nothing much of interest to culture existed
prior to humans by the time culture was generating monotheistic
myths.

Monotheistic religion, however, precipitates its own demise in
rationalizing human supremacy over the natural world. Religion
paves the way for empirical detachment from nature, and survives
upon the two remaining mysteries in nature that flummox human
intelligence. Neither the origin of life, nor death, can be fathomed
by empirical methods, and so religion steps in to provide stories
for the human spirit's fear of these dark regions at either end of
its own personal history. The theory of evolution arrives now to
remove the sense of the personal from life and death, and vastly
expands the history that is of interest to humankind. An imaginable animal once again sits at the source of human existence; and
personal death is troubled by the idea of natural selection which
calmly consigns whole species to extinction. The neutralization of
death is probably the primary reason that myth-making still appeals to modern culture. Humans do not wish to die like animals;
it feels like a great injustice that a life vivified by culture should
disappear meaninglessly. Modern re-enactments of myth are faced
with the choice, then, of either asserting the sacredness of the
death of individual animals or risking falsity in continuing to
fortify the imagined gap between humans and animals.

The power of myth over death introduces the theme of the
victimization of animals into this discussion. A motive behind the
creation of myths could well be the desire to bypass the finality of

death. In theory, that desire might salvage animals from the demotion to which empiricism has subjected them. Viewing each animal as part of the stream of life, as holding, that is, some deathless mystery tapped by myth, could lend to animals value beyond their usefulness to humankind. Regrettably, at least as far as known myths go, the ahistorical approach to animals has a habit of disavowing animal death. Myths from hunter-gatherer societies seem designed to justify the killing of animals, inasmuch as the generic spirit of the animal killed absolves the hunter of guilt. A certain denial of the material death of any individual animal hovers around the myths of hunter-gatherer societies. The mystery of the animal lives on, and so the death of the individual animal seems inconsequential. The animal victim of extant myths is thus a decidedly different order of being from the animal victim decried by, say, the anti-vivisection movements of the nineteenth and twentieth centuries. The animal victim of myths is clearly not the pitiable creature produced by sentimental anthropomorphism but a powerful being demanding supplication. Leaving aside the permission myths give to kill actual animals, one might argue that myths empower animals by placing their essential nature beyond the reach of that most powerful enemy of living beings, death. This effect is certainly soothing to the human desire for immortality. It may even produce larger-than-life animals. Nevertheless, in their own way, the myths of hunter-gatherer societies yield a similar result to the empirical approach. They create a kind of collective animal for each species which minimizes responsiveness to the suffering of the individual.

One modern story which shows the effect that faith in the power of myth to keep animals immune to death has upon animal victims is Ursula K. Le Guin's 'Buffalo Gals Won't You Come Out Tonight?' Le Guin's story honours the animistic world-view of North American aboriginal people and makes a compelling critique of the speeded-up, burned-out world created by modern people. There is an animal victim in the story: a personified coyote dies of poisoning by the evil world of humankind. This death, however, turns out to be no death at all: a wise Spider-woman says that grief over the coyote is unnecessary because 'Coyote' dies all the time. With 'Buffalo Gals' representing a modern acknowledgment of mythic holism, it is apparent that the idea of the timelessness of the animal interferes in the urgent need for us to recognize that coyotes and other species of animals can in fact disappear forever. The assertion that there is a spiritual place in which some transcendent being called 'Coyote' lives in immortal harmony with a perfect natural order leaves myth looking all too optimistic for the real world to bear, however burned-out and spiritually impoverished current notions of the real world might be. It is difficult to see how the immutability of the spiritual world is meant to serve the actual coyotes dying under the assaults of humankind. Cultural enhancement occurs at the cost of the natural animal. The intention behind Le Guin's story and other modern invocations of myth is healthy enough, and yet the ultimate implication appears to be a dangerous denial of material realities.

Myth is most alive in its intention to articulate the holistic vision. The profundity of mythic intention would place myths at the summit of story-telling. Their power comes from active telling and retelling, not from automatic revelation. A comment made by Bronislaw Malinowski enhances this sense of the vigorous purposefulness of myth: 'Myth is ... a vital ingredient of human civilization; it is not an idle tale, but a hard-worked active force; it is not an intellectual explanation or an artistic imagery, but a pragmatic charter of primitive faith and moral wisdom' (p 101). Myth aims beyond transience to the permanent and universal. In fact, it appears that the aim in myth is what excites the modern imagination. With its innocent but emphatic intentionality, myth opposes the empirical methods that go on churning out answer after answer to life's mysteries. As the spirit of Romanticism implies, modern culture needs and wants from the natural world opposition to the seeming omniscience of the powers of reason. Yet in the twentieth century, reason has undermined Romanticism to the extent that trust in mythic consciousness now depends upon the intentions of myth rather than its achievement.

This is one reason that pagan animism cannot be retrieved in modern fiction. If animism does close the gap between animals and humans, then it does not truly represent present circumstances either in the real world, where animals are wholly dominated, or in the world of the imagination, where myth always falls short of expressing the truth about animals. That science also falls short of expressing the truth about animals restores life to mythic renditions of modern ways of experiencing animal reality, and yet there is always an unbridgeable rift between narrative and animal reality, a rift which myth fails to cross, however wistfully it may gaze across at the unreachable animal. Myth does gaze wistfully at the animal, but narrative reflects scepticism and conflict. In terms of content, modern fiction cannot help but depict human dominance over nonhuman animals. Gestures towards animism negate monotheism's censure of the animal, but myth cannot break through the reality of human dominance and empower animals. What myth tempered by sceptical narrative can empower is the victimization of animals. Modern approaches to myth, that is to say, separate culture from dependence upon psychic oppression of animals. The incorporation of myth into narrative shows that the victimization of animals is not necessary to culture's survival. In turn, as a product of narrative instead of a product of myth, the animal victim destabilizes mythic constructions that reinforce the rift between culture and nature. The question of power arises here, the power of myth to capture the truth of animals and, conversely, the power of animals, or animal victims in this case, to undermine human cultural constructions.

As we try to fathom relations between myth and narrative, a nod in the direction of postmodernism becomes pertinent. Postmodernism revels in the conceptual systems spawned by the mind of humankind and places reality even further beyond the reach of story-telling than other theories of aesthetic creation. From a postmodern point of view, myth would be a 'lie' of sorts, but its fallaciousness does not matter. Postmodernism has the undeniable virtue of pointing out the degree and depth to which ideas that we take for truths depend, in fact, upon elaborate, culture-based constructions unconsciously agreed upon but only vaguely related to reality, if at all. It has the further virtue, in this context, of establishing the extreme difficulty of putting into words a truthful account of animals in light of the many ways in which culture can miss animals and reify images out of temporary needs and desires. Postmodernism would deny, however, that the literal animal has the power to seize narrative and bend it towards acknowledgment of its, the animal's, reality. In removing the test of reality and the censoriousness of value-testing, postmodern theory leaves the human mind in the position of creating freely, with the kind of playfulness and self-celebration that Andrew Lang detected and denounced in animism. The literal animal is almost irrelevant to the cultural enterprise from a postmodern perspective. Indeed, we have only slight access to the literal animal in any event, and thus we need not worry a great deal if the abstraction in a work of art that substitutes for the animal is in or out of harmony with the genuine being who comes trotting along at the sound of its dinner-dish or utters a distress call to warn its young of the presence of danger.

This line of thought returns discussion to the initial observations of the obvious distance between myths and empirical and historical accounts of reality. Postmodernism places literature closer to the mythic end of the spectrum than to the empirical/historical end. It may even place literature on the side of myth opposite to whatever nebulous idea of reality one uses as a reference point and effect the liberation of literature in that fashion. Myth, that is, purports to speak about realities, and perhaps even about ultra-real realities, whereas from a postmodern perspective literature is only indifferently related to the real world. In fact, the 'real world' is yet another cultural construction, and nonhuman animals, or the multifarious representations of animals, are equally so. Postmodernism therefore places literature in a position of power by reducing the influence of significance in the abstract. If any literary image of an animal, for example 'Coyote' in Le Guin's story, bears little relation to the genuine animal, the misrepresentation does not matter to the cultural enterprise. Animal victims in literature derive meaning, such as it is, from the concentric layers of the literary system in which they exist, and not from those animal victims that live and die out there in the real world. Postmodernism is the ultimate in anti-Darwinism in that it severs culture from nature. It puts culture in a position of infinite regress, moving back layer after layer of explanation but disallowing utterable contact with nature. Myth might well exist in a similarly onanistic state, with truth not revealed so much as transmitted in some pre-linguistic intention. The kinds of vacancies that postmodernism takes to be suggestive of realities that language can only indirectly tap can be seen as similar to the truths existing not in but as a result of mythic narrative.

Depending on one's point of view, then, myths can exist in a discontinuous state, stemming from, addressing, and satisfying purely cultural ends, or they can serve mysteries in the world denied by science and history. Taking the latter position, literature is akin to myth in so far as it lends power and significance to a world flattened and rationalized by empirical and historical explanation. Unlike myth, and unlike poetry, however, fiction concedes to empirical and historical explanations if only as far as to address them. When fiction introduces myth, it does so with a kind of hopeful scepticism. It borrows the gravity of myth to enhance meaningfulness, but remains sufficiently worldly to withhold endorsement of metaphysical assertions. While myth receives its impetus directly from mystery, fiction does not yield easily to the mysterious and ineffable. In varying degrees, disillusionment always informs fictional invocation of the mythic perspective, whatever desire for the unifying power of myth may also be present.

It will be apparent from this discussion that myth thrusts us into irresolvable paradoxes where animal victims are concerned. The power that animal victims undeniably have in fiction may be manufactured, may be a product of mythical illusions like those that once lent power to the pitiable sacrificial animal of primitive ritual. On the one hand, if the animal victim is simply a literary tool serving a cultural end, then mystical significance is human not animal in origin, is artificial and hence a further imposition on animals. On the other hand, the totemically magnified image may serve the reality of the animal victim's anti-human significance better than the image of the pathetically oppressed creature. Myth itself tells us indirectly that we and natural animals exist apart and in conflict. Yet the hope, the intention, of fiction appears to be to establish an equality in difference. However one views myths, as spiritual pointers or as fallacies, the fiction that addresses the problem of myth places the demand before culture to undergo self-examination. Under earnest questioning, the mythic aim devolves to the animal's advantage, for it makes us work to understand the animal's place both in and out of culture. Because of its aim towards unity, myth in modern narrative proves that the effort to bring the natural animal into art is a strenuous one. It is appropriate, therefore, to begin analysis with the epitome of the tortured artist, Gustave Flaubert.

GUSTAVE FLAUBERT: MYTH, THE TORTURED ARTIST, AND HEAPS OF ANIMAL VICTIMS

Of the three writers discussed in this chapter, Gustave Flaubert is the most aggressive in his drive to force myth to break through rational explanation and mirror life in its totality. Of the stories discussed in this chapter, his *Salammbo* and 'The Legend of St Julian Hospitator' contain the most animal victims, and the most sadistic violence against animals. No compassion occurs in these stories to castigate the violence against animals. No modern rationalism occurs to relieve the historical moment of the relentless oppression of mysticism. A comment Flaubert makes during the composition of *Salammbo* reveals that, in writing the novel, he felt himself subjected to the tortures he was recording. The creation of *Madame Bovary* generated agonies, but none were quite as focused as that which Flaubert depicts in his letter of 19 December 1858 to Ernest Feydeau. He is explaining his unhappiness at having to repeat a certain literary effect in *Salammbo*:

Clever writers would think up tricks to get out of the difficulty, but I'm going to plunge straight into it, like an ox. Such is my system. But how I'll sweat! And how I'll despair while constructing said passage. Seriously, I think that no one has *ever* undertaken a subject so difficult as regards style. At every line, every word, language fails me, and the insufficiency of vocabulary is such that I'm often forced to change details. It will kill me, my friend, it will kill me. No matter; it begins to be fun.

In short, I have finally achieved erection by dint of whipping and manipulation. Let's hope there's joy to come. (*Letters,* pp 198–9)

Many aspects of this statement merit comment, not the least among them being the masochistic metaphor which seems to represent a kind of fulfilment for Flaubert. With characteristic ardour and self-parody, he expands fussing over a minor literary problem into a matter of life, death, impotence, and flagellation. He imagines that he is beating *Salammbo* out of his unliterary animal corpus. The right style, the style that will accurately convey life in ancient Carthage, equals an erection – not insemination, not ejaculation or orgasm, as one might expect were Flaubert a Romantic writer, but the pre-creative stage in which fertilization or pleasure hang in suspension, awaiting the movement of the phallus. Few images could better reflect frustration with language, and the painful process of wresting truth from language. No image could explain better why Flaubert piles up animal bodies in *Salammbo*. He does not quite believe in his art; his body is an actual obstacle to artistic creativity and yields art only under torture. Neither does he believe in the sacred reality that myth is supposed to tap, although he wants to. The decadence of the mythic content in *Salammbo* discloses Flaubert's disgust and his faith. He drives life to sickening violence to force life to reveal the holiness he doesn't believe in.

It is almost a pity to use Flaubert in this examination of animal victims. Outside of his literary works, he expressed fellow-feeling for animals. In one entry in his *Intimate Notebook*, recorded when he was barely out of adolescence, he observes that 'There are days when the sight of animals fills me with tenderness' (p 41). 'At times,' Flaubert says in a letter of 1845, 'I look on animals and even trees with a tenderness that amounts to a feeling of affinity; I derive almost voluptuous sensations from the mere act of seeing – when I see clearly' (*Letters*, p 32). 'I attract mad people and animals,' he notes in the same letter: 'Is it because they sense that I understand them, because they feel I enter into their world?' (p 33). In another letter, written in 1846, he says, 'I am as sorry for caged birds as for enslaved human beings' (p 49) He also writes in his *Intimate Notebook*, 'I love to see humanity humbled. That spectacle cheers me when I am tired' (p 49). These youthful expressions of misanthropy and of affinity for the animal metamorphose into violence as even the language of art fails to articulate the lucid sense impression of reality.

In his philosophical biography of Flaubert, Jean-Paul Sartre links Flaubert's persistent feeling of tiredness with his sensitivity to the animal state. Sartre sees the child Gustave's response to the household pets as foundational to the shaping of the novelist's psyche. The family fiction, Sartre explains, was that Gustave was intellectually and verbally incapable. Gustave's acceptance of that fiction manifests itself in affinity for the domesticated animal. Early in the biography, Sartre notes that 'reality is the animality that cannot be decomposed, it keeps its silence' (p 27). The young Gustave's muteness begins to attain philosophical significance in the later experience of boredom which he shares with pets:

The experience of universal monotony he will later call *ennui* – with good reason; but 'pure boredom with life' is a pearl of culture. It seems clear that household animals are bored; they are homunculae, the dismal reflections of their masters. Culture has penetrated them, destroying nature in them without replacing it. Language is their major frustration: they have crude understanding of its function but cannot use it; it is enough for them to be *objects of speech* – they are spoken to, they are spoken about, they know it. This manifest verbal power which is denied to them cuts through them, settles within them as the limit of their powers, it is a disturbing privation which they forget in solitude and which deprecates *their very natures* when they are with men. (Sartre's italics, p 137)

Sartre's analysis is eminently valuable in explaining Flaubert's frustration with language and his awareness of the failure of culture to penetrate reality. The product of culture that broaches nature for humans is not language but ennui. The undomesticated animal embodies the hope for life without culture, without language. If Gustave the child felt like a 'dismal reflection' of the adults who believed him to be simple-minded, and felt his 'very nature' deprecated by his family, his art manifests striving for freedom from oppression. That striving also has reference to animals, as Sartre suggests:

Without culture the animal would not be bored – he would live, that is all. Haunted by the sense of something missing, he lives out the impossibility of transcending himself by a forgetful relapsing into animality; nature is discovered through resignation. Boredom with life is a consequence of the oppression of animals by man; it is nature grasping itself as the absurd end of a limiting process instead of realizing itself as biological spontaneity.

If Gustave shares this nostalgia with the beast it is because he too is domesticated. (pp 138–9)

'Biological spontaneity' is ruled out for Flaubert. Culture is ever an obstacle to nature. Flaubert can see and feel the silent reality of the animal; he can struggle to find words that approximate reality in general. Ultimately, however, culture fabricates reality, and the best that can be achieved is rage at culture.

Sartre locates the quintessential problem for Flaubert, the man and the artist, in a story Flaubert wrote when he was fifteen years old. This story is about the life of an ape-man, Djalioh, product of a scientist's experiment which has an orangutan mate with a female slave. 'It is clear that Djalioh,' Sartre says, 'represents Flaubert himself' (p 21). The narrative unfolds around the question of how to '*situate* Djalioh in society' (Sartre's emphasis, p 20); that question is complicated by the ape-man's inability to speak for himself. Djalioh can do little more than utter a tremulous word or a sigh: 'Whether it was a word or a sigh,' Sartre quotes, 'was of little consequence, but inside him there was a complete soul.' Sartre makes frequent reference to this story, *Quidquid volueris,* throughout this first volume of his biography of Flaubert. Later, Sartre uses the story to explain Flaubert's interest in Pascal's understanding of post-lapsarian humanity. 'By his origin, in effect,' Sartre notes in this context, 'Djalioh, the son of a woman, escapes the *general essence* which characterizes orangutans; the son of an ape, he escapes what the young author believes to be *human* nature' (Sartre's italics, p 201). Djalioh comes in handy again, much later, as Sartre describes the double-sided scepticism of Flaubert's response to ideology – his reaction to the materialism inherent in images of the dissection of corpses, and his contempt for priestcraft's manipulations of spirituality. Djalioh's linguistic difficulties predict Flaubert's refusal to accede to either ideology: Flaubert, Sartre notes, 'is wrong in *Quidquid volueris* when he refuses to give his incarnation, Djalioh, the capacity to make 'logical connections'; it is not these connections that he lacks but the determined, practical intention of using them to say yes or no' (p 530). Djalioh is more than a convenient metaphor in Sartre's analysis of Flaubert. Djalioh is truly an 'incarnation' of life experiences otherwise unamenable to articulation.

If Flaubert is sensitive to animal reality, if he has an affinity for animals and embodies his adolescent frustrations in a being who is half animal, why, then, does his fiction depict such gruesome violence towards animals? In his novel *Flaubert's Parrot,* Julian Barnes offers an answer to the observation that a lot of animals are slaughtered in Flaubert's stories:

He isn't Walt Disney, no. He was interested in cruelty, I agree. He was interested in everything. As well as Sade, there was Nero. But listen to what he says about them: 'These monsters explain history for me.' He is, I must add, all of seventeen at the time. And let me give you another quote: 'I love the vanquished, but I also love the victors' ... There is an earthquake in Leghorn: Flaubert doesn't cry out in sympathy. He feels as much sympathy for these victims as he does for slaves who died centuries earlier turning some tyrant's grindstone. You are shocked? It's called having a historical imagination. It's called being a citizen, not just of the world but of all time. It's what Flaubert described as being 'brother in God to everything that lives, from the giraffe and the crocodile to man.' It's called being a writer. (pp 134–5)

Novelistic licence is clearly in evidence in Barnes's explanation. Granted, Flaubert isn't Walt Disney; nor is he Mary Webb, or D.H. Lawrence, or John Steinbeck, or Henry Williamson, or Giorgio Bassani, or any of the other writers whose stories permit an untroubled empathic response to animals. That he has a 'historical imagination' constitutes a partial excuse for confronting the reader with scenes of slaughter which doubtless occurred. That he is a writer and not a moralist also alters the task he has to perform as he surveys life. Yet Flaubert is not making a neutral choice among historical phenomena; where animals come into play, he is selecting periods in history and cultural conflicts that necessitate cruelty. This is not to argue that animals are all in all to Flaubert, that he chooses historical periods on the basis of whether or not he can display animals in torment. Still, there is a wide separation between his personal tenderness for animals and the slaughter that goes on in some of his stories. The sympathy he supposedly feels for both human and animal victims is deeply troubled by sadism. As to the 'victors' he supposedly loved, there are none in *Salammbo*: bloodshed and torture wash out whatever sense of victory in battle there might be in *Salammbo*. Myth makes this history what it is, but Flaubert also perceives the unreality of myth. The violence comes from myth beating its head against the wall of nature. Flaubert concurs in the effort of myth to coerce meaning out of silence; he is willing to sink into the mythic mode to 'get down to the depth of matter – to be matter,' in the words that his St Antony utters at the close of *The Temptation of St. Antony*. Still, one does not need the external knowledge of Flaubert's affinity for animals to see that the animals in *Salammbo*, however oppressed and brutalized, do not submit completely to the mythic intention.

Anthony Thorlby has described *Salammbo* as 'a kind of soundless scream, silent violence, sensations burningly intense yet quite abstract.' Referring to the critical impression that the vision in *Salammbo* is static, Thorlby says that because the novel 'does not move us in any human – let alone humane – fashion, all its violent action does not move at all; it is all aimless, except as aesthetic spectacle' (p 483). If the reader were particularly sensitive, *Salammbo* might move him or her to revulsion, but that is beside the point. The novel does preclude humane sensibilities; the lavish decadence of the aesthetic spectacle, however, bars only the sentimental and romantic among human responses. Flaubert's attempt to reduce humanity to matter, to 'open entrails, scattered brains and pools of blood' (*Salammbo*, p 216), argues with the dazzling and sometimes ludicrous adornments the Carthaginians heap upon themselves for their religious ceremonies, even when their bodies are too emaciated to support the finery. Observing the ornaments of a crowd of priests attempting to worship Moloch at the height of the siege, Flaubert points out that 'nothing could have been more lugubrious than this silent crowd, with earrings swinging against pale faces, and golden tiaras encircling brows racked with atrocious despair' (p 237). There is indeed some equality between the decorative items of worship and the hacked-off limbs and burned torsos that litter the battlefield; one set of items produces the other. This is not to suggest, however, that religious zeal produces the corpses, or fear of violent death produces the engines and images of worship. Rather, the corpses and priestly artifacts represent conflicting sides in a characteristically Flaubertian quarrel with materialism and spirituality. All of these objects, corporeal and mystical, are swept up in neutrality. That neutrality might well offend those who want spirituality to conquer materialism, or materialism to conquer spirituality; but Flaubert refuses victory to either reading of life. Indeed, in a general way, as Kitty Mrosovsky observes in her introduction to *The Temptation of St. Antony,* Flaubert refuses 'to regard human life as the most important fact in the universe' (p 55). If one wants an epistemology that is indifferent to human life, science and history could qualify. Science and history are immune to the sympathies critics find lacking in *Salammbo*. But *Salammbo* is obviously not a work of science or of history; the extreme violence of the deaths and the inhuman extravagance of the trappings of worship make the novel something quite distinct from exercises in scientific or historical anatomization. Science and history do not exactly *refuse* 'to regard human life as the most important fact in the universe,' as Flaubert does. To make his novel art, he needs to surpass the trivially neutral in human experience; and he does so by extending battlefield injuries into a carnival of gore and intelligible myth into an orgy of garish symbols. Polarized merely, the conflict of materialism and spiritualism might lead to aesthetic stasis, but Flaubert drives his images into a progressively reckless refusal of human meaning to the body and to mysticism.

The elephants in *Salammbo* contain the historical struggle between rationality and myth. They participate in both the disease of decoration and the carnage. The 112 elephants Hanno equips for military service are loaded up with useless gear, which, one would imagine, would hinder their performance in battle. But since the people 'cherished them, and no treatment was too good for these old friends,' Hanno decks them out with bronze breastplates, adorns their caparisons with heavy purple material, and enlarges the towers the beasts are supposed to carry on their backs. He also has their trunks gilded (p 93). Despite the weight of equipment, the elephants perform well; they storm the Barbarian troops, disembowelling soldiers and hurling bodies into the air, 'so that long entrails hung round their ivory teeth like bundles of rigging on a mast' (p 148). The elephants go a little too wild, in fact, and their drivers are forced to kill them with the mallets and chisels provided for that purpose. At an earlier point in the war, the use of elephants has backfired on the Carthaginians. The Barbarians send pigs soaked in oil and set aflame into the midst of the elephants, whereupon the elephants trample the Carthaginians with enthusiasm equal to that which marks their assault upon the Barbarians. Beneath the gilding and military display, they are democratic beasts, well prepared in the heat of battle to crush any human body.

At the mid-point of the novel, in a chapter on the Carthaginian general Hamilcar, Flaubert juxtaposes a grisly scene of human torture with tender sentiments for elephants. It is worth pointing out that, early in the chapter, Hamilcar has 'tried to banish from his thoughts every form, every symbol and name of the Gods, the better to grasp the unchanging spirit hidden behind appearances' (p 107). In this effort, he is an admirable character, though he participates fully and readily in the cruelty that permeates every aspect of life in this novel. Enraged by the memory of 'hundreds of odious things' he had seen in battle, Hamilcar orders mass flogging and branding with irons for slaves and masters who had allowed the necessary work of flour-grinding and sword-making to deteriorate in his absence. Victims are flogged beneath the plane-trees; blood from the flogging 'showered up into the foliage, and red shapeless masses howled as they writhed at the foot of the trees' (p 134). Hamilcar turns from this scene to the elephant pen, where three lonely and maimed elephants survive, the others having died of wounds:

One had its ears split, another a large wound on the knee, the third had had its trunk cut off.

However they looked at [Hamilcar] sadly, like rational beings; and the one who had lost its trunk, lowered its huge head, bent its knees, and tried to fondle him gently with the end of the hideous stump.

At the animal's caress two tears sprang from his eyes. (p 135)

Ironically, this elephant with the mutilated trunk is the locus of the humane feelings Anthony Thorlby says are missing from *Salammbo*; its caress constitutes the one moment of recognizably civilized tenderness that occurs in the novel. The power of the innocent beast's gentleness may be measured by the tears of the man who has just sentenced human beings to horrible torments. Untouched by the agonies of the people and obviously accustomed to cruelty, this man is moved to pity by the animal. Of course, the result is that he has the elephant-keeper condemned to death. Nevertheless, for this brief instant, one finds Flaubert's affinity for animals breaking through the sadism. This moment brings to mind one more observation from Sartre on Flaubert's childhood closeness to animals: the child, Sartre says, 'can love others and believe himself loved only on the level of common subhumanity' (p 15). There is no genuine love in *Salammbo* apart from this one caress from the domesticated elephant. Perhaps that is why Flaubert has this one, mutilated elephant remain alive at the conclusion of the universal slaughter.

It would be easy to read castration symbolism into the elephant's stumpy trunk. Such a reading would fit in neatly with some of the modern associations of tenderness towards animals with sexual dysfunction, as is demonstrated in Giorgio Bassani's *The Heron* and Mary Webb's *Gone to Earth*. Whatever sexual energies there are in *Salammbo,* they are certainly cut off before actual sexual intercourse can take place. Rape is mentioned incidentally, but Salammbo and Matho, the sole candidates for meaningful sexual coupling, stand lusting for each other at a distance. In place of conjugal union, there is the final scene of the much-tortured Matho dying at Salammbo's feet, and Salammbo herself dying of grief at the celebration of her wedding to a different man. Matho, it should be noted, is carried captive into Carthage, tied with 'his arms and legs in a cross' (p 273) on the back of the elephant with the mutilated trunk. While there is too much crucifixion in *Salammbo* to view Matho as a Christ-figure, and too much sadism to find nostalgia for regenerative phallicism in the sadly shortened trunk of the elephant, it can be argued that the image conjoins the triumph of the crippled beast (Flaubert himself, if Sartre's psychoanalysis is accurate) with the ghoulish victory of a perverse religion. The elephant is not culpable; it serves its masters regardless of their allegiances. It innocently caresses the torturer, and innocently transports the man whose capture signals the final blow to the Barbarians' cause. The animality of the elephant has been co-opted by the inhuman purposes; the member, its trunk, that identifies it fundamentally as elephant has been brutally disfigured. The stubby trunk is a travesty of elephant trunks. In the final battle, this elephant climbs a pile of corpses, waving its trunk which in this moment looks like 'an enormous leech' (p 272). For all the frightening statues of animal-gods, and for all the mystic or sacrificial animals they keep around them, the true animal is non-existent to the Carthaginians. The image of the elephant carrying Matho multiplies corruption upon corruption, beginning with the core impairment of animal being, spreading to the perverse, anti-sexual victory over the lover, then further to the rout of the almost-healthy heathenism of the Barbarians, and ultimately to the subsumption of any sense of humanity under feverish worship of the god Moloch and the goddess Tanit.

Swept up in the human disease, animals can nonetheless be seen as the saving grace of *Salammbo,* were one inclined to dismiss the work as simply decadent and abstract. In the second chapter of the novel, the mercenaries, the Barbarians, who have done battle for Carthage and will lay siege to the city, encounter a long row of crosses with lions crucified upon them. The reason local peasants have crucified the lions is not especially strange: they hope that the display of lion corpses will scare away other lions. Nor are the mercenaries especially oppressed by the sight of the lions; they mock the first carcass they have come across, addressing it as 'consul' and 'citizen,' and throwing stones at its head to keep away the flies, evidently aware that the lion is past caring about a few flies. Gruesome details compose the picture of the lion; Flaubert has visualized the animal completely, the 'huge muzzle,' the forepaws 'widely separated like the wings of a bird,' the visible ribs, the hind legs nailed together at the base of the cross, and the black blood flowing through the hair and 'collected in stalactites at the bottom of its tail.' Other, half-eaten, lion corpses have their faces 'contorted in hideous grimaces.' At this point in the novel, evidently, Flaubert is much more impressed with the crucified lions than are the peasants or the mercenaries. Is he aiming to shock readers, to rattle their bourgeois sensibilities? Perhaps he is. But he is also interested in communicating the full sense of the animal body, splayed, nailed and bloody. The lions are not sacrificial animals for the peasants – they would have to have been killed before being hoisted onto the crosses – and are not taken to be so by the Barbarians. They are sacrificial animals for the novel's purposes, bearing the savage and not the sentimental connotation of sacrifice. Plain ignorance replaces the religious significance they would have for a Christian culture; yet it is an ignorance obsessively acted upon, for there are many crucified lions and they have been on display long enough for some to have decayed into skeletons only. There is no symbolic point to the crucifixion. The lions do, however, establish the gravity of the violence in *Salammbo*.

The crucified lions return again as a memory, in the second to last chapter of the novel. Dozens of people are crucified in this chapter, Carthaginians and Barbarians alike. Two leaders of the Barbarians are dying side by side on crosses. Spendius, the runaway slave who had sought revenge on his captors and has proven himself loyal and brave in battle, has the highest cross. Vultures are hovering around him. With an 'indefinable smile,' he asks the other crucified man, 'Do you remember the lions on the road to Sicca?' The man catches Spendius' meaning: 'They were our brothers!' he says, as he dies (p 265). Spendius is the most likeable character in the novel. He has useful skills; he can make sandals and spears and nets; he is said to be able to tame wild beasts (p 37). He has been loyal to Matho, whose love for Salammbo has driven him to rash exploits. Spendius comforts Matho, and guides him through the dangerous adventure to steal the veil of the goddess Tanit from the temple inside the walls of Carthage. A practical man, Spendius does not believe in the mystical powers of the veil; he has no 'confidence in its virtues' (p 76). He wants only to drive the Carthaginians to despair. Spendius 'would have spat upon the images of Olympian Jupiter; yet he was afraid to speak loudly, and never failed every day to put his right shoe on first' (p 96). He is a superstitious man, much as the peasants who crucified the lions are superstitious; but the elaborate ritual and decadent observances of Carthaginian faith provoke neither fear nor attraction in him. While the crucified Carthaginians, among them the Elders of their religious worship, are dying ignobly, Spendius experiences 'a strange courage.' At this point, when there is no hope of escape, he 'despised life, certain as he was of an almost immediate and eternal liberation, and he waited impassively for death' (p 265). Spendius, then, is the human link to the lions. His death matters, while the deaths of thousands of others mean little more to Flaubert than the rending of corpses into charred or bloody pieces of flesh. Spendius goes as far into mysticism as Flaubert himself might license. Spendius' brand of mysticism still has reference to kindly feeling for the body, such as is expressed in the memory of the lions. The novel does progress; it is not a static, aesthetic vision merely. The crucified animal leads towards the crucified human, with 'human' here having sensible significance, beneath the pathetic straining for spiritual aggrandizement evident in the gadgetry and human sacrifices in Carthaginian worship.

Flaubert gives the ultimate victory to lions. Crucified at the start of the second chapter, lions sit amongst Barbarian bodies, replete and drowsy from consuming human flesh, at the close of the second to last chapter. The live animals and the dead soldiers are promiscuously intermingled: 'All over the plain lay lions and corpses' (p 274). The dead men are heaped up in piles:

In one of the heaps which made uneven humps over the plain something vaguer than a ghost rose up. Then one of the lions began to walk, silhouetted with his monstrous shape as a black shadow against the background of the crimson sky; when he was close to the man he knocked him down with a single blow of his paw.

Then lying flat on him he slowly pulled out the entrails with the end of his teeth.

This unexpected bounty of human flesh has been a great boon to the wild beasts; they have multiplied, especially the lions. Humanity, in its animal and corporeal meaning, dissolves into meaningless hummocks on a open plain. What faint life stirs among the hills is easy pickings for the robust predatory creatures that prevail over the scene.

The book closes, as it opened, with a celebration. The impression from the first chapter is that these people are like wide-open mouths, consuming every creature that moves on the surface of the planet. Anything that crawls through the bushes, or burrows in the earth, or hides beneath stones, these Carthaginians will snare and perfume and decorate for their feasts. It is little wonder that they succumb easily to worship of Moloch the Devourer. In the final chapter, they are supposedly worshipping Tanit, the female adversary of Moloch – Tanit the never-hungry versus Moloch the ever-hungry. In either case, worship means, as one has come to expect, an orgy of sadism. The citizens line the streets, waiting to torture Matho in whatever way possible. Matho's 'body was something special for them, endowed with an almost religious splendour' (p 279). With their understanding of religion, this splendour excites them to subject Matho's body to lavish cruelties. As Matho nears Salammbo, he has ceased to resemble a human being:

Except for his eyes his appearance was no longer human; he was just a long shape, completely red from top to bottom; his broken bonds hung along his thighs, but could not be distinguished from the tendons of his wrists which had been completely stripped of flesh; his mouth remained wide open; two flames came from his eye sockets which seemed to go up into his hair; and the wretch kept walking!

The novel has been aiming all along to convert bodies into animate matter. Flaubert seems driven to discover what of substance remains when pain and mutilation efface all vestiges of recognizable humanity in the person. Incredibly, Salammbo looks into Matho's flaming eyes and recalls the loving words this entity has spoken to her when he was still a man: 'she did not want him to die!' If this love, which sees past the horribly disfigured flesh and conceives a hope for continued life, is meant to represent the novel's answer to sadism, it comes after too much carnage and ugliness to be plausible. Certainly, Salammbo's wish that Matho should live runs wholly contrary to everything animal or human that has gone before, with the exception of the elephant's caress. Up to this point, the goal has been nothing but death, and the bloodier the death, the better. It is really too late, however, for Flaubert to pull out of the course he has set for himself: Salammbo's tenderness is flyweight opposition to the great rolling machine that has crushed and dismembered countless bodies. There is no credible transcendent vision for the human players in this novel. The animals suggest a way of life that does not depend upon torture, but the mass of people are too deeply swayed by their depraved fetishism to even begin to look at the animal in the way that Flaubert does. The culture in *Salammbo* is quite simply a death-loving culture.

By way of transition to discussion of Timothy Findley's *Not Wanted on the Voyage,* I wish briefly to mention a story by Flaubert which, like Findley's novel, is a response to Christian belief. Where the popular version (see Thurston, pp 314–16) of the medieval legend of St Julian the Hospitaller focuses upon the acts of mercy St Julian performs as penance for killing his parents, Flaubert's 'The Legend of St Julian Hospitator' expands greatly upon the bloodlust in Julian prior to his crime. The popular version notes Julian's fondness for hunting in a scant two sentences; in Flaubert's version, the origin and exercise of Julian's lust to kill animals takes up almost two-thirds of the narrative.[1] The fulfilment of the prophecy of the stag who, with Julian's arrow lodged in his forehead, curses him three times and tells him he will kill his parents, is not accidental for Flaubert, but rooted in Julian's thirst for animal blood.

It is a thirst that originates in his childhood, when Julian, 'seized with hatred' (p 61) for a mouse, kills the creature. His second victim is a pigeon, whose neck he wrings and whose convulsions 'make his heart beat wildly, filling him with a savage, passionate delight' (p 62). Flaubert describes at length the many animals that fall victim to Julian's passion as Julian grows up. He exemplifies the wantonness of this passion when Julian lops the feet off a sleeping wood-grouse (p 65) and blithely goes on his way. The moment of the stag's prophetic utterance is preceded by a scene of incredible slaughter, reminiscent of such scenes in *Salammbo,* but here with moral overtones. Julian is in the woods, killing animals right and left. In fact, they come to him in great numbers, circling round him, 'all trembling and gazing at him with gentle, supplicating eyes' (p 66). Suddenly, he comes upon an enclosed valley filled with stags. He shoots arrows into the herd, his appetite for death seemingly insatiable:

The maddened stags fought, reared up in the air, and climbed on each other's backs, their bodies and tangled antlers making a broad mound which kept shifting and crumbling.

At last they died, stretched out on the sand, their nostrils foaming, their entrails gushing out, and the heaving of their bellies gradually subsiding. (pp 66–7)

The stag who delivers the prophecy is part of a family; Julian kills the fawn, and when the doe gives 'a deep, heart-rending, human cry,' Julian kills her too, out of exasperation. Nothing provokes a change of heart in Julian, neither the scene of carnage he causes, nor the manifest personal grief of the individual animal.

The stag's prophecy changes only Julian's habits; his desire for animal blood remains intact. He has dreams of being in Paradise, surrounded by animals; Julian's 'paradise,' however, presupposes no accord with animals but only endless slaughter (p 72). Flaubert predicates the murder of Julian's parents upon the frustration of Julian's desire for bloodshed. On the night before the prophecy is fulfilled, Julian is out in a forest, having decided to begin hunting again. Now, despite his most determined efforts, the animals that appear to him will not die from his arrows; they disappear at the instant he thinks he has scored a hit. Animals surround him again, taunting him this time: a bear knocks his hat off his head; a panther scornfully drops an arrow at his feet. These animals 'seemed to be thinking out a plan of revenge' (p 77). Thus, his 'lust for blood took hold of him again, and since animals were lacking he would gladly have slaughtered men' (p 78). Ironically, of course, the people he kills in his state of thwarted lust are his parents. Such is the revenge of the animals upon cruelty that is suppressed merely, and not authentically relinquished. Flaubert imputes power to animals; even at the stage at which they fall victim to one man's ability to spread death amongst them, the extravagance of that man's success mocks the whole idea of the hunt and reflexively discredits the motive for killing animals. That their resistance to being killed takes civilized form – the form of ridicule, or simply vanishing, rather than paying back hatred with hatred – similarly returns the evil in Julian's character to Julian himself.

The remainder of Flaubert's retelling is similar enough to the popular version of the legend to render description unnecessary. It is interesting to note, though, that Flaubert's alterations to this part of the legend – the fact that Julian's wife does not go with him into exile, or that Flaubert's Leper carries Julian to heaven instead of preceding him there – are the sources of concern mentioned by Robert Baldrick in his introduction to the Penguin edition, and not the extraordinarily attenuated scenes involving animal victims. In view of the lengths Flaubert goes to in the examination of St Julian's bloodlust, these other changes seem trivial. The idea that they could ever provoke reader resistance suggests a certain area of blindness, if only on the part those who speculate upon how Christians would receive the story. That said, Flaubert's version does indicate a critique of Christianity, structurally, through filling in what is omitted in the legend, and philosophically, through showing that the change in Julian hinges upon an authentic renunciation of an inveterate passion for slaughter. Flaubert is not complacent about the killing of animals; he does not treat this act as negligible, as a point that can be glossed over in a sentence or two. While it may be true that the scenes of animal slaughter add drama to what was a bloodless and rather flat story (as legends of saints often are), it cannot be denied that the enhancement of imaginative power occurs not at the expense of the animal, but by means of a magnification of animal significance. Flaubert subordinates the spiritual message of the Christian legend to dramatic elucidation of the human/animal connection. The dismissive line at the end of the tale – 'And that is the story of St Julian Hospitator' – signals Flaubert's honest admission that he cannot really reconcile the extant legend with all the cultural material he has incorporated into his version. The anemic, authorized legend cannot be brought to account for the bloodlust which Flaubert reveals is hidden behind the deceptively innocent opening lines.

Flaubert has taken up a considerable proportion of discussion in this chapter, and with good reason. He has by far the most complex attitude towards animals of any author examined to this point. As well as demonstrating conflicts in the modern approach to myth, Flaubert exhibits an acutely tortured responsiveness to animal victims. Animals are not animals in the abstract for him. When he writes about immense animal suffering (including that of the human animal), he is cognizant of the reality of the animal's experience, of the real pain and real fear animals undergo. Yet however hard he drives his fiction into carnage, he cannot wrest real pain out of the flesh in the artistic context. That he wants to realize suffering in art is clear enough. Had he been able to do so, he might have permitted himself to express the tenderness for the animal that he feels outside his art. He is unwilling, though, to manufacture pain and indulge false compassion. Myth in its historical context gives him a pretext for looking into a cruelty towards the animal which he himself does not feel. The broken world of myth lets him hunt for a holism which he knows would be false in any cultural context.

TIMOTHY FINDLEY'S ALLEGORY OF A WORLD WITHOUT MAGIC

In *Not Wanted on the Voyage,* Timothy Findley uses the myth of the Flood and critique of this myth to arrive at an allegory of the current state of human relations with nature. The ark manifests literally the hierarchical power structure given by Judaeo-Christian belief. Large animals and some mythical monsters dwell on the darkest and lowest deck, while presiding over all the creatures, on the open, upper deck, is Dr Noah Noyes, patriarch, self-declared 'reverend,' magician, and vivisector. Towards the end of the novel, the 'lower orders' do manage to disrupt the literal arrangement, but the fundamental evils of the belief system have produced other, more permanent iniquities. Much that is magical is lost from the world even before the further degeneration of the sacred and magical which occurs on the voyage itself. As the ark sails forth, at the end of book two, leaving all the lovely, vital world to drown, it condemns to extinction, also, the Faeries. The Faeries beat upon the walls and roof of the ark, but 'the ark, as ever, was adamant. Its shape had taken on a voice. And the voice said: *no*' (p 193). At the novel's conclusion, the ark's '*no*' has become literal, one sign of its triumph being the loss to the animals of their voices. The sheep, which used to sing hymns, can only repeat 'Baaaa's,' and the whispers which had produced dialogue in the mind of the cat Mottyl have died. Since God, Yaweh, has also died earlier in the novel, the silencing of the animals' voices leaves humankind alone in a mute world just like that which anthropocentrism gives us.

Talking animals will no doubt be discomforting to the modern sensibility which seeks appreciation of the anti-human qualities of animals. There is, nevertheless, a qualitative difference between the context in *Not Wanted on the Voyage* that presupposes animal speech and that of the animal fable, which imposes speech upon personified animals. That difference resides partly in motive. Findley has the animals speak to drive home the loss to culture when animals stop talking. Here, too, the influence of modern ethics and hopefulness is seen, since modern culture, in its own inept fashion, is attempting to penetrate the silence of the animal and comprehend animal language. One can view *Not Wanted on the Voyage* as an ethical work which fabricates animal dialogue for the purpose of discomposing settled belief in the blankness of animal consciousness. The difference between animal speech in *Not Wanted on the Voyage* and that in the animal fable is determined, furthermore, by conception. Whereas the point of the animal fable is to render morals palatable to humans, or to please human needs in some other way, the point of *Not Wanted on the Voyage* is to raise the value of the animal against human beliefs. Animals are an end in *Not Wanted on the Voyage,* not a means. Animal language, then, is only to a small degree tendentious; the mythical, magical context naturalizes animal language. It seems, simply, right that in the 'blooming, buzzing' world before the flood, animals should participate in the community of discourse. The change that silences animals is a world-change, not merely a cultural change. Reversing modern epistemology's confident assumption that culture has abandoned myth and found nature, this novel says that culture has dropped out of myth and lost nature.

Different as the two novels are, there is one curious point of similarity between *Salammbo* and *Not Wanted on the Voyage.* Just as a moment of deep tenderness occurs in *Salammbo* when an elephant caresses Hamilcar with its mutilated trunk, so too does an elephant in *Not Wanted on the Voyage* prove itself morally superior by rescuing the cat Mottyl when she has fallen to the lowest deck of the ark. While the context for Flaubert's brief invocation of the gentleness of these large beings is naturalistic and historical, and the context for Findley's appeal to animal virtue is fabulous and therefore permits narrative extension, the scenes are central in both novels. Human violence and ignorance rage all around these peaceable creatures. Granted, the capacity of Flaubert's elephant to become aggressive in battle suggests a dimensionality that is missing from Findley's conception of elephants and from his conception of animals in general. Findley barely mentions wildness in animals; he could be charged, that is, with stereotyping animals for moralistic purposes. The central episode with the elephant could be cited as the clearest example of such stereotyping, in the same way that his attribution of language to animals could be said to indicate an underlying, anti-animal moralism. Yet in the sense that animal ways of being in the world put to shame human ways of being in the world, the implicit argument in *Not Wanted on the Voyage* that the supposed absence of animal virtue is a function of human blindness is valid. By means of the fabulous, Findley performs the same act of casting humankind as the enemy as later writers of the wild animal's story do. It is up to the reader to translate his allegory into conflict between nature and culture. As with *Salammbo,* the elephant's gentleness in Findley's novel represents an instance of grace in which the natural clearly outclasses the feverish effects of human delusion.

'Delusion' is the operative word for the legacy of Judaeo-Christian ideology as Findley represents it. Dr Noyes is a noxious character, and yet there is pathos in the madness he displays as, at the end of the novel, he is left all alone to invent Yaweh's edicts in a flat, godless world . The decree from 'Yaweh' that Noah delivers is the biblical one that 'everything that lived and breathed and moved had been delivered into their hands [the hands of humans: the hands, more precisely, of men] – *forever*' (p 351). The decree is based on nothing at all. In essence, the natural world, like Yaweh (p 242), says 'no' in turn to the negations it suffers from religion and science. The sign, the olive branch, that Dr Noyes takes for the re-emergence of the natural world in fact comes from the Dove's cage on board the ark itself. The rainbow, which Dr Noyes says is the symbol of God's covenant with humankind, is a paper rainbow, a prop from a magic show Dr Noyes created to entertain Yaweh. With the destruction of mythic consciousness, the living correspondence of humans and nature is also destroyed. Human language is rejected by the natural world and loses meaning. All that humans are left with is the 'noise' of Dr Noyes and his kind.

Dr Noyes reduces nature to a paste-and-paper magic show, to a fabrication of his own crazed brain. What is more, allegorically speaking, the natural world in the form of the animals gathered on the ark either refuses or has lost the power to correct Dr Noyes. 'Holy' really does mean 'no way out' (p 270); the ark is stalled; and we, humans and animals, are a sadly diminished, captive but indifferent, audience to the pathetically arbitrary edicts of the Dr Noyeses of the world. *Not Wanted on the Voyage* allegorically re-enacts the historical progress that has left culture chattering away to itself in the midst of a silent world.

Pitiful as it is at the end of the novel, the meaninglessness of Dr Noyes's utterances and acts reveals a deadly side in the ugliest scene in the novel. The 'sacrifice' of the Unicorn leaps out of *Not Wanted on the Voyage* as markedly cruel and perverse. In this respect, it appears to violate the sense of the fabulous that Findley sustains, despite the occurrence of other animal deaths like that of an ape-child or a sacrificial lamb early in the novel. The departure from the generally wholesome and tolerable, however, drives home both the savagery and the madness of a world controlled and interpreted by Dr Noyes. The rationale that Dr Noyes invents for the unjustifiable transgression against the fragile, barely embodied Unicorn underscores the unreality of all the explanations he and his kind will give in the future.

Throughout the novel, Findley's ethical concern for animals is combined with feminism; women and animals are victimized in the sacrifice of the Unicorn. Dr Noyes forces the Unicorn to participate in the defloration of Emma, the girl-bride whose natural aversion to her repulsive husband rather than her anatomy is source of the failure of sexual relations in their marriage. The violence done to Emma's vagina is an act of aggression against love; with the triumph of rape over conjugal love, there can be no place for Unicorns in the world that Dr Noyes creates. Already dying from savage treatment and psychic abuse of its shy existence, the Unicorn receives the final blow from Emma's husband; furious, Japeth hacks off the Unicorn's horn with his sword: 'Later, Japeth would come to understand he had acted as the arm of God. Noah would explain this for him' (p 266). The blatant malignancy of this whole episode compels the desperate Dr Noyes to manufacture a transparently factitious ritual to sanctify his deed. Cloven-hooved, the Unicorn is not a proper sacrificial animal, and so he hits upon the expedient of sacrificing the horn instead. The horn becomes 'the sacred Phallus,' and thus the male organ becomes a fetish. Ironically, the 'sacred Phallus' is ground into golden dust as part of the ritual sacrifice. The whole craven, faithless performance Dr Noyes names the *'Ritual Ceremony of the Holy Phallus, in Remembrance of Yaweh's Holy Beast, the Sacred Unicorn'* (p 273). In highly convoluted and post hoc fashion, then, Dr Noyes blames the victim under the pretence of sanctifying it.

For the reader, it is the impression of the Unicorn as an animal, and not as a symbol or even as a magical creature, that makes the circumstances of its death unerringly abhorrent. As Findley depicts it, the Unicorn is an especially delicate animal, so retiring as to be almost unearthly. Dragging such an animal into the sordid act of ravaging a female child constitutes an assault on the whole of animality, including that which humankind shares in common with other species. In fact, the novel is generally so empathetic towards animals that only a deep rage against human uses of animals could have permitted Findley to drive his art towards the ugly scene of the Unicorn's death. With this episode, Findley reveals, furthermore, the corruption in the male fantasy, mentioned in chapter 5, likening the killing of animals to the sexual conquest of women. Findley inverts the fantasy: men do not stride bravely through the world penetrating living beings with phalluses and spears, but instead meanly usurp the animal's vitality and pervert it for use as a weapon against women, killing both animals and love in the process.

Not Wanted on the Voyage effects several significant reversals of this sort. One can note, as another example, the reversal of evolutionary relations, such that it is not apes which 'give birth' to humankind, but humankind which gives birth to apes. In effect, Darwinian evolution does try to give birth to apes, to bring them into the family of beings presumed to have significance in the conceptual world. Many of Dr Noyes's acts are designed to negate the familial connection between humans and apes. In his family, ape-children are murdered. From an allegorical perspective, one can observe that the living patrimony of the ape is denied even in the modern age; despite the assertion of continuity between ourselves and, specifically, apes, apes and all other animals are still held firmly in some void which permits our treatment of their interests as inconsequential. Hence, the visionary, transvestite

Lucifer/Lucy's assertion that humans 'will go on throwing all the apes and all the demons and all the Unicorns overboard for as long as the voyage lasts' (p 349). '[A]n ape was only an animal. Nothing human' (p 170), Japeth argues to himself after he has killed an ape-child loved by another family and rescued from the flood by Mrs Noyes. In her anger, Mrs Noyes utters a blasphemy: 'There is no God ... There is no God worthy of this child' (p 170). It is perhaps possible, since this is fantasy, to miss the seriousness of Mrs Noyes's denunciation. Findley is not effecting a light or playful rearrangement of traditional hierarchies. With Mrs Noyes's assertion, he elevates an animal who has yet to make it into the community of respected beings over the 'Being' whom religion treats as the most meaningful in all of creation. The suggestion that we can look to the essentially anathematized animal to understand what is valuable challenges both the illusory transcendence of religion and the reductionism of science. Findley's challenge, furthermore, hinges upon the biological connection between humans and apes which fantasy allows him to reveal as literal rather than theoretical or metaphoric.

Here, then, is another connection between *Salammbo* and *Not Wanted on the Voyage:* both Flaubert and Findley use the real, embodied in animals, to discompose belief systems and their effects upon the world. The animal victims are not figurative, as myth would have them, but representatives of a genuine conceptual world which disputes the authenticity of myth and especially of the acts which find their justification in myth. Findley differs from Flaubert in infusing the good, natural world that is lost with animistic vitality. Flaubert, as indicated earlier, wants to reach in art the materiality of all living beings. Yet disagree as they might upon what reality is, both authors realize that, divorced from nature, human belief can only produce myths that are synonymous with lies. And both realize that, ungrounded, myth needs to victimize the living body, human and animal, to declare its materiality.

MYTHIC INFLATION AND HISTORICAL DEFLATION IN FAULKNER'S 'THE BEAR'

In 'The Bear,' William Faulkner equivocates upon the recognition that myth seeks to prove its authenticity in the victimization of living bodies. Faulkner loves myth and mourns the collapse of myth into history. He does, however, treat the physical death of the totemic bear which draws hunters to the woods year after year as one stage in the disintegration of mythic consciousness. But, in marked contrast to Timothy Findley, he seeks virtue in virility: combined with the death of the bear, and the sale and destruction of the bear's woods, is the disappearance of the 'real man.' Faulkner sees, rightly, that historical progress has undermined the myth of masculine psychopomp, such that modern men can only go ignobly into the woods to hunt. Yet he seems also to want to predicate the now-lost myth of the hunt upon the failure to kill the totemic animal. Certainly, the annual hunt, as Faulkner depicts it, stands as an admonishment to life in Memphis, where 'men in starched collars and neckties' and 'ladies rosy in furs' stroll hard pavements and dine in restaurants. These city people 'had never heard' of the great dog Lion or the legendary bear Old Ben, 'and didn't want to' (p 234). Nostalgia for the demise of the hunting ethos informs 'The Bear.' But nostalgia for the living bear conflicts with the remembered sanctities of the hunt. Ironically, as Mary Allen astutely observes, all the stories in Go Down, Moses, including 'The Bear,' 'substantiate the hunt as an *immoral* activity' (p 153). While Memphis life is inferior to the life of the hunt, the hunt demonstrates its own unworthiness in taking the life of the revered animal.

Faulkner's story, as it is currently published, has a long passage of McCaslin family history inserted into it. In an interview in the late 1950s, Faulkner said that this passage, section IV, 'doesn't belong in ['The Bear'] as a short story.' He encourages the reader to 'skip that when you come to it' (in Utley et al, eds, *Bear, Man, and God,* p 116). Section IV, however, has several beneficial effects upon the text, not the least among them being that it provides, in Irving Howe's words, 'an abrasive disruption of the idyllic nostalgia previously accumulated' (p 257). In section IV, after Ike McCaslin has related the tale of his meeting with Old Ben and his failure to shoot the bear when he could, his cousin quotes Keats's 'Ode on a Grecian Urn' at him: 'She cannot fade, though thou hast not thy bliss, / Forever wilt thou love, and she be fair!' (p 297). These lines from Keats are quoted also in the original, 1935 version of 'The Bear.' In that version, the boy's father speaks the lines to explain to the boy why he (the boy) did not shoot Old Ben. The boy's encounter with Old Ben is the climactic moment in the 1935 version of the story: Old Ben does not die in this version. By a process of successive distancing, then, the lines from Keats come to ring hollow in the extended version of 'The Bear.' They are delivered by a man whose relation to Ike is more distant than that of the father to the boy in the original. They are isolated from the primary text by the shift in mood and range characterizing the historical passage. More important, the lines are uttered against the reader's knowledge that Old Ben has been killed. The memory of the long-dead bear, which the assertion in 'Ode on a Grecian Urn' should enshrine, in fact makes feeble compensation for the living animal. It can also be granted, with some reluctance, that the masculine myth of the hunt is sufficiently convincing to eclipse Keats's delicate, poetic sentiment. The hunters have the totemic Old Ben; future generations have only the anecdotal bear. As Irving Howe indicates, the whole of section IV leads up to the disenchantment driven home by the last section of the story, in which Ike returns to the scene of the hunt and finds that 'hunting' in the abstract has been desecrated.

The conclusion of 'The Bear' comes as a surprise, in view of the mythic ponderousness Faulkner has infused into the hunt in the first three sections of the story. Everything about the hunting trips appears at first to speak of an immutably superior way of existence. The hunters compose a community of men, bonded together so perfectly as to negate the racial differences that Faulkner himself cannot overlook. At least, that is, a transcendence of racial prejudice is one of Faulkner's opening flourishes in praise of the hunt: part of the 'best of all talking' to which Ike is exposed on these trips to the woods concerns 'men, not white nor black nor red but men, hunters with the will and hardihood to endure and the humility and skill to survive' (p 191). Even the whiskey these men drink has to be robed in mythic significance:

[I]t would seem to him that those fine fierce instants of heart and brain and courage and wiliness and speed were concentrated and distilled into that brown liquor which not women, not boys and children, but only hunters drank, drinking not of the blood they spilled but some condensation of the wild immortal spirit, drinking it moderately, humbly even, not with the pagan's base and baseless hope of acquiring thereby the virtues of cunning and strength and speed but in salute to them. (p 192)

Clearly, for Faulkner, these are not just a bunch of men off on a toot in the woods. They participate annually in a mystic ceremony, a ritual affirming the potent spirit of the wilderness and the 'humility and pride' – a keynote – of the hunter in the face of that spirit.

The totality of that spirit is summed up in Old Ben. All the other animals are fair game. Shooting a buck and being daubed with the buck's blood is a mystic rite for the boy. This initiation is described in Faulkner's 'The Old People'; in this story, as Ike anticipates shooting the buck, he thinks that soon 'he would draw the blood, the big blood which would make him a man, a hunter.' Other animals, evidently, have 'little blood': rabbits are the target of boys in 'apprenticeship' to manhood (p 195). In the course of time, killing animals has virtually disappeared as a rationale for the hunt. Major de Spain and old General Compson, who preside over the yearly excursion, have already demonstrated their prowess as hunters and men, and seem to spend the whole time back at camp, sharing the 'best of all talk' and the mystic whiskey, and not shooting animals. Only inferior men, and the boy, go off to kill the lesser beasts:

Boon and the negroes (and the boy now too) fished and shot squirrels and ran the coons and cats, because the proven hunters ... scorned such other than shooting the wild gobblers with pistols for wagers or to test their marksmanship. (pp 204–5)

'Gobblers' (note the uneasy childishness in the designation: these are not 'turkeys'), evidently, are nothing better than moving objects for the lazy whim of the proven hunter. Neither 'big blood' nor little blood runs through turkey veins; if it did, the proven hunter would be sinking to the level of boys and people of colour in shooting the birds. The power that continues to draw these men into the woods, then, is concentrated in Old Ben. The men return to the woods, 'not to hunt deer and bear but to keep yearly rendezvous with the bear which they did not even intend to kill' (p 194) – or at least that is the impression the boy has. Later, he realizes that the men 'had no actual intention of slaying' the bear, 'not because it could not be slain but because they had no actual hope of being able to' (p 201). Already, mythical import is beginning to succumb to disillusionment. The hunters, who will not deign to shoot lesser animals, are in fact brave, or short-sighted, enough to kill Old Ben if it could be done, and thus to bring an end to the mighty, spiritual quest of which only Old Ben could be the object. Testifying to the immorality of the intent to slay Old Ben is the fact that the inferior man, Boon Hogganbeck, kills the bear, and not the distant white hunters. Only a mortal man, it appears, can prove the bear likewise mortal and defile its totemic meaning.

'The Bear' is, in fact, a *Bildungsroman*. In the eyes of the innocent boy, Old Ben is

not even a mortal beast but an anachronism indomitable and invincible out of an old dead time, a phantom, epitome and apotheosis of the old wild life which the little puny humans swarmed and hacked at in a fury of abhorrence and fear like pygmies about the ankles of a drowsing elephant; – the old bear, solitary, indomitable and alone; widowered, childless and absolved of mortality – old. (pp 193–4)

When Old Ben wounds a female dog with its claws, 'it was still no living creature but only the wilderness which, leaning for a moment, had patted lightly once her temerity' (p 199). When the boy grows into the realization that this bear is mortal and can be destroyed, he undergoes physical sensations denoting both fear and lust: he experiences 'a flavor like brass in the sudden run of saliva in his mouth, [and] a hard sharp constriction either in his brain or his stomach' (p 200). He realizes, simultaneously, 'his own fragility and impotence': he too is mortal; the hunt does not distinguish him above the animals he kills.

The mortal bear is still far enough removed from the state of the natural animal to be invoked by mystic rites. By some uncanny telepathy, the bear knows when the boy has jettisoned the trappings of civilization. First, the boy leaves his gun behind to walk unarmed into the bear's territory. This weaponlessness is 'a condition in which not only the bear's heretofore inviolable anonymity but all the ancient rules and balances of hunter and hunted had been abrogated' (p 207). When, after nine hours, the boy has not yet encountered Old Ben, he realizes that the watch and compass he carries are signs of impurity which repel the bear. Once he rids himself of these remaining instruments, he at last sees the bear. Even so, the bear is not an animal but a metaphysical emanation defying natural law:

It did not emerge, appear: it was just there, immobile, fixed in the green and windless noon's hot dappling, not as big as he had dreamed it but as big as he had expected, bigger, dimensionless against the dappled obscurity, looking at him. Then it moved. It crossed the glade without haste, walking for an instant into the sun's full glare and out of it, and stopped again and looked back at him across one shoulder. Then it was gone. It didn't walk into the woods. It faded, sank back into the wilderness without motion. (p 209)

Despite having been called up by magic, and despite its physical nebulousness, the bear behaves as a real bear would most likely behave on encountering a human in the woods. Old Ben's nonviolent retreat in this instance marks one distinction between 'The Bear' and conventional hunting stories. Old Ben is not the ferocious beast of hunting lore, which threatens humans with its wicked claws and fangs and tests the hunter's virility. While it would be wrong to say that the boy's state of spiritual awe and passivity has drawn the bear to him, it would not be wrong to suspect reluctance on Faulkner's part to approve of victimization of at least this one animal. The mysticism that surrounds Old Ben, the fact that the bear safeguards the last vestiges of the genuine wilderness, seems in this passage to join forces with an unacknowledged empathy for the simple animal who wants to go its own way undisturbed.

This brief instant of communion with the natural animal quickly disappears under narrative preparation for the Battle of the Titans, which will see Old Ben pitted against Lion, the wild dog whose eyes express 'a cold and almost impersonal malignance like some natural force' (p 218). Obviously, something has to be done, narratively speaking, to shift the onus of Old Ben's death away from human beings, if only partially: humans, however humble and proud, are after all too puny to bring down the myth Faulkner has built up around the bear. Besides that, this year's hunt has to be quintessentially different from the hunts of other years: Old Ben cannot die by mischance alone. Thus Faulkner introduces Lion, an animal who equals Old Ben in strength and mystery. It is a foregone conclusion that Lion will also fall victim to this battle and die. Humankind has to be deprived utterly of mythic beasts; it would be a violation of progressive disillusionment if Lion were left in human hands, to keep alive the spirit of the untame and inhuman.

Boon Hogganbeck is a kind of scapegoat to Faulkner's need to eliminate the bear and show myth in collapse. The other men are too pure to commit the awful deed; if the myth of male bonding in the wilderness is to remain pristine, none of the proven hunters can assume the guilt of invalidating the hunt and consigning the wilderness to human authority for good. Boon Hogganbeck is a peculiar hybrid. He is something of a hero in having saved Ike's life by throwing him out of the path of a runaway horse and wagon (p 233). He attends so faithfully to Lion that their relationship is almost marital; the man and the dog sleep together, and when Boon caresses Lion, it is unclear which of the two, Lion or Boon, is the woman in this relationship (p 220). Boon kills the bear in the approved mythic manner: with a knife, not a gun. Yet Boon is of mixed blood, part Indian, part white, and has the mentality of a child. He has 'the ugliest face the boy had ever seen. It looked like somebody had found a walnut a little larger than a football and with a machinist's hammer had shaped features into it and then painted it, mostly red' (p 227). Faulkner has clearly worked hard to compose this face; natural and machine imagery clash to create a picture that is hardly human. At one point, Boon's face is described as a 'huge gargoyle's face' (p 225). In sum, Boon is both a likely and an unlikely challenger for the bear. He has the desperate heroism of the oppressed; he is a born victim, stigmatized by his mixed racial origins and his physical ugliness. He possesses both the psychological and the literary qualities that make him suitable for sacrifice to narrative pressure to nullify myth. Boon has to bear final guilt, too, for reducing the hunt to a pettiness.

Two years after the events which bring about the death of Old Ben, Ike returns to the woods. The annual hunting ritual has come to an end: Major de Spain has sold the timber-rights for the woods to a Memphis lumbering company, and the wilderness itself is about to be destroyed. Trains and city mentality are going to wreck the land. Ike recalls a time when the trains passing through the wilderness had been 'harmless' (p 320). Faulkner links the harmless coexistence of industry and wilderness with sympathy for the animal: he inserts a memory from the distant past in which a locomotive frightens a bear into a tree, and Boon sits beneath the tree for hours, waiting for the bear to come down and making sure that no one shoots the vulnerable creature. Only at this point, when the destruction of the woods will wipe out all the

mythic potence of the hunt, does Faulkner introduce compassion
for the animal. Before this point, compassion for the animal would
have undermined the value of the hunt. Now, with the demise of
the hunting myth, it is possible for Faulkner to indulge sentimentality over the animal victim, albeit somewhat speciously. Nostalgia now demands that the hunt appear truly innocent and truly
mindful of the life of the animal.

There is a further loss of innocence to come. Passing the graves
of Lion and of Sam Fathers, who had guided him through his first
hunting experiences, Ike thinks that these beings have not ultimately died, but have merely been 'translated into the myriad life
which printed the dark mold of these secret and sunless places
with delicate fairy tracks' (p 328). Old Ben, he thinks, has also become inviolable. The crippled paw they have buried with Lion and
Sam Fathers will be returned to the mighty bear:

Old Ben, too; they would give him his paw back even, certainly they
would give him his paw back, then the long challenge and the long
chase, no heart to be driven and outraged, no flesh to be mauled and
bled – (p 329)

One detects Keatsian romanticism in Ike's fantasy, from the
spiritualization of Old Ben down to the 'delicate fairy tracks' that
cross the once virile wilderness. Fortunately, Faulkner is wise
enough not to let this idyllic delusion stand. While he finds it
necessary to introduce a rather obvious snake at this moment, he
is also going to sever all sentimental attachments to the myth of
the hunt. The 'snake' in this wild Eden is realism; the snake
foreshadows the last scene in the woods that Ike will encounter.
In this scene, bear-slayer Boon is sitting under a tree, as he had
sat under a tree previously protecting a frightened bear from
attack. This time, however, Boon is frantically trying to repair his
rifle so that he can shoot the multitude of squirrels running about
in the branches above him. He seems barely to recognize Ike, or
at least to view Ike only as a competitor for the inferior animals
he has singled out as his own personal prey. 'Get out of here!' he
yells at his friend; 'Dont touch them! Dont touch a one of them!
They're mine!' With these words, the hunt is reduced to the mean-
est of human terms, to avarice and selfishness, to a mundanely
lustful act whose only object is to kill animals.

CONCLUSION

With the final scene in 'The Bear,' Old Ben falls into mortality. Like all the other animal victims, in *Salammbo* and 'The Legend of St. Julian Hospitator,' and in *Not Wanted on the Voyage,* Old Ben pulls down with him human faith in myth. Whether the debunking of myth is a healthy process, as it is with Flaubert, or an occasion for sadness, as it is with Findley and Faulkner, animal bodies have borne the brunt of modern disillusionment. The struggle to resurrect myth as dynamic, creative narrative meets its match in the mortal animal. The animal reminds us of our own death. Where myth articulates the hope that humans are not merely material beings, that by some magical power the right kind of language will confer immortality upon natural beings, modern fiction remains sceptical. Animals carry the force of realism. Their silence acts as a barrier to linguistic intention. Their death closes the gap between nature and culture.

While it is good that some quality in fiction's use of myth can bring the literal animal into contact with cultural representation, it is a pity that the reminder of the natural animal has to be death. The hope that modern people place in myth is a hope for rapport with the whole world of living creatures. Modern culture gives us, instead, rapport with the dying animal, the animal victim. Though one cannot discount myth as forming a link between culture and nature, it is largely by means of the attitude which treats myth as synonymous with fallacies that modern narrative establishes that link. The idea of myth is of vital strategic significance, nonetheless. In the next chapter, we find that narrative can convert even the death of the natural animal into a cultural commodity. The remarkable aspect of this turn within the argument is that few modern narratives actually do perform this double oppression upon animals, where one would think that the culture-bound nature of any artistic enterprise would automatically divest animals of natural import. The danger of using animal death to serve cultural ends is ever-present in mythic intention, yet it seems that only especially strained aesthetics, distinct from culturally fostered and authorized myth, distorts animals so greatly as to denaturalize death.

7 The Doubly Victimized Animal

By way of rounding off this analysis of animal victims in modern fiction, I turn now to stories in which qualities of the narrative itself perpetrate literary aggression against animal victims. Discussion thus far has traced animal victims accordingly as they are more and more deeply implicated in cultural conflicts, ranging from efforts to derive heroic values from a mute natural world to the foundering of myth upon animal bodies. In all of the stories, animals serve to illuminate and intensify thematic concerns. It is precisely that aspect of the use of animals in stories discussed to this point that might well arouse the argument that none of these animals are animals in fact but only cultural images manufactured to fit into various human problems. Animal victims in fiction work so well to uproot profound complications in human experience that their very utility appears to argue against the position I have taken: that a great many post-Darwinian authors really do manage to incorporate animal resistance to human culture into their works. Animals are present in all works of fiction, it could be argued, primarily to illuminate the human condition, and they are twisted out of their natural state accordingly. Admittedly, the meaningfulness of animal death in the previously discussed works of fiction has reference to human culture and may even be said to derive from human culture. It must be admitted, as well, that culture penetrates the images of animals in these stories at least as far as to supersede the complete indifference of natural animals to culture. Parts of the animal, that is to say, are co-opted: the animal innocence, vitality, suffering, and, most often and paradoxically, the selfsame indifference to culture that makes them meaningful to a modern writer in the first place. Nevertheless, in so far as the animal victim confounds resolution of the human dilemmas to which they have reference, they can be said to stand apart from the cultural field and to preserve at least some of their natural autonomy. The totality of the animal is not assimilated into the fictional world. An ethic which would prevail against the victimization of animals is somewhere in evidence, however remote that ethic may be from the necessity to articulate honestly the nature of actual experience. In other words, aggression against animals is not a given in these stories. Aggression against animals is essential for the expression of the profundity of conflict, but conflict is disclosed *as* conflict by means of animal qualities that remain aloof and unimplicated. The ethic of regard for nonhuman animals does not stand alone, either; it is supported by a literary drive to force culture towards contact with the natural animal.

In the stories now to be discussed, the shaping vision prescribes what looks like victimization of what look like animals. There is little evidence of an ethic which would inhibit the liberties taken by the text in its depiction of violence against animals. More important, however, the absence of such an ethic detracts from the literary image of animals. Animals are clearly a device in these stories used to explore and frequently to inflate the human image. Animals in these stories are, in essence, scarcely animals at all but schematic elements in an aesthetic or psychological design. It is here that the argument that all animals in fiction are merely figures of human construction, merely metaphors, and lack autonomous meaning is disconfirmed. When literary animals are wholly subject to human design and lose a living connectedness with their own world, they cease to communicate values important to culture and operate instead to reinforce artificial aims in culture. Why victimize them, then, if cruelty means nothing? The fact is that violence against animals in stories falling into this final category is in essence fake violence. It is akin to the violence in recent movies which make the counting of bodies part of the fun for some members of the audience. Like the humanity of the bodies that drop in these movies, the animality of the animal victims in these stories is negligible or non-existent. Just as these movies clear a space for the hero and establish him as the consummate target of aggression, these stories affirm the central importance of humankind. Because real life seems determined to inform us as a species and as individuals that we are insignificant, there is a kind of gratification to be had from imagining ourselves as the object of enemies, however anonymous, who are hell-bent on annihilating us. While it can be reasonably argued that fiction cannot truly escape the anthropocentrism on which it is founded, stories in this chapter go further and exploit animal victims to reinforce the illusion that human beings are set apart as the special object and focus of fate. This is not to say that cruelty to animals is rendered innocuous by the aesthetic rationalization of illusion. Quite the reverse is true: these stories tacitly encourage aggression against real animals by implying that nonhuman animals are devoid of experience worthy of human consideration. Because human subjectivity is likewise bound to formalities of narrative, the obligation to heed the voice of compassion evaporates. These stories reflect that deadening of sensibility which in life allows humans to victimize animals without scruple. The reification of anti-animal and anti-human values makes these stories dangerous, since there is a sense in which modern culture would like nothing better than to be relieved of responsibility to the natural animal and to the animal in each human being.

Commentary begins with Ernest Hemingway's *The Sun Also Rises*. Hemingway makes an interesting case because the famous stripped style of writing he affects should in theory articulate well the elementary state in which animals are presumed to live. That this style has the opposite result, that it negates instead of realizing the animal, suggests either that culture has acknowledged the complexity of animal experience or that the style itself manifests a deliberate refusal on Hemingway's part to confront life squarely. The irony, of course, is that both the style and content of his stories boast of their superior authenticity over more tangled perspectives on life, when in fact Hemingway uses the bluff style of writing to screen animal identity from view.

Since naked prose cheats the animal of its proper experiential scope, one might think that surrealism[1] would convey the full strangeness of animal being and its influence upon human consciousness. Surrealism should grasp the irrational in the human/

animal connection, where the irrational defies the sterility of empirical conceptions of animals. Franz Kafka's animal stories and the brilliant, recently translated novel *Cow,* by Beat Sterchi, demonstrate that departures from realism can produce striking benefits for the status of animals. Yet it takes a sustained act of conscience, rare in self-consciously surreal works, for the writer to yield aesthetic power to animals. Enamoured of the act of creation itself, surrealists fall too easily into exploiting the animal victim simply to prove that they are assaulting normal perceptions of life. Freed from commitment to representationalism, surrealistic narrative finds itself freed from the liabilities of conscience as well. Nothing in the narrative impedes violence against animals. That violence, indeed, serves an artistic end primarily in that it enhances the distinctiveness of the surreal vision. Mangled animals reinforce the impression of narrative deviation from common reality. I have chosen Graeme Gibson's *Communion* and Jerzy Kosinski's *Painted Bird* to illustrate how the surrealistic mode can co-opt the shock value inherent to violence against animals. No doubt, if we looked at life from the animal's perspective, persistent human aggression would indeed yield madness of the sort Gibson and Kosinski invoke. In *Communion* and *The Painted Bird,* however, the victimization of animals is not explored for the animal's sake, but simply feeds a narcissistic fantasy of persecution. Cruelty to animals is predictable, not because that is the reality for animals, but because the author has designed the imagined world to substantiate the protagonist's personal suffering. What should be inexplicable – violence against animals – becomes all too intelligible when one looks at artistic motivations for the kind of vision that these fictions construct.

Horror tales take similar liberties with animals. Despite the fact that the past few years have seen werewolves, giant insects, and enraged prehistoric creatures giving way to disfigured psychotic killers and demons from hell as images of terror in popular horror, it is still possible to manipulate animals to make them frightening. The movies *Jaws* and *Alien* attest to the continuing popularity of animal monsters; the shark's musical motif and the image of the 'alien' bursting out of the stomach fell quickly into common parlance, indicating an abiding fondness in the public for the creatures that frighten. Though I have argued elsewhere[2] that a significant number of modern works of horror lend power to animals to remind humankind that other beings besides ourselves occupy the planet, it is also true that the attribution to animals of a capacity to terrorize human beings supports a reactionary justification for continuing hostilities against them. The representation of the relation between humans and nonhuman animals as warlike has ancient roots. Indeed, though the collection of stories in this chapter is eclectic, the horror stories highlight a failing in Hemingway's works and in the two surreal works under consideration: all of the stories ultimately perpetuate the retrograde belief that animalkind and humankind exist in a state of war with one another. World-view and aesthetic mode conspire to render the victimization of animals inevitable. Among works of horror, those that are most satisfying to a modern desire to restore power to animals are those that go overboard and imply that animals are victorious over humankind. Daphne du Maurier's *The Birds* falls into this category, as does the film *The Frogs* and, in effect, Arthur Herzog's novel *The Swarm*.

The horror story chosen for discussion in this chapter pits only one human being against one animal and, of course, the animal is dead at the end of the story. I have selected Stephen King's *Cujo* because it does some interesting work with paranoia about animals. Naturally enough, *Cujo* cannot incorporate critique of that paranoia or it would lose the power to frighten people and fall out of the genre of horror. One thing that distinguishes this story from others of the same genre is that the animal it uses is an ordinary domestic pet. The ordinariness of the St Bernard dog highlights the violence to which he is subjected. King labours to infuse the familiar animal with sinister qualities menacing to humanity. He strives to lend plausibility to the threat the animal must embody. Finally, however, the act that ends the familiar animal's life is of a violence that surpasses whatever justification there may be in the threat the animal represents. By means of fictional devices, *Cujo* distorts the animal *per se* into an object eminently deserving of the gruesome punishment which humankind ultimately carries out upon it.

The variety of stories that contrive to support anthropocentric pride at the expense of animals suggests the multiplicity of fronts on which efforts to affirm the inherent value of natural animals can be thwarted. The failure of these stories to include critique of the anthropocentric ideology that informs them indicates the significance to the image of animals of the cultural debate even as that debate remains on cultural plane. The self-enclosed and self-justifying nature of these stories constitutes the overarching victimization which negates and denaturalizes the suffering animal, much as does isolation of humankind from animals, not to mention that conceit which locates our species as the source of all meaning in life. It must be pointed out, however, that within these terms, fiction evidently has a great deal of flexibility. There is much that is interesting and even complicated about these stories, despite their deleterious effect upon animals. Indeed, this variety of interest would have to obtain; how else could one explain the many centuries of pleasure anthropocentrism has given to humankind?

MAKING ANIMAL VICTIMS DISAPPEAR: ERNEST HEMINGWAY AND EMPTY MACHISMO

It is easy to accuse Ernest Hemingway of perpetuating the anachronistic ideology of machismo. Certainly that ideology mandates insensitivity to animals, since the power to shed animal blood without squeamishness is fundamental to the establishment of virility under the terms of a macho approach to life. With his admiration for the bullfight and the safari, Hemingway does flaunt masculine prowess. But the quality of his vision, as Margot Norris discerns, runs counter to the attitude he professes to uphold. His animals are not the full-blooded beings that fall before the power of the male, but aesthetic objects with so scant a genuine presence in the narrative as to render manly posturing pathetic.

In *Beasts of the Modern Imagination,* Margot Norris provides a superb and detailed critique of Hemingway's attitudes as they appear in the prose works *Death in the Afternoon* and *Green Hills of Africa.* My own critique of *The Sun Also Rises* uses Norris' as a springboard. Although its tendency would be to convert animals into abstractions, the postmodern literary theory Norris applies does make an admirable tool for paring away the psychological and ideological mechanisms that obscure aesthetic aims. Instead of proposing, as one could, that the reduction of the animal to an object immune to injury and pain reveals an underlying sentimentality on Hemingway's part, Norris implies that the language he employs manifests greater sadism than the ideology he preaches. Remarking upon Hemingway's assertion in *Death in the Afternoon* that pain to the bull is 'incidental' to the artistry of the bullfight, Norris writes: '[t]he language itself enacts an order of mental or rational cruelty by stripping the inflicted pain of any intrinsic importance, by denying its centrality to the event, by dismissing it, with a sadist's arrogance, as a mere detail in a larger, abstract project' (p 199). Art, then, conspires with the rationalizations bullfighting needs to adopt in a culture anxious to recognize animal identity. The language is defensively barren; it seeks to fool the potentially hostile reader into believing that no animals are hurt in the arena, because, really, there are no animals present. The bulls are only animate objects in an artistic spectacle. Seen as art, the spectacle in the bullring does not merely override animal pain; it in fact causes that pain to disappear, since the whole event is just a geometric interplay of abstract forces in any case.

If that defence does not work, Hemingway erects the next barrier to empathy, which is empiricism. Effectively undermining the assertion that the bull's pain is 'incidental,' Hemingway argues that, anyway, pain is not really felt until half an hour after an injury is inflicted. Bulls are killed before they experience pain. Norris sees this argument as equally specious to that which tries to represent the bullfight as art. Hemingway, she says, assumes the role of 'neutralizer of violence,' when in fact his defensive strategies are designed to sanction cruelty to bulls. Whether the scientific assertion about the onset of pain is true or untrue, Hemingway's argument is factitious in that it is deployed only for the purpose of defending indefensible callousness.

As Norris realizes, the suffering of horses gored in the bullfight stands as a particularly strong contradiction to Hemingway's defence. Should a reader be convinced that the bullfight is an aesthetic event, or that bulls, as Hemingway asserts in *Toros Celebres,* in fact love the combat, the injuries to horses might still elicit the reader's indignation. Horses do not enjoy combat; they do not ask for the violence done to them, as a Hemingway bull supposedly does. They are innocent victims of a spectacle in which they do not participate psychically or aesthetically. Because of their innocence, Hemingway distances himself from them in a manner that exposes the disingenuousness of his argument as a whole. He has to treat the horses as comical beings, the clowns of the arena. In her critique of this gesture, Norris cites key descriptions from the first chapter of *Death in the Afternoon.* Hemingway writes:

There is certainly nothing comic by our standards in seeing an animal emptied of its visceral content, but if this animal instead of doing something tragic, that is, dignified, gallops in a stiff, old-maidish fashion around a ring trailing the opposite of clouds of glory it is as comic when what is trailing is real as when the Fratellinis give a burlesque of it in which the viscera are represented by rolls of bandages, sausages and other things. If one is comic, the other is. (*Death in the Afternoon*, p 7)

In keeping with the tendency of his language to convert the bull-fight into an abstraction, Hemingway here unites actual steaming bowels with vaudeville props under the same schematic principle. The vaudeville routine he describes does not seem particularly funny, but even if one did find it amusing, the desensitization necessary to find the goring of live horses equally amusing borders on the delusional. If Hemingway's description of the horses' gait as 'stiff' and 'old-maidish' is accurate, there is even greater cause for anger and compassion, for here is an animal of inherent dignity and bodily grace forced by pain and the weight of its own spilling intestines into an unnatural stride. Aesthetic distance is all very well, but some events call out so clearly for emotional response that aesthetic distance becomes unethical. Margot Norris bases her critique of Hemingway's description on the distinction between inside and outside:

Having established the horses' ridiculous and comic character, their disembowelings become 'burlesque visceral accidents,' more embarrassing than painful, and very funny, like shitting. 'I have seen it, people running, horses emptying, one dignity after another being destroyed in the spattering, and trailing of its innermost values, in a complete burlesque of tragedy ... '

In order to pull us from the inside to the outside, to disengage us from our site of empathy inside the terrified body of the blindfolded horse, dazed with pain, plunging desperately to expel the horn tearing at its bowels, Hemingway conjures up the metaphor of the comic theater, of circus, in order to make us appreciate only the visual exterior of the spectacle, 'the most picturesque incident' in the bullfight, and to distance us emotionally by making us laugh, as though the pain, fear, injury and death we see were no more real than in a theater performance. (pp 205–6)

Hemingway's blatantly strained rhetorical display in this instance is necessitated by the high probability that readers will identify with the horses, even when culturally fostered misconceptions about the ferocity of bulls prepare readers to accept the cruelty of the bullfight proper. Ridiculing the horses, whose innocence is unmistakable, Hemingway simultaneously makes fun of the empathic response to animals as a whole. Any indignation at the scene of animal pain he implicitly attributes to feeble-mindedness. His brand of virility and realism demands the callow response of literally laughing at pain. One is tempted to suggest that Hemingway finds the scene of the horses' injuries actually threatening and laughs out of nervousness.

At one point, Norris' critique of Hemingway expands into a global critique of culture in general:

Hemingway ultimately demystifies the bullfight by creating a new myth. He solves the mystery of how the killing of the animal can be great art by creating its tautological opposite: the mystery of how great art can be founded on animal torture and killing. Hemingway's specious answer, that killing can be done with courage, skill and technical brilliance to create a spectacle of incomparable beauty, masks another answer, that the bullfight epitomizes the anthropocentric bias upon whose consequent suppression of Nature (the animal, the body, pain) the Western tradition founded culture and art. (pp 200–1)

Placed in the context of Western culture as a whole, Hemingway's defence of the bullfight does reflect pre-modern anthropocentrism. Hemingway might not be displeased by this critique, since he scorns the sensitive modern male as an effeminate entity who deserves the contempt of the Hemingway female. That Hemingway cannot face the animal blood he spills, and must convert the human experience of animal death into art, also says a great deal about cultural process. Honouring animal symbols or the personified animal of fables, pre-modern culture could remain indifferent to the real animal body, which suffers from injuries, convulses in pain, and bleeds when it is stabbed. The living experience of the animal was kept isolated from the natural animal by aesthetic displacement. The many stories we have seen in which art strives for the reverse effect, strives to contain the suffering of real animals and comprehend the emotions that follow from that suffering, attest to the disintegration of the methods of negation Hemingway employs. Indeed, without meaning to, Hemingway articulates the deadness of anthropocentric culture.

The reader expecting to find his or her nerve tested upon great lashings of gore in a Hemingway story is going to be disappointed. The polemical demands of the essay require honest description of cruelty. His fiction elides even that basic level of confrontation. *The Sun Also Rises* promises to rise to a crescendo of violence, with most of the narrative moving purposefully towards the bull-fight; but the novel finally opts instead for a show of technical prowess displayed mostly in pedantic verbiage. Were Hemingway himself not given to machismo, one might suspect him of parodying the attitudes behind the lore of the bullfight. The anticlimactic presentation of the much-lauded bullfight could be seen to bespeak authorial irony sympathetic to his narrator's sexual impotence. In other words, the transfer of virility from actual gore to verbal ostentation could imitate the tragedy of Jake Barnes's physical affliction. Barnes could be an anti-hero, pathetic in his neurotic fondness for bull-fights and even more pathetic in the pride in didacticism he inflicts upon the other characters.

As a novelistic device, Barnes's impotence in fact serves the opposite purpose of saving him from being dragged down by wom-ankind. It relieves him of the burden of sexual performance and protects his psychic manhood from possible deterioration in an affiliation with a woman. The other male characters lose their manly aloofness in various courting rituals from which Jake is exempt. In addition, the war injury which has left him impotent has the literary value of making a mystery out of Barnes's man-hood. The novel hints at personal tragedy long before the secret comes out. Even then, the disclosure takes allusive form, with vague references to an accident and an airplane (pp 115–16). The lack of candour is meant to speak less of Jake's embarrassment and more of his toughness. Here is a man who means to brave out his impotence all alone. Let lesser men leak out their fears in verbal confessions: Jake will bear the stigma without the consola-tion of talk. This war wound is in fact so enigmatic that Jake's penis remains a mystery throughout the novel. The critical con-sensus is that Jake is impotent, possibly castrated, but some crit-ics are not willing to commit themselves to this opinion. While the whole issue may seem somewhat absurd, it is of great consequence within Hemingway's gender-based belief system. His secrecy draws critical attention to the significant locale, whether there is a penis there or not.

The literary act of drawing consciousness to a place and then doing a locutionary dance around what seems to be a vacancy pretty well sums up the essential narrative ritual of *The Sun Also Rises*. Evidence confirming that Jake is an 'aficionado' (Hemingway makes a considerable fuss over this word [pp 131–2], as if it might be too technical for the reader to understand) comes early in the novel when Jake receives two bullfight papers, one yellow, and the other orange (p 30). Hemingway deliberately withholds information as to the contents of these papers, and the writing takes on a Pinteresque absurdity. Apparently, he means to signal masculine aloofness: 'aficion' clearly entails a lack of emotional engagement. Perhaps his aim is to reproduce 'aficion' in the reader. Whatever his purpose might be in showing the reader the bullfight papers and then refusing to reveal the contents, the effect is to evade the protest of reason that could form in the reader's mind as a consequence of genuine confrontation with the fatuousness of the aficionado's pleasures.

The bullfight itself is marked by similar omission. The bullfight should constitute a kind of climax; it has been the aim of the characters' travels for at least two-thirds of the novel. While one does not exactly hope for carnage, certainly one could expect some increase of emotional intensity or heightening of activity as the action comes to the bullfight. That expectation increases as Hemingway seems to be revealing the details of the fiesta slowly, with the purpose of reaching a dramatic height in the scene in the arena. Let me repeat: anticipation does not necessarily hang upon a vision of a bloodbath in the bullring. Hemingway's ideology, furthermore, rules out any ascent into the tragic mode over the scene in the arena. The least one expects is some sort of ceremony, some confrontation with the reality of the bullfight, if only at a ritualistic level.

Hemingway does pay some attention to the bulls as they are released from their cages into corrals. This scene finds bulls pitted against steers. Hemingway treats the scene as a kind of boxing match: Jake points out that the bulls use their horns like boxers, with a right and left thrust (p 139). But even with the implicit humanization of this analogy, the herding of the bulls by the steers is an anticlimactic event. A few brief manoeuvres, a perfunctory poking of a steer by a bull, and the episode is over. All Jake, the man with 'aficion' – that is, a 'passion' for the bullfight – can say after the all-important bulls are revealed is, 'They were nice bulls' (p 144). Perhaps the true aficionado is supposed to be taciturn; perhaps it is bad form to express enthusiasm over the bulls. In any event, it is left to the reader to infer that they are healthy, vigorous bulls worthy of the bullfight, and not 'nice' polite bulls that would prefer to stand peacefully in a field instead of being harassed into displays of aggression.

The scene of the running of the bulls is even further stripped of literary effort. Jake watches the running of the bulls from a balcony. From this perspective, he sees a crowd of men running:

Behind them was a little bare space, and then the bulls galloping and tossing their heads up and down. It all went out of sight around the corner. One man fell, rolled to the gutter, and lay quiet. But the bulls went right on and did not notice him. They were all running together. (p 160)

These five sentences are the sum total of Hemingway's description of the famous running of the bulls at Pamplona. A later repetition of the event, in which a man is killed, receives attention no more animated than the first. The bulls are 'heavy' and 'muddy-sided'; their horns are 'swinging' (p 196). One bull separates itself from the herd and gores a man. And then the ritual is over for that day, too. Hemingway's literary approach to the bull-running shuts off analysis; it represents a frustrating impediment not only to insight, but also to a simple visual grasp of what is going on.

It hardly seems possible that description could be further stripped down than this, but Hemingway manages to effect greater uncommunicativeness as he arrives at the first bullfight. 'It was a good bullfight' (p 164), Hemingway observes, and that is all. Something about this 'good bullfight' supposedly establishes the young matador Romero as 'a real one.' What is meant by Romero being 'a real one' is held suspended until the second bullfight. Yet in this second bullfight, most of the literary action takes place in the stands between Jake and Brett, a woman who is being introduced to bullfighting for the first time. That action, of course, is not emotional or psychological action. It takes the form of Jake telling Brett what to look at in the arena: 'I told her about watching the bull, not the horse ... I had her watch how Romero took the bull away from a fallen horse ... I pointed out to her the tricks the other bull-fighters used ... She saw why she liked Romero's cape-work and why she did not like the others ... ' (p 167). Sublimated sexual aggression hovers around Jake's instruction. He is forcing the woman's attention here and there, and, in true pornographic style, winning her appreciative submission to being educated. We do get some clues as to why Romero's performance is superior to that of other matadors: 'Romero's bull-fighting gave real emotion, because he kept the absolute purity of line in his movements' (p 168). But where is that 'real emotion'? What does it feel like? And what on earth happened to the bulls? They have disappeared. Romero could be a ballet dancer, proving his abilities alone on stage. If 'purity of line' is the primary excitement of the event, a reader would be justified in thinking that the skills of the bullfight would be demonstrated just as well, if not better, without the bull.

The third and last bullfight focuses upon the contrasting performances of the aged matador Belmonte, who has lost the spirit of the arena, and Romero, the 'real one.' Description of Belmonte surveys the artificiality of his flourishes, his demoralization and the hostility of the crowd. The bull comes in as an afterthought: 'after his second bull was dead ... [he] handed his sword over the barrera to be wiped' (p 214). In other words, Belmonte has driven his sword into the bull's body, has killed the bull, and has pulled out his sword now covered in blood. The passive voice diminishes the act of killing the bull to a nullity. The bull's blood is not even mentioned; it is only implied in the wiping of the sword.

Since Romero's performance is a virtual *raison d'être* for the novel as a whole, it is clearly impossible to omit the bull from this last foray into meaning. After all, Romero 'loved the bulls' (p 216), and it would do his fighting techniques a disservice to leave out the animal opponent. Possibly, the inclusion of the bull this time foreshadows the sexual liaison Brett and Romero will share afterwards. Hemingway must infuse Romero with some sense of animal carnality, or Romero's participation in the sex act becomes inconceivably abstract. Hemingway is in a similar fix to that of Lawrence in *The Fox*: having made the animal into a mystery, he now must struggle to introduce carnality. Lawrence at least has the intelligence not to imply that the aggressive male is also the ideal lover.[3] In any event, Hemingway has the bull actually appear in the last bullfight, at least to respond dutifully to the matador's tricks. The peak moment arrives:

The bull charged as Romero charged. Romero's left hand dropped the muleta over the bull's muzzle to blind him, his shoulder went forward between the horns as the sword went in, and just for an instant he and the bull were one, Romero way out over the bull, the right arm extended high up to where the hilt of the sword had gone in between the bull's shoulders. Then the figure was broken. (p 218)

Presumably the effortlessness of the kill is to be attributed to Romero's great talent. The image of Romero charging the bull appears to be something of a lapse from the artistic refinement Hemingway means to present, but his ideology could not allow the bull any unanswered display of power. Apart from this one, swiftly countered act of resistance, the bull falls in line nicely with the choreography of the fight. It plays partner to Romero's moves, as if the pair were on a dance floor. It does not resent the persecution, or suffer, or rebel and act upon its own animal in- stincts. It even cooperates in death, dropping over in the pre- scribed manner, with its 'four feet in the air' (p 219). 'It was like a course in bullfighting' (p 219), Jake observes. Indeed, the descrip- tion is something like a course in bullfighting. It is not much like literature. One would imagine, however, that even in a course on bullfighting the instructor would want to impress upon his stu- dents the possibility that bulls might respond badly to harass- ment and injury. Simple appreciation of a skilful performance in the bullring should demand attention to the physical mass and the hostility of the bull. Otherwise, the bullfight is a game, and the killing of the bull stands in total violation of the spirit of the sport. Apparently, detailed attention to the killing of the bull would detract from Hemingway's literary style. The writing is bloodless; the bull, too, must be a bloodless entity, because Hemingway's aesthetic does not know what to do with a suffering animal subject. Because the whole performance passes by with the serenity of an afternoon of bird-watching, one has little faith in the observation that Jake and his friend Bill 'both took a bull- fight very hard' (p 221). As with the bullfight itself, there is here a gesture towards feeling, but it is feeling without content: no experience has occurred to ground the feeling in reality.

One kind of animal does preoccupy Hemingway, however, and that is the horses he depicts as comical in *Death in the Afternoon*. Comparing the attitude towards the horses in *The Sun Also Rises* with that of *Death in the Afternoon,* written some six years later than the novel, one senses that the language of farce represents a post-hoc rationalization for discomfort Hemingway previously recognized. Certainly, in the earlier work, he displays distress over the goring of the horses. In fact, he repeats so often that a spectator to the bullfight should not look at the horses that the whole subject takes on a fetishistic aura. True to form, Hemingway never actually mentions what happens to the horses in the bullring; he never even shows the horses, injured or uninjured, running around the arena. He simply repeats obsessively the advice to avoid looking at the horses, and then repeats after the event how shocking it was that whatever happened to the horses did happen.

With this compulsive repetition, the aficionado's capacity to suffer the never-disclosed injuries to the horses becomes an obvious source of conceit. The horses rather than the bulls turn the bullfight into an ordeal, a test of mental prowess, for the spectator. The following conversation among Jake and his friends manifests the furtive pride underlying all the protestation over the horses:

Bill said something to Cohn about what to do and how to look so he would not mind the horses ...

'I'm not worried about how I'll stand it. I'm only afraid I may be bored,' Cohn said.

'You think so?'

'Don't look at the horses, after the bull hits them,' I said to Brett. 'Watch the charge and see the picador try and keep the bull off, but then don't look again until the horse is dead if it's been hit.'

'I'm a little nervy about it,' Brett said. 'I'm worried whether I'll be able to go through with it all right.'

'You'll be all right. There's nothing but that horse part that will bother you, and they're only for a few minutes with each bull. Just don't watch when it's bad.' (pp 161–2)

After the fight, Brett has proven herself 'a lovely, healthy wench' (p 166) in enduring the event. She goes off into ecstasies:

'Simply perfect [she exclaims]. I say, it is a spectacle!'

'How about the horses?'

'I couldn't help looking at them.'

'She couldn't take her eyes off them,' Mike said. 'She's an extraordinary wench.'

'They do have some rather awful things happen to them,' Brett said. 'I couldn't look away, though.'

'Did you feel all right?'

'I didn't feel badly at all.'

'Robert Cohn did,' Mike put in. 'You were quite green, Robert.'

'The first horse did bother me,' Cohn said ... (p 165)

The way these people fuss about their own feelings would be humorous if it weren't so puzzling. The reader is left absolutely in the dark as to what the dreadful 'horse part' is. All the self-congratulation for having endured the true test of strength, which obviously has more to do with the horses than with the bulls, is completely meaningless.

It could be proposed that Hemingway has cleverly excluded animal subjectivity from *The Sun Also Rises* in order to show why his human subjects are part of a 'lost generation.' The loss of the animal to these people leaves their conversations inane, their pleasures destructive, and their friendships trivial. This interpretation is valid if one places the novel in the larger literary context in which authors are honestly striving to grasp the significance of the victimized animal to the modern condition. In the larger literary context, the superficiality of Hemingway's characters and the atonality of his narrative speak to the importance of animal vitality in modern works of fiction. Internally, however, Hemingway's narrative works in the retrograde direction, predicating the wholeness of the human psyche upon delight in the negation of the animal. Jake is 'lost' only because he is impotent. Were he sexually capable, his love of the artistry of the bullfight would be final confirmation of the perfection of his manhood. That his 'manhood' would remain an abstraction because of the omission of bulls from the narrative is entirely consistent with Hemingway's ideology. By eliding the bull, Hemingway puts himself in the convenient position of not having to test his theories of masculinity.

What is important to Hemingway plainly has little to do with animals. One irritating aspect of his narrative, then, is the pretence that animals are crucial to his purposes when in fact they are negligible. Even more irritating is the discovery that one is likely to end up arguing against empathy for animals in demanding realism from Hemingway. *The Sun Also Rises* has this effect of cornering a reader who wishes to debate the bullfighting issue. Contend that Hemingway does not give a realistic presentation of animal injuries in the bullring, and one finds oneself supporting the aggression that lies at the heart of the bullfight. Hemingway can turn the tables and say that those who want realism are the vicious ones: he, he could assert, has shown due consideration in refraining from focusing upon animal injuries. He thus achieves an ideological sleight of hand, managing to encourage the victimization of animals while appearing merely to be making inoffensive use of a few, not very real animals for the purpose of exploring the human condition. He does not realize, however, that the ideology of machismo rests upon the unreality of his animals and would collapse if he truly faced animal pain.

SELF-PITY AND THE SURREAL: USING ANIMAL VICTIMS TO FEED HUMAN NARCISSISM

Graeme Gibson's *Communion* and Jerzy Kosinski's *The Painted Bird* are as deceptive as Hemingway's stories, but their deceptiveness runs in the opposite direction. Where Hemingway mutes violence against animals with the apparent point of resurrecting lost virility amongst the superficially civilized, Gibson and Kosinski amplify violence against animals with the apparent point of denouncing violence in the human sphere. In a way, the vision in *Communion* and *The Painted Bird* is more treacherous than Hemingway's, since Hemingway does not pretend to speak for an ethic of gentleness, while Gibson and Kosinski depict cruelty to animals in their narratives under the guise of moral purposes. In assaulting their readers' sensibilities with the ugliness of life, they seem to have remedial motives in mind. They seem bent on discomposing shallow sanctities to show the reader that a bourgeois and mentalized ethic is not good enough for countering the seething mass of violence that life engenders. Instead of opposing cruelty, however, Gibson and Kosinski luxuriate in it. The surrealism in their narratives is predicated upon violence. Violent episodes are multiplied gratuitously. In this sense, *Communion* and

The Painted Bird are similar to *The Sun Also Rises*: they attain a kind of thrill from cruelty. The surreal, free-floating, and compulsive terrorism which produces animal victims fuels a gratifying sense of the misery life inflicts upon the human ego.

The central episode in Gibson's *Communion* involves the attempt made by the protagonist Felix Oswald to free an epileptic husky from captivity and impending death in a laboratory. It is a given that this supposed act of charity is misconceived and futile. Felix is afflicted with incredible ignorance of animals. Animal experience is impenetrable to him. He cannot engage with physical reality. In light of the fact that the dog is crippled, the daydream that prompts Felix to mimic the merciful act is more foolish than a Disney fantasy:

He'd like to take it back to the woods. That appears to be the natural course of action: it would be the best thing. Driving north as far as the roads go, if he had a car, past towns and villages, back into winter until somewhere, in a clearing perhaps, by the edge of the bush, he releases it. That's the best thing, the natural thing: it pleases him, seeing it slip from the car, pausing to smell the air curiously, defensively, then breaking into the tireless searching run of wild dogs, the wolf ... (p 48)

He wants to transform the sick domestic dog into a creature of the wilderness. The intention might be honourable, however absurd, were it not that Felix is drawn by the fantasy instead of being pushed by true feeling for the animal. He takes the media image of kindness to animals and informs himself, by rote, that this image represents 'the natural course of action.' He is enamoured with the thought of himself as liberator, and with the picture of the dog running free. There is no correspondence between reality and image. There is, in fact, no correspondence between Felix and the dog. The title, *Communion,* points ironically to the absence of affinity at the heart of the novel. Kindness becomes a matter of performance only.

In his terrible state of emptiness, Felix stands allegorically for 'Everyman.' Cynicism informs Gibson's depiction of the common man, particularly with respect to the common man's sex life. Felix's sexual activity parallels his conduct towards the husky. The form his sexual expression takes is not, strictly speaking, sexual, just as his act of kindness is not an act of kindness. Felix works off his sexual desires by licking and fondling two stone statues of women erected in a graveyard. In this feature of Felix's character, Gibson resurrects the association of sexual dysfunction with compassion for animals. He perceives the artificiality of a compassion grounded in antipathy to the body, but holds out no hope of authentic feeling for animals. In the world *Communion* creates, all humane acts are manufactured. They are forced upon unresponsive objects and reluctant living beings.

For Felix, the husky dog is as inanimate an object as the statues. Felix goes through the motions of communion with the animal. He begins looking into the dog's eyes:

At first there was nothing in those eyes, not a thing: no shadows, no light, just yellow diminishing without depth. Then one morning, several days ago, Felix saw something shiver inside the pupil, it was like something opening, something flashing deep beneath the surface. It happened very quickly. Most people would have missed it completely. Indeed it might not have happened for anyone else; it may well have happened *because* of him. Felix hardly dares to think about it, hardly dares to hope. (pp 24–5)

The consciousness that stands right up front in an animal's eyes eludes Felix. He has to struggle to perceive response in the husky's eyes, and when he does perceive it, he takes it as communication directed at him specifically. All the violent signs the dog gives of having internal experiences – the epileptic fits during which it howls and convulses and foams at the mouth – mean nothing to Felix until he, Felix, receives what seems to be the reaction of consciousness to himself alone. Like the depiction of sexuality, this analysis of standard human relations with animals is fair enough. It criticizes our species for failing to recognize life in animals until human egos want such recognition for their own purposes. It goes further to suggest that the self-flattery arising from this ego-centred, and hence bogus, communion sends the person off into displays of kindness to the animal which totally ignore the animal's needs. The course of action Felix takes with the husky serves the desires of his own ego and imagination. In the larger domain, Felix represents his culture by imitating the falsified, self-gratifying pattern of events in popular imagery which show the animal responding gratefully to human benevolence.

Although there is justice in this scepticism, it fosters a vision in which all kindness to animals is narcissistic and doomed to failure. The disastrous consequences of this one sentimental act, performed by one person towards one dog, suggest the futility of any human attempt to make altruistic contact with animals. In effect, the novel indicates that no animal wants to be set free because human belief in the animal's desire for freedom is an invention of culture. Understanding between humans and animals is completely impossible.

The novel forces Felix into victimizing the husky in order to fulfil his fantasy of releasing the dog into the wilderness. Driving the dog out of the city, he tries to execute the moves dictated by his fantasy: 'Clearly he must acknowledge the animal's fear, he must reassure it with everything at his disposal' (p   59). He speaks kindly to the dog, to no avail. When it comes time for the dog to run away, the dog only wants to stay in its cage. Felix grows impatient:

If he upended the cage he could shake the son-of-a-bitch out onto the road. That's a possibility: at least it's something he might be able to do. Standing against the car he closes his eyes; the dog should appreciate, at least understand that its freedom is being restored, it should, no matter how cautiously, he recognizes that suspicion is natural and therefore desirable, it should at least poke its fucking head out of the cage, it should see what Felix has done, is doing ... (pp 63–4)

The fantasy degenerates further into a contest of wills between Felix and the dog. Out of the cage, the dog climbs back into the car. Felix has to pry it out of the car with a jack:

[H]e leans on the red metal jack, it presses cruelly into the sinews, bones and muscle, the whimpering grows in strength. They are both without anger. Felix bending into the car, forcing methodically, he doesn't think, he has no sensation, the husky resists. It's only a matter of time, it can't win. Felix knows that. The only question is how much, what kind of pain will he have to inflict before the animal finally capitulates? (pp 66–7)

In light of the pleasant vision of bestowing freedom upon a grateful animal, this turn of events takes on farcical overtones. The distance between the fantasy of liberation and the cruelty perpetrated upon the uncooperative dog is meant, it seems, to be laughable. The pain Felix causes to the husky is factitious pain, designed less to provoke compassion for the animal than to destroy the fiction of beneficence.

It is almost unnecessary to relate what happens to the husky. Once cars and highways are introduced into the scheme for liberating the dog, the nature of the novel's conception of life makes it a foregone conclusion that the husky will be struck down and killed by a car. It is possible that Felix himself has accidentally driven over the husky: that outcome would certainly conform admirably to the novel's purposes. But as Felix observes, 'Even if he did kill it, it doesn't matter' (p 73). In an absolute sense, it doesn't matter who killed the husky because the husky is only the novel's device for casting cynicism over sentimental ideals. That an animal is the focus of those ideals is unimportant. The ideals themselves are the aim of the novel's disillusionment. The novel runs through the scene of the dog's death several times (pp 71, 82, 92, 98). Description is realistic: the dog 'struggles in small circles.' It 'flops from side to side like a fish ... Bone protrudes from its side, and the snow is black with its blood' (p 71). The recurrence of the scene imitates well the workings of any consciousness that has suffered such a humiliating assault upon its illusions. Yet a suspicious quality of fervour hangs about the repetitions of the scene. As the fate of Felix at the conclusion of the novel reveals, the fervour attaching to the husky's death is not sadistic delight in the torments of the animal but luxuriance in pity for 'Everyman' and the futility of Everyman's fine intentions.

The surreal world of *Communion* inevitably converts humanitarian gestures into dust and ashes. The world's cruelty does not end, however, with disabusing Felix of his altruistic fantasies. Finally, the cruelty of the novel's world concentrates itself into a group of street children, who pour gasoline on Felix and set fire to him (p 118). Self-pity reaches its zenith in this development. The closing *auto-da-fé* is so comically novelistic that one comes to doubt that any part of the novel is intended as verisimilitude. Perhaps Felix does not really go into a graveyard and fondle statues. Perhaps he never really tried to free the husky. Perhaps the repetitions, and the novel as a whole, take place only in someone's imagination. In that case, of course, getting worked up about the dog and its pain, about the defeat of humane intentions and about any challenge to cultural myths, is purely pointless. One is left only with an 'I' who feels so sorry for itself that it must generate a world that will satisfy its need to feel abused.

Likewise, the litany of tortures in *The Painted Bird* serves the desire of the individual ego which deplores the world's mistreatment of itself. As with Hemingway, however, protest against Kosinski's vision traps the reader in an uneasy position. Culture since World War II has not recovered from the shock of the magnitude of state-supported evil that civilization can still spawn. Dismissal of the meaning of the images from the concentration camps is rightly judged an evil in itself. When Kosinski translates the abominations of this war into a personal saga of unrelenting persecutions, rejecting his vision swerves uncomfortably close to denial that this war was, at base, as abhorrent as *The Painted Bird* makes it out to be. Indeed, defending animals against a background of nakedly loathsome tortures inflicted upon persons becomes something of an embarrassment. It is necessary to remember, then, that judgment is being made upon a novel, and not upon the war the novel purports to illuminate. No one denies that people suffered terribly during the war years; nor does one wish to suggest that the torments Kosinski depicts are not a realistic representation of the suffering real people experienced. What can be criticized is Kosinski's pornographic interest in the events he describes, and that narcissism which focuses the misery of millions of people upon one ego. *The Painted Bird* would have been a very different novel if it had been written in the third person. In fact, it seems fair to say that the novel would not exist at all but for the all-important 'I' that is subjected to continuous torture.

After the initial impact that any cruelty inherently possesses, the succession of torments the boy undergoes in *The Painted Bird* becomes predictable and loses dramatic power. The boy's loss of speech under torment and recovery of the power to speak after the war are clearly dramatic expedients. There is a detectable narrative difficulty in the novel: tortures interest the author but will only occur serially and will not drive the story; the mechanisms that will drive the story along take away the pleasures Kosinski derives from victimization. Fortunately, it is not necessary for the purposes of this discussion to detail the constant rapes, gougings, beatings, killings, and castrations that occur in *The Painted Bird*. Humans endure many more terrible agonies than animals do in

this novel. Isolation of the animals, however, discloses the fraud-
ulence of the surreal world Kosinski creates. The errors revealed
are errors of omission. The macabre, which animals can certainly
enhance, is impoverished by sensationalism, as when a wicked
carpenter falls into a pit of rats and is eaten alive (p 56). In conformity with anachronistic convention, Kosinski transmutes the
alien quality of animals into hostility, as when, for hours at a
time, a wolfhound named Judas stands guard over the boy hung
suspended from a hook in the ceiling and threatens him with dire
injury should he drop to the floor (pp 115–19). The lack of thought
evident in such uses of the animal goes hand in hand with a lack
of feeling. The absence of compassion for animals in turn underscores the dehumanization of the human characters, both perse-
cutors and victims. None of the beings in *The Painted Bird* have
genuine life-stories, not even the narrator; their presence is determined solely by their utility in the repetition of one scene of
pain after another. It could be argued, of course, that this is
precisely what the horror associated with war does to living beings,
converts them into disembodied ciphers in the schematics of torture. The omission of a countervailing narrative interest, however,
negates the emotional engagement with persons and events that
is necessary for true insight into the evils of war and a true
assault upon bourgeois complacency.

One episode seems to counter the critique that the novel lacks
feeling. On this occasion, Kosinski invites the reader to feel pity
for a malnourished horse with a broken leg. Needing affection as
much as anything, the horse nudges the boy with his muzzle; the
boy gives the horse his sympathy. A farmer, of course, responds
quite differently to the horse, not merely slaughtering it for its
hide and bones, but actually shaming the creature beforehand for
its gestures of friendship: 'the cripple suddenly turned his head
and licked the farmer's face. The man did not look at him, but
gave him a powerful, open-handed slap on the muzzle. The horse
turned away, hurt and humiliated' (p 71). The farmer then proceeds to strangle the horse, having two other horses slowly draw
the rope tight around its neck by pulling in opposite directions.
The humanization of the horse is not the problem with this episode;
indeed, Kosinski's awareness of a capacity in animals to suffer
from rebukes to their appeals for love represents a strong counter-
argument to the charge that he divests animals of genuine sig-

nificance. Nevertheless, two aspects of this episode taint an otherwise cogent depiction of animal suffering. The predictability of unnecessary cruelty to the horse sours emotional identification; pity seems to have been aroused factitiously, to be assaulted. In view of that level of design, one comes to suspect, furthermore, that the object of the episode is less the horse than the boy. The boy's humane impulse has to be traduced. The horse's misfortune is turned to the boy's account.

That the primary role of animal victims is to enhance the impression of the boy's afflictions is confirmed by overt analogies. When some children pour gasoline on the boy's pet squirrel and set it aflame (p 6), the image returns later in the form of the boy's belief that some soldiers mean to pour gasoline on him and set fire to him (p 63). In a less subtle episode, the agonies of a half-skinned rabbit produce an immediate comparison between the animal's pain and the boy's. The rabbit tears frantically around the yard; every time 'her loose hanging skin caught on some obstacle she halted with a horrible scream and spurted blood' (p 133). Infuriated at this scene, a farmer kicks the boy in his stomach: 'The world seemed to swirl. I was blinded as if my own skin were falling over my head in a black hood' (p 134). The extreme pain suffered by the half-skinned rabbit is transmuted ultimately into a metaphor for the boy's pain on being kicked in the stomach.

The most insidious metaphoric use of the animal victim is that of the painted bird. The title of the novel refers to the habit of a man named Lekh of daubing paint on a live bird and then watching birds of its own kind turn upon and kill it. As with the horse, Kosinski infuses pathos into the plight of the painted bird. Set free in the woods, the bird warbles joyfully in response to the song of its fellows, 'its little heart, locked in its freshly painted breast, beating violently' (p 44). The flock tries to drive the painted bird away, and when the bird persists in its efforts to join them, they peck it to death. Kosinski singles out a raven to illustrate the general outcome of Lekh's routine. Lekh and the boy find the raven still alive: its 'eyes had been pecked out, and fresh blood streamed over its painted feathers' (p 45).

The boy, needless to say, suffers the same treatment from members of his own species. Dark-skinned, he is taken for a Gypsy or a Jew, and endures prolonged miseries of rejection and torture at the hands of beings who are human like himself. It is only as he relates the boy's experiences after the war, however, that Kosinski makes an explicit connection between the boy and the painted bird. Kosinski re-invokes the painted bird to explain the boy's experience on meeting his parents, who had handed him over to the protection of the peasants at the start of the war: 'I suddenly felt like Lekh's painted bird,' the boy observes, 'which some unknown force was pulling toward his kind' (p 206). The analogy works well to demonstrate that this boy has been permanently stigmatized by his suffering. His humanity lies hidden beneath the overlay of cruel experience. It takes a considerable leap to extend the analogy to all the children and all the people who passed through the miseries of this particular war. If the novel had assisted in the effort to generalize the consequences of the war from the one boy to human beings at large, it would have been a better novel. But that narcissism which prevents the inclusion of other people in narrative empathy applies also to Kosinski's use of animal victims. Certainly, as we have seen in Giorgio Bassani's *The Heron,* correspondence between human and animal victims can substantiate grief for both beings. Kosinski, however, reduces the painted bird's suffering to a metaphor and in the process, I would argue, loses an opportunity to push the experiential boundaries of victimization.

If all that the surreal mode finds itself able to do with animal victims is capitalize upon them, it would be far better if it did not victimize the animal at all. In fact, another novel set in World War II, Louis-Ferdinand Céline's *Castle to Castle,* demonstrates the benefits to the surreal vision of leaving the animal wholly unaffected by human chaos: Céline's cat Bébert moves along his own autonomous path as the war-time world disintegrates, and by his natural sanity, highlights the grotesqueness of events. The animals in *The Painted Bird* and *Communion* do not convey independent meaning into the narrative; they do not challenge or alter the course of the narrative. In this sense, they are not 'real' animals because their suffering is patently a means to an artistic end and not an object of contemplation significant in itself. Their presence as victims is part of the surreal routine, taking 'routine' to mean both habit and performance. Used merely as ciphers in the production of art, animal victims cast doubt upon the integrity of the surreal vision as a whole.

MODERN HORROR RESURRECTS 'THE BEAST'

In effect, Hemingway, Kosinski, and Gibson evince fear of the demand that genuine recognition of the animal would place upon their imaginations. That fear and the various conventions which deflect it are firmly based in pre-Darwinian thought. Discounting animal subjectivity springs from human defensiveness just as surely as does the pre-modern move to cast animals as beasts threatening to the aims of civilization. A self-serving need to set animals at a distance from the human species informs both reduction of the animal to a nullity and magnification of the animal into a menacing alien beast. The obvious fear that attaches to the beast image illuminates the motive behind the corresponding method of invalidation. Indeed, if one were going to be psychoanalytic about it, one might speculate that a huge, lowering, and ferocious beast stands behind the schematic animal substitute inhabiting Hemingway's, Gibson's, and Kosinski's novels. The almost obscenely victimized animals in the latter two works already possess an element of beastly menace. That horror stories can still capitalize upon the fear provoked by animals indicates the resilience of the beast image and the extreme ambivalence of modern culture's attitudes towards animals. Where other literary works inadvertently slide into invocation of the beast, however, horror makes conscious use of both the convention and the anxieties that the convention taps.

Because animals represent almost no threat whatsoever to the modern person, horror generally relies upon the total corruption of the animal's image. Horror stories and horror films normally do little else but project human fears into the stereotypic beast. The genre, typically, does not care a whit about the genuine animal beyond its, usually exaggerated, physical appearance. The animal monster, then, isolates evil from the human species and contains that evil safely in an alien image. It also, in a way, forgives the evil, because the animal monster cannot help itself. The disownment of such human hostilities as the animal monster embodies produces the pleasant effect of simultaneously frightening and reassuring the spectator. The animal monster removes collective guilt from the spectator, isolates and affirms the innocence of the humans that fall victim to the monster, and thus satisfies the polarized urges in the human psyche towards whole-hearted disobedience of social laws and absolute innocence conferred upon the individual by the nature of the world.

As horror stories that use animals go, Stephen King's *Cujo* is surprisingly clever. *Cujo* conforms to the genre in exploring simple and fundamental concepts of guilt and innocence by shuffling human and animal attributes. Following the usual practice, the animal is central, and order is restored once the animal is killed. Where King breaks from tradition, as mentioned earlier, is in his use of a familiar, scarcely manipulated animal to terrorize the human subject. King works consciously and subtly with the horror story's projection of human guilt onto animals. The familiar animal highlights the processes and effects of projection. In addition, he loads his story with particulars of contemporary life, with current issues such as the frustrations of the stay-at-home mother and with the constant reference to brand-name commercial products that has become one of his trademarks. These two departures from standard form, the modern details and the use of the familiar animal, are not unconnected. *Cujo* manufactures fear out of the well-known material of everyday experience. King takes features of modern experience that are supposed to be friendly and makes those features hostile to the individual. He transforms the tediously safe world of the modern person into a place that can turn on the person at any moment and wreck his or her happy, boring life. *Cujo* thus satisfies a need in modern individuals to have the over-controlled elements of routine existence come to life and threaten them personally. One of the seemingly innocent elements of everyday life which, *Cujo* indicates, can rise up against us is the companion animal we have invited into the heart of our families.

In order to place within the bounds of possibility the transformation of the friendly, compliant pet into a menacing beast, King offers a natural cause as the reason for the change in Cujo. Cujo's treacherousness is not the result of witchcraft or ecological disaster; he is simply a very large Saint Bernard infected with rabies – infected, of course, by a bat. Yet since the possibility of rabies alone is unlikely to cause the typical consumer of horror to look warily at placid household pets, King astutely incorporates suggestions of the supernatural into Cujo's metamorphosis. King knows his readership; he knows that fans of horror will appreciate manipulations of customary features of the genre. The natural diagnosis of Cujo's depravity must therefore compete with hints that Cujo is the reincarnation of one Frank Dodd, a local policeman who murdered several women five years before the events of the novel, and then killed himself. King carefully juggles the rational cause with insinuations of the demonic, so that part of the pleasure of the novel comes from deciding whether plain rabies or undying human evil is the most appealing reason for Cujo's malevolence. The course of the natural explanation through the reader's resistance is eased by veiled association with the diabolic. The resulting synthesis in Cujo of beast and family pet is calculated to appeal simultaneously to ancient fears of the animal and modern common sense. While the fictional devices engendering the dog's image may be obvious, immersion into the novel is facilitated by uncertainty. Cujo's hostility is credible on two conflicting fronts, then: on the modern, rational front which demands a plausible explanation, and on the old, pre-conscious front where irrational anxieties about animals still reside.

The threat in *Cujo* is pointedly directed at the individual. The pointed assault serves a different psychological need than the image of the monster flailing about and wrecking whole cities: it converts each reader into a potential victim of the animal. It is less important that Cujo savagely kill a few other persons than that he subject the main character to a prolonged period of terrorization. The gory deaths of Cujo's other victims serve to prove the animal's power and determination. Since the main character in *Cujo* is a woman, King has available to him intimations of rape, most obvious when Cujo climbs on top of Donna Trenton, his tail still wagging, and starts 'biting her bare stomach just below the white cotton cups of her bra, digging for her entrails' (p 228). Horror arises from the synthesis of the familiar and the hidden. The bra King describes is a utility bra, of the sort any woman might put on in the morning; that such a garment should be involved in a quasi-pornographic scene invokes the terror of a woman's having the ordinary and innocent intimacies of her life suddenly and violently exposed, as in rape. The idea of hidden, unpredictable, and personal menace also informs the note that Cujo is wagging his tail. Can an animal be so severely divided that he attacks with one end of his body while remaining friendly with the other? Does the true, beastly nature of the domestic dog obtain delight from acting on a secret desire to ravage human flesh? In either case, we are invited to doubt our reading of the friendly gesture:

perhaps when dogs wag their tails at us, they have designs upon our entrails. King breaks through the psychological defences which sustain a normal world for the common reader and opens the individual to fear of the animal.

Any attempt to read an animal's mind contravenes the cultural orthodoxy which denies consciousness to animals. On the scale of creative effort to understand animals, King's recreation of Cujo's thoughts stands a notch above facile humanization. King has given enough thought to the dog's mind to work with basic feelings and significances. Cujo's response to the members of the family that own him is indicated, for example, in upper case letters; these people enter the dog's field of perception not by name, but only by species and gender, as THE BOY, THE MAN, and THE WOMAN (p 20). A reasonable analysis of animality also informs King's recreation of the mental changes caused by rabies. He brings the voices in Cujo's mind to an increasingly heightened tone of specific command as the disease progresses. Blame shifts within the dog's mind. At first, Cujo just wants to get rid of the 'BADDOG' feeling (p 21) he experiences from having nosed his way into the bats' cave. Next he starts dreaming about ripping open the bowels of the boy he loves (p 94). When he sees the boy at this stage in the disease, the boy looks like 'a monster on two legs' (p 98). Sickness converts the world into horror for him. Finally, the voices in his head inform him that every person he encounters is the one who has made him ill; self-consciousness articulates and legitimates the desire of Cujo's diseased body to tear into the flesh of the human being. To the degree that speech may ever be supposed to belong to nonhuman animals, Cujo's thoughts remain within the bounds of imaginable animality.

Thus we have a relatively plausible animal, whose malevolence has a relatively plausible origin, used to terrorize a person whose life is probably much like the reader's own. In the same sense that King plays with but does not affirm the idea of demonic possession, however, he also dangles before the reader the potential moralization of Cujo's aggression. Cujo's malice is loosely related to the guilt of some of his victims. Cujo takes the role of avenger in at least one of the three cases in which he kills a human being. His second victim is his owner, Joe Camber. The tyranny Camber exercises over his wife and son constitutes a subplot in the novel. The man is vulgar and mean; he threatens to beat his wife with his belt, and she finds it necessary to stifle the rare orgasm she achieves in their love-making because Joe wouldn't understand what was going on (p 86). The note on his wife's sexual dissatisfaction is necessary because when Cujo kills Joe Camber, he does more than tear the man's throat to shreds, as he has done with his first victim. While the downed man protects his throat with his arms, Cujo charges him once again: 'And this time he came for Joe Camber's balls' (p 129). One can assume that the disease eventually causes Cujo to lose all sense of discrimination, since he later savages the balls of a perfectly innocent sheriff. On this occasion, we are given one of the hints at supernatural agency. As Sheriff Bannerman lies ruined on the ground with the grinning dog standing over him, he thinks, *'Hello, Frank. It's you, isn't it? Was hell too hot for you?'* (p 272)

When it comes to Donna Trenton's guilt, King is careful never to make an explicit connection between the illicit affair she has had and the torment Cujo inflicts upon her. Guilty of adultery, Donna has already introduced evil into the happy nuclear family. Her conscience converts the rabid Cujo into an agent of divine justice. Trapped in that by-now classic horror device, the car that will not start, Donna tries to reassure herself that there is no moral intent behind the dog's assault: Cujo 'is merely a sick animal' and not 'four-footed Fate' (pp 203–4). This highly reasonable observation, however, cannot supersede her impression that the dog is determined to enact vengeance upon *her* personally. She experiences the feeling that Cujo is 'looking at her, not at a woman who just happened to be trapped in her car with her little boy, but at *Donna Trenton,* as if he had just been hanging around, waiting for her to show up' (p 150). Later, she observes that Cujo's eyes 'were fixed on hers: dumb, dull eyes, but not without – she would have sworn it – not without some knowledge. Some malign knowledge' (p 207). Looking at Cujo, she *'knew* that the dog was something more than just a dog' (p 207). Later still, as Cujo looks up from worrying the body of the sheriff, Donna sees on the Saint Bernard's face 'an expression (could a dog *have* an expression? she wondered madly) that seemed to convey both sternness and pity ... and again Donna had the feeling that they had come to know each other intimately' (p 275). Donna is not mistaken, either, in detecting personal aggression in Cujo's countenance. King discloses the thoughts running through the diseased mind of the Saint

Bernard. The dog seeks to blame someone for its suffering and Donna seems a likely candidate:

It was THE WOMAN most of all. The way she looked at him, as if to say, *Yes, yes, I did it, I made you sick, I made you hurt, I devised this agony just for you and it will be with you always now.*
    Oh kill her, kill her! (p 220)

That Cujo subsequently decides that the sheriff is the one responsible for his misery (p 270) because he, Cujo, feels hatred towards the man, does not absolve Donna of guilt. The external world verifies the psychological projection. For one thing, Cujo really is bent on killing her, and for another, the sin she has committed is part and parcel with the evil spirit that invades the community and, as a supernatural explanation would have it, spawns the rabid dog. Following the logic of the demonic element in the novel, Donna is indeed the source of Cujo's sickness. The covert warning to unfaithful women is reinforced by the fact that Donna's four-year-old son dies from heat-stroke as the ordeal in the car reaches its climax. Truly innocent people seldom die in horror stories, not even from the supposedly anarchic violence of the beast. Since King acknowledges, here and there, the amorality of Cujo's assault, but simultaneously raises questions of guilt and innocence, the implicit culprit in the boy's death is the mother who has wrecked his home-life and exposed him to danger.

Given that *Cujo* is a work of popular horror, one should wonder why it is significant in any respect that a little boy dies at the end of the story, or that a fairly credible animal is co-opted into the manufacture of fear. It is the utility of conventions that counts in the creation of horror, not their conformity to moral or artistic standards. If a certain convention becomes predictable, well then, it is time to stretch the convention. If the nuclear family's guaranteed survival and return to happiness begins to pall, or the mechanisms of the one-dimensional, vicious beast begin to show through its fur and hide, then adjustments must be made to keep the enthusiast pleasantly on edge. With parental guilt at a peak, and people more than ever inclined to treat household animals as intimates, King hit upon perfect devices for modernizing the horror story. Yet it is precisely because of the reality of these modern developments that the departures from old-fashioned conventions cannot be passed over simply as new strategies. One cannot argue against criticism of the novel, that is, with the observation that the death of boy is not real, but simply a contrivance of horror, or that Cujo is not a dog, but a lifelike puppet of the author's purposes. Perhaps King cannot be faulted for capitalizing upon current trends to write an effective story, but the reactionary consequences of his exploitation of realities to generate horror need airing. The novel supports traditional family values, those that have threatened women with violence should they step out of line. It also reactivates phobias about animals which have been slowly fading away. The pernicious aspect of King's use of the animal resides with that selfsame realism which is gaining ground in common understanding of animals: this is no fantastic creation that provokes fear, but a recognizable dog, with his animal nature intact. The point with respect to the animal, then, is not that King's depiction of Cujo is self-serving, or that it is shoddy, but that it compels a plausible animal to act as the enforcer for a set of values that are anti-feminist and a set of beliefs that are anti-animal.

The fact that we can accept Cujo as a natural dog renders the violence used on him all that more gruesome. When the time comes to punish the animal aggressor, King utilizes symbols of the elements of civilization against which Cujo has transgressed. Cujo has turned one of the foremost symbols of human power, the car, into a torture chamber. At one point in the novel, Donna smashes the dog's body and head repeatedly with the car door. The dog's body makes a 'heavy *whopping* sound' (p 229) as the car door thuds against it; his neck and head make crunching noises, but still Cujo does not die. At last, after many more hours of torment, Donna climbs out of the car and attacks Cujo with a baseball bat. The baseball bat breaks in half and she jams the jagged edge into Cujo's eye: 'The splintered handle of the bat wavered and jiggled grotesquely, seeming to grow from his head where his eye had been' (p 288). Cujo dies, and Donna crazily goes on bludgeoning the corpse with the broken bat. The baseball bat is a suitable symbol of vengeance because of the child's death. Once the friendly companion of children, Cujo has committed the ultimate crime against playfulness and innocence. The baseball bat epitomizes the forces Cujo has violated in changing from a friend to a murderer of children. Common sense, of course, absolves

Cujo, but the cruelty of the injuries to which he is subjected transfigures him by implication into the beast of traditional horror against whom the use of every available method of inflicting injury is justified. The excessiveness of the violence brought to bear upon the dog imitates the logic of the torturer's slogan reported by Elaine Scarry: 'If they are not guilty, beat them until they are' (*The Body in Pain*, p 41). If the animal is not a beast, then the horror story will punish him until he is.

Death is not, however, the final punishment for Cujo. Leaving the corpse whole apparently does not fulfill the need for revenge against the upstart animal. Perhaps it is standard practice to remove the head of a dead rabid animal, but since we have been shown that Cujo's brain spawned vicious intentions towards human beings, observation that a veterinarian saws off Cujo's head and drops the offending object into a garbage bag has significance greater than simple reportage. It is only after this final insult, furthermore, that Cujo is said to have 'gone' (p 295). Blame, then, falls upon the literal head of the animal, upon the location of thought and of animal identity. The novel converts the animal's head into garbage. That act alone, it seems, constitutes sufficient retribution upon the dog for his attack on humankind.

There are subtleties and clever fusions in *Cujo*. King makes skilful use of the ambivalent feelings and incompatible beliefs about animals that permeate popular culture. To a certain extent, the fact that *Cujo* does not represent itself as a work of high culture exonerates it from the rigours of the conflict between the natural animal and human culture. Shoddy uses of animals are less excusable in works that purport to reveal the truth about life. In the long run it is difficult to say whether works of high culture which victimize the already victimized animal or those of popular culture are the more dangerous. *Cujo* delivers the message that animals deserve to be killed since they threaten us, but Hemingway, Gibson, and Kosinski put so much artistic effort into proving that, in truth, animal victims are negligible that their stories could easily be judged much more pernicious than any popular work of horror. Nevertheless, one does not like to see paranoia about animals and retrograde conventions reinforced. If *Cujo* is taken as an icon rather than an agent of modern experience, it too capitalizes upon the natural animal in ways that authorize aggression. King's astute exploitation of current issues in human and animal relations obscures the countervailing effort to appreciate the anti-cultural status of animals. Indeed, he takes the anti-cultural status of animals and returns it to its pre-modern shape of antagonism to humankind. He creates horror out of the animal resistance that should test rather than reinforce cultural conventions.

CONCLUSION

Cujo overtly express modern hostility to the growing power of the natural animal. Human culture wants to preserve its supremacy; it does not like having to cope with animals. It experiences the animal's demand for recognition as aggression against itself. The animal victim instils guilt in the cultural mind. In fiction, animal victims present culture with an incarnate image of both culpability and limitation. The living, autonomous animal knows the world in ways that are impenetrable to culture. The animal victim discloses to culture the debilities culture does not want to confront. Real-life victimization of animals reveals the pettiness of human culture, the aggression it has not overcome and the artificiality of its pride in dominance. Works of fiction in which narrative enacts a double victimization upon already victimized animals unconsciously illuminate cultural guilt. They adopt specious mechanisms to minimize the animal victim and efface human accountability. Hemingway's stories tell us that the animal victim does not truly exist. Graeme Gibson's *Communion* also suggests ultimately that the animal victim does not exist, or if it does, it does so only to magnify the great weight of tragedy that falls upon the individual person. Animal victims may well exist for Jerzy Kosinski, but their pain operates primarily as a convenient metaphor for human suffering. *Cujo* ends up relishing the victimization of animals; the message is that animals ask for the violence that culture commits daily against them. These stories illustrate the ways in which narrative can cooperate in cultural self-deception.

By means of contrast, these stories which negate the animal victim also reveal the integrity of most of the other stories examined in this book. In their highly diverse ways, the narratives discussed in the previous chapters, from Jack London's wild animal adventures to William Faulkner's mythic representation of the bear, accept the challenge to culture that the animal victim intrinsically articulates. Where Hemingway, Gibson, Kosinski, and King work to protect culture from acknowledgment of its aggression against nonhuman animals, most of the writers covered in the foregoing categories expose readers to the conflicts culture initiates when it victimizes animals. The works of fiction analysed in this closing chapter use artifice to reinforce cultural alienation from animals. Although alienation from animals is a deeply entrenched factor in pre-modern culture, modern thought seeks ways in which that alienation can be transcended. Writers representing widely divergent periods in the post-Darwinian age, from Gustave Flaubert to Giorgio Bassani and Timothy Findley, attest to the fact that culture continues to victimize animals at a cost to both conscience and authenticity.

A salutary conclusion that can be drawn from discussion in this chapter is that works of the imagination practising the duplicitous act of aggression upon animals reveal themselves fairly readily. They reveal themselves, for one thing, in the extraordinary gymnastics they have to perform to efface or distort the animal. The strains they manifest suggest that animals in their natural state inherently present to us an argument against our aggression. Animals are not naturally our victims. Without meaning to, these stories prove that this is so: that it requires a highly unnatural vision of life to ignore the claims upon our sensibilities that animals, and especially animal victims, intrinsically communicate.

Conclusion

If this survey has done no more than demonstrate that there is a valuable body of ideas associated with animals in modern fiction, then it has satisfied one of its primary aims. 'Value' is a crucial term in the argument offered in this discussion because pre-Darwinian conventions in belief sought to deprive nonhuman animals of full value and to affirm, thereby, the primacy of our species. The irony, of course, is that our species has assumed for itself the power of deciding what is and is not valuable, and so it is hardly surprising that we bent belief in favour of our own attributes and habits. The conceptual tangle facing modern culture is how humankind can break out of its own ways of appraising life and concede to the influence of the other animals. Taking animals into account means more than making a few modifications in preconceived values: it requires radical rethinking of the methods we use to arrive at value systems in the first place. Alienation from animals is a deeply entrenched condition in cultural values. Such alienation, indeed, has represented one of the defining qualities of culture. Human belief now must accept a genuine argument from animals. In more than a metaphorical sense, the animal subjects culture itself to assessment. Obviously, our attitudes towards other species stand in need of examination. Those attitudes are, in fact, being examined, in life partly, but more intensely in fiction. Fiction roots through human attitudes, pointing out those that are self-serving and false. It confronts the conflicts inherent to human presuppositions about other animals, and tries to meet the animal on its own terms. By showing that the ideas associated with animals are substantial, I have attempted, then, to establish that the animal itself is a source of value to modern culture, and not just the ideas the animal generates.

Conscious of the self-sufficiency of the animal, modern fiction rattles human complacency. It does so almost helplessly, since the post-Darwinian age is, in a certain respect, intrinsically 'rattled,' even if the bulk of the human race appears to be unaware of the historical change we are undergoing. Fiction discerns and reflects the historical upheaval. One can see that the natural animal has infiltrated culture from the seriousness of the conflicts that develop when fiction seeks to assimilate animals. The conflicts centred upon the animal are genuine conflicts, not conflict invented to satisfy fondness for tribulation: the tensions invoked by the presence of the animal in fiction penetrate deep into accepted patterns of familiar existence and displace them from their regular courses. As we have seen – to reiterate – discord results from personification of the wild animal; only in combination with misanthropy does morality stretch into the wild animal's domain. The mere sight of the natural animal in the city environment produces instant dissonance; that dissonance, in turn, gives access to the oppression of the human psyche by urban values. When the theme is sexuality, attention to the natural animal intensifies sexual anxieties; sexual performance becomes performance more obviously with animals as witnesses to the human drama. Likewise, myth becomes self-conscious as it seeks to enfold animals; the holistic life of the animals discloses the imperfection of putatively global myths. Finally, fiction unwittingly exposes its own contrivances when it pretends to deal with natural animals but is in fact only reinforcing cultural illusions. Animals will not allow narrative to get away with fakery at any level of experience, neither in contemplation of specific environments like the wild or the city, nor in the realms of the psychosexual and of myth-making, and particularly not in the act of constructing fiction itself.

The works of fiction examined here reveal that even our best efforts at breaking down cultural constructions and realizing an authentic vision of life rely oftentimes upon the victimization of nonhuman animals. The revolution that fiction effects is to confront aggression against genuine animal subjects. Indeed, the full significance of victimization of animals can hardly be attained where animals are merely literary mechanisms or symbolic figures. Conceiving of animals as symbols protects culture from awareness of its hostility towards real animals. Symbolic animals are immune to suffering because they express as they stand the totality of cultural victimization. In overcoming the perceptual habits that accepted animal metaphors as a true relation to animals, modern fiction shakes conscience out of its indifference towards mistreatment of flesh-and-blood creatures living around us. Living animals are not a resource, neither in life, nor in literature. The subversion of comfortable imaginative uses of animals is a precondition for ethical conduct towards other species.

Modern works of fiction leave us with vivid images of individual animal victims. We have images of anguished animals brought down as they strive to take flight from human aggressors: of Tarka the otter expending his last strength and last breath in his search for a hiding place from the crowd of hunters with their pack of dogs invading his river; of the very last great auk as envisioned by Allan Eckert in its wobbling attempt at escape from hunters; of the pig in Roald Dahl's story struggling to keep its feet against the pull of the conveyor belt in the slaughterhouse; of the rabbit in Mary Webb's *Gone to Earth* fleeing in terror from the farmers' clubs out of a last stand of wheat; of the fly in Katherine Mansfield's story, dry and on the point of flight, stopped by a blob of ink falling on it from above.

No wonder that literary speculation into the animal victim's experience encounters utter bewilderment. As effective as images of unwilling victims are images of those whose incomprehension divests them of the power to resist: the last curlew, of Bodsworth's story, who loses his mate and does not realize that no other mate will ever come to replace her; Kehonka, the Canada goose in Roberts' story, who tries to force his clipped wings into flight so that he can join the migrating flock but ends up the victim of a fox when his wings fail him; the Unicorn in Findley's *Not Wanted on the Voyage,* less magical creature than delicate animal, who dies wordlessly while the human madness rages on above him; the wounded heron in Bassani's novel, who seeks the shelter of the hogshead where the novel's hero hides and who gazes curiously into the eyes of the man.

Then there are the images of trusting, responsive animals that remind us of our inhumanity and hint at the deep fulfilment that could be had from true kinship: the epileptic husky in Graeme

Gibson's *Communion* which does not want to be abandoned by the side of the highway; the Percheron horse Jock in Grove's novel who nickers in friendly greeting at the man who shoots him; the horse in Kosinski's *Painted Bird* asking for love and receiving only insult and death; the elephant in *Salammbo,* destined to be used in war, who caresses the torturer of men with its stump of a trunk; and, most painful for those who live with companion animals, the boisterous, loving dog Esau stabbed by Tobias Mindernickel in Thomas Mann's story.

These images receive their power from the author's appreciation of the individual subjectivity of the animal. They receive their power, more specifically, from an underlying realization that animals do not want to die. The shock or sadness provoked by these images is not conferred upon the helpless creature by sentiment but claimed as a right owed to a being who has its own courses in life. The resistance of these animal victims to being dragged into human and cultural dilemmas is precisely the quality which challenges the validity of these dilemmas. Each animal embodies a whole world of senses and perceptions which defies our species' belief that its activities are the most important concern on the face of the planet. The fact that animals would live on quite contentedly without us suggests that even our much-vaunted conquest of nature is a product of our own fantasy. Whatever its intended exploitation of animals might be, fiction endangers faith in culture when it invokes the animal's state of being. As subjects with meaning and consequence in narrative, animal victims inherently protest the vested anthropocentrism which seeks to negate them.

It remains to be seen whether or not cultural mistrust of anthropocentrism will influence social institutions. The grasp of reason and sentiment upon the real animal is clearly precarious. Current destabilization of what once passed for knowledge of animals, however, is all to the good. The less secure we are in our conceptions of animals, the more hazardous it becomes to victimize them. Our age is too close to the conventions that permitted indifference to the identity of other animals for optimistic belief that instituting a new myth would work to their benefit. The danger lies not so much in philosophical prematurity as in the likelihood that the question of animal reality would be resolved in favour of continuing exploitation. Management attitudes, for example, such as those seeking to preserve a few environmental corners for animals and regulate ecological balances among animal populations, seem to represent concessions from our species, but they manifest the same tiresome assumption as of ages past that human notions of order possess final authority over the rest of nature. The modern age is still a long way from realizing the extent to which the idea of continuity between humans and animals undermines human power structures. If the idea that human beings are custodians of the planet is a necessary stage in the process of deposing our species, one hopes that greater humility on our part is to come. Some day, perhaps, the intellectual recognition that we are animals will filter down to the experiential level and such distinctions as exist between ourselves and other species will lose the power to reify the anthropocentric bias that isolates us from nature. Modern fiction tells us that the ideological and epistemological methods we are currently employing do not cross the gap between nature and culture. What modern fiction can and does achieve is the sanctification of the individual animal's life against all the numerous contradictions that rationalize physical and ideational abuse.

In the meantime, humankind can go on arguing about the nature of animals, about the nature of the ethic that should embrace them, and about the animal or anti-animal nature of the human species. We do so in the modern age with other animals as spectators. The animals' power to throw back at us the cultural dilemmas in which we implicate them finds its way into modern works of fiction. In one sense, the claim made by the animal who watches us is extraordinarily simple. We need only to return the gaze of the animal to realize that we are arguing all on our own. Animals do not ask for or authorize the variety of ways in which we victimize them. Animals do not even participate in the conflict between nature and culture which splits the human animal in two. We cannot bestow rights upon them, for they stand there watching us fully possessed of those rights already. In their very being, animals repudiate our efforts to subjugate them to cultural purposes. When we ask them to affirm the importance of human existence, their silence is more articulate than any of the words we impose upon them.

Notes

1 Traditional uses of animals in cultures other than modern Western
culture lie outside the scope of the present study. Obviously, pre-
modern, aboriginal and non-Western cultures pose obstacles to
modern, European, or European-derived sensibilities. For some
purposes, those obstacles can be overcome; intensive analysis of
representations of animals, however, demands a deeper acquaintance
with fundamental world-views than is necessary with other subjects.
It has to be pointed out, nonetheless, that all cultures manage to
victimize animals with, as yet, relatively little disturbance to basic
assumptions about the ways of the world. Indeed, as a speculation,
people from modern Western culture distinguish themselves in the
degree to which their consciences are troubled by the victimization of
animals. While it would be wrong to credit one theorist with creating
doubts in the Western mind, it seems fair enough to propose that
Charles Darwin has had considerable influence upon Western culture.
Whether one argues that Darwinian theory emerges out of pre-
existing forces in Western culture, or that Darwin originates ideas
which then go on to trouble human belief, the Darwinian idea of
continuity between humans and animals has attained greater than
theoretical import in Western culture. Perhaps the idea of continuity
is gradually becoming a reality to other cultures as the influence of
Western culture itself spreads beyond geographical boundaries. That
idea has had the time in Western culture to become an increasingly
real presence and an increasingly meaningful site of discomfort.

Darwinian belief and other forces in Western culture create that paradoxical state of straining towards and straining against animal victims which is the focus of this study. If one is looking for genuine perplexity over the animal victim, as I am, products of Western culture are, it appears, best suited to the purpose.

CHAPTER ONE

1 My remarks in this section are of necessity somewhat general. Readers seeking further detail are advised to consult the following works, which give comprehensive interpretations of particular periods in the cultural history of animals: Dix Harwood, *Love for Animals and How It Developed in Great Britain;* John Passmore, 'The Treatment of Animals'; Keith Thomas, *Man and the Natural World: Changing Attitudes in England 1500–1800;* John Turner, *Reckoning with the Beast: Animals, Pain and Humanity in the Victorian Mind;* Harriet Ritvo, *The Animal Estate: The English and Other Creatures in the Victorian Age*; and Coral Lansbury, *The Old Brown Dog: Women, Workers, and Vivisection in Edwardian England.*
2 Some useful sources on the happy beast, or 'theriophily,' in history are: James E. Gill, 'Theriophily in Antiquity: A Supplementary Account' *Journal of the History of Ideas* 30 (July–Sept 1969) 401–12; George Boas, *The Happy Beast in French Thought of the Seventeenth Century* (New York: Octagon Books 1966); George Boas and Arthur O. Lovejoy, *Primitivism and Related Ideas in Antiquity* (New York: Octagon Books 1965 [1935]); and George Boas' entry 'Theriophily' in the *Dictionary of the History of Ideas.*
3 Leonora Cohen Rosenfield describes the philosophical extension of the machine analogy from animal to human, as it occurs in France, in *From Beast-Machine to Man-Machine: The Animal Soul in French Letters from Descartes to La Mettrie.* Wallace Shugg's 'The Cartesian Beast-Machine in English Literature (1663–1750)' shows that the debate was just as lively in England as it was in France.
4 See Thomas' *Man and the Natural World,* pp 129–34.
5 In his prescient book, *Animals' Rights, Considered in Relation to Social Progress,* published in 1895, and then revised in 1905 and again in 1922, Henry S. Salt includes an appendix of extracts from philosophical works written between 1723 and 1921. This appendix and Salt's book as a whole make a fine starting point for readers wishing to fill out their knowledge of the issue and its history in the last two

and a half centuries. The book was republished in 1980 by the Society
for Animal Rights, Clarks Summit, Pennsylvania, with a preface by
Peter Singer and an updated biblography compiled by Charles R.
Magel.

6 See John Turner's history of this period in *Reckoning with the Beast*,
chapter 3.

CHAPTER SIX

1 Denise Colonna D'Istria gives a superb close reading of the integration
of human and animal images in Flaubert's 'Legend' in her article 'Sur
"la legende de saint Julien l'Hospitalier.'"

CHAPTER SEVEN

1 I am using the term 'surreal' loosely to suggest works of the imagination which move through disrupted worlds, either formally in
accordance with the standard definition of surrealism or intrinsically
because the natural/historical world has, as in a state of war, become
surreal. In either case, the created work must shape itself to account
for the bizarre. Deviancy becomes the norm; normal experience is
violently disturbed.

Since the subject is animal victims, I make no mention of surreal
works of fiction which violate the animal's world in other ways. It
seems to me that Gunther Grass' *The Flounder* warrants criticism for
simply humanizing the flounder and failing to tackle the fish's
animality. His *The Rat* commits a similar error, and probably should
not be exonerated on the grounds that he develops a vision of the
global triumph of the rats over humankind. Similarly, Charles
Williams' *The Place of the Lion* seems to lend power to animals by
having numerous symbolic creatures appear by magic during a kind of
spiritual convulsion in the English landscape. The sole purpose of
these symbolic animals, however, is to provide a mystical revelation to
the novel's protagonist.

Outside of fiction, other, perhaps familiar, examples of the artistic
abuse of animal victims within the surreal mode may be observed in
the stage version of Peter Shaffer's *Equus* and Francis Ford Coppola's
film *Apocalypse Now*. Though it is based upon a genuine incident,
Equus enacts an obvious denaturalization of horses; the play plunders
animal anguish for the sake of artificially magnifying human suffer-

ing. Real life is also brought to serve art in Coppola's film: a live water buffalo is beheaded on screen. While it is important that audiences be exposed to the usually clandestine slaughter of animals, the film-makers' purpose in recording the sacrifice of this particular water buffalo is to enhance the general aesthetic impression of horror and madness.

2 'The Animal at the Door: Modern Works of Horror and the Natural Animal,' *State of the Fantastic*, ed Nicholas Ruddick.

3 As mentioned earlier, Lawrence himself notes the bullfight in *The Plumed Serpent,* wherein he apparently concurs with the disgust expressed by his female protagonist. Among Lawrence's stories is one, 'None of That,' in which a woman is raped by a gang of bullfighters. His attitude in this story, unfortunately, is similar to Hemingway's in that he implies that the woman has asked for such treatment with her arrogance. Nevertheless, Lawrence makes explicit what Hemingway disguises in the sublimated sexual aggression of Jake's didactic tyranny over Brett.

Selected Bibliography

Adams, Carol J. *The Sexual Politics of Meat: A Feminist-Vegetarian Critical Theory.* New York: Continuum Publishing Company 1990

Allen, Mary. *Animals in American Literature.* Urbana: University of Illinois Press 1983

Atwood, Margaret. *Survival: A Thematic Guide to Canadian Literature.* Toronto: Anansi 1972

Auxter, Thomas. 'The Right Not to Be Eaten.' *Inquiry* 22 (Summer 1979) 221–30

Barnes, Julian. *Flaubert's Parrot.* London: Pan Books 1985

Bassani, Giorgio. *The Heron.* Translated by William Weaver. San Diego: Harcourt Brace Jovanovich 1970 (originally published in 1968)

Beer, Gillian. *Darwin's Plots: Evolutionary Narratives in Darwin, George Eliot and Nineteenth-Century Fiction.* London: Ark Paperbacks 1983

Bentham, Jeremy. *An Introduction to the Principles of Morals and Legislation.* With an introduction by Laurence J. Lafleur. New York: Hafner Publishing Co 1948 (originally published in 1789)

Berger, John. 'Animal World.' *New Society* 34 (25 November 1971) 1042–3

– 'Animals as Metaphor.' *New Society* 39 (10 March 1977) 504–5

– 'Vanishing Animals.' *New Society* 39 (31 March 1977) 664–5

– 'Why Zoos Disappoint.' *New Society* 40 (21 April 1977) 122–3

Berman, Morris. *Coming to Our Senses: Body and Spirit in the Hidden History of the West.* New York: Bantam Books 1990

Boas, George. 'Theriophily.' In *Dictionary of the History of Ideas* vol 4. Ed Philip P. Weiner. New York: Charles Scribner's Sons 1973

Bodsworth, Fred. *Last of the Curlews.* Toronto: New Canadian Library, 1963 (originally published in 1954)

304 Bibliography

Bramwell, Anna. *Ecology in the Twentieth Century: A History.* New Haven: Yale University Press 1989

Bruner, Jerome S. 'Myth and Identity.' In *Myth and Mythmaking* ed Henry A. Murray, pp 276–87. Boston: Beacon Press 1968

Burgess, Anthony. *Flame into Being: The Life and Work of D.H. Lawrence.* London: Heinemann 1985

Campbell, Joseph. 'Mythological Themes in Creative Literature and Art.' In *Myths, Dreams, and Religion* ed Joseph Campbell, pp 138–75. New York: E.P. Dutton and Co 1970

Cirlot, J.E. *A Dictionary of Symbols.* Translated by Jack Sage, with a foreword by Herbert Read. New York: Routledge and Kegan Paul 1962

Clark, Kenneth. *Animals and Men: Their Relationship as Reflected in Western Art from Prehistory to the Present Day.* Toronto: McClelland and Stewart 1977

Clark, Stephen R.L. *The Nature of the Beast: Are Animals Moral?* Oxford: Oxford University Press 1984

– 'The Rights of Wild Things.' *Inquiry* 22 (Summer 1979) 171–88

Coombs, David. *Sport and the Countryside in English Paintings, Watercolours and Prints.* Oxford: Phaidon Press 1978

Culler, A. Dwight. 'The Darwinian Revolution and Literary Form.' In *The Art of Victorian Prose* ed George Levine and William Madden, pp 224–46. New York: Oxford University Press 1968

Dahl, Roald. 'Pig.' In *Kiss Kiss.* Harmondsworth, Middlesex: Penguin Books 1980 (originally published in 1959)

Darwin, Charles. *The Expression of the Emotions in Man and Animals.* With an introduction by Konrad Lorenz. Chicago: University of Chicago Press 1965 (originally published in 1872)

– *The Origin of Species by Means of Natural Selection or the Preservation of Favored Races in the Struggle for Life* (1859) and *The Descent of Man and Selection in Relation to Sex* (1871). New York: Modern Library, Random House Publishers nd

Day, Thomas. *The History of Sandford and Merton.* 3 vols. With a preface by Isaac Kramnick. Garland Series, ed Alison Lurie and Justin G. Schiller. New York: Garland Publishing 1977 (facsimile reproduction of the editions of 1783 [vol 1], 1786 [vol 2], and 1789 [vol 3])

D'Istria, Denise Colonna. 'Sur "la legende de saint Julien l'Hospitalier."' *Bulletin de l'Association Guillaume Budé* 4 (December 1988) 365–78.

Dombrowski, Daniel A. *The Philosophy of Vegetarianism.* Amherst: University of Massachusetts Press 1984

Eaton, Randall. 'The Hunter as Alert Man: An Overview of the Origin of the Human/Animal Connection.' In *The Human / Animal Connection*

ed Randall L. Eaton. Incline Village, Nevada: Carnivore Research
Institute 1985

Eckert, Allan W. *The Great Auk.* Toronto: Signet Books, New American
Library 1963

Eliade, Mircea. *Myth and Reality.* Translated by Willard R. Trask. New
York: Harper and Row 1968

Elman, Robert. *The Great American Shooting Prints.* With an introduction by Hermann Warner Williams, Jr. New York: Alfred A. Knopf
1972

Evans, E.P. *The Criminal Prosecution and Capital Punishment of
Animals.* New York: E.P. Dutton and Co 1906

Fallaci, Oriana. 'The Dead Body and the Living Brain.' *Look*
(28 November 1967) 99–114

Faulkner, William. 'The Bear.' In *Go Down, Moses.* New York: Vintage
Books 1973 (originally published in 1942)

Findley, Timothy. *Not Wanted on the Voyage.* Harmondsworth,
Middlesex: Penguin Books 1984

Flaubert, Gustave. *Intimate Notebook 1840–1841.* Translated with an
introduction and notes by Francis Steegmuller. New York: Doubleday
and Co 1967

– 'The Legend of St. Julian Hospitator.' In *Three Tales.* Translated with
an introduction by Robert Baldick. Harmondsworth, Middlesex:
Penguin Books 1965 (originally published in 1877)

– *The Letters of Gustave Flaubert, 1830–1857.* Selected, edited, and
translated by Francis Steegmuller. Cambridge, Massachusetts:
Belknap Press of Harvard University Press 1980

– *Salammbo.* Translated with an introduction by A.J. Krailsheimer.
Harmondsworth, Middlesex: Penguin Books 1983 (originally published
in 1862)

– *The Temptation of St. Antony.* Translated with an introduction and notes
by Kitty Mrosovsky. Harmondsworth, Middlesex: Penguin Books 1980

Foster, Richard. 'Criticism as Rage: D.H. Lawrence.' In *D.H. Lawrence:
A Critical Survey* ed Harry T. Moore. Toronto: Forum House Publishing Co 1969

Freud, Sigmund. *Totem and Taboo: Some Points of Agreement between
the Mental Lives of Savages and Neurotics.* Translated by James
Strachey. New York: W.W. Norton and Co 1950 (originally published
in 1913)

Friedrich, Carl J., and Zbigniew K. Brzezinski. *Totalitarian Dictatorship
and Autocracy.* Second edition, revised by Carl J. Friedrich. New York:
Praegar Publishers 1969 (original edition published in 1956)

Fuller, B.A.G. 'The Messes Animals Make in Metaphysics.' *Journal of Philosophy* 46 (22 December 1949) 829–38

Garcia, John, and Robert A. Koeling. 'The Stimulus Fittingness Principle.' Quoted in *Learning: Systems, Models and Theories* ed William S. Sahakian, pp 360–4. Chicago: Rand McNally College Publishing Co 1970 (originally published in 1966)

Gibson, Graeme. *Communion.* Toronto: Anansi Press 1971

Girard, René. *Things Hidden since the Foundation of the World.* Translated by Stephen Bann and Michael Metteer. Stanford: Stanford University Press 1987

Godlovitch, Stanley, Roslind Godlovitch, and John Harris, eds. *Animals, Men and Morals: An Enquiry into the Maltreatment of Non-Humans.* New York: Grove Press 1971

Goethe, Johann Wolfgang von. *Elective Affinities.* Translated with an introduction by R.J. Hollingdale. Harmondsworth, Middlesex: Penguin Books 1978

– *'The Sorrows of Young Werther' and Selected Writings.* Translated by Catherine Hutter, with a foreword by Hermann J. Weigand. New York: New American Library 1962

Gold, Joseph. 'The Ambivalent Beast.' In *Proceedings of the Sir Charles G.D. Roberts Symposium, Mount Allison University* ed Carrie MacMillan, pp 77–86. Halifax: Nimbus Publishing 1984

Goody Two-Shoes. A Facsimile Reproduction of the Edition of 1766. With an introduction by Charles Welsh. London: Griffish and Farran 1881

Griffin, Donald R. *The Question of Animal Awareness: Evolutionary Continuity of Mental Experience.* Los Altos, California: William Kaufmann 1981

Grove, Frederick Philip. *Settlers of the Marsh.* With an introduction by Thomas Saunders. Toronto: New Canadian Library, McClelland and Stewart 1966 (originally published in 1925)

Hallie, Philip P. *Cruelty.* Middletown, Connecticut: Wesleyan University Press 1969; rpt 1982, with a new introduction and postscript

Haraway, Donna. *Primate Visions: Gender, Race, and Nature in the World of Modern Science.* New York: Routledge 1989

Harrison, Brian. 'Animals and the State in Nineteenth-Century England.' *English Historical Review* 88 (1973) 786–820

Hartshorne, Charles. 'Can Man Transcend His Animality?' *Monist* 55 (April 1971) 208–17

Harwood, Dix. *Love for Animals and How It Developed in Great Britain.*

PH D dissertation. New York: Columbia University Press 1928

Hauser, Arnold. *The Social History of Art.* Vol 3: *Rococo, Classicism and Romanticism.* London: Routledge and Kegan Paul 1977 (first published in two volumes in 1951; four-volume edition 1962)

– *The Social History of Art.* Vol 4: *Naturalism, Impressionism, The Film Age.* New York: Vintage Books nd (first published in two volumes in 1951; four-volume edition 1962)

Haverstock, Mary Sayre. *An American Bestiary.* New York: Harry N. Abrams 1979

Hebb, D.O. 'Emotion in Man and Animal: An Analysis of the Intuitive Processes of Recognition.' *Psychological Review* 53 (1946) 88–106

Heiman, Marcel. 'The Relationship between Man and Dog.' *Psychoanalytic Quarterly* 25 (1956) 568–85

Hemingway, Ernest. *The Sun Also Rises.* New York: Charles Scribner's Sons 1970 (originally published in 1926)

Henkin, Leo J. *Darwinism in the English Novel 1860–1910: The Impact of Evolution on Victorian Fiction.* New York: Russell and Russell 1963

Himmelfarb, Gertrude. *Darwin and the Darwinian Revolution.* New York: W.W. Norton and Co 1962

Horkheimer, Max, and Theodor W. Adorno. *Dialectic of Enlightenment.* Translated by John Cumming. New York: Herder and Herder 1972 (originally published in 1944)

Houghton, Walter E. *The Victorian Frame of Mind, 1830–1870.* New Haven: Yale University Press 1957

Howe, Irving. *William Faulkner: A Critical Study.* New York: Vintage Books 1952 (a revised and expanded edition)

Huxley, Thomas Henry. *'Evolution and Ethics' and Other Essays.* New York: D. Appleton 1902 (*Evolution and Ethics* originally published in 1894)

Hyman, Stanley Edgar. *The Tangled Bank: Darwin, Marx, Frazer and Freud as Imaginative Writers.* New York: Atheneum 1962

Jelliffe, Smith Ely, and Louise Brink. 'The Role of Animals in the Unconscious, with Some Remarks on Theriomorphic Symbolism as Seen in Ovid.' *Psychoanalytic Review* 4 (July 1917) 253–71

Kellert, Stephen R., and Joyce K. Berry. *Knowledge, Affection and Basic Attitudes towards Animals in American Society: Phase III.* Yale University: School of Forestry and Environmental Studies. Reproduced by the National Technical Information Service, United States Department of Commerce 1980

King, Stephen. *Cujo*. New York: New American Library 1981

Kirk, G.S. *The Nature of Greek Myths*. Harmondsworth, Middlesex: Penguin Books 1974

Klaits, Joseph, and Barrie Klaits, eds. *Animals and Man in Historical Perspective*. New York: Harper and Row 1974

Klingender, Francis. *Animals in Art and Thought to the End of the Middle Ages*. Ed Evelyn Antal and John Harthan. Cambridge, Massachusetts: MIT Press 1971

Kosinski, Jerzy. *The Painted Bird*. New York: Pocket Cardinal edition, Simon and Schuster 1967 (originally published in 1965)

Lansbury, Coral. *The Old Brown Dog: Women, Workers, and Vivisection in Edwardian England*. Madison: University of Wisconsin Press 1985

Lang, Andrew. *The Making of Religion*. New York: AMS Press 1968 (originally published in 1898)

Lawrence, D.H. *The Fox*. In *Four Short Novels*. New York: Viking Press 1965 (originally published in 1923)

– 'Reflections on the Death of a Porcupine.' In *Phoenix II: Uncollected, Unpublished, and Other Prose Works by D.H. Lawrence*. Collected and edited with an introduction and notes by Warren Roberts and Harry T. Moore. New York: Viking Press 1970

Lawrence, John. *A Philosophical and Practical Treatise on Horses and on the Moral Duties of Man towards the Brute Creation*. 2 vols. London: T.N. Longman 1796–1798

Le Guin, Ursula K. *Buffalo Gals and Other Animal Presences*. New York: New American Library 1987

Levin, Harry. 'Some Meanings of Myth. In *Myth and Mythmaking* ed Henry A. Murray, pp 103–14. Boston: Beacon Press 1968

London, Jack. *The Call of the Wild* and *White Fang*. Toronto: Bantam Books 1981 (originally published in 1903 and 1906, respectively)

– *Jerry of the Islands*. New York: Macmillan Co 1917

– *Michael: Brother of Jerry*. New York: Macmillan Co 1917

– The Other Animals.' In *Revolution and Other Essays*. New York: Macmillan Co 1912 (originally published in 1908)

Lorenz, Konrad. *On Aggression*. Translated by Marjorie Latzke, with an introduction by Sir Julian Huxley. London: Methuen and Co 1974 (originally published in 1963)

Lucas, Alec. 'Nature Writing in English.' In *The Oxford Companion to Canadian Literature* general ed William Toye. Toronto: Oxford University Press 1983

Lutts, Ralph H. *The Nature Fakers: Wildlife, Science and Sentiment.*
Golden, Colorado: Fulcrum Publishing 1990

MacDonald, Robert H. 'The Revolt against Instinct: The Animal Stories
of Seton and Roberts.' *Canadian Literature* 84 (Spring 1980) 18–28

Magee, William H. 'The Animal Story: A Challenge in Technique.'
Dalhousie Review 44 (1964) 158–64

Malinowski, Bronislaw. *Magic, Science and Religion and Other Essays.*
With an introduction by Robert Redfield. New York: Doubleday and
Co 1954

Mandeville, Bernard. *The Fable of the Bees: Or, Private Vices, Publick
Benefits.* With a commentary, critical, historical, and explanatory by
F.B. Kaye. Oxford: Clarendon Press 1924; rpt 1966

Mann, Thomas. 'Tobias Mindernickel.' In *Stories of Three Decades.*
Translated by H.T. Lowe-Porter. New York: Alfred A. Knopf 1941
(this story originally published in 1897)

Mansfield, Katherine. 'The Fly.' In *Selected Stories.* Chosen and introduced by D.M. Davin. London: Oxford University Press 1967
(originally published, with other stories, in *The Dove's Nest* in 1923)

Midgley, Mary. *Animals and Why They Matter.* Harmondsworth,
Middlesex: Penguin Books 1983

– *Beast and Man: The Roots of Human Nature.* Ithaca: Cornell
University Press 1978

Mill, John Stuart. *Whewell on Moral Philosophy.* In *Collected Works,* vol
10: *Essays on Ethics, Religion and Society.* Ed J.M. Robson. Toronto:
University of Toronto Press 1969 (essay originally published in 1852)

Millett, Kate. *Sexual Politics.* New York: Avon Books 1971

Montaigne, Michel de. *Apology for Raimond Sebond.* In *The Essays of
Montaigne.* Trans E.J. Trechmann. New York: Modern Library 1946

Morris, Richard Knowles, and Michael W. Fox, eds. *On the Fifth Day:
Animal Rights and Human Ethics.* Washington, DC: Acropolis Books
1978

Morton, Peter. *The Vital Science: Biology and the Literary Imagination
1860–1900.* London: George Allen and Unwin 1984

Mushet, David. *The Wrongs of the Animal World, with the Speech of
Lord Erskine on the Same Subject.* London: Hatchard and Son 1839

Nash, Christopher. 'A Modern Bestiary: Representative Animal Motifs in
the Encounter between Nature and Culture in the English, American,
French and Italian Novel, 1900–1950.' PH D dissertation, New York
University 1970

Norris, Margot. *Beasts of the Modern Imagination: Darwin, Nietzsche, Kafka, Ernst and Lawrence.* Baltimore: John Hopkins University Press 1985

Noske, Barbara. *Humans and Other Animals: Beyond the Boundaries of Anthropology.* London: Pluto Press 1989

Ortega y Gasset, José. *Meditations on Hunting.* Translated by Howard B. Wescott, with an introduction by Paul Shepard. New York: Charles Scribner's Sons 1972 (originally published in 1942)

Oswald, John. *The Cry of Nature; or, An Appeal to Mercy and to Justice on Behalf of the Persecuted Animals.* London: J. Johnson 1791

Passmore, John. 'The Treatment of Animals.' *Journal of the History of Ideas* 36 (April–May 1975) 195–218

Rachels, James. *Created from Animals: The Moral Implications of Darwinism.* Oxford: Oxford University Press 1991

Rappaport, Ernest A. 'Zoophily and Zooerasty.' *Psychoanalytic Quarterly* 37 (1968) 565–87

Regan, Tom. *The Case for Animal Rights.* Berkeley: University of California Press 1983

– 'Honey Dribbles Down Your Fur.' In *Environmental Ethics: Philosophical and Policy Perspectives* ed Philip P. Hanson. Burnaby, BC: Institute for the Humanities/SFU Publications 1986

– ed. *Animal Sacrifices: Religious Perspectives on the Use of Animals in Science.* Philadelphia: Temple University Press 1986

Ricoeur, Paul. *The Symbolism of Evil.* Translated by Emerson Buchanan. Boston: Beacon Press 1969

Ritvo, Harriet. *The Animal Estate: The English and Other Creatures in the Victorian Age.* Cambridge, Massachusetts: Harvard University Press 1987

Roberts, Charles G.D. *Earth's Enigmas: A Book of Animal and Natural Life.* Boston: I.C. Page and Co 1903

– *The Feet of the Furtive.* New York: Macmillan Co 1913

– *Kindred of the Wild.* New York: Stitt Publishing Co 1905

– *Thirteen Bears.* Ed Ethel Hume Bennett. Toronto: Ryerson Press 1947

– *Watchers of the Trails.* Illustrated by Julek Heller. London: Kestrel Books 1976 (originally published in 1904)

Rollins, Bernard. 'Animal Consciousness and Scientific Change.' *New Ideas in Psychology* 4 (1986) 141–52

Rosenfield, Leonora Cohen. *From Beast-Machine to Man-Machine: Animal Soul in French Letters from Descartes to La Mettrie.* 1940. Enlarged Edition, with a Preface by Paul Hazard. New York: Octagon Books 1968

Ruskin, John. *Modern Painters.* Vol 2 (containing part of pt 2, 'Of truth,' and pt 3, 'Of the idea of beauty'). London: J.M. Dent nd (originally published in 1856)

Salt, Henry S. *Animals' Rights, Considered in Relation to Social Progress.* With a preface by Peter Singer and an updated bibliography prepared by Charles R. Magel. Clarks Summit, Pennsylvania: Society for Animal Rights 1980 (originally published in 1892)

Sartre, Jean-Paul. *The Family Idiot: Gustave Flaubert, 1821–1857.* Vol 1. Translated by Carol Cosman. Chicago: University of Chicago Press 1981 (originally published in 1971)

Scarry, Elaine. *The Body in Pain: The Making and Unmaking of the World.* New York: Oxford University Press 1985

Scholtmeijer, Marian. 'The Animal at the Door: Modern Works of Horror and the Natural Animal.' In *State of the Fantastic* ed Nicholas Ruddick. Westport, Connecticut: Greenwood Press 1992

Schopenhauer, Arthur. *On the Basis of Morality.* Translated by E.F.J. Payne. Indianapolis: Bobbs-Merrill Co 1965 (originally published in 1841)

Schopenhauer, Arthur. *The World as Will and Representation.* Vol 1. Translated by E.F.J. Payne. Indian Hills, Colorado: 1958; rpt, with minor corrections, New York: Dover Publications 1969

Serpell, James. *In the Company of Animals: A Study of Human-Animal Relationships.* Oxford: Basil Blackwell 1986

Seton, Ernest Thompson. *Animal Heroes.* New York: Grosset and Dunlap 1905 (originally published in 1901)

– *Lives of the Hunted.* London: David Nutt 1901

– 'The Natural History of the Ten Commandments.' *Century Illustrated Magazine* 75 (November 1907) 24–33

– *Wild Animals I Have Known.* Toronto: New Canadian Library, McClelland and Stewart 1977 (originally published in 1898)

Shepard, Paul. *The Tender Carnivore and the Sacred Game.* New York: Charles Scribner's Sons 1973

Shugg, Wallace. 'The Cartesian Beast-Machine in English Literature (1663–1750).' *Journal of the History of Ideas* 29 (April–June 1968) 279–92

Sinclair, Upton. *The Jungle.* Harmondsworth, Middlesex: Penguin Books 1982 (originally published in 1906)

Singer, Peter. *Animal Liberation.* New York: Avon Books 1975

Singer, Peter, ed. *In Defense of Animals.* New York: Harper and Row 1985

Skinner, B.F. *About Behaviorism* New York: Alfred A Knopf 1974

Smith, Anne. 'A New Adam and a New Eve – Lawrence and Women: A Biographical Overview.' In *Lawrence and Women* ed Anne Smith. New York: Barnes and Noble 1978

Spilka, Mark. *The Love Ethic of D.H. Lawrence.* Bloomington: Indiana University Press 1955

Sprigge, T.L.S. 'Metaphysics, Physicalism and Animal Rights.' *Inquiry* 22 (Summer 1979) 101–43

Steinbeck, John. *The Log from the Sea of Cortez.* New York: Viking Press 1951

– The White Quail.' In *The Long Valley.* Harmondsworth, Middlesex: Penguin Books 1986 (collection originally published in 1938)

Stevenson, Lionel. 'Darwin and the Novel.' *Nineteenth-Century Fiction* 15 (June 1960) 29–38

Tapper, Richard. 'Animality, Humanity, Morality, Society.' In *What Is an Animal?* ed Tim Ingold, pp 47–62. London: Unwin Hyman 1988

Tester, Keith. *Animals and Society: The Humanity of Animal Rights.* London: Routledge 1991

Thomas, Keith. *Man and the Natural World: Changing Attitudes in England 1500–1800.* Harmondsworth, Middlesex: Penguin Books 1984

Thoreau, Henry David. *Walden; or, Life in the Woods.* In *The Annotated Walden.* Edited with an introduction, notes, and bibliography by Philip Van Doren Stern. New York: Clarkson N. Potter 1970 (originally published in 1854)

Thorlby, Anthony. 'The Cult of Art.' In *The Modern World* vol 2: *Realities* general eds David Daiches and Anthony Thorlby, pp 461–90. London: Aldus Books 1972

Thurston, Herbert, S.J., and Donald Attwater, eds. *Butler's Lives of the Saints.* Vol 1. New York: P.J. Kenedy and Sons 1963.

Tuan, Yi-Fu. *Dominance and Affection: The Making of Pets.* New Haven: Yale University Press 1984

Turner, John. *Reckoning with the Beast: Animals, Pain and Humanity in the Victorian Mind.* Baltimore: Johns Hopkins University Press 1980

Utley, Francis Lee, Lynn Z. Bloom, and Arthur F. Kinney, eds. *Bear, Man, and God: Eight Approaches to William Faulkner's 'The Bear.'* New York: Random House 1971

Watson, John B. *Behaviorism.* Chicago: University of Chicago Press 1958 (originally published in 1924)

Webb, Mary. *Gone to Earth.* With an introduction by Erika Duncan. Toronto: Lester and Orpen Dennys 1982 (originally published in 1917)

White, Lynn, Jr. 'The Historical Roots of Our Ecologic Crisis.' *Science* 155 (10 March 1967) 1203–7

Williams, George C. 'Huxley's Evolution and Ethics in Sociobiological Perspective.' *Zygon* 23 (December 1988) 383–407

Williamson, Henry. *Tarka the Otter.* Illustrated by C.F. Tunnicliffe. Harmondsworth, Middlesex: Penguin Books 1959 (originally published in 1927)

Wollstonecraft, Mary. *Original Stories from Real Life.* With a preface by Miriam Brody Kramnick. Garland Series, ed Alison Lurie and Justin G. Schiller. New York: Garland Publishing 1977 (facsimile reproduction of the edition of 1788)

Wynne-Tyson, Jon, ed. *The Extended Circle: A Commonplace Book of Animal Rights.* New York: Paragon House 1989

Index